Shojo Beat

kimi ni todoke
From Me to You

Vol. 18
Story & Art by
Karuho Shiina

Volume 18

Contents

Story Thus Far

Sawako Kuronuma has always been a loner. Though not by choice, this optimistic 16-year-old girl can't seem to make any friends. Stuck with the unfortunate nickname "Sadako" after the haunting movie character, rumors about her summoning spirits have been greatly exaggerated. With her shy personality and scary looks, most of her classmates will barely talk to her, much less look into her eyes for more than three seconds lest they be cursed. Thanks to Kazehaya, who always treats her nicely, Sawako makes her first friends at school, Ayane and Chizu. Eventually, Sawako finds the courage to date Kazehaya.

On a school trip to Okinawa, poor Sawako and Kazehaya's attempt at a first kiss is interrupted, leaving them stiff and awkward around each other. Also during the trip, Ryu confesses his long-held romantic feelings to Chizu, who turns him down. But during the Christmas party, Chizu and Ryu end up exchanging gifts that bring them closer. Also during the party, Ayane finally accepts Kento's feelings for her. After the party, Sawako and Kazehaya walk home together, so uncomfortable around each other that Sawako breaks down crying, thinking he no longer cares for her. It is in that moment that Kazehaya finally kisses her!

kimi ni todoke

From Me to You

Episode 72: Forty-Five Minutes

Karuho Shiina

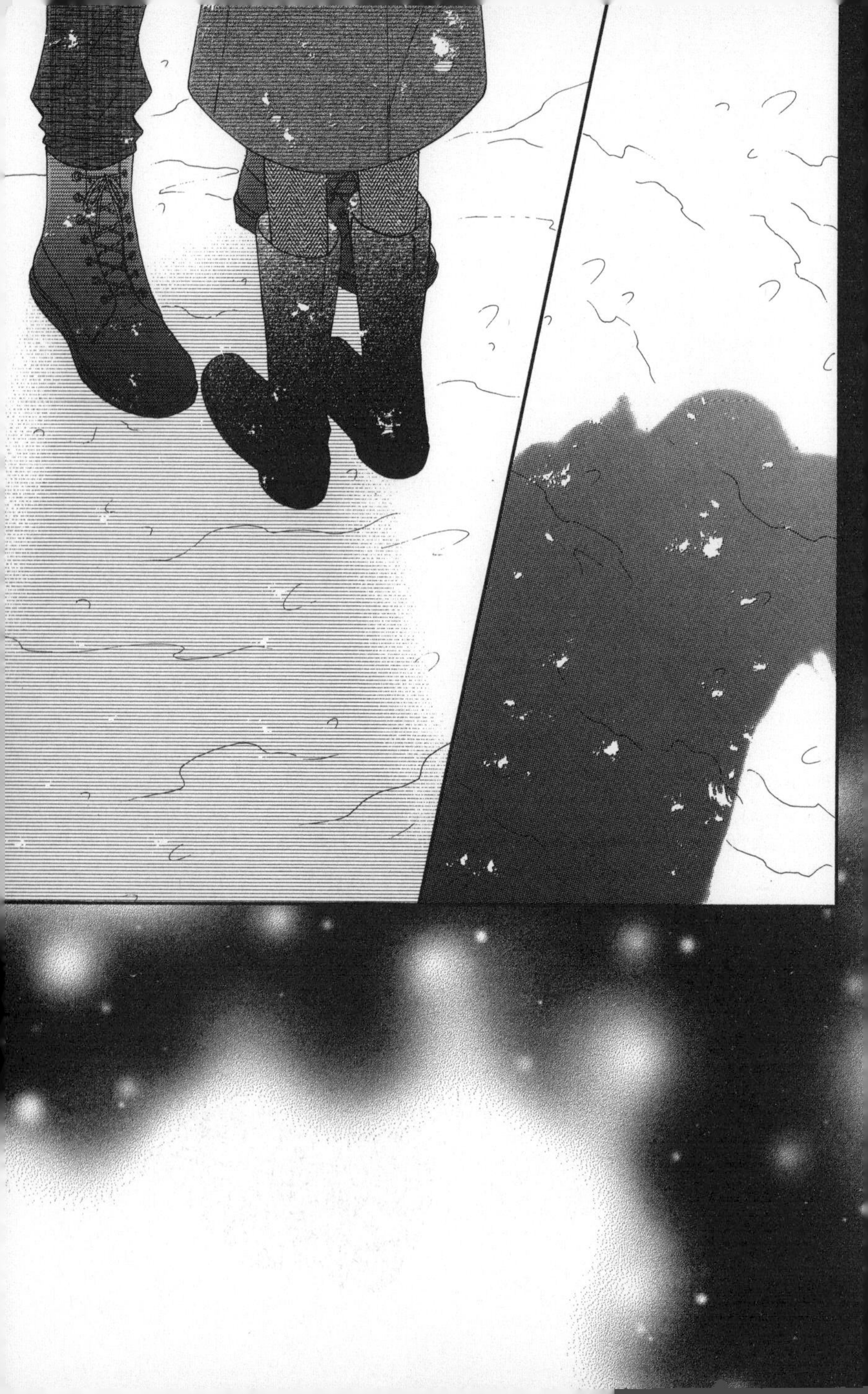

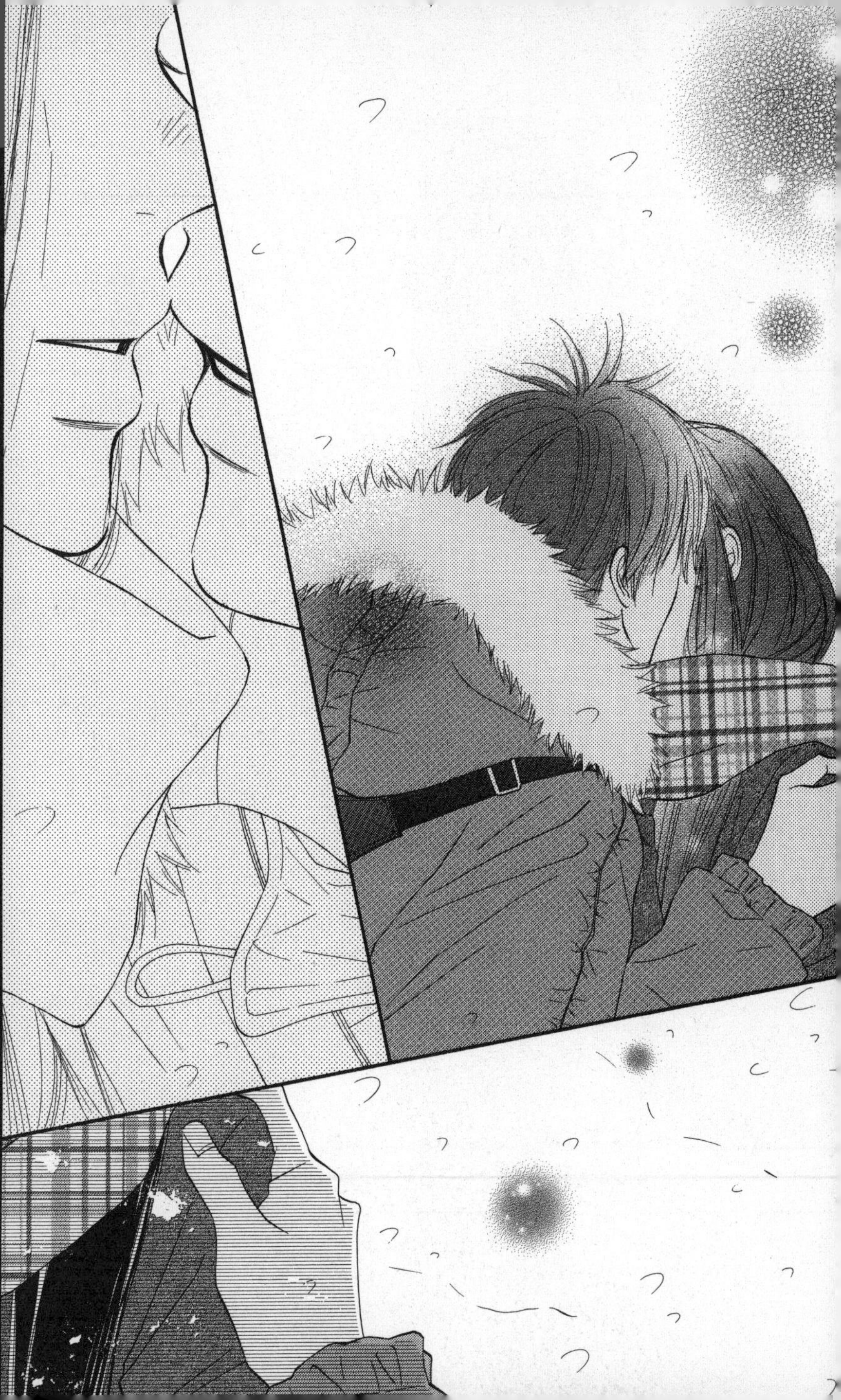

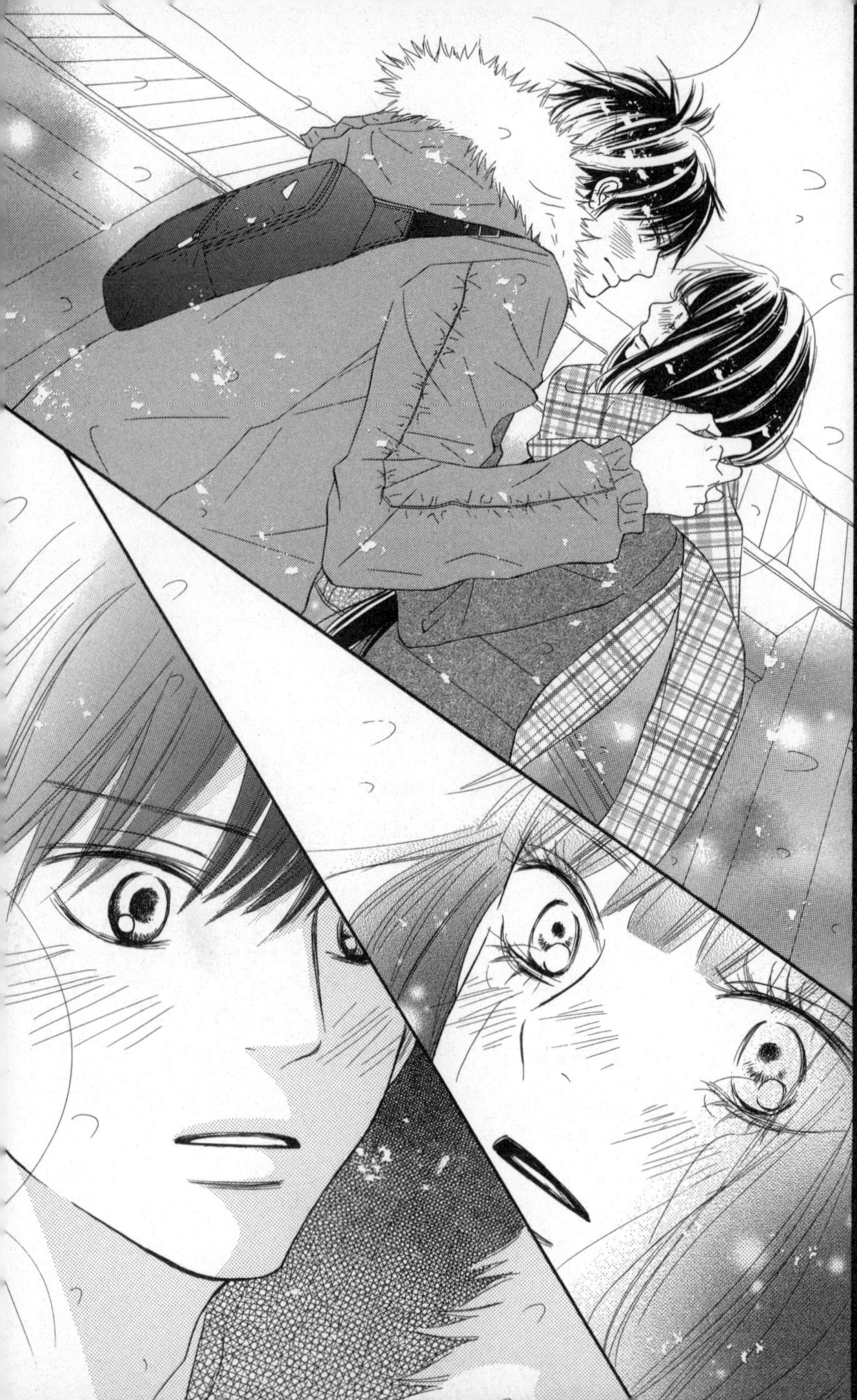

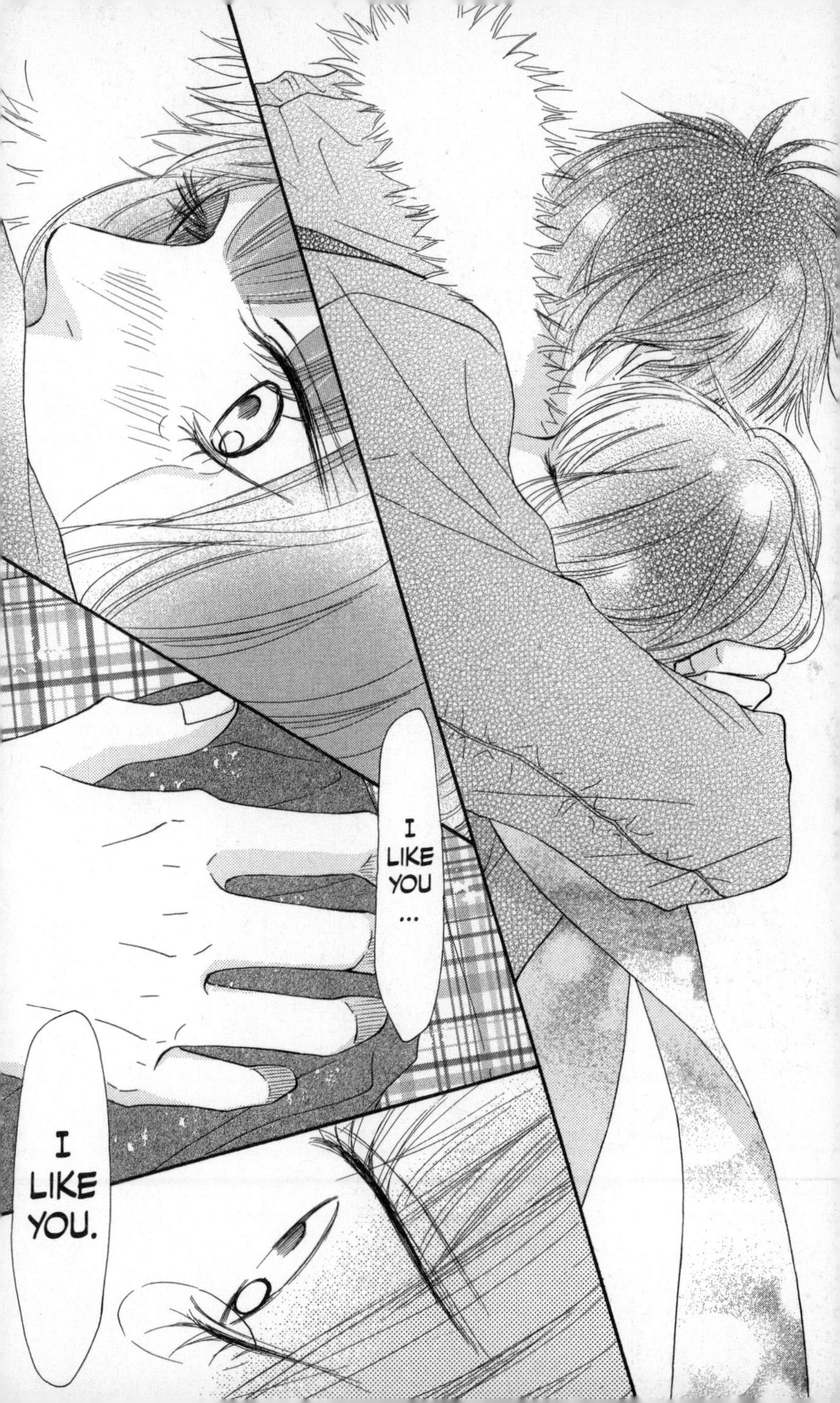
I LIKE YOU ...
I LIKE YOU.

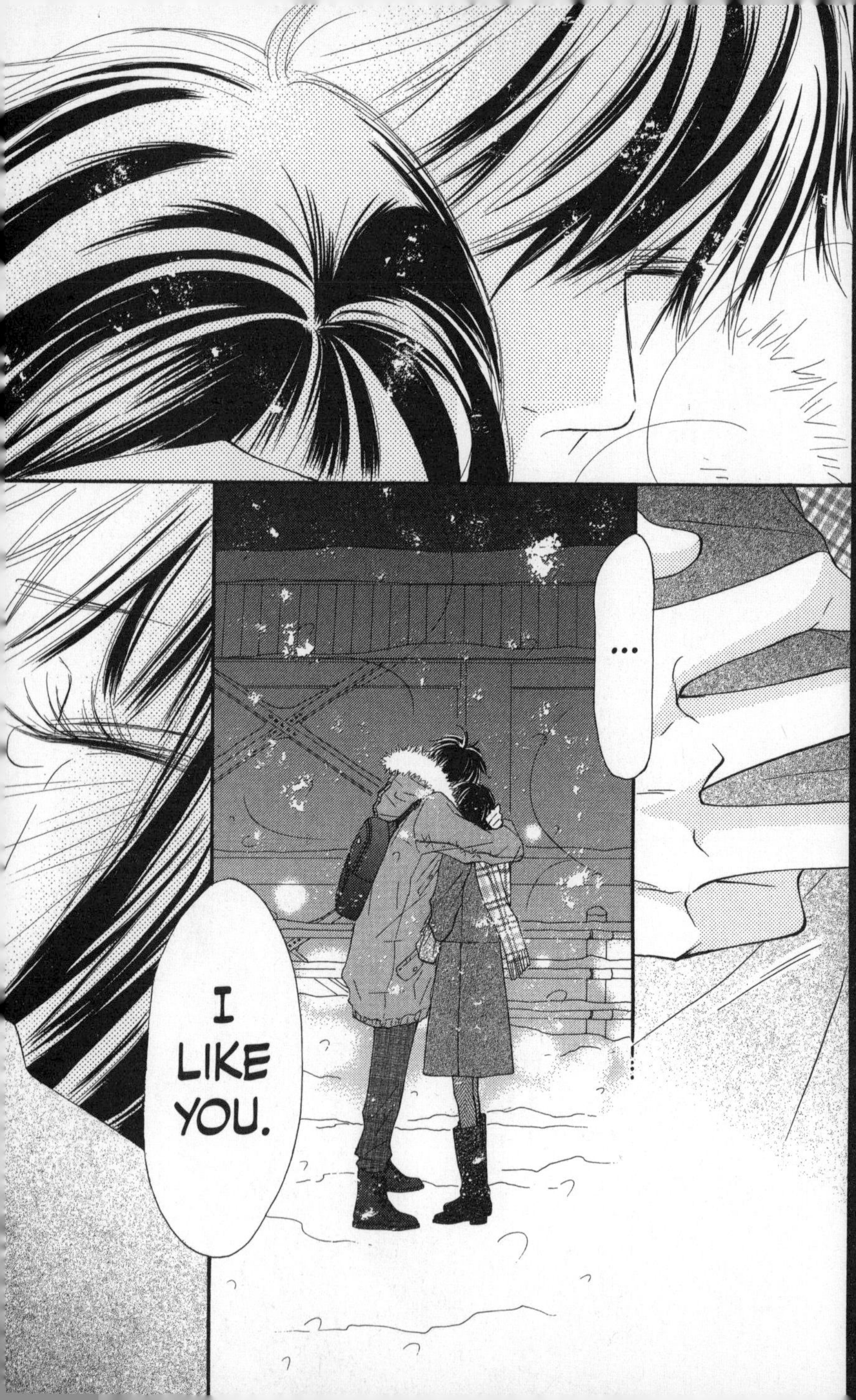
...
I LIKE YOU.

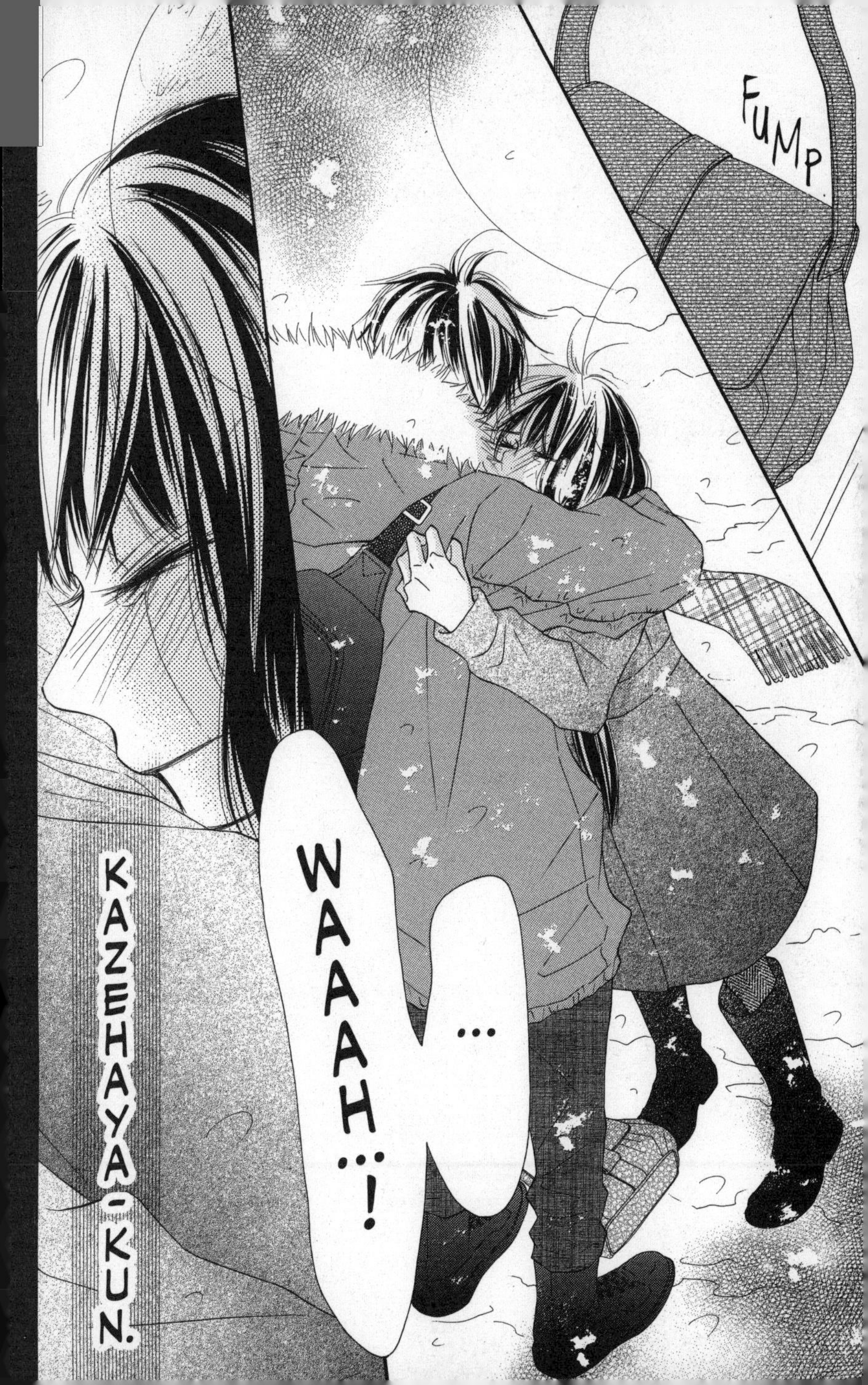
FUMP
...
WAAAH...!
KAZEHAYA-KUN.

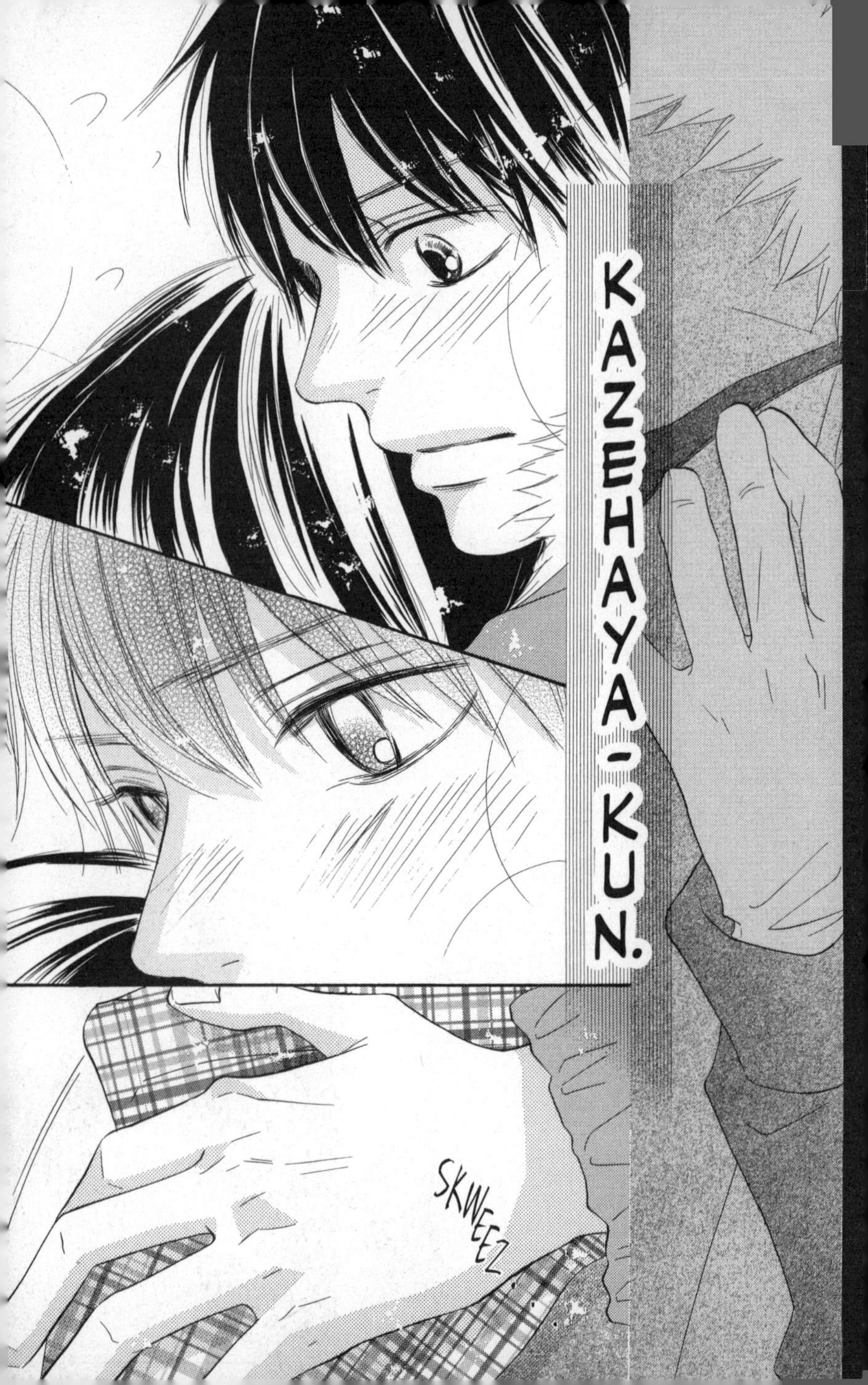
KAZEHAYA-KUN.
SKWEEZ

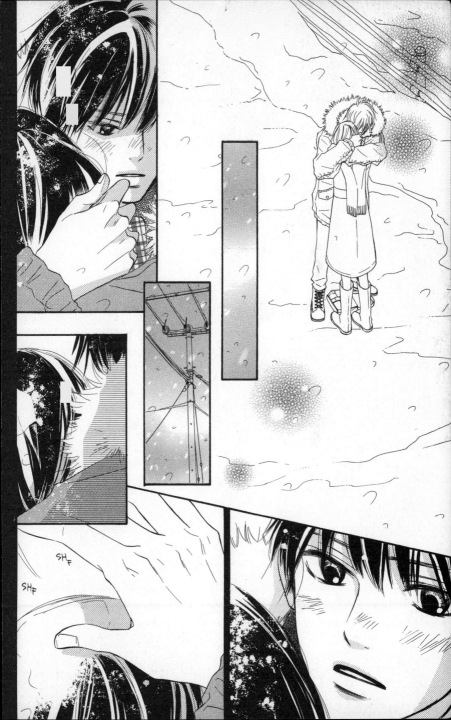

SHF

SHF

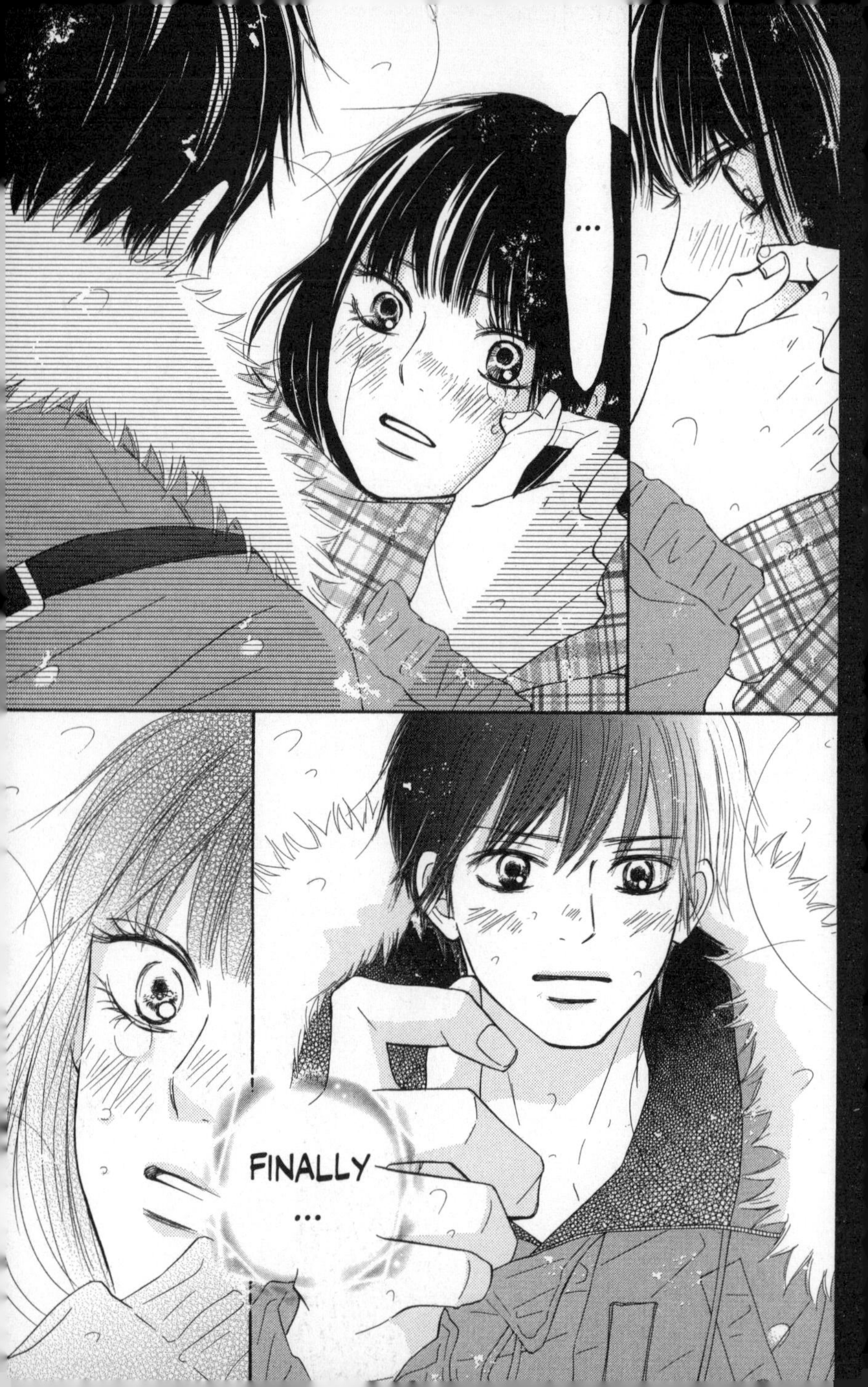
...
FINALLY
...

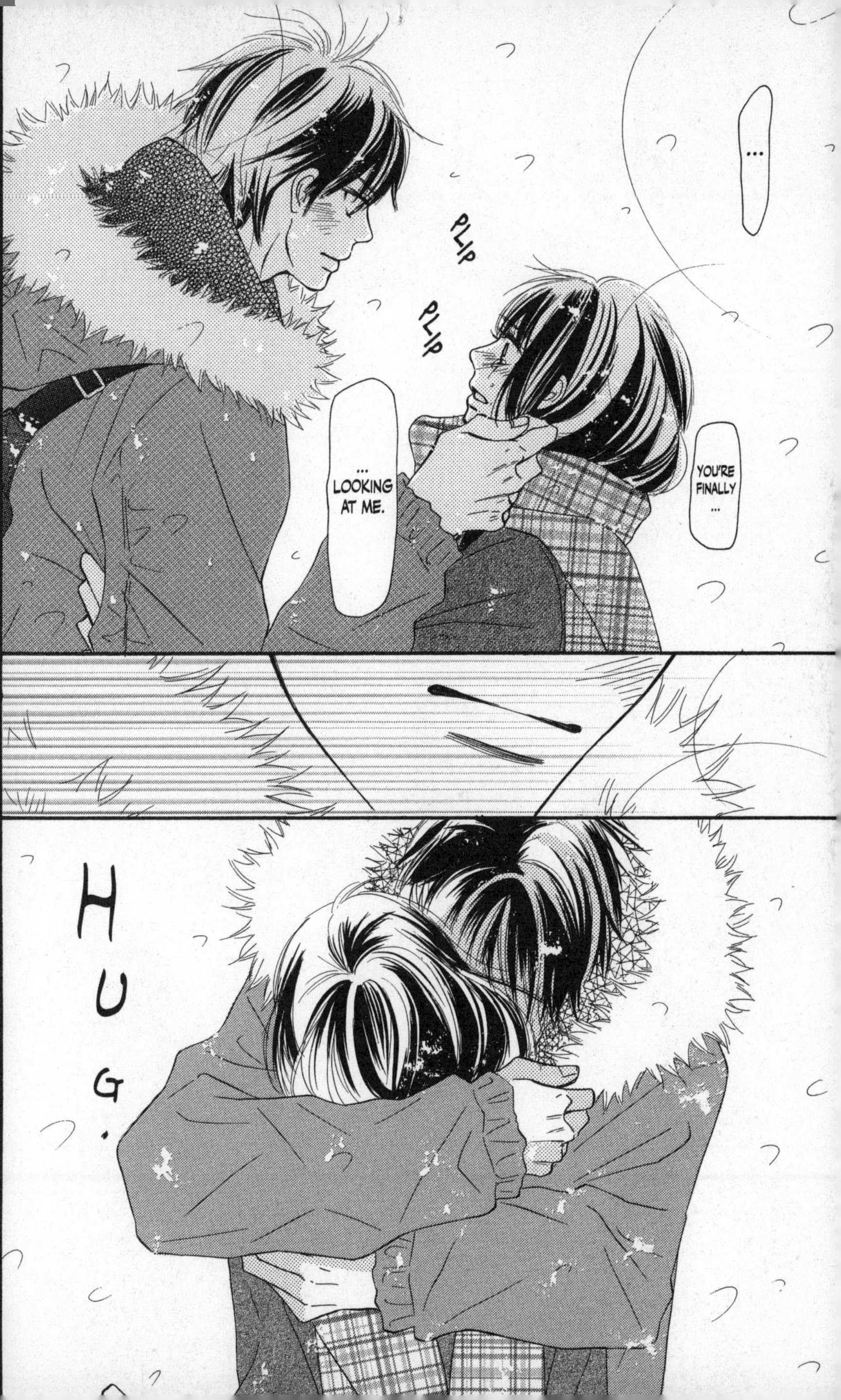
...
PLIP
PLIP
YOU'RE FINALLY ...
... LOOKING AT ME.
HUG.

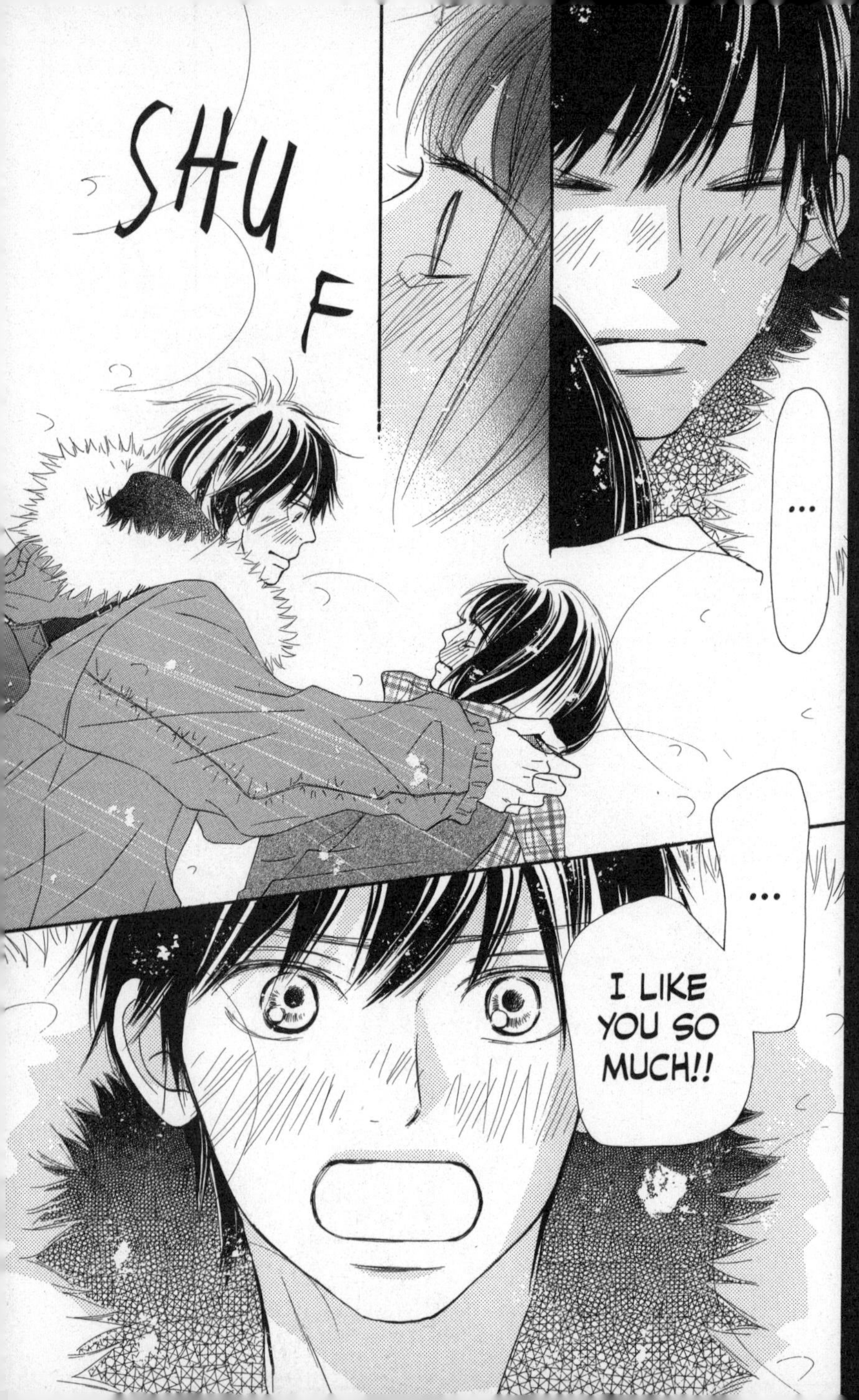
...
SHUF
...
I LIKE YOU SO MUCH!!

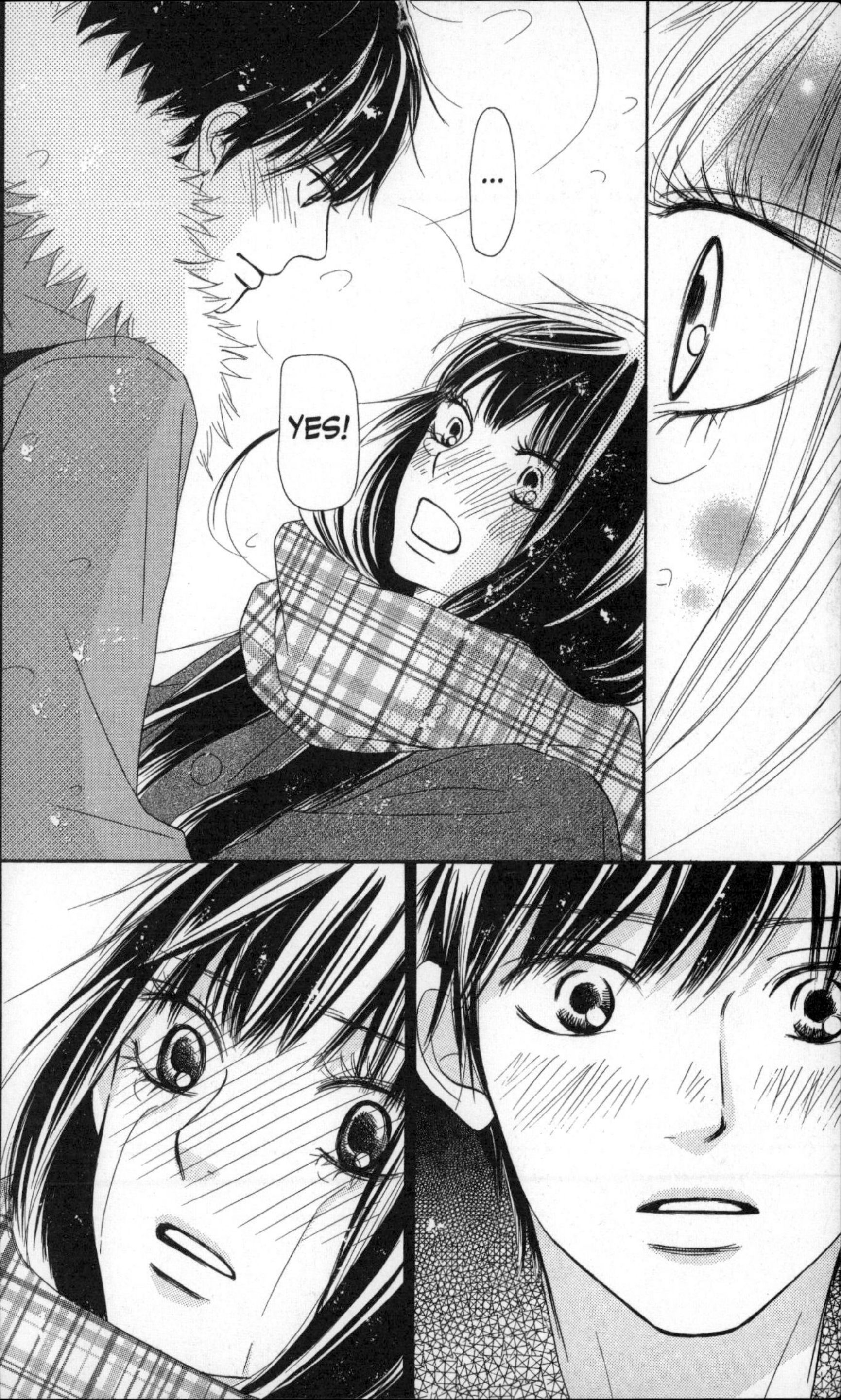
...
YES!

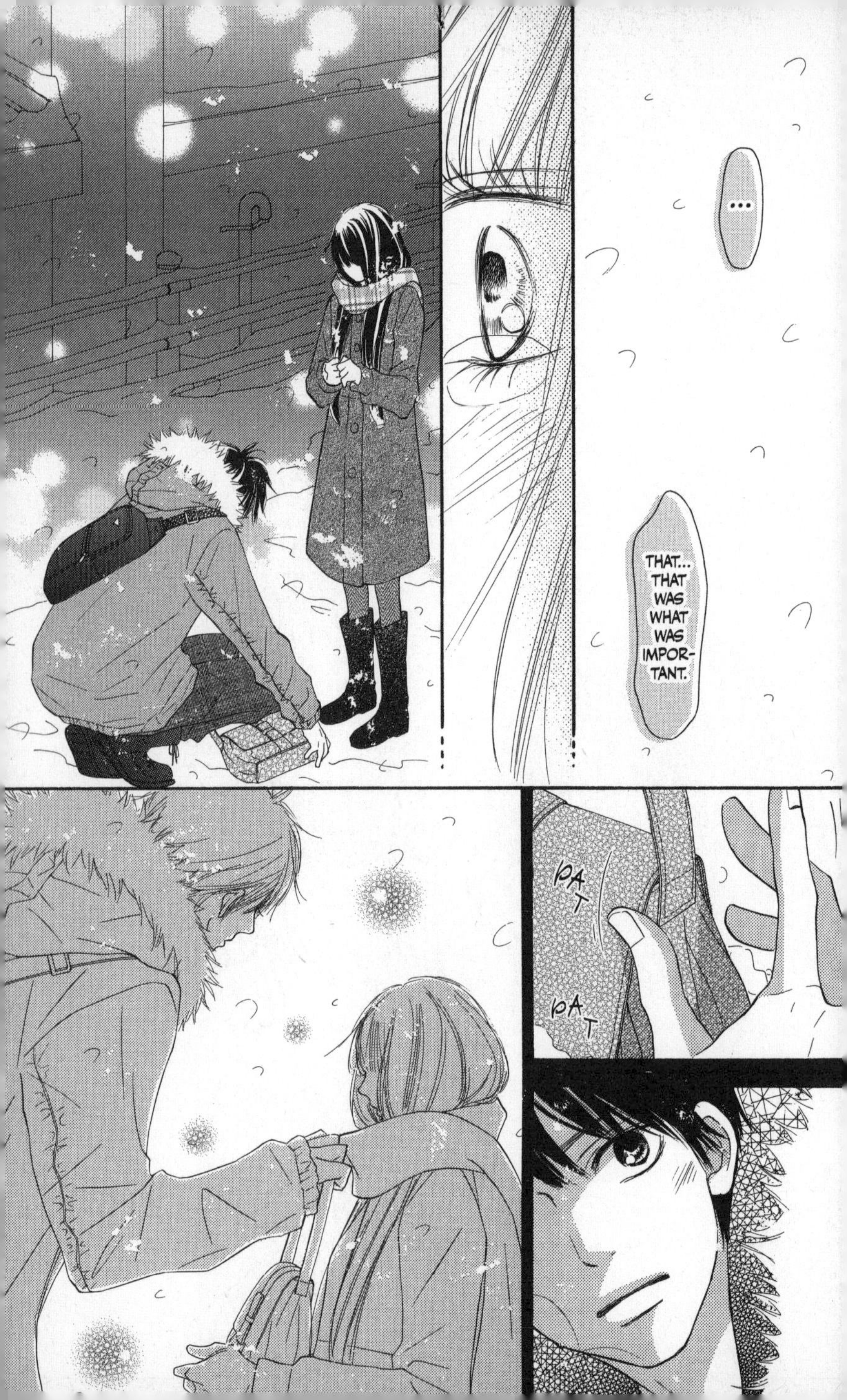
...
THAT... THAT WAS WHAT WAS IMPOR-TANT.
PAT
PAT

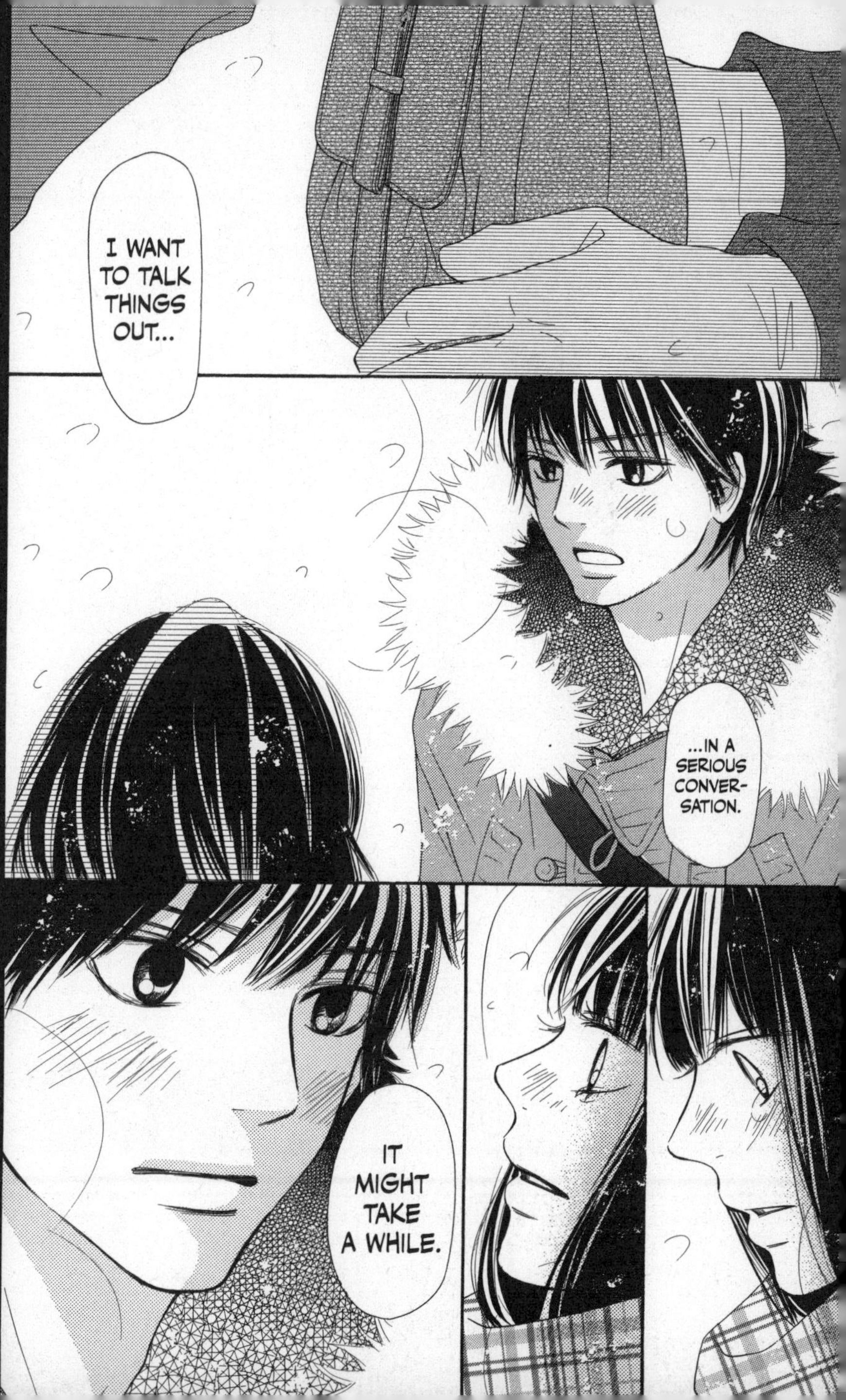
I WANT TO TALK THINGS OUT...
...IN A SERIOUS CONVER-SATION.
IT MIGHT TAKE A WHILE.

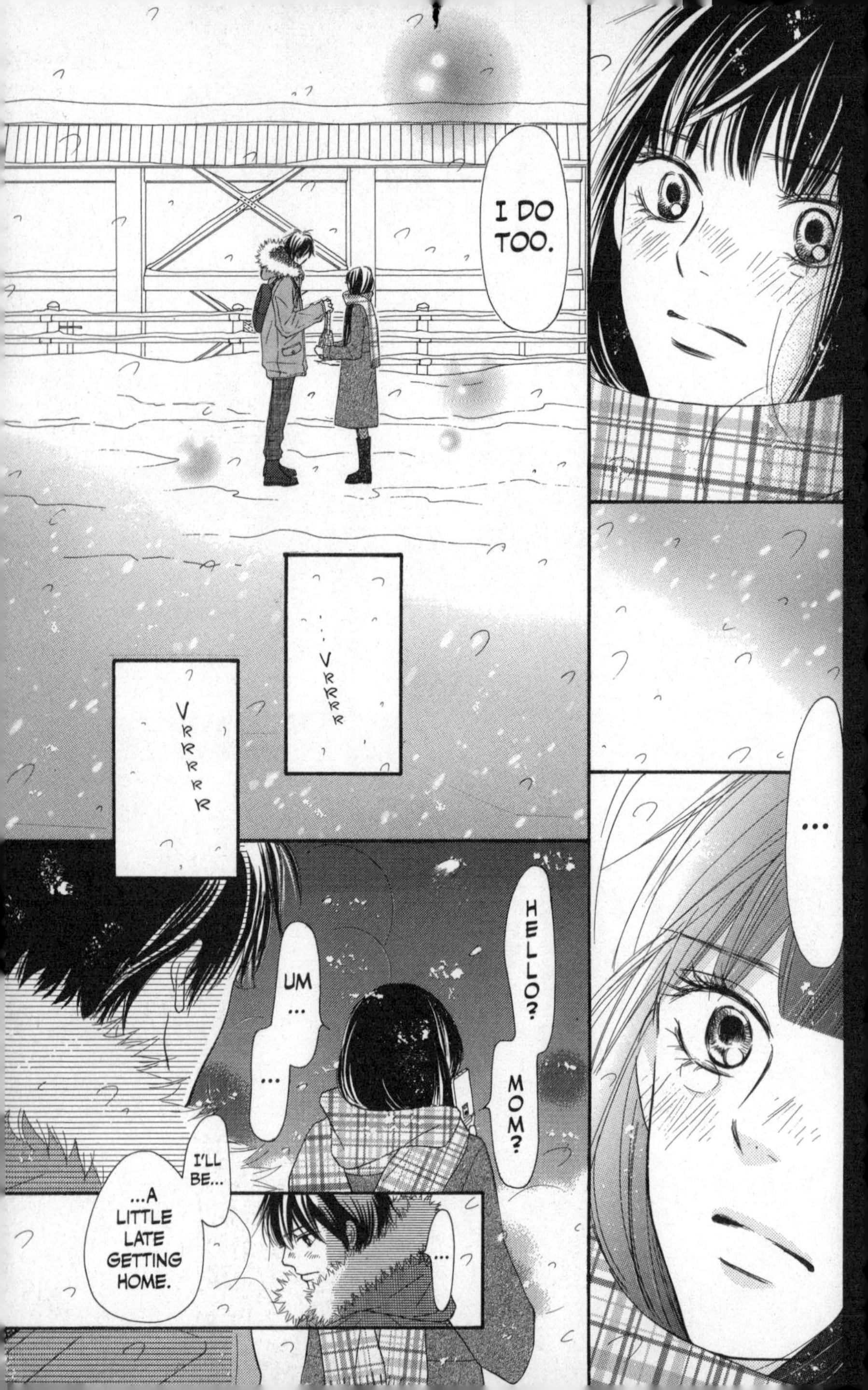
I DO TOO.
...VRRRR
VRRRRR
...
HELLO? MOM?
UM ... ...
I'LL BE...
...A LITTLE LATE GETTING HOME.
...

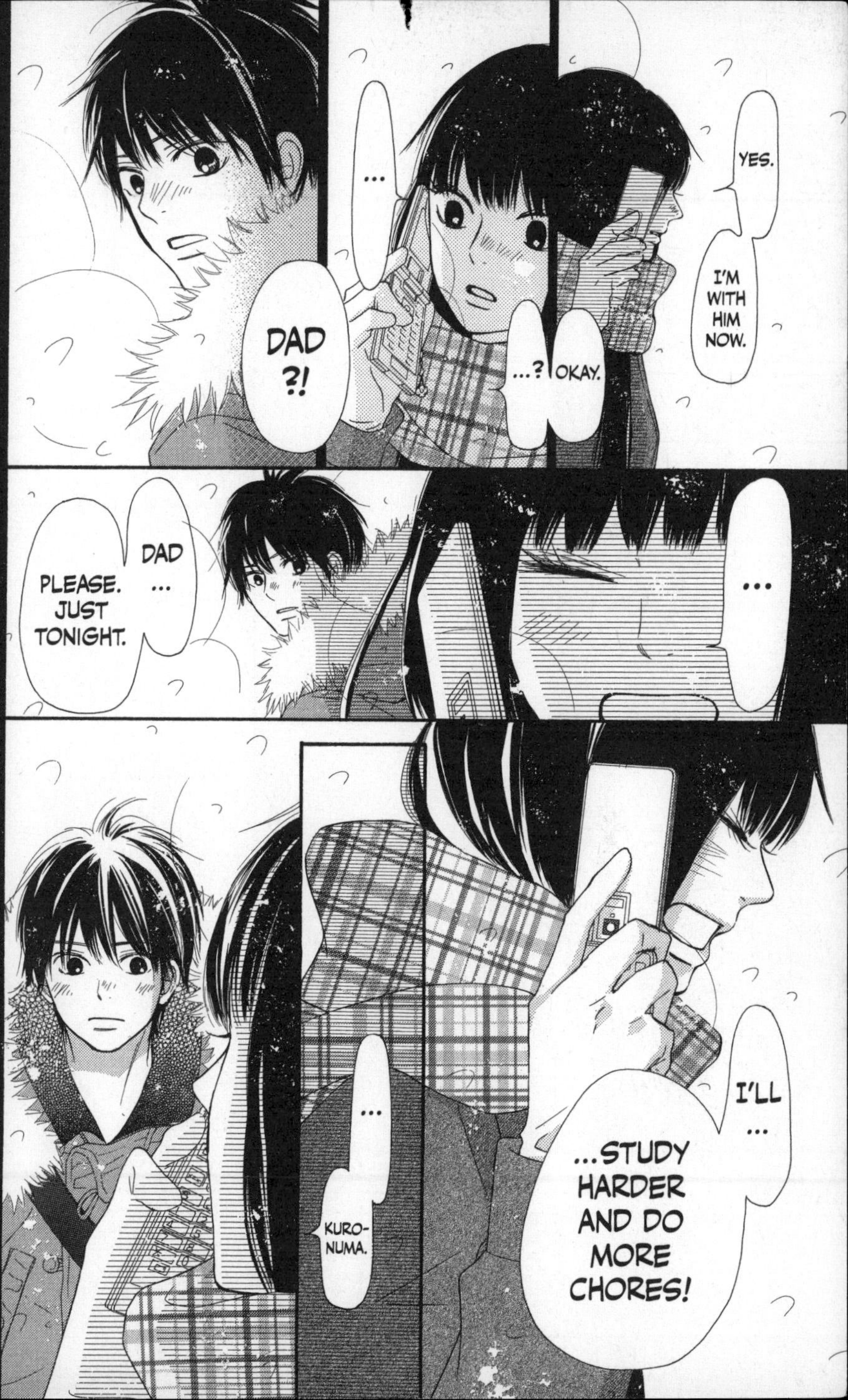
YES.
I'M WITH HIM NOW.
...
OKAY.
...?
DAD ?!
...
DAD ...
PLEASE. JUST TONIGHT.
I'LL ...
...STUDY HARDER AND DO MORE CHORES!
...
KURO-NUMA.

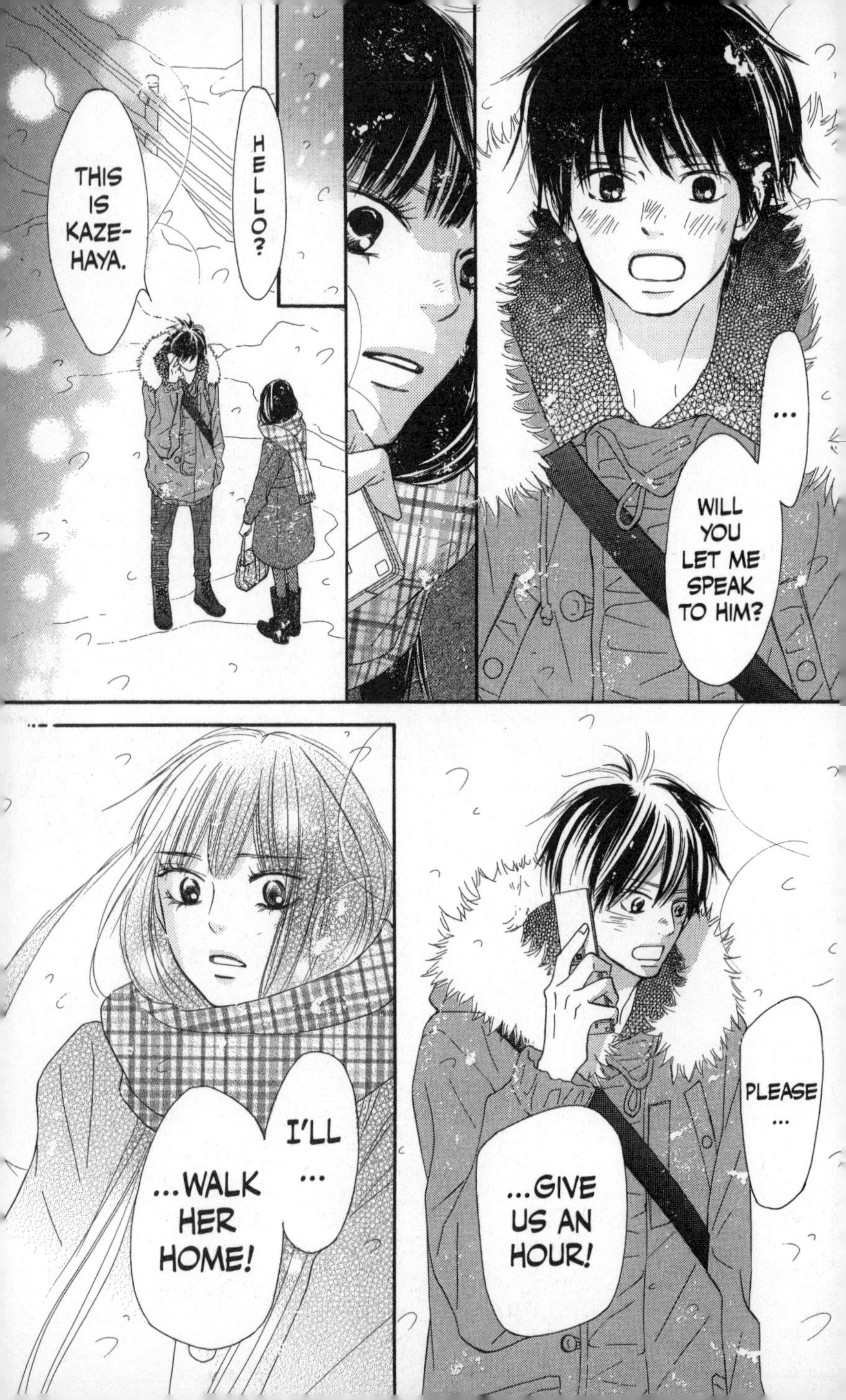
...
WILL YOU LET ME SPEAK TO HIM?
HELLO?
THIS IS KAZE-HAYA.
PLEASE ...
...GIVE US AN HOUR!
I'LL ...
...WALK HER HOME!

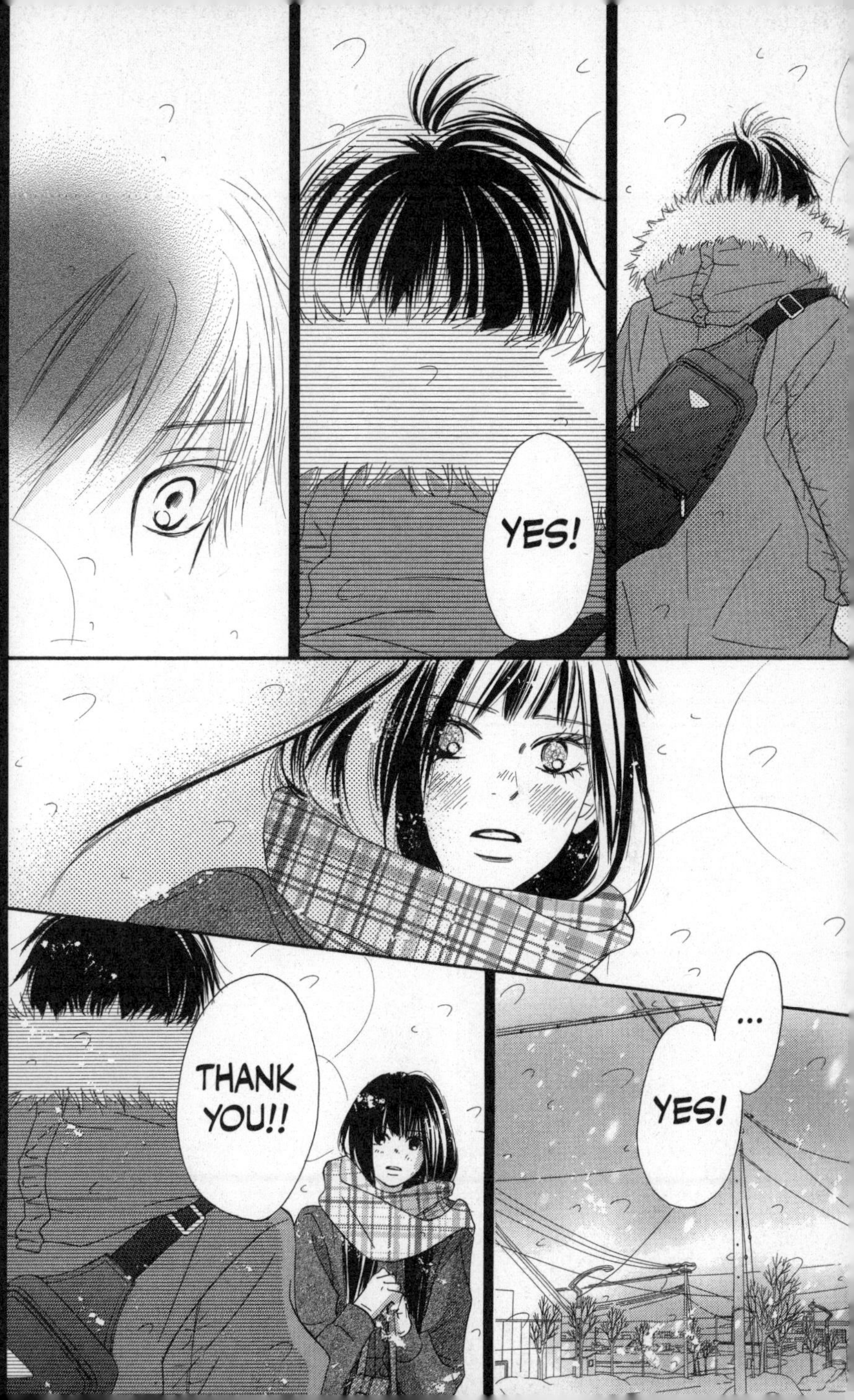
YES!
...
YES!
THANK YOU!!

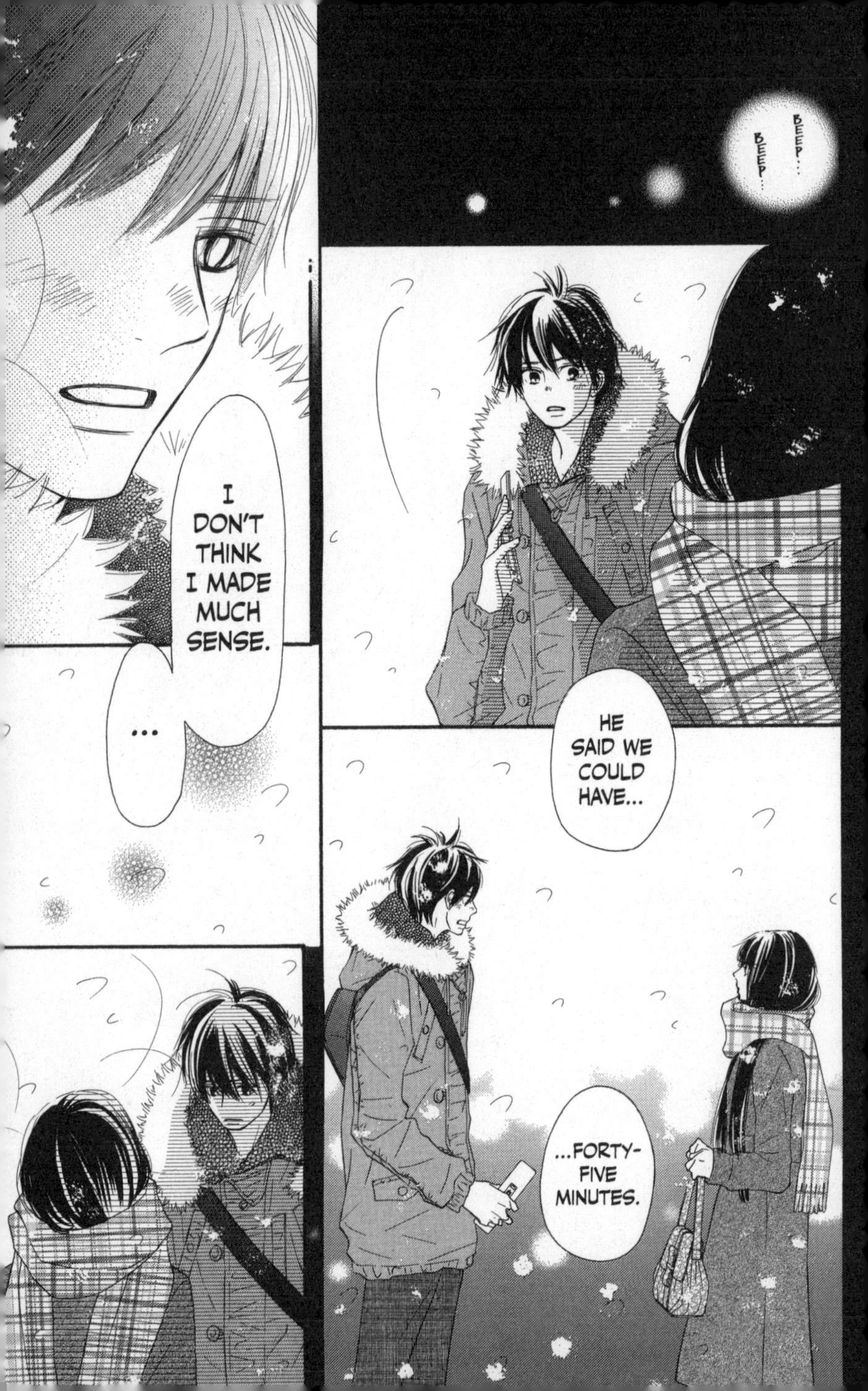
BEEP... BEEP...
HE SAID WE COULD HAVE...
...FORTY-FIVE MINUTES.
I DON'T THINK I MADE MUCH SENSE.
...

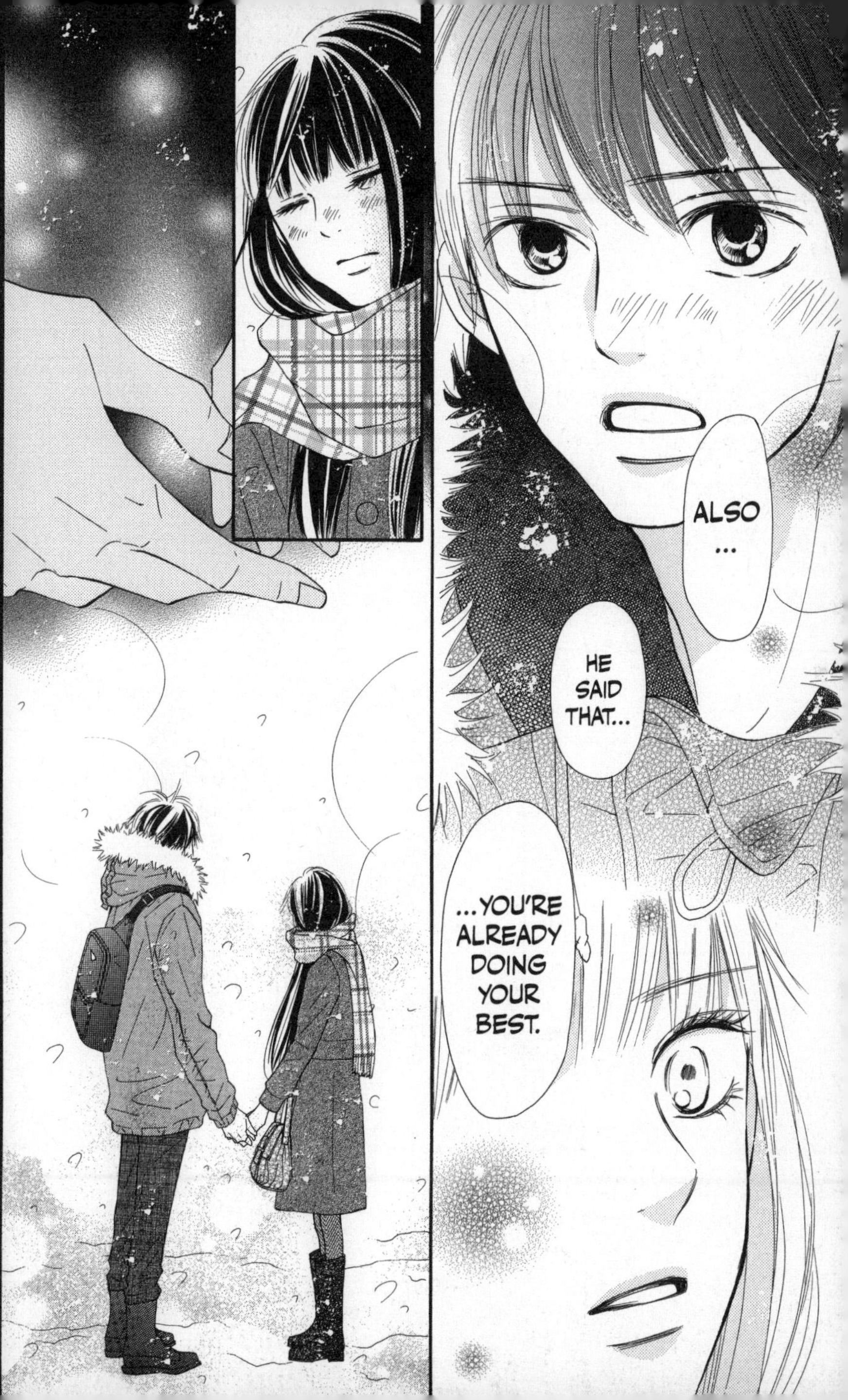
ALSO ...
HE SAID THAT...
...YOU'RE ALREADY DOING YOUR BEST.

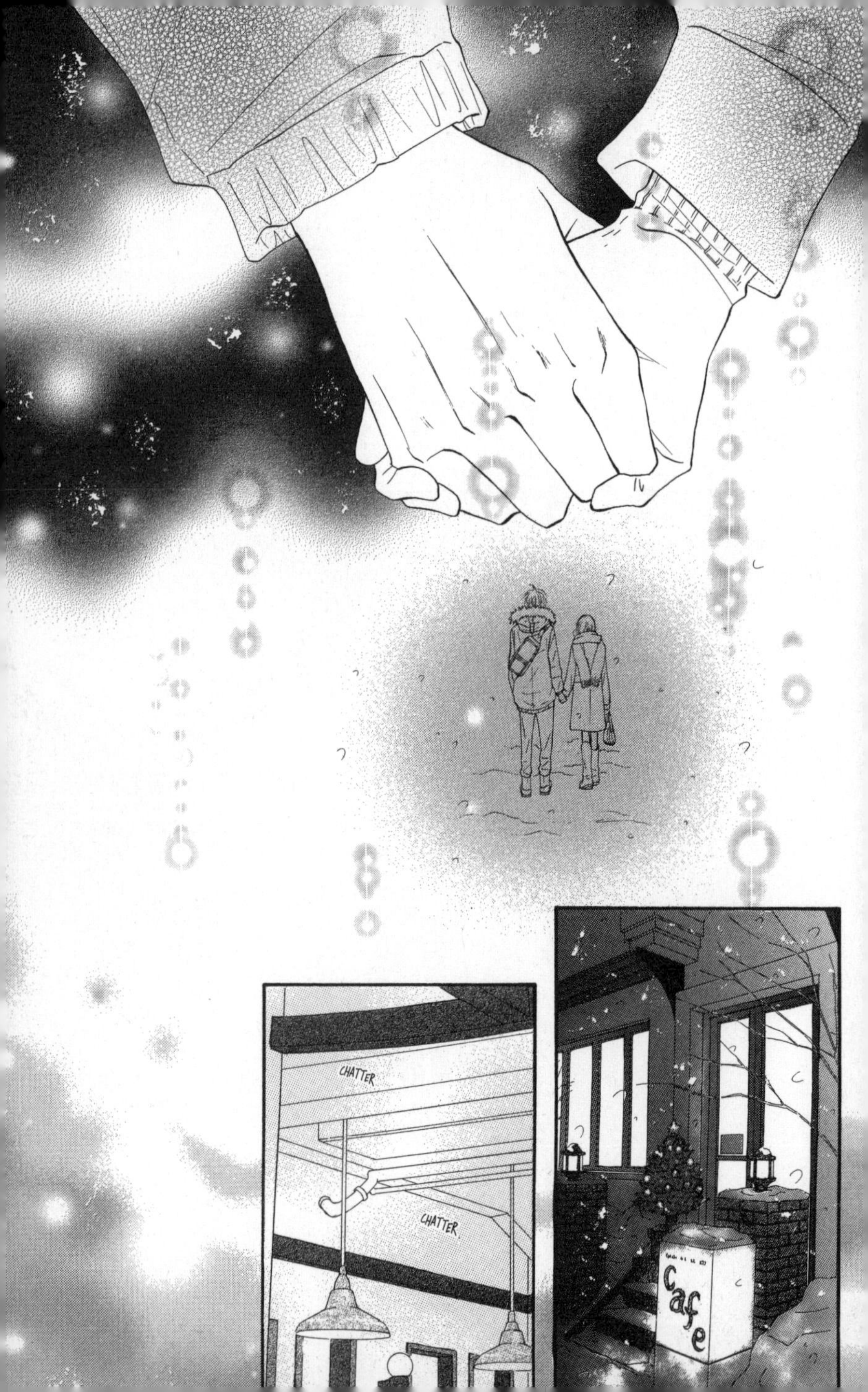
Cafe
CHATTER
CHATTER

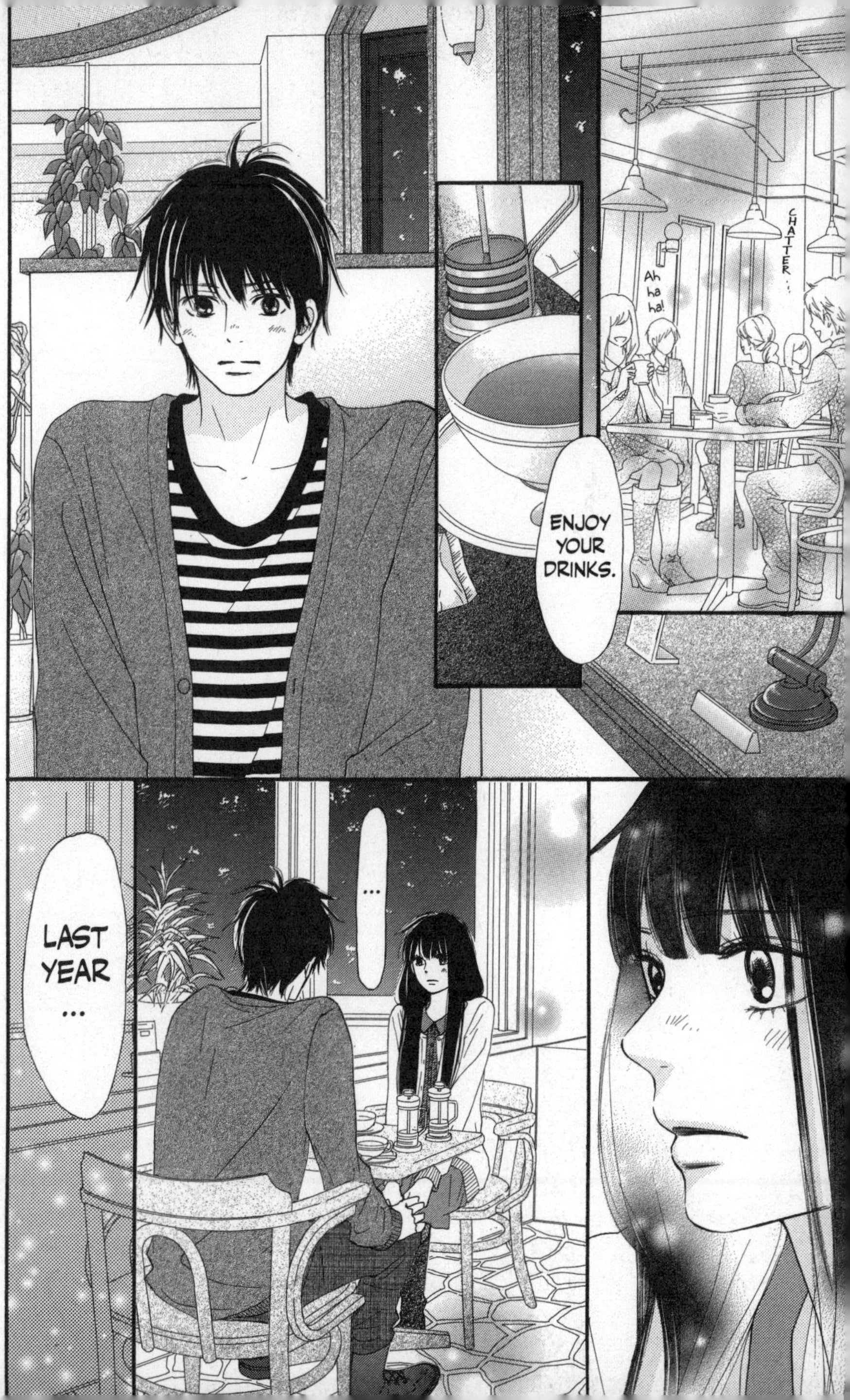
CHATTER...
Ah ha ha!
ENJOY YOUR DRINKS.
...
LAST YEAR ...

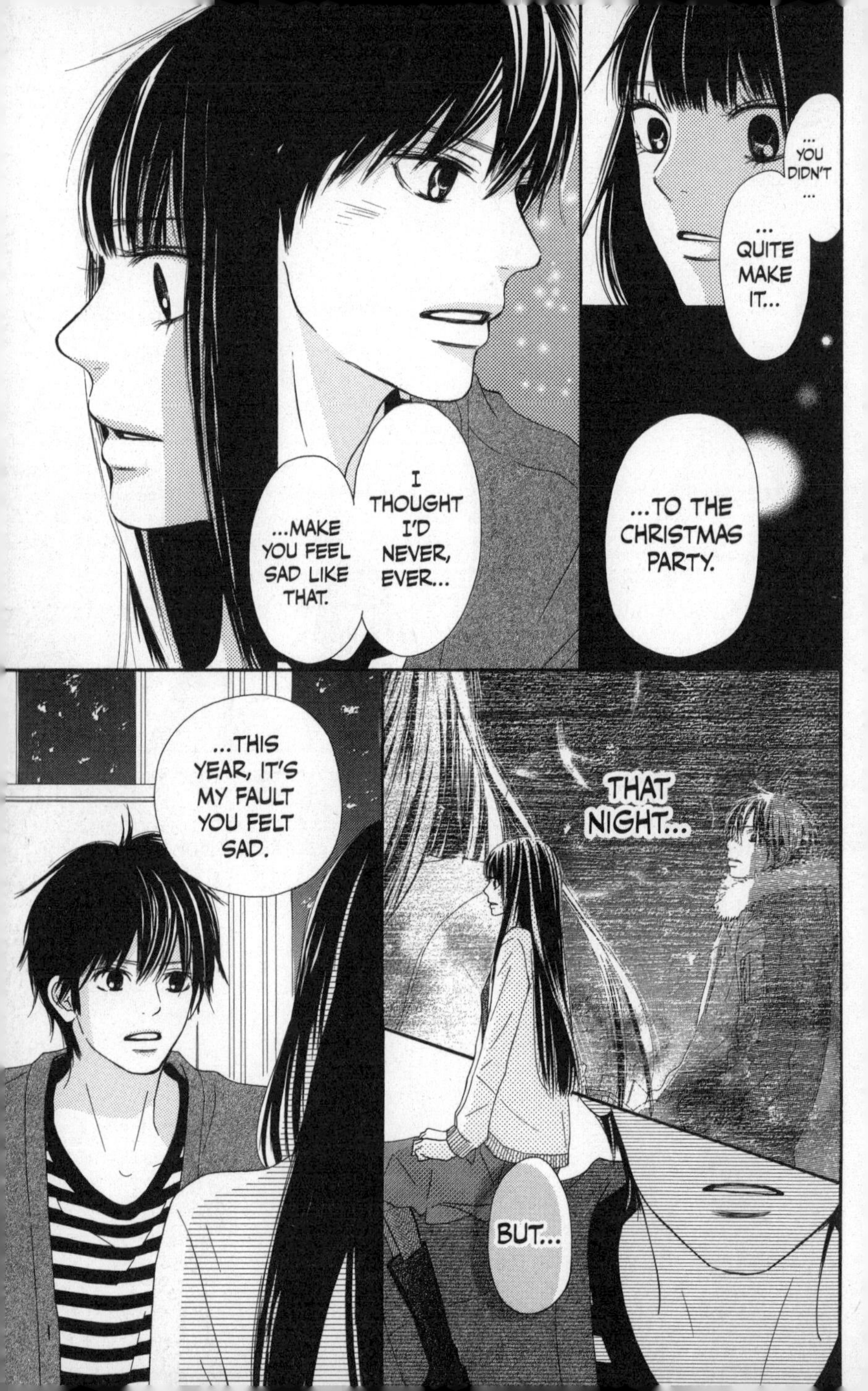
... YOU DIDN'T ...
... QUITE MAKE IT...
...TO THE CHRISTMAS PARTY.
I THOUGHT I'D NEVER, EVER...
...MAKE YOU FEEL SAD LIKE THAT.
THAT NIGHT...
BUT...
...THIS YEAR, IT'S MY FAULT YOU FELT SAD.

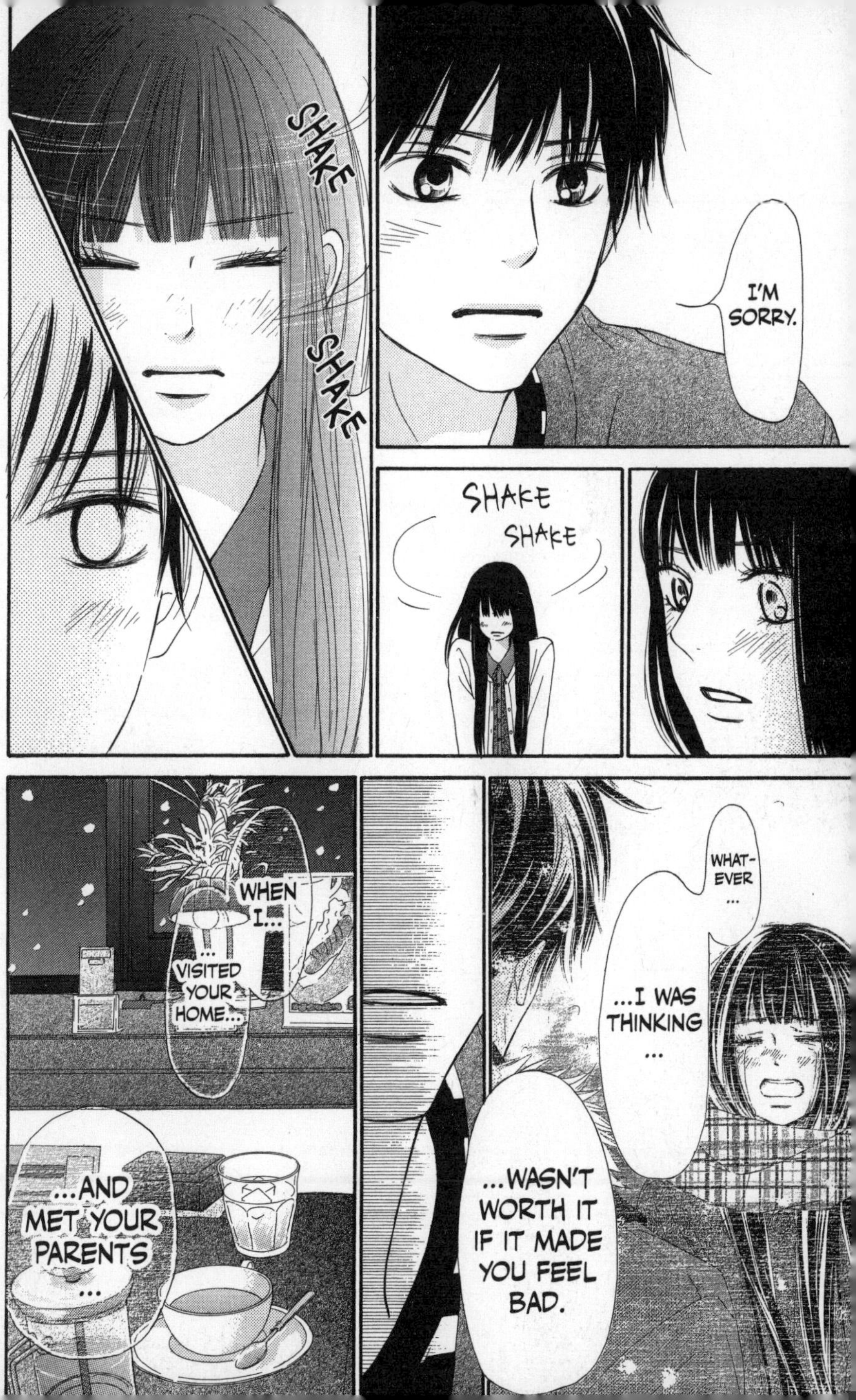
I'M SORRY.
SHAKE
SHAKE
SHAKE
SHAKE
WHAT-EVER ...
...I WAS THINKING ...
...WASN'T WORTH IT IF IT MADE YOU FEEL BAD.
WHEN I...
...VISITED YOUR HOME...
...AND MET YOUR PARENTS ...

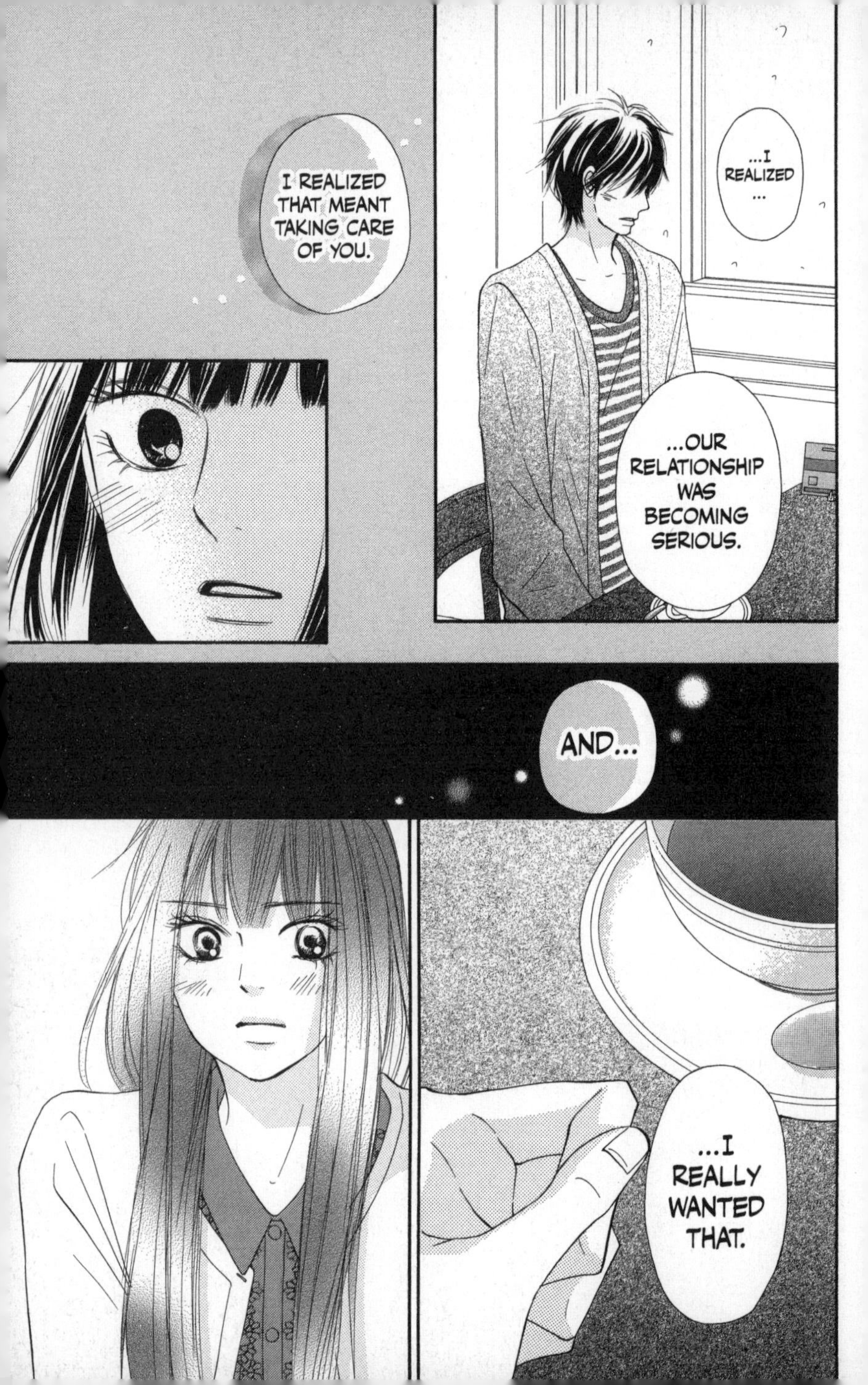
...I REALIZED ...
...OUR RELATIONSHIP WAS BECOMING SERIOUS.
I REALIZED THAT MEANT TAKING CARE OF YOU.
AND...
...I REALLY WANTED THAT.

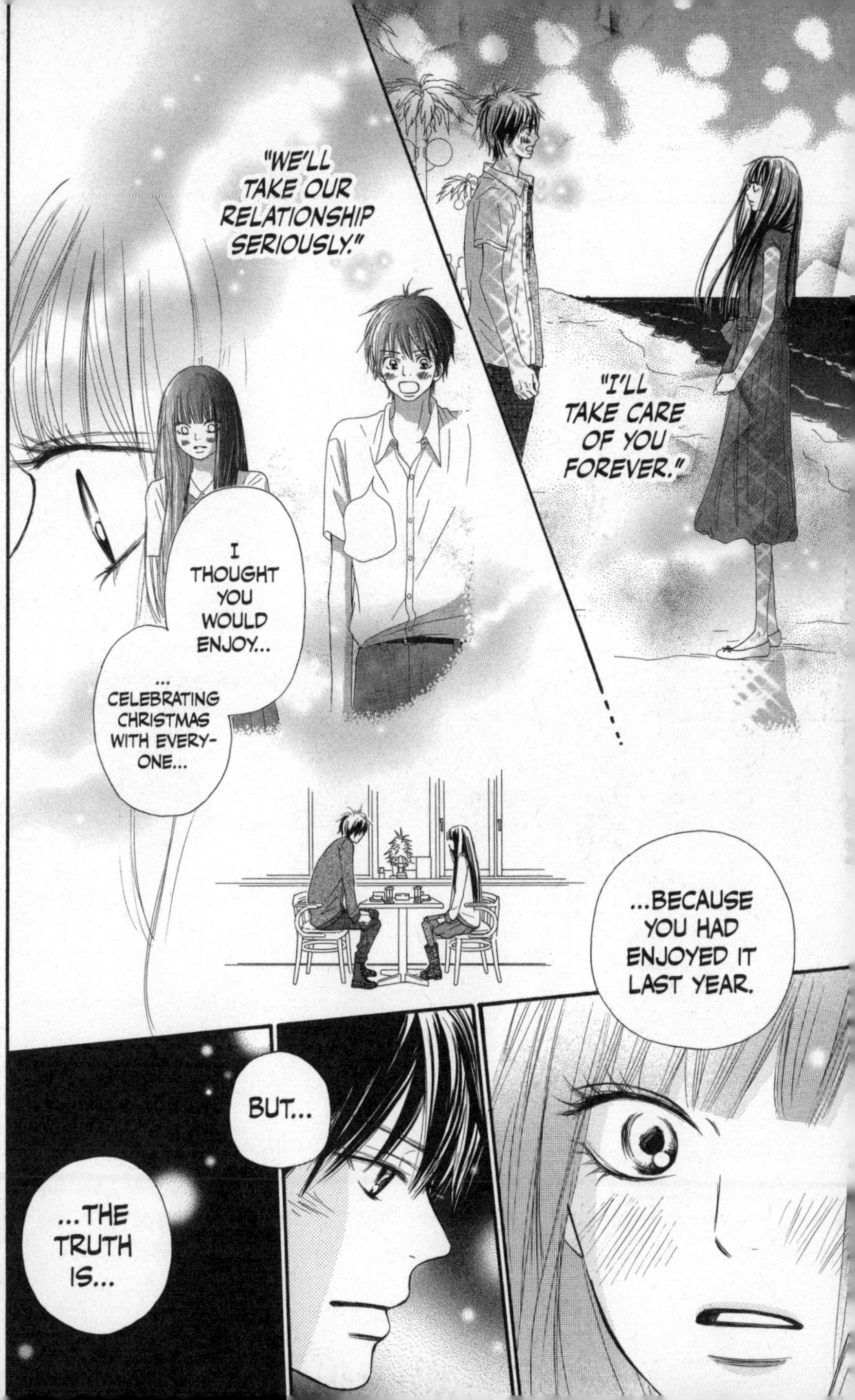
"I'LL TAKE CARE OF YOU FOREVER."
"WE'LL TAKE OUR RELATIONSHIP SERIOUSLY."
I THOUGHT YOU WOULD ENJOY...
...CELEBRATING CHRISTMAS WITH EVERY-ONE...
...BECAUSE YOU HAD ENJOYED IT LAST YEAR.
BUT...
...THE TRUTH IS...

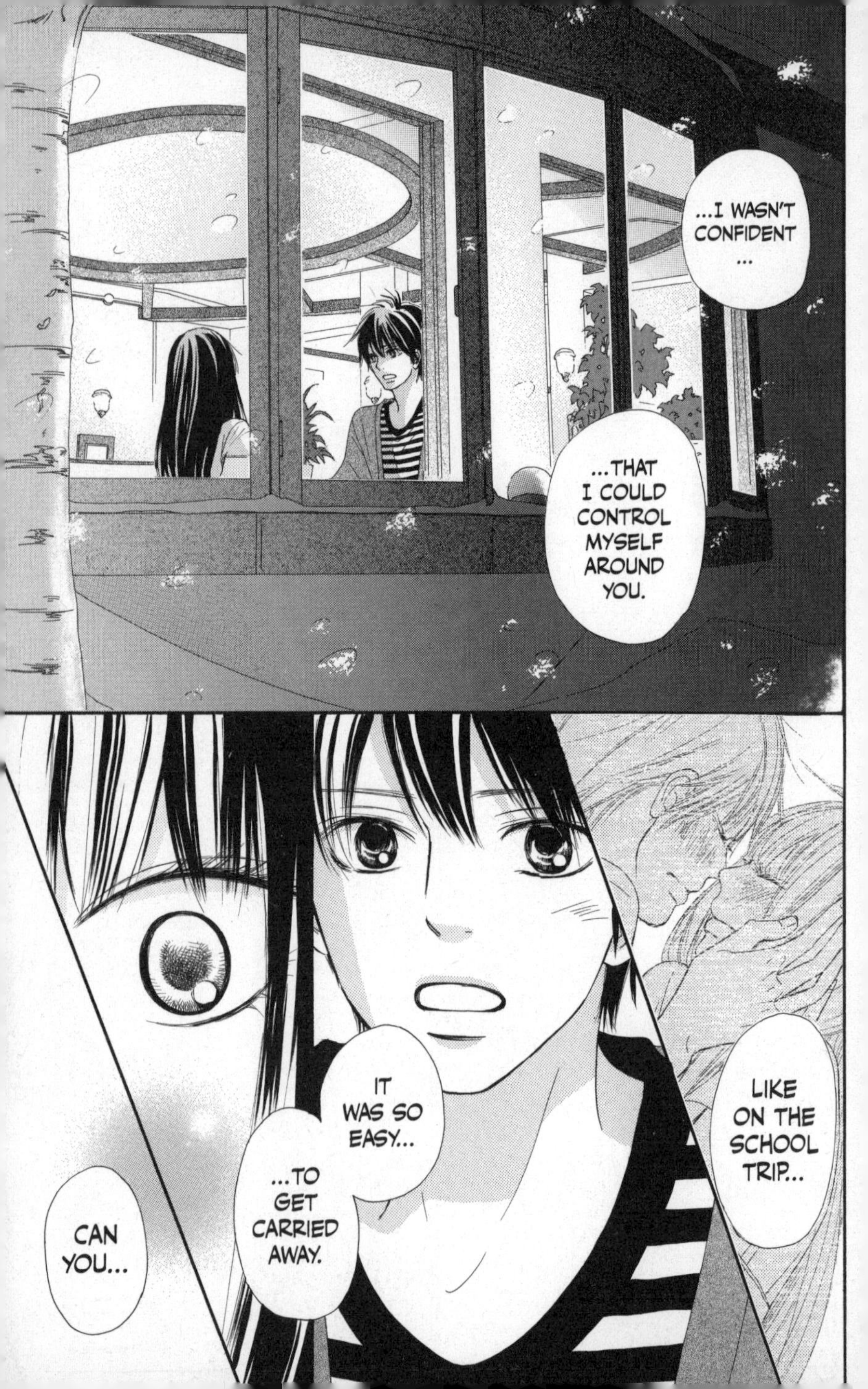
...I WASN'T CONFIDENT ...
...THAT I COULD CONTROL MYSELF AROUND YOU.
LIKE ON THE SCHOOL TRIP...
IT WAS SO EASY...
...TO GET CARRIED AWAY.
CAN YOU...

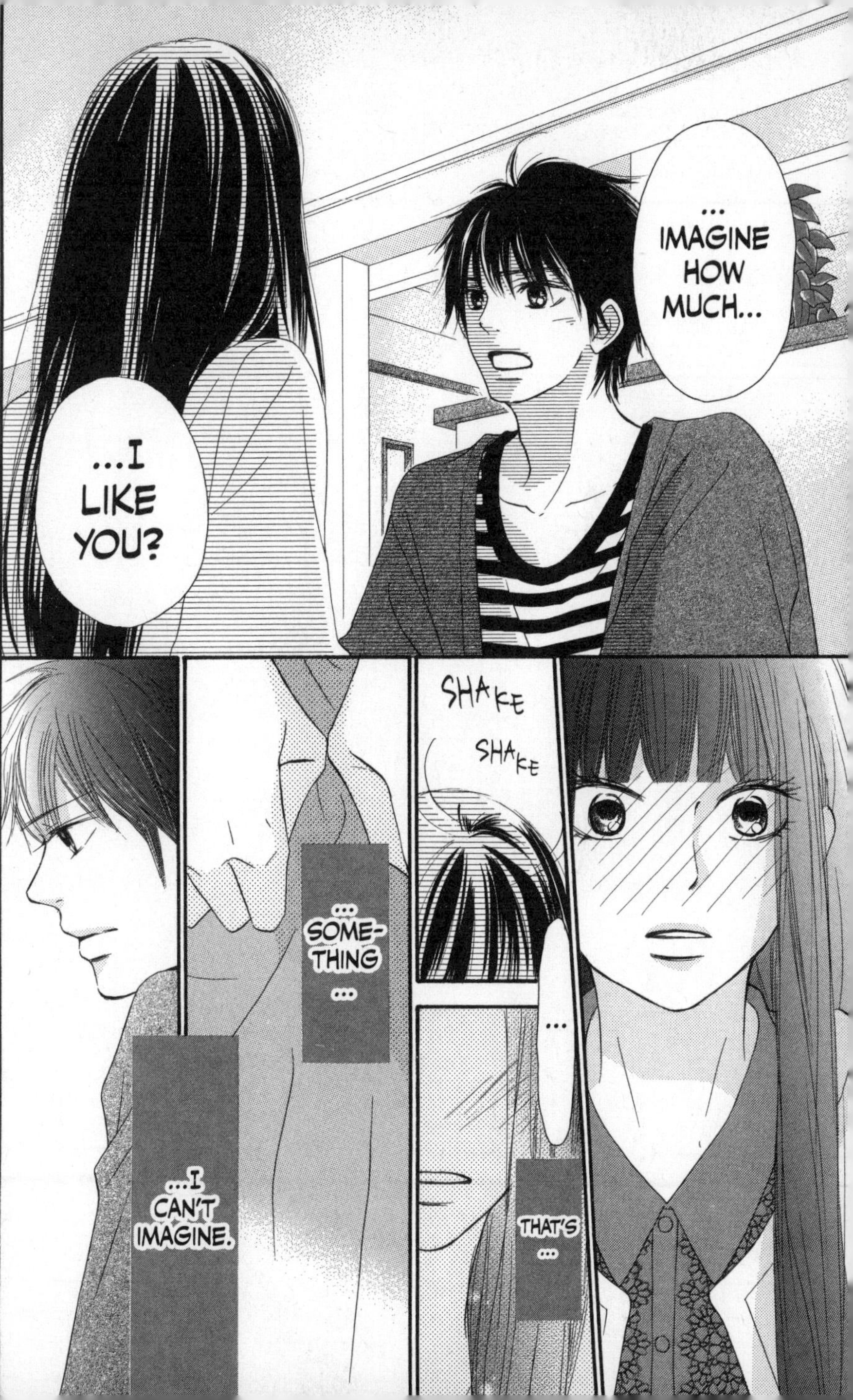

... IMAGINE HOW MUCH...
...I LIKE YOU?
...
THAT'S ...
SHAKE
SHAKE
... SOME-THING ...
...I CAN'T IMAGINE.

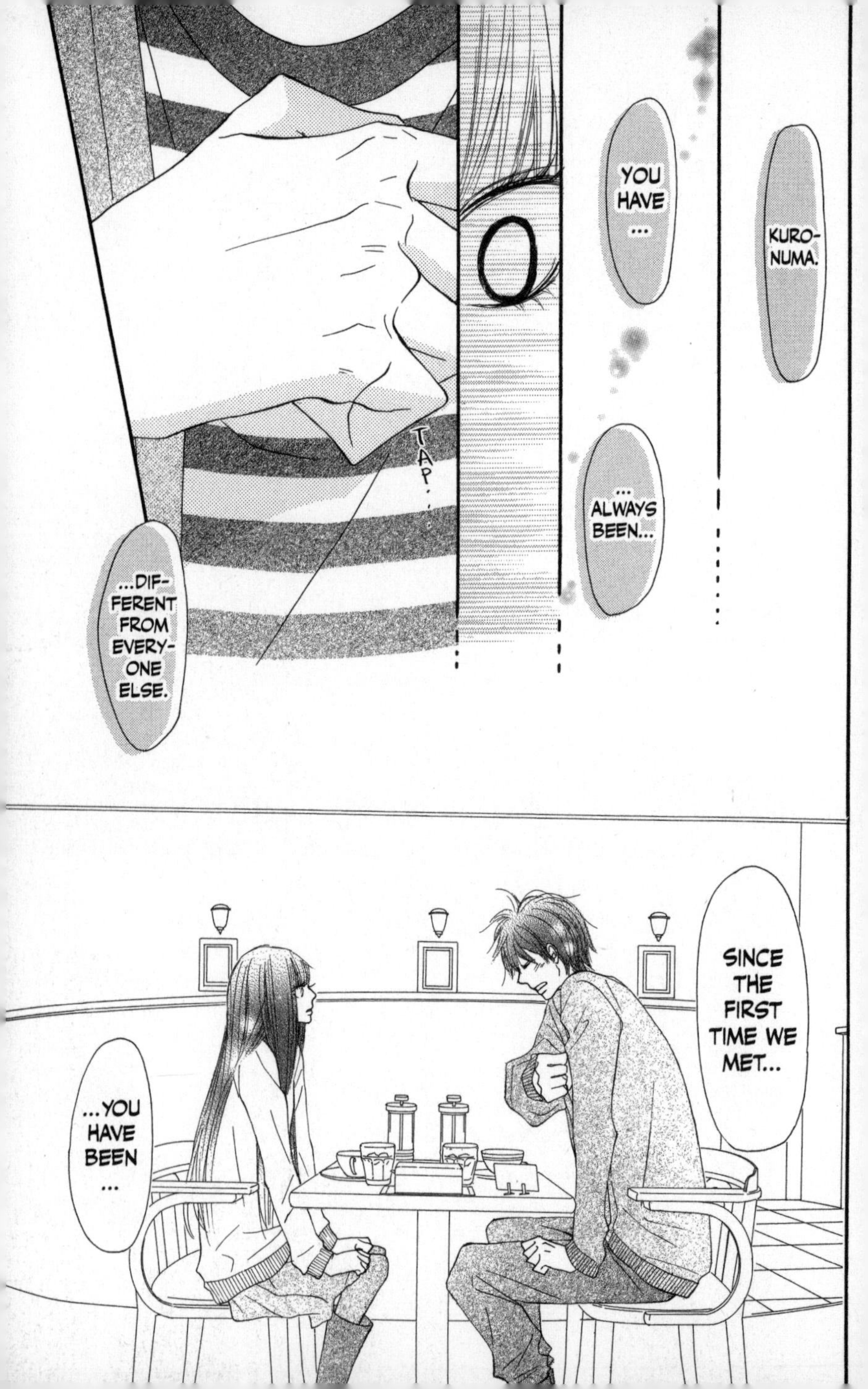
KURO-NUMA.
YOU HAVE ...
... ALWAYS BEEN...
TAP . .
...DIF-FERENT FROM EVERY-ONE ELSE.
SINCE THE FIRST TIME WE MET...
...YOU HAVE BEEN ...

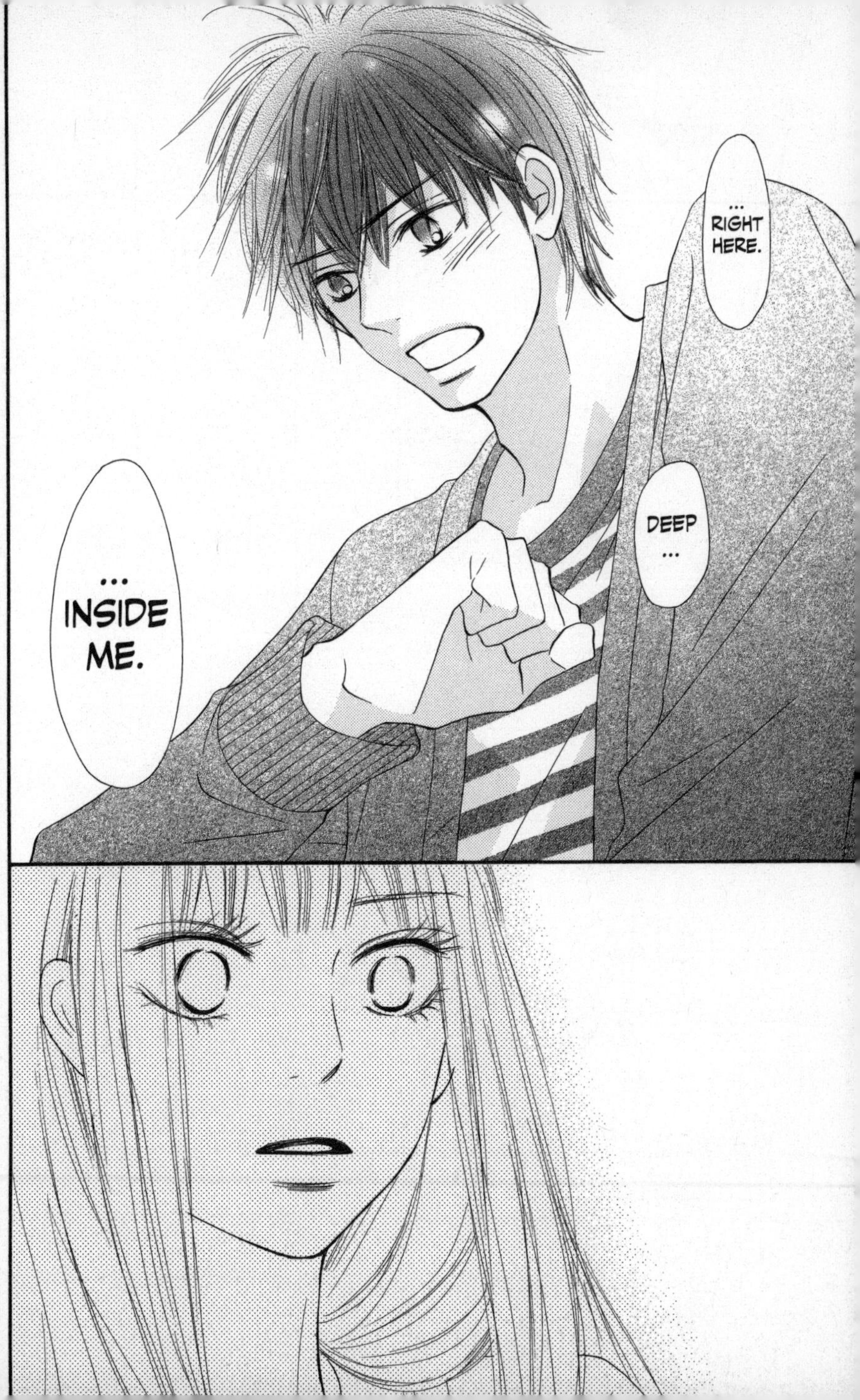
... RIGHT HERE.
DEEP ...
... INSIDE ME.

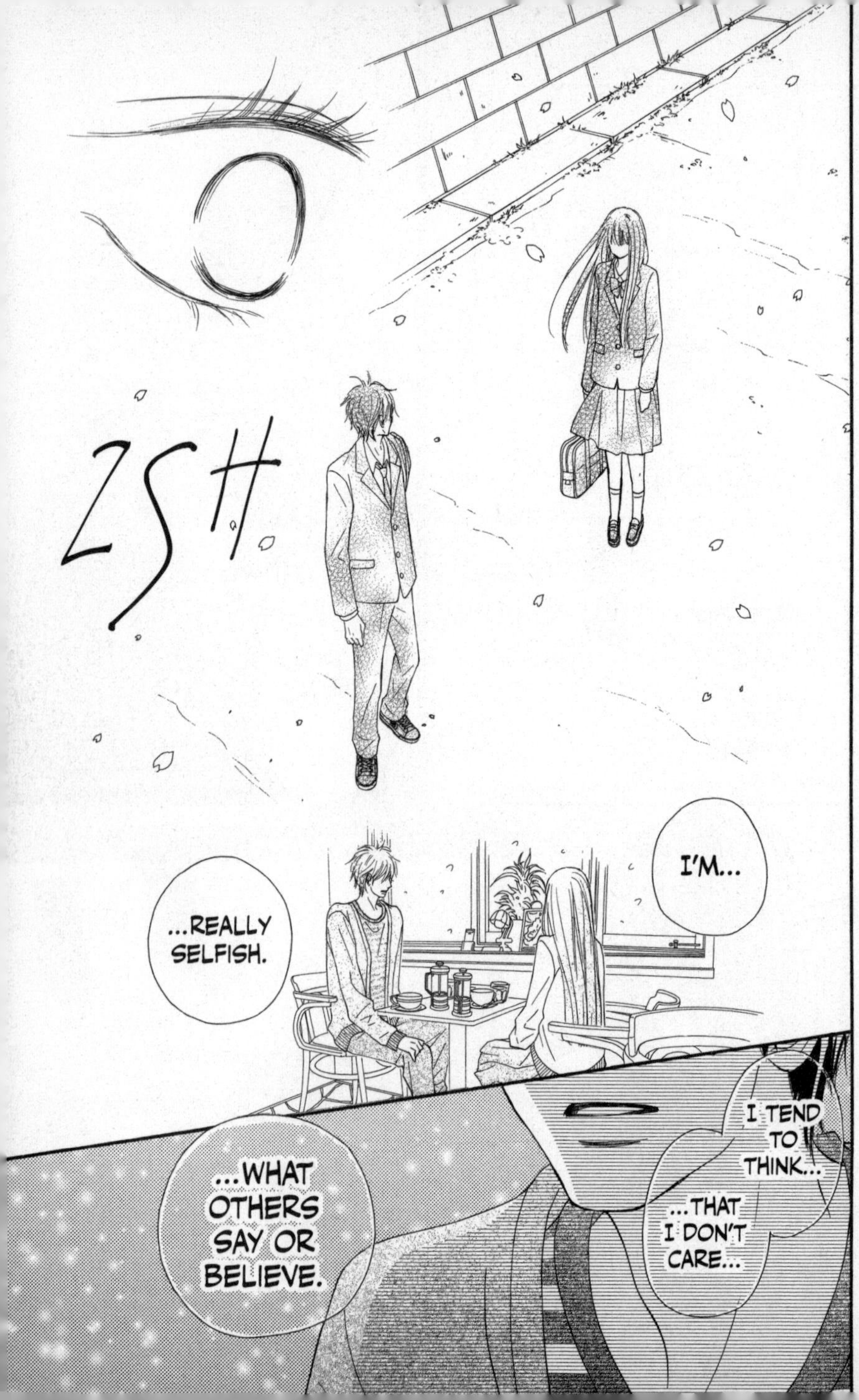
ZSH
I'M...
...REALLY SELFISH.
I TEND TO THINK...
...THAT I DON'T CARE...
...WHAT OTHERS SAY OR BELIEVE.

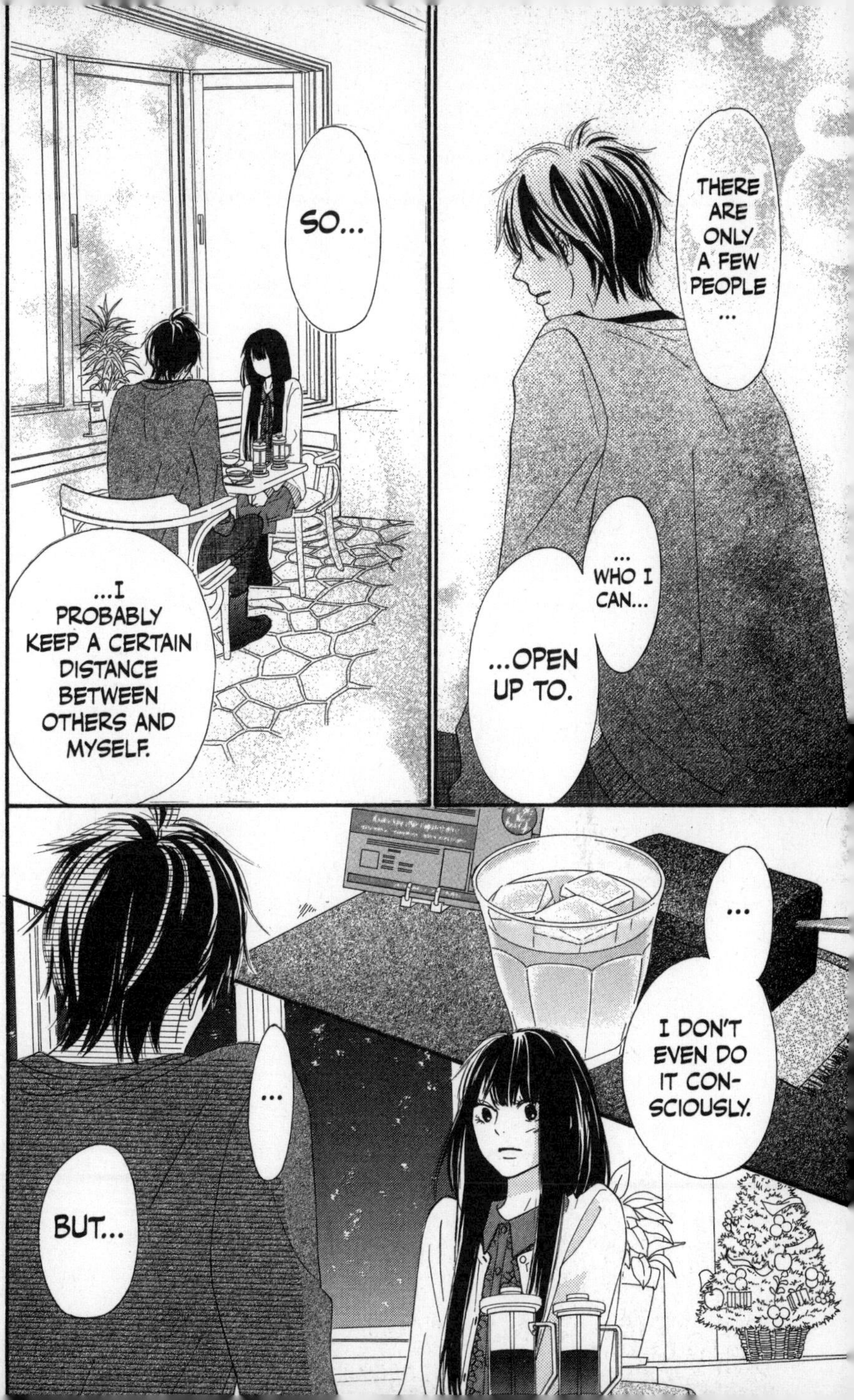
THERE ARE ONLY A FEW PEOPLE ...
... WHO I CAN...
...OPEN UP TO.
SO...
...I PROBABLY KEEP A CERTAIN DISTANCE BETWEEN OTHERS AND MYSELF.
...
I DON'T EVEN DO IT CON-SCIOUSLY.
...
BUT...

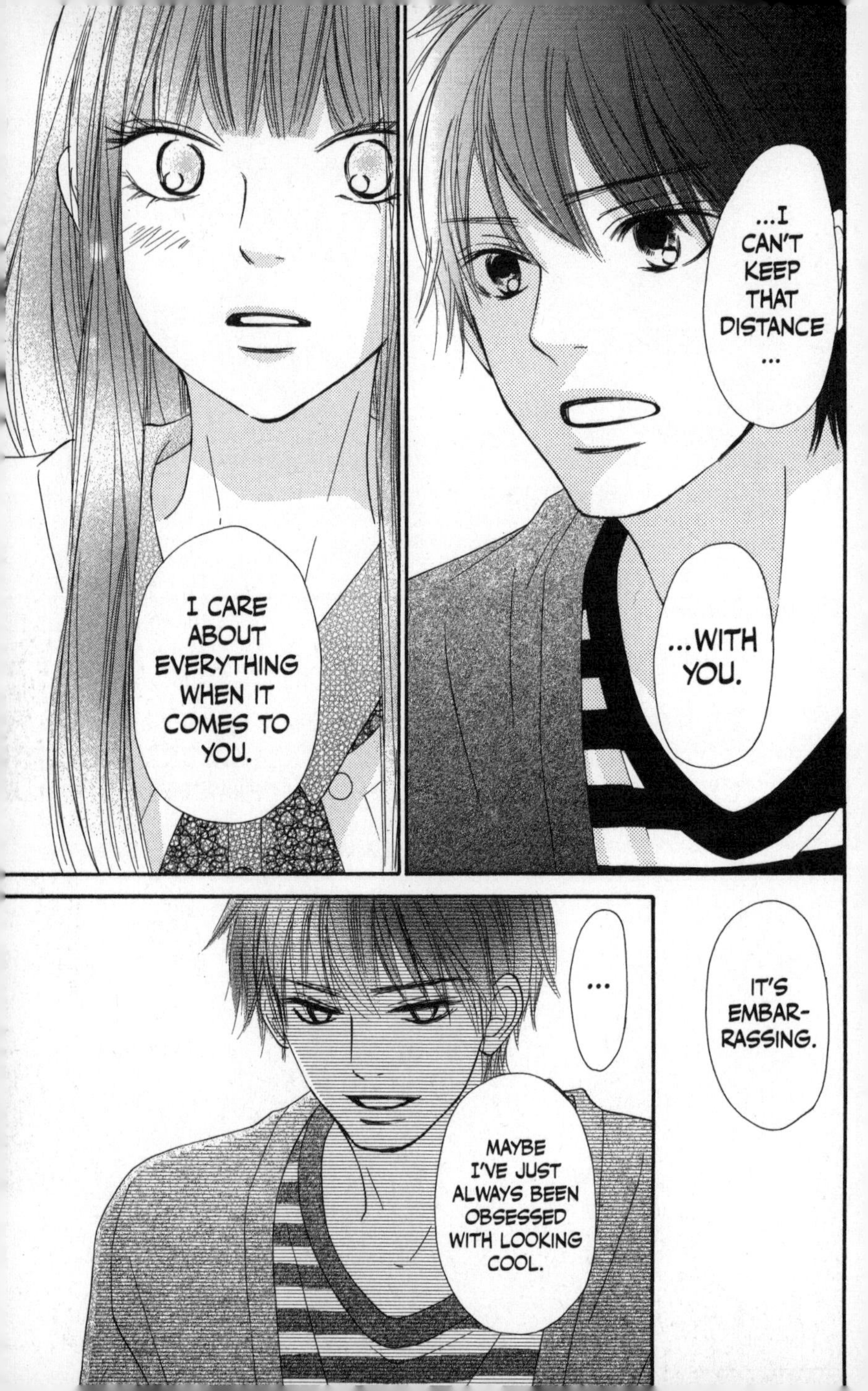
...I CAN'T KEEP THAT DISTANCE ...
...WITH YOU.
I CARE ABOUT EVERYTHING WHEN IT COMES TO YOU.
IT'S EMBAR-RASSING.
...
MAYBE I'VE JUST ALWAYS BEEN OBSESSED WITH LOOKING COOL.

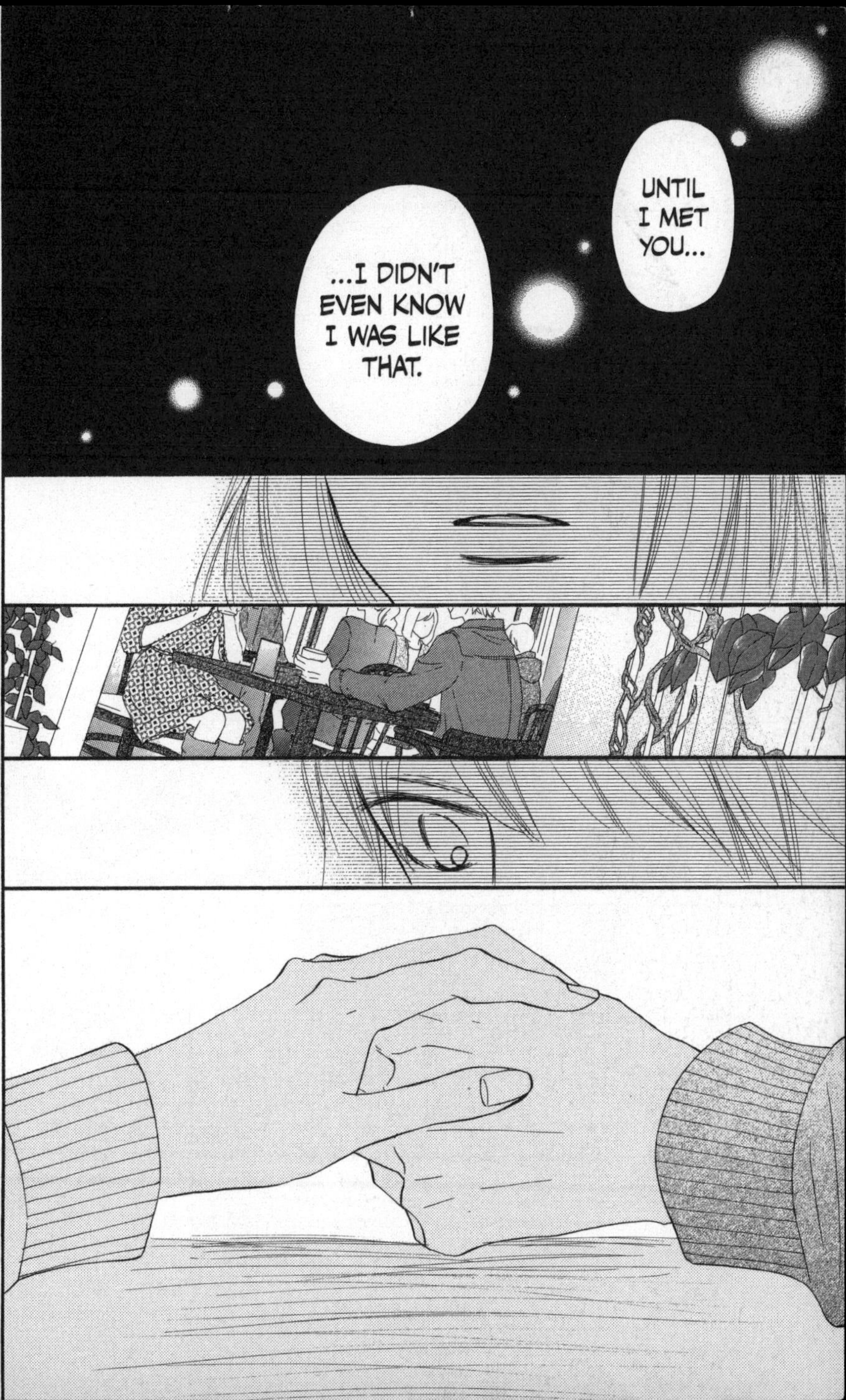
UNTIL I MET YOU...
...I DIDN'T EVEN KNOW I WAS LIKE THAT.

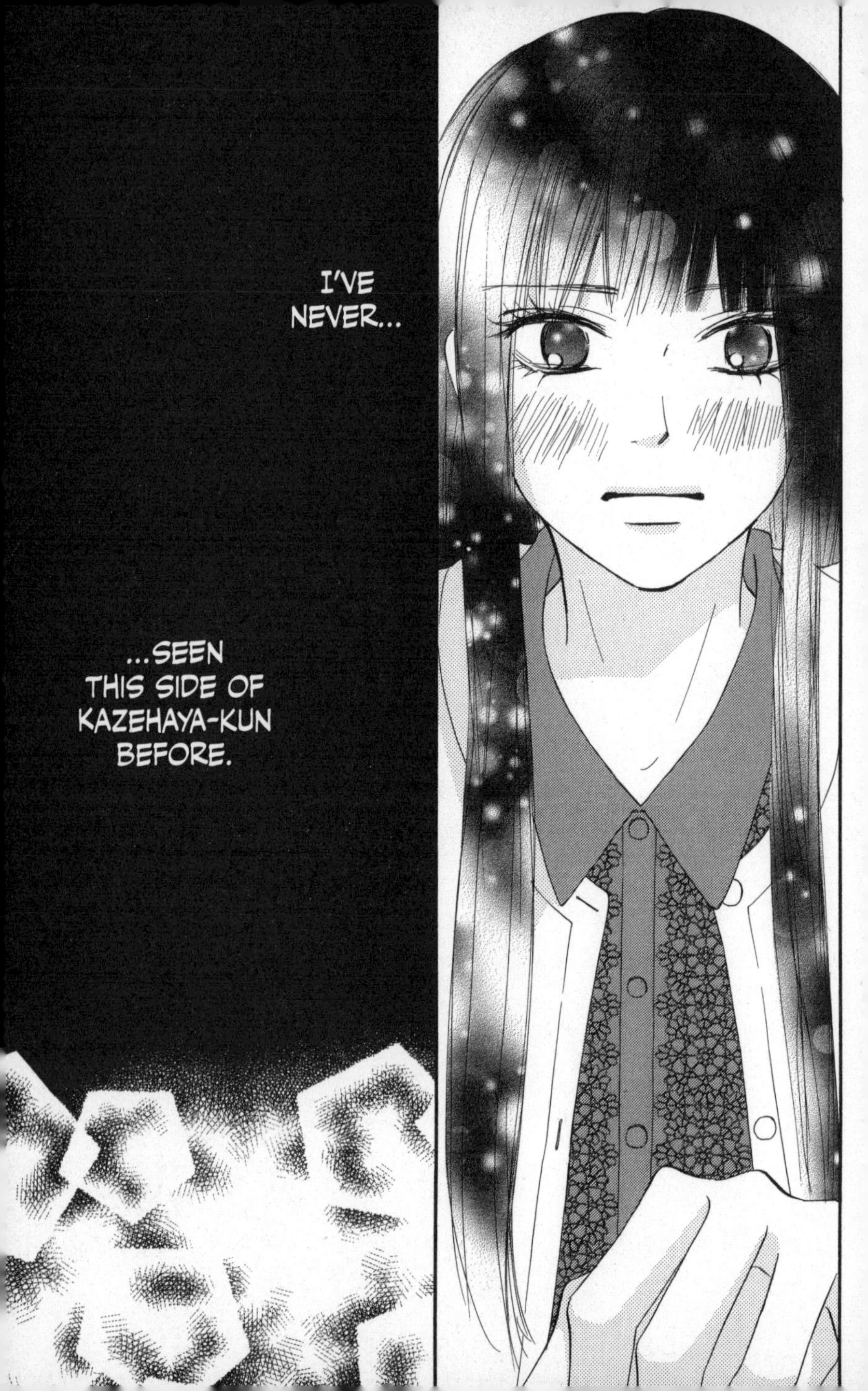
I'VE NEVER...
...SEEN THIS SIDE OF KAZEHAYA-KUN BEFORE.

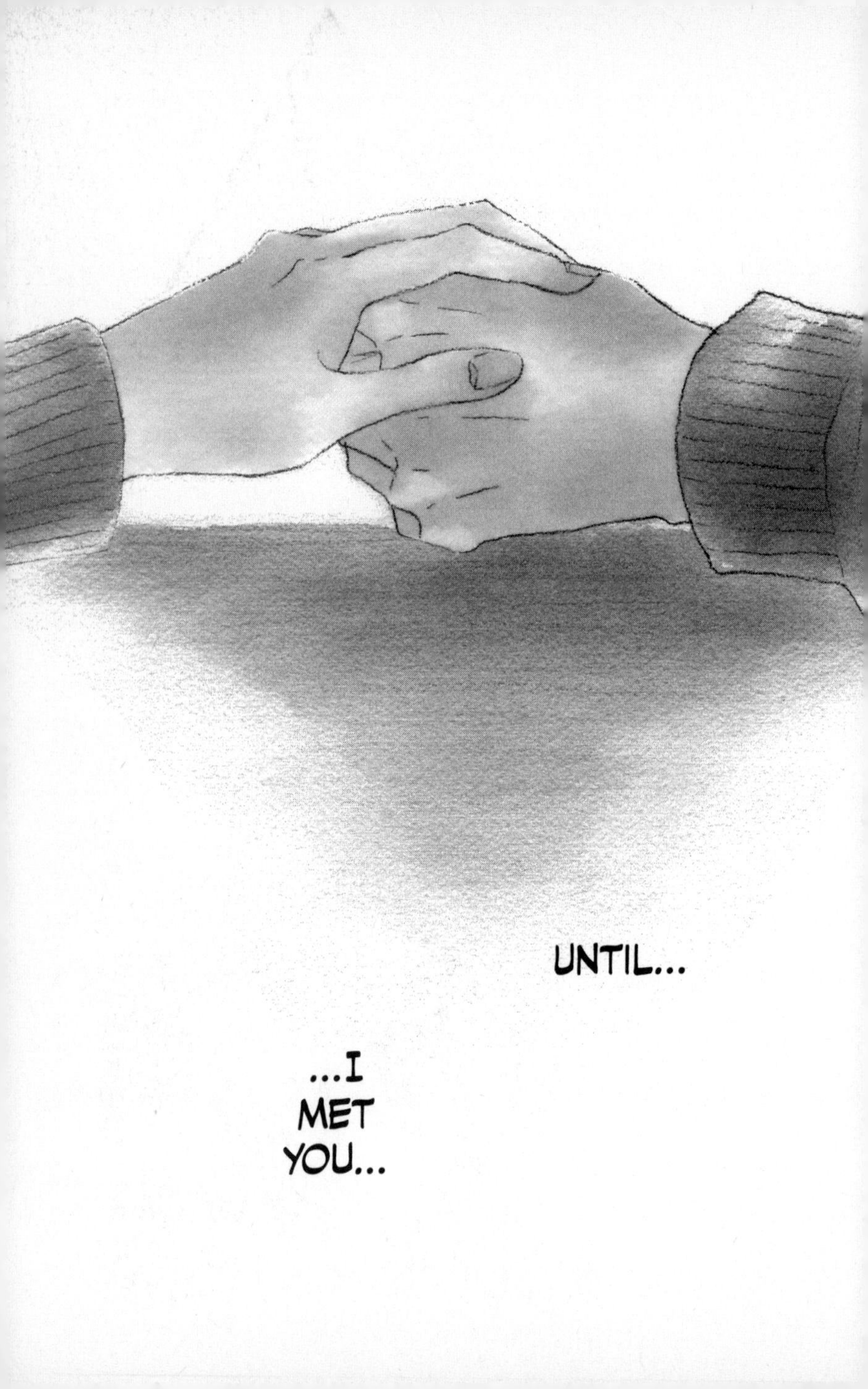
UNTIL...
...I MET YOU...

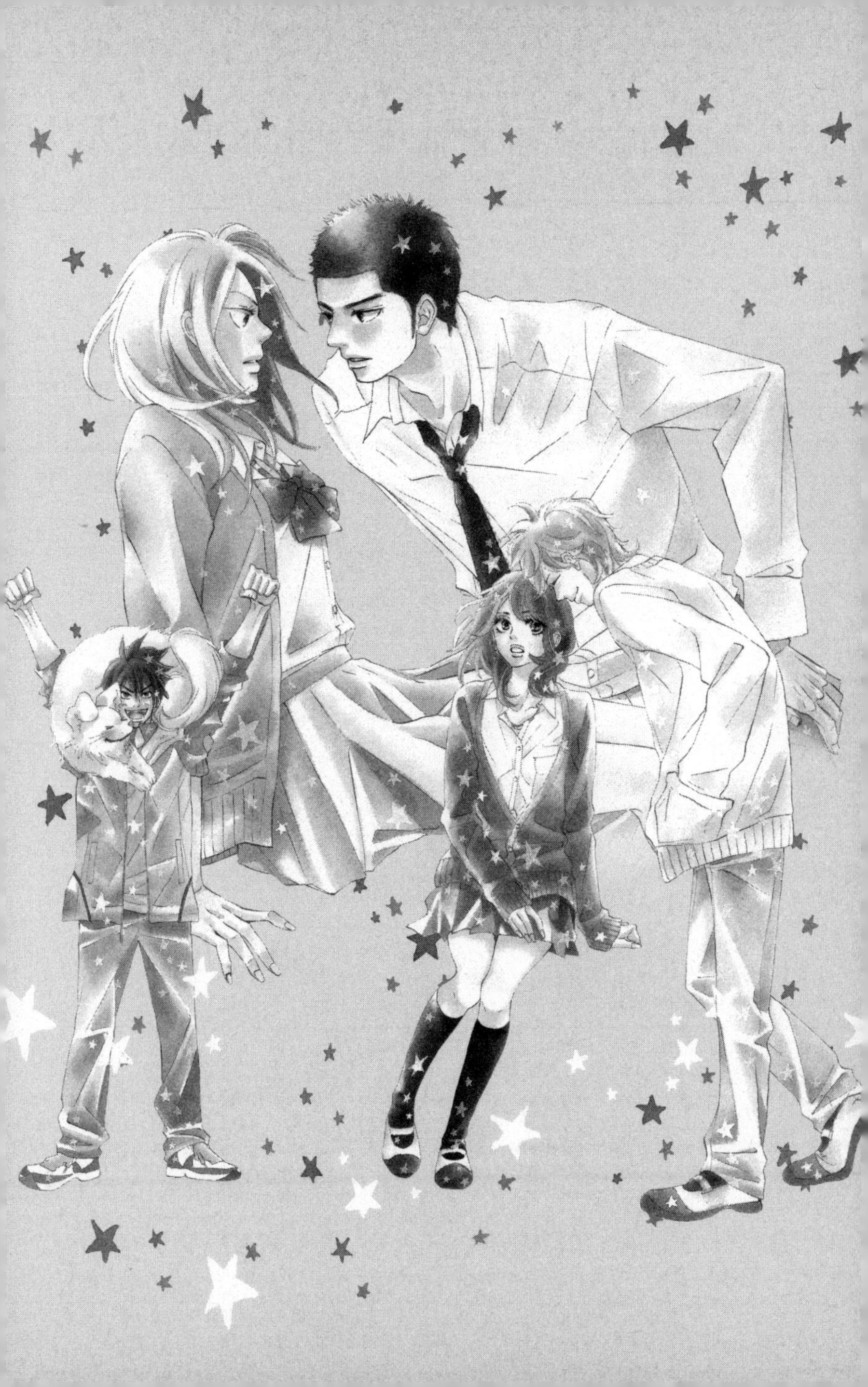

Episode 73: Paying Attention

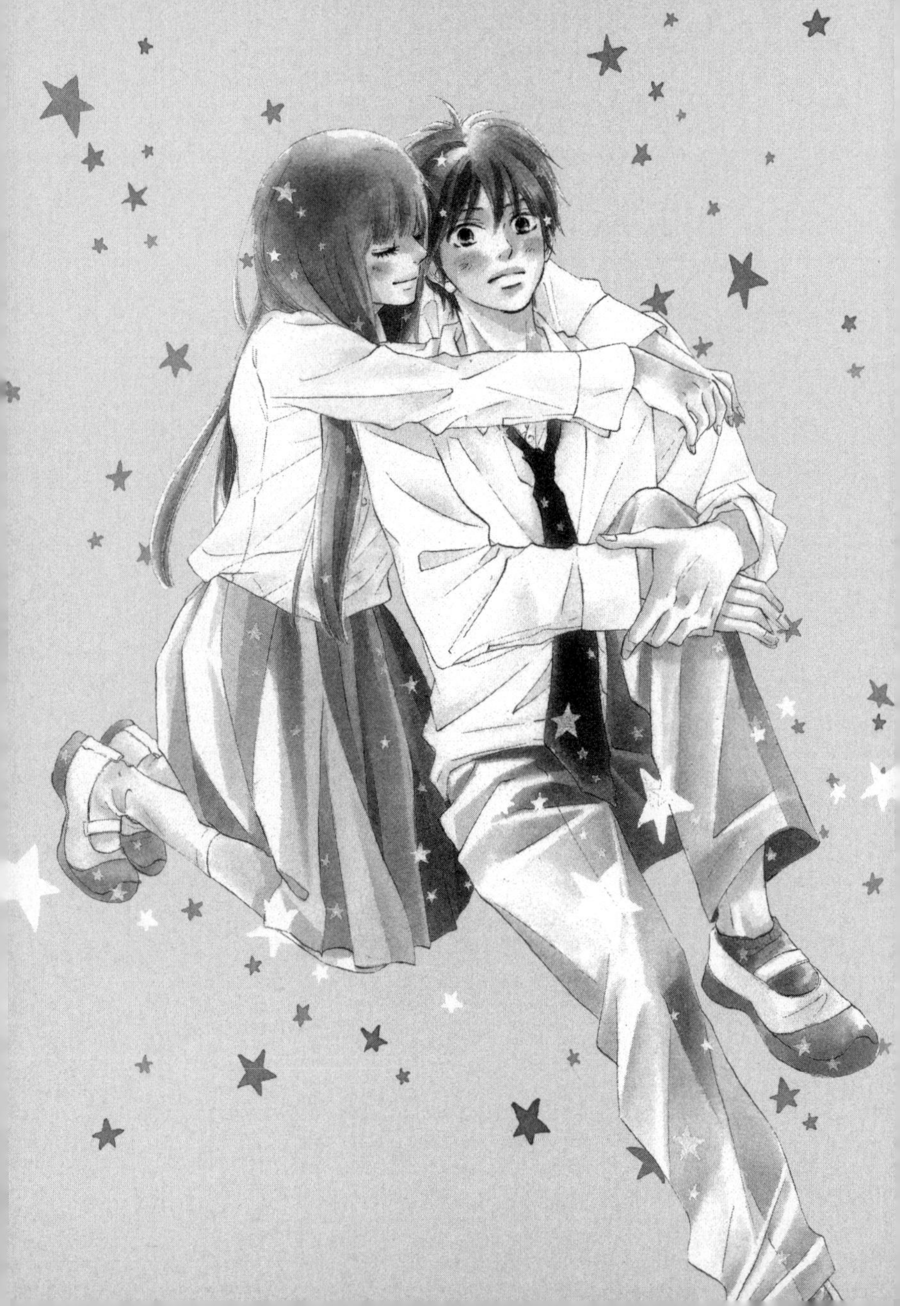

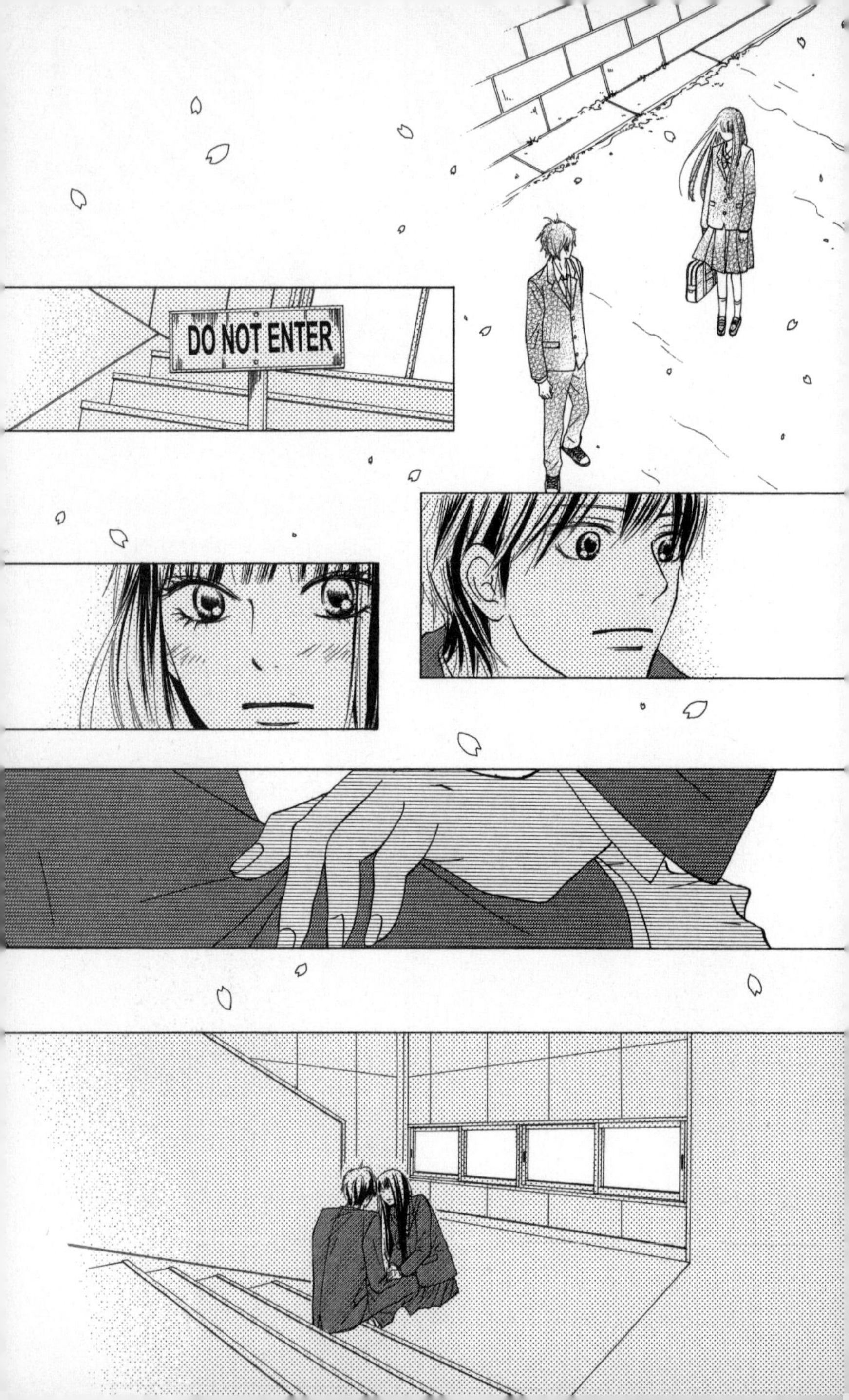
DO NOT ENTER

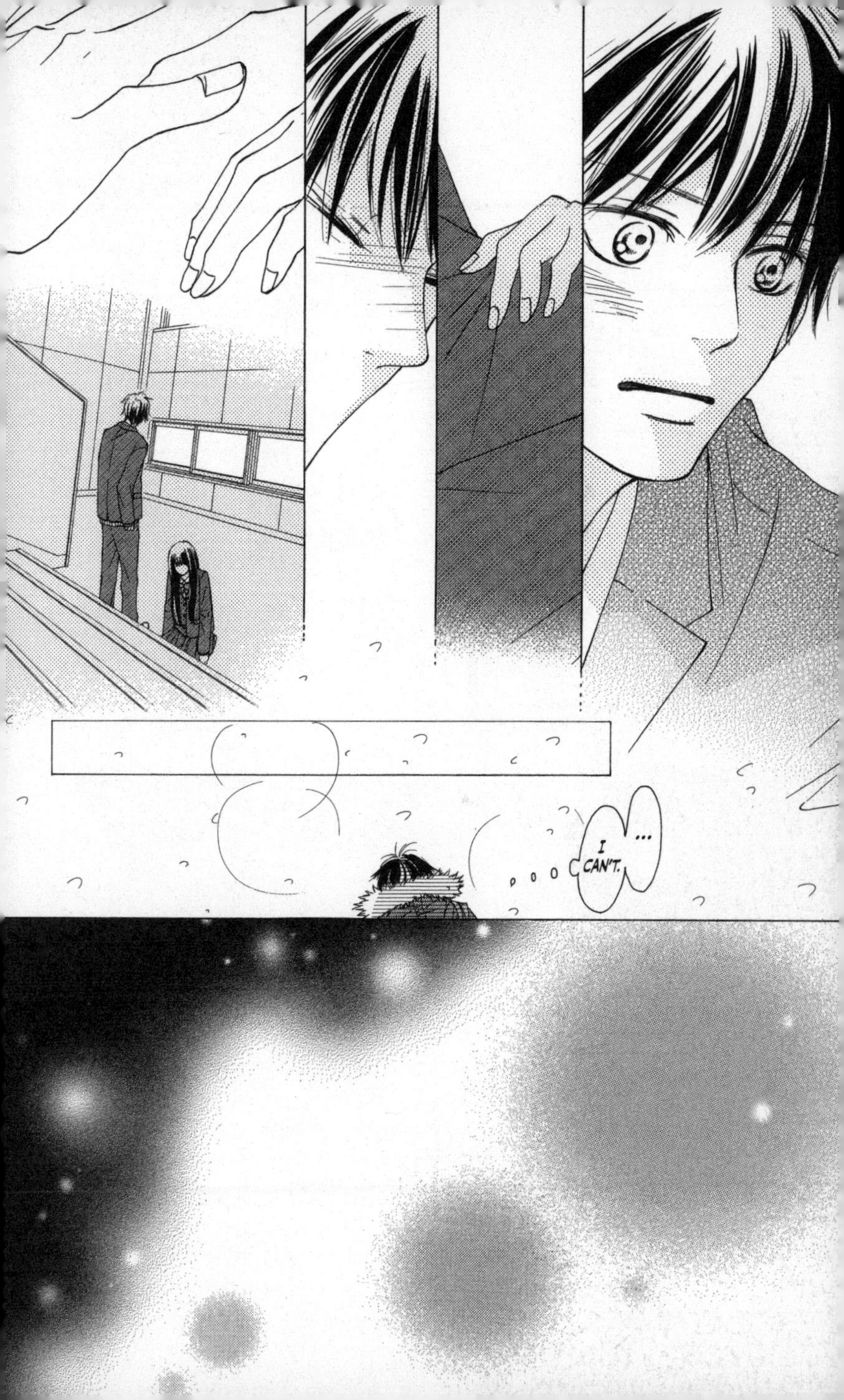

...
I CAN'T.

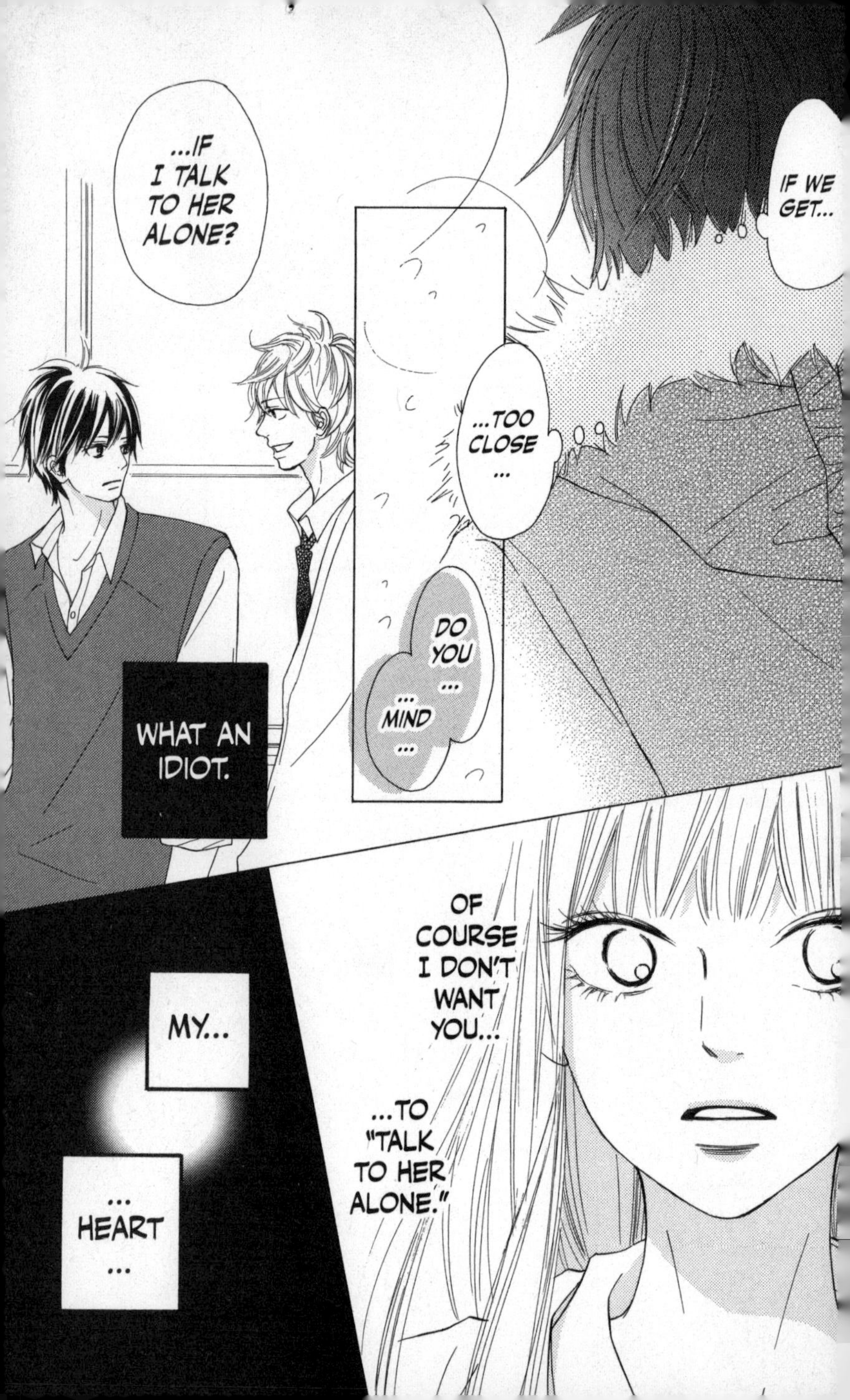
IF WE GET...
...TOO CLOSE...
DO YOU... ...MIND...
...IF I TALK TO HER ALONE?
WHAT AN IDIOT.
OF COURSE I DON'T WANT YOU...
...TO "TALK TO HER ALONE."
MY...
...HEART...

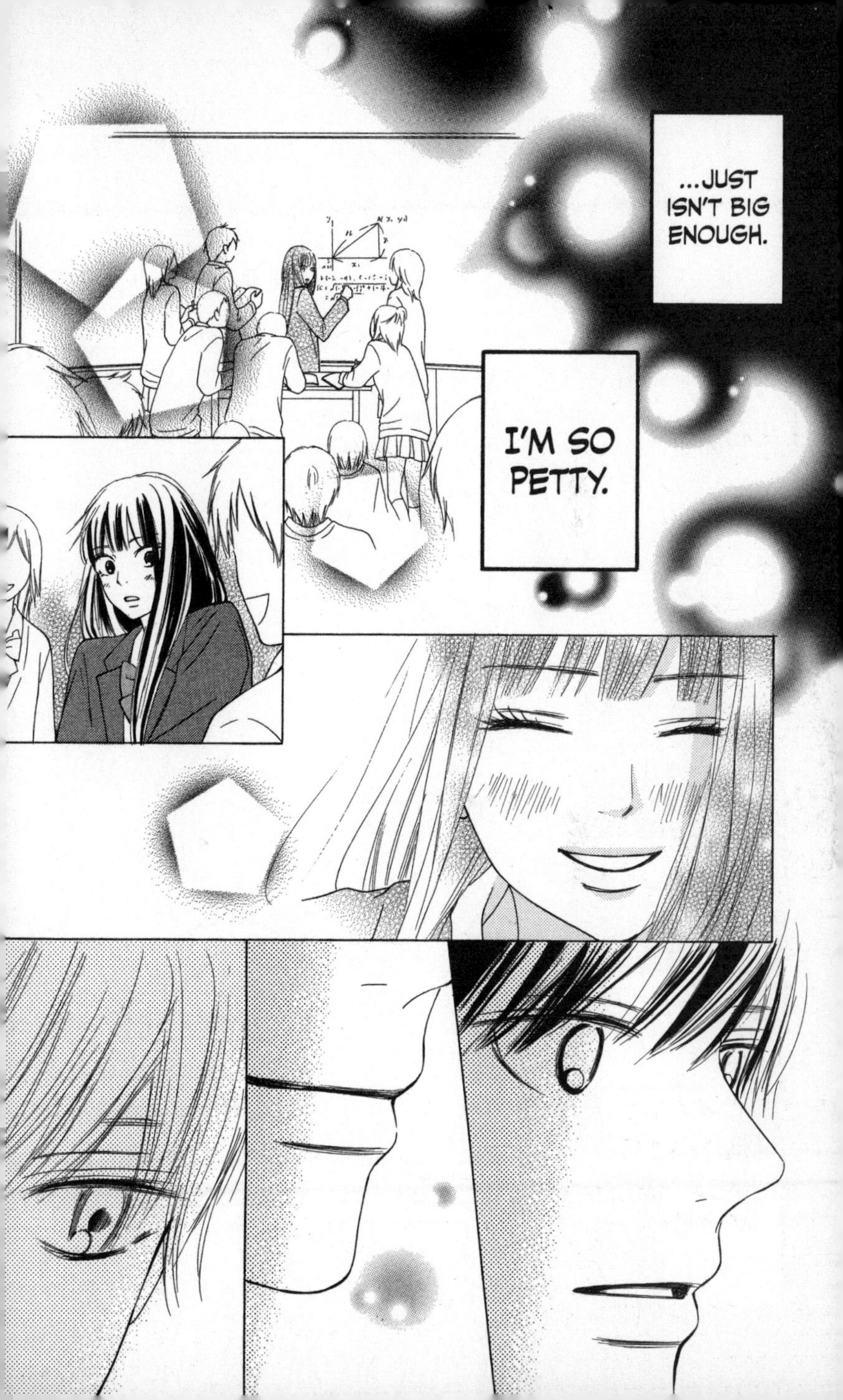
...JUST ISN'T BIG ENOUGH.
I'M SO PETTY.

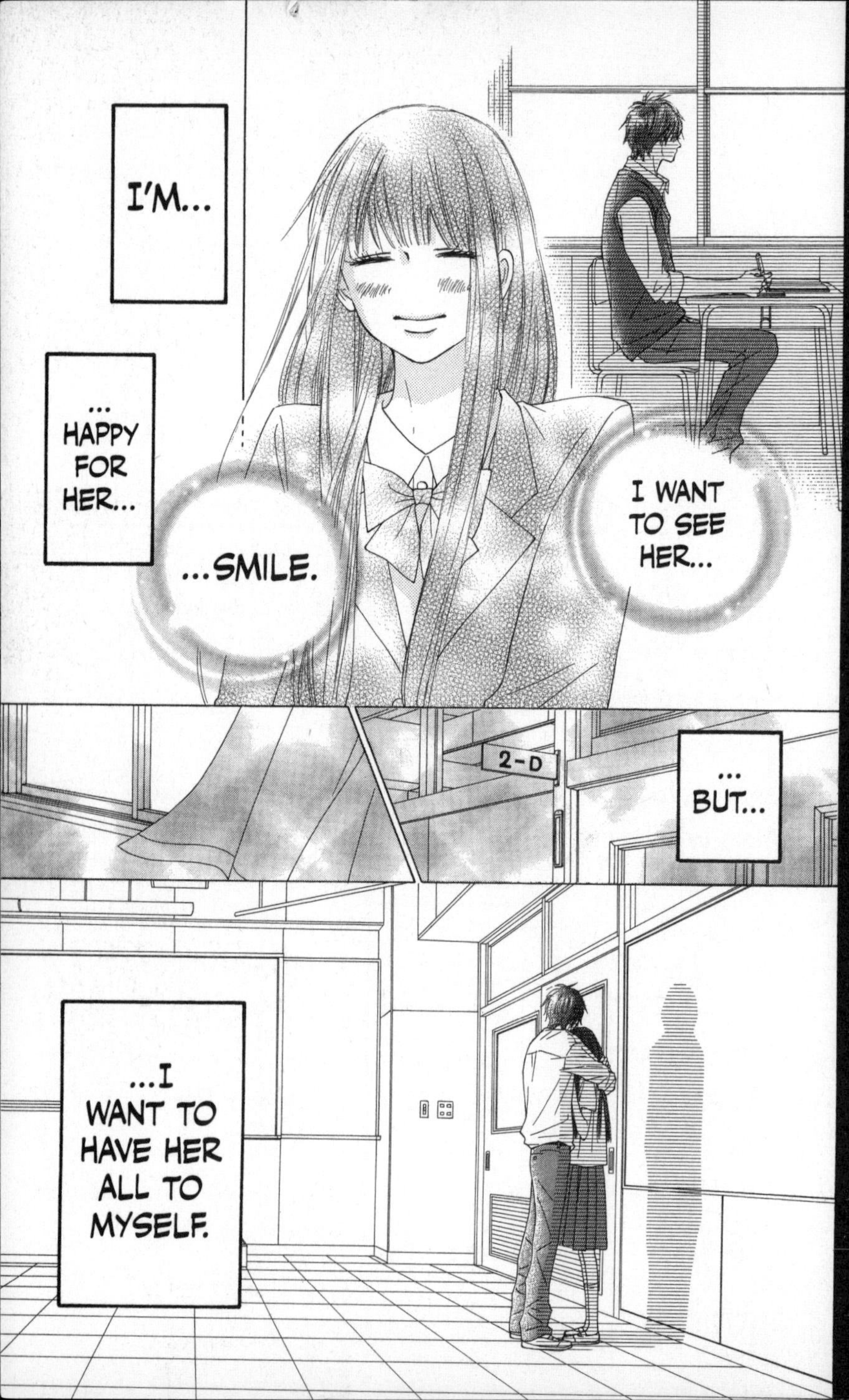
I WANT TO SEE HER...
...SMILE.
I'M...
...HAPPY FOR HER...
2-D
...BUT...
...I WANT TO HAVE HER ALL TO MYSELF.

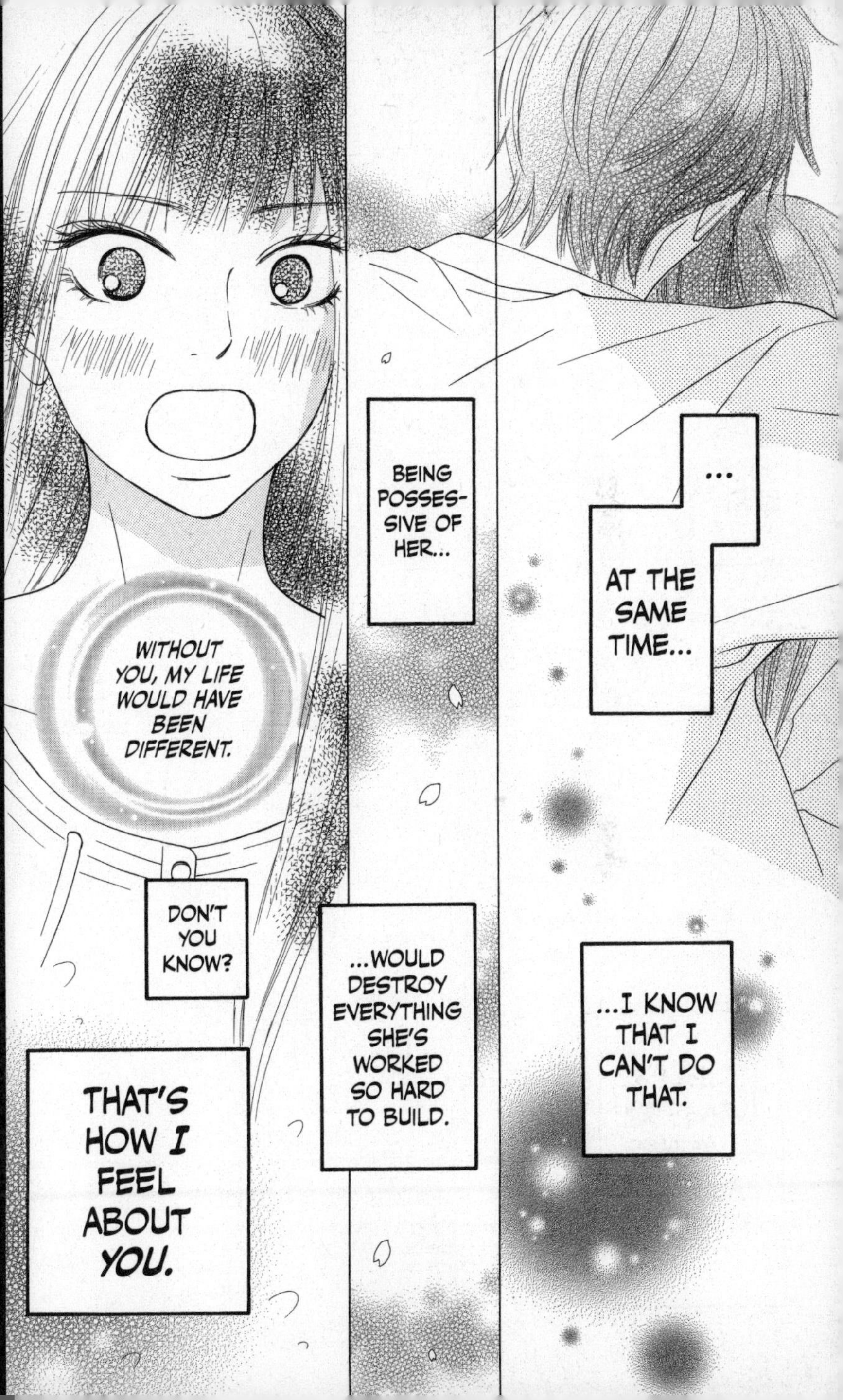
...
AT THE SAME TIME...
...I KNOW THAT I CAN'T DO THAT.
BEING POSSES-SIVE OF HER...
...WOULD DESTROY EVERYTHING SHE'S WORKED SO HARD TO BUILD.
WITHOUT YOU, MY LIFE WOULD HAVE BEEN DIFFERENT.
DON'T YOU KNOW?
THAT'S HOW *I* FEEL ABOUT *YOU.*

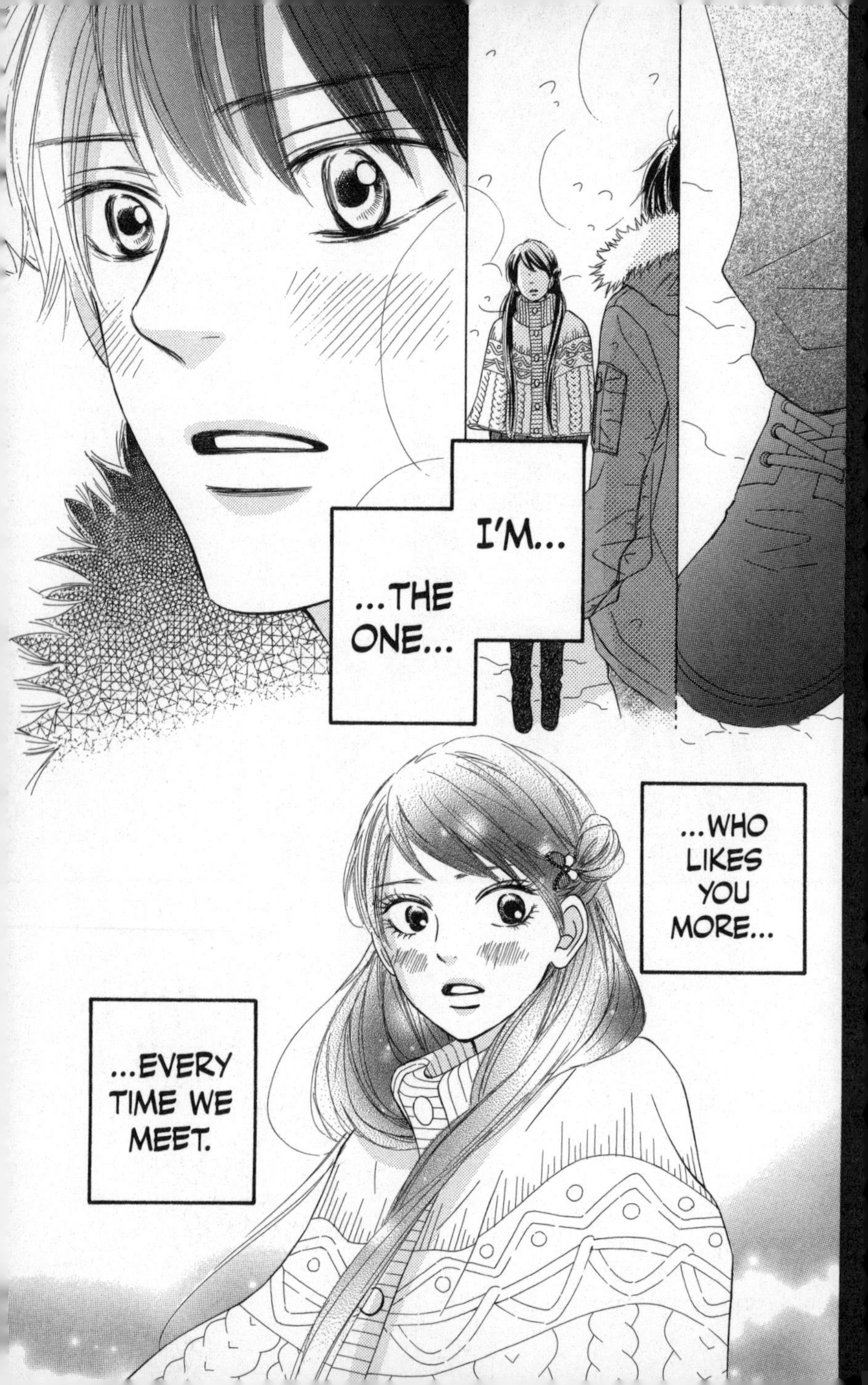
I'M...
...THE ONE...
...WHO LIKES YOU MORE...
...EVERY TIME WE MEET.

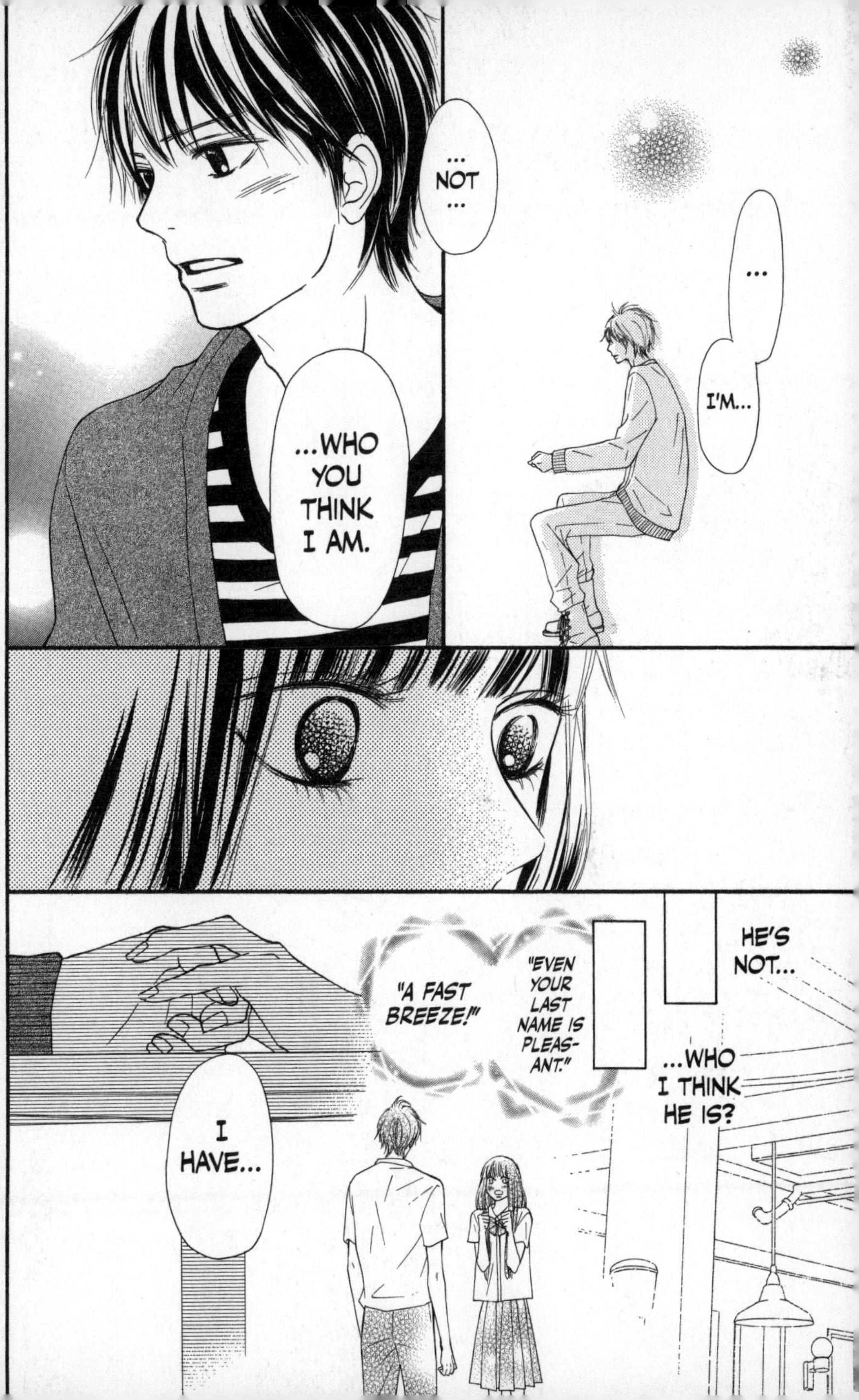
...
I'M...
...NOT...
...WHO YOU THINK I AM.
HE'S NOT...
...WHO I THINK HE IS?
"EVEN YOUR LAST NAME IS PLEAS-ANT."
"A FAST BREEZE!"
I HAVE...

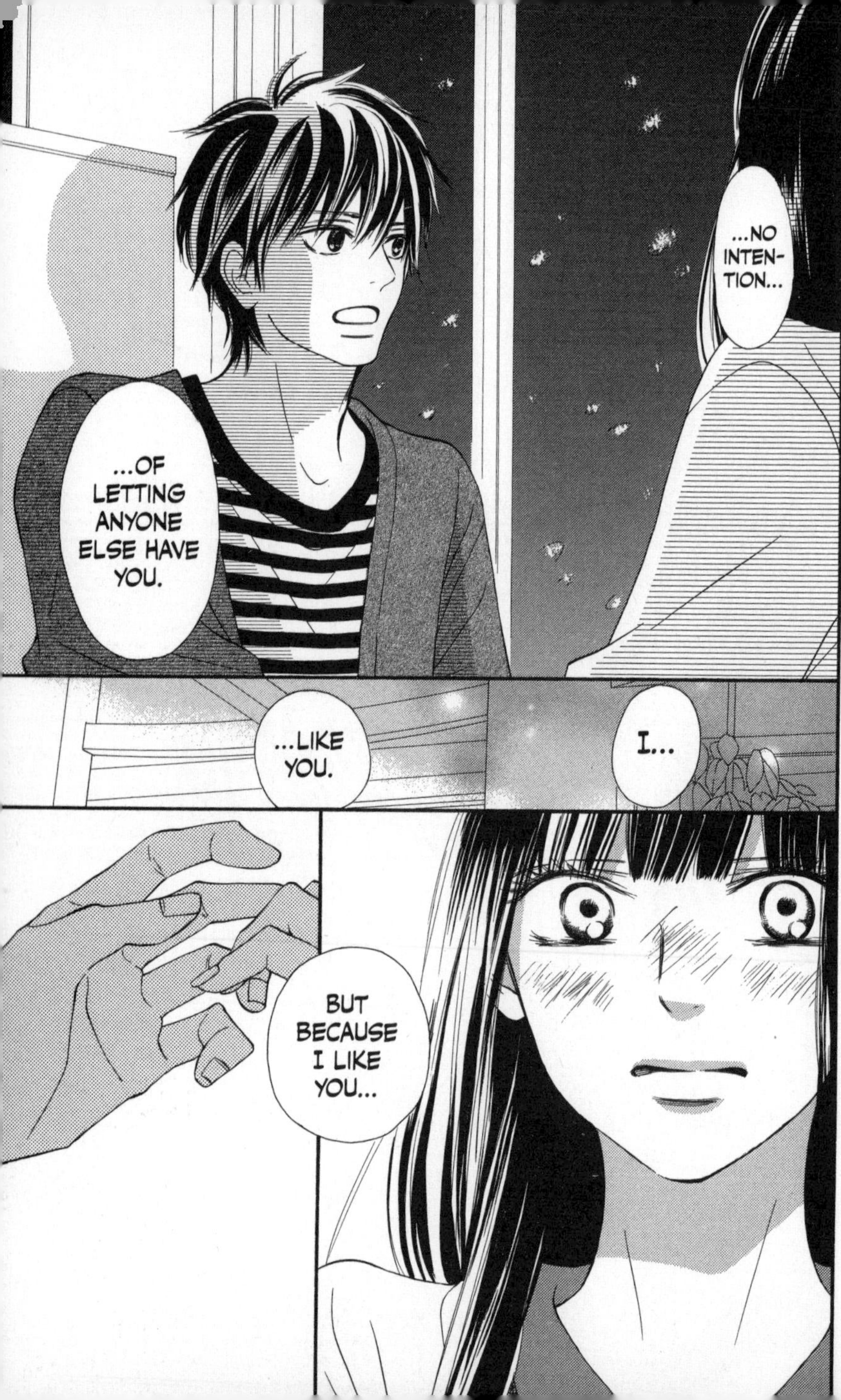
...NO INTEN-TION...
...OF LETTING ANYONE ELSE HAVE YOU.
I...
...LIKE YOU.
BUT BECAUSE I LIKE YOU...

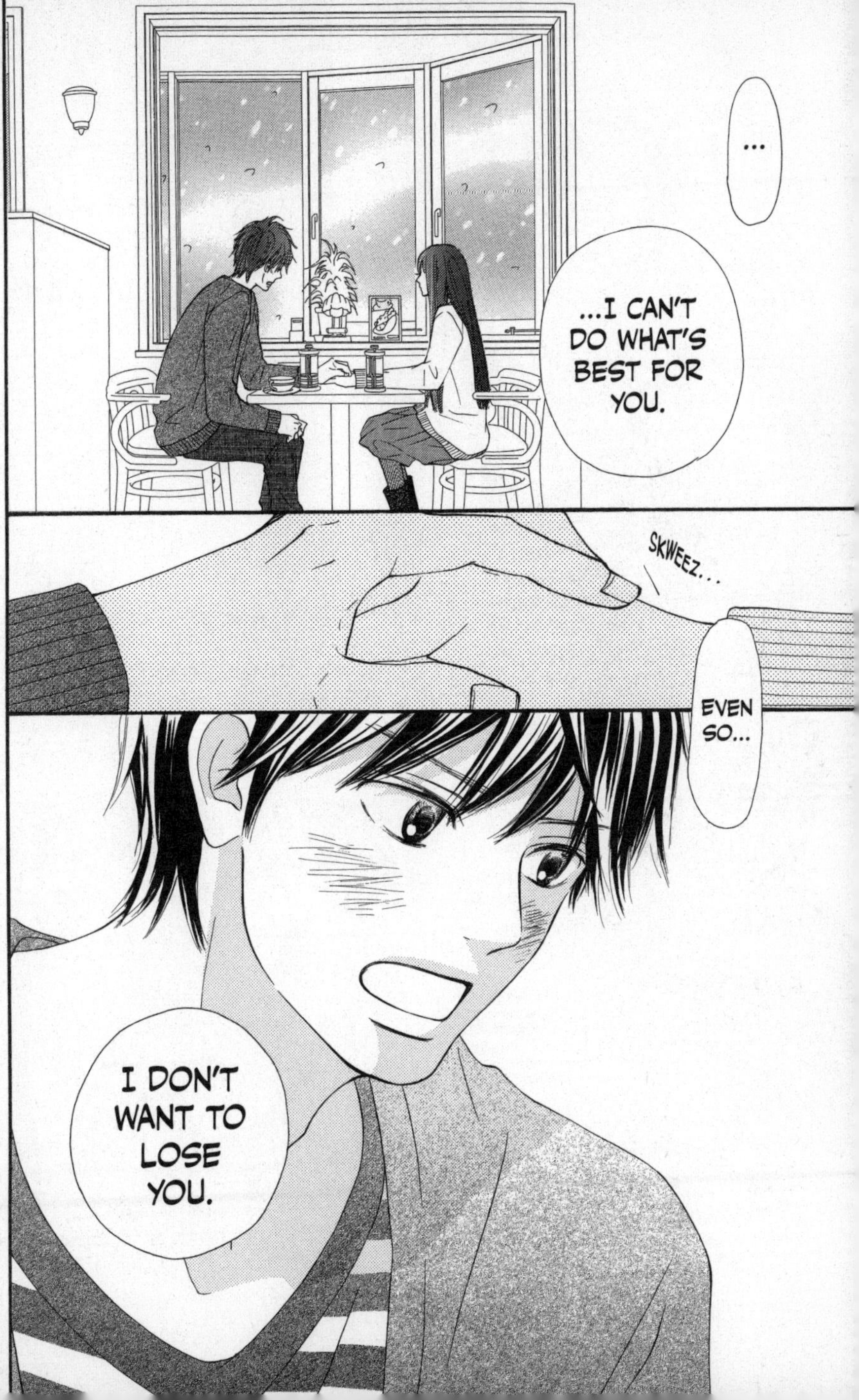
...
...I CAN'T DO WHAT'S BEST FOR YOU.
SKWEEZ...
EVEN SO...
I DON'T WANT TO LOSE YOU.

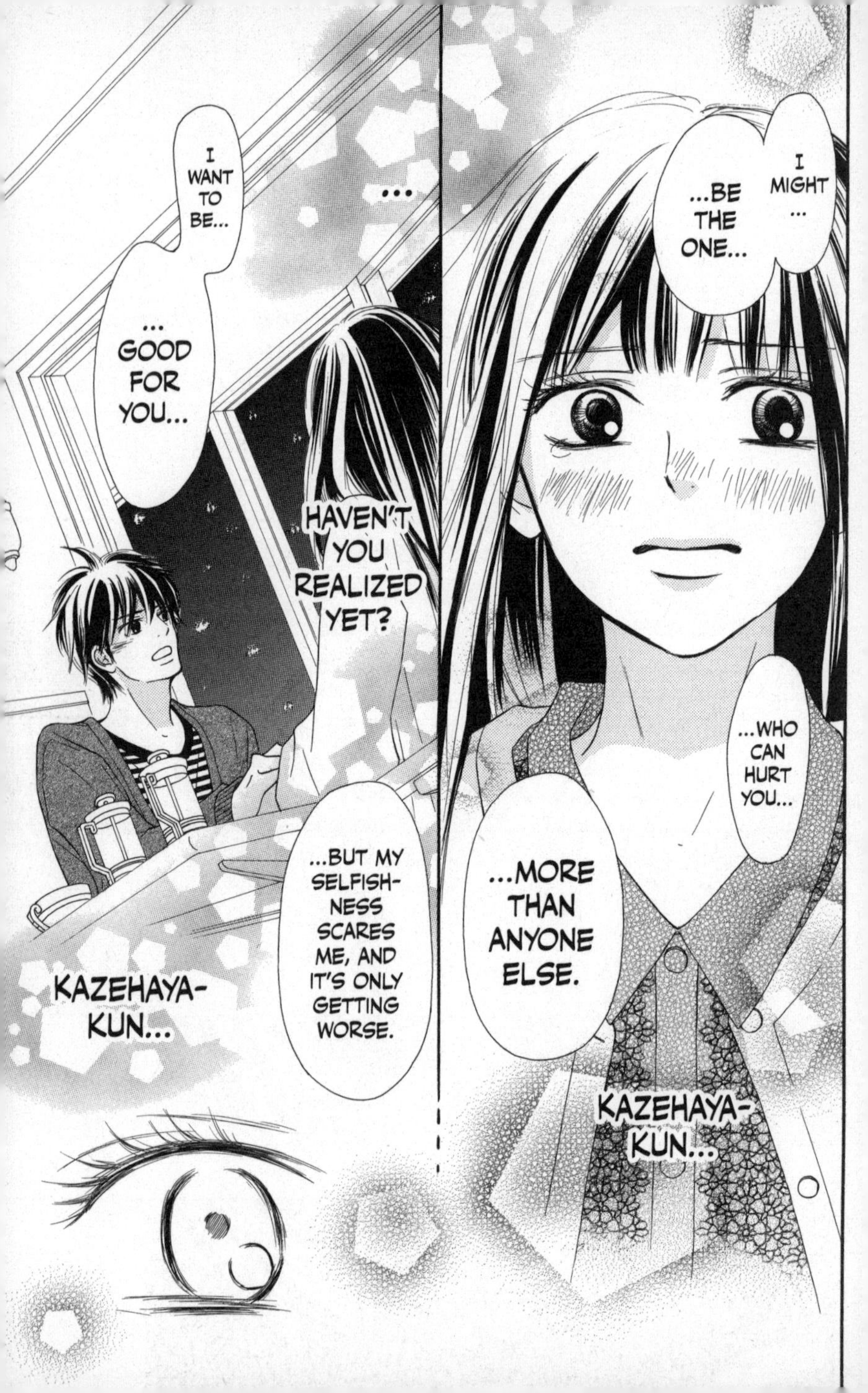

I MIGHT...
...BE THE ONE...
...WHO CAN HURT YOU...
...MORE THAN ANYONE ELSE.
KAZEHAYA-KUN...
...
I WANT TO BE...
...GOOD FOR YOU...
HAVEN'T YOU REALIZED YET?
...BUT MY SELFISHNESS SCARES ME, AND IT'S ONLY GETTING WORSE.
KAZEHAYA-KUN...

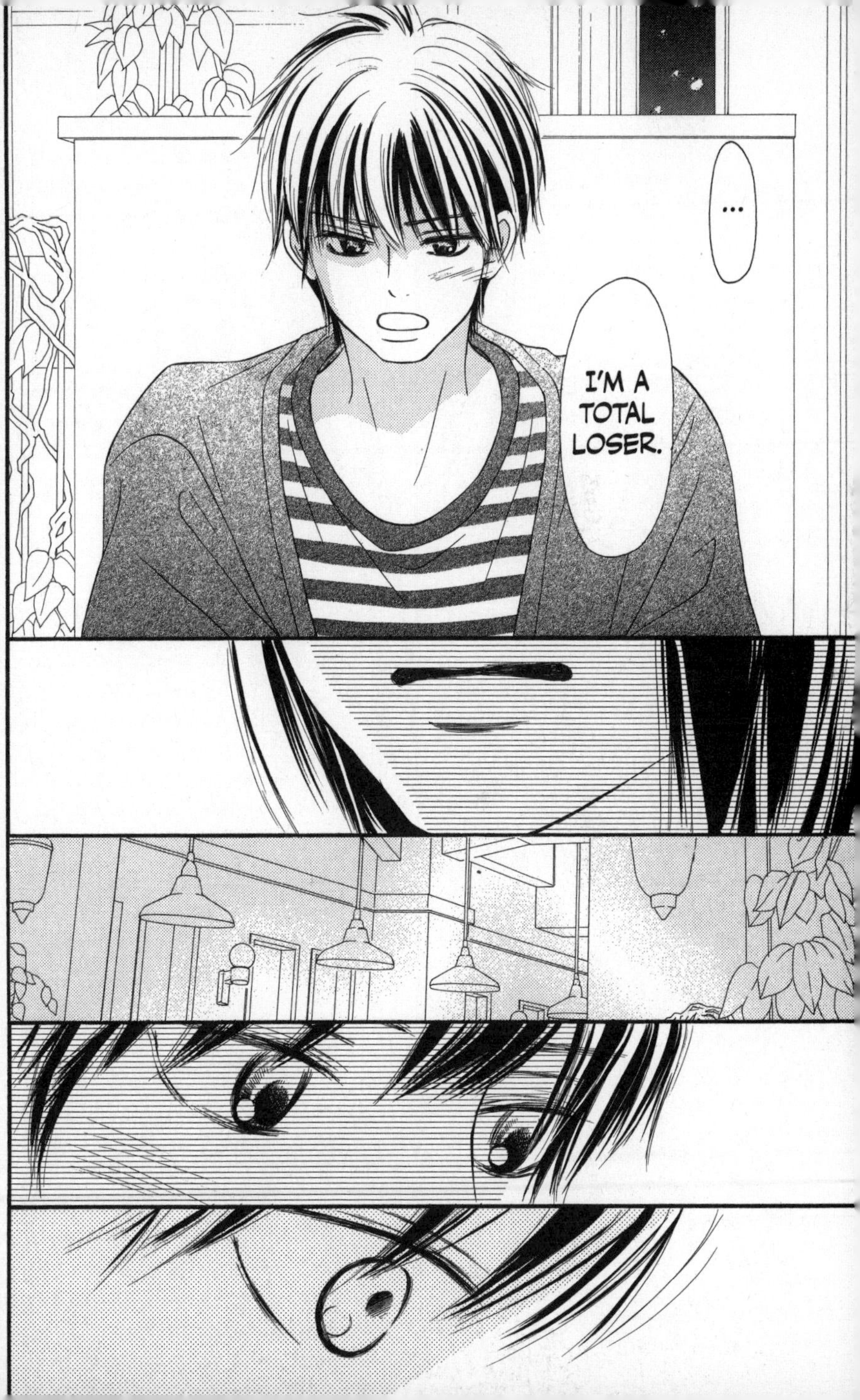
...
I'M A TOTAL LOSER.

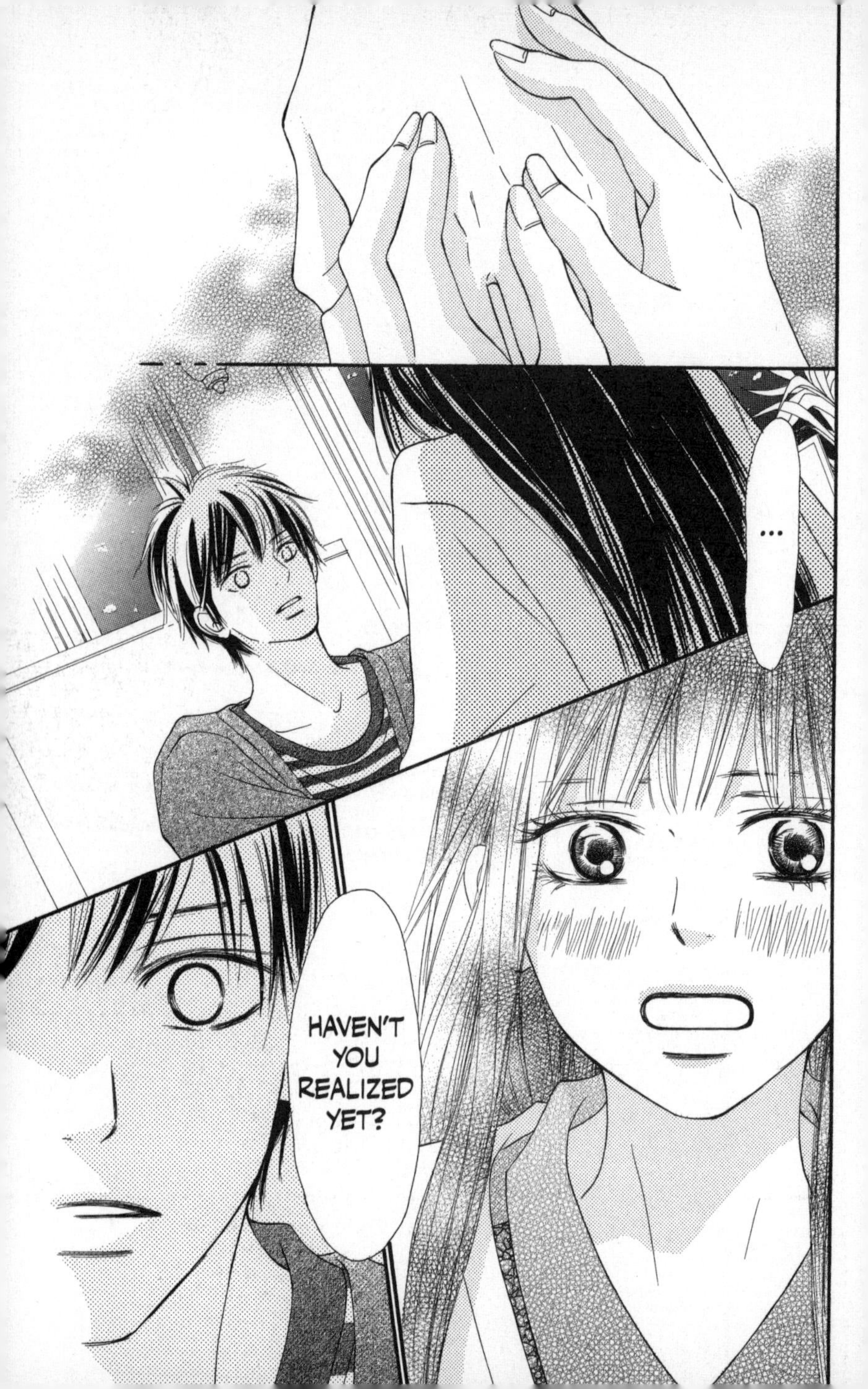
...
HAVEN'T YOU REALIZED YET?

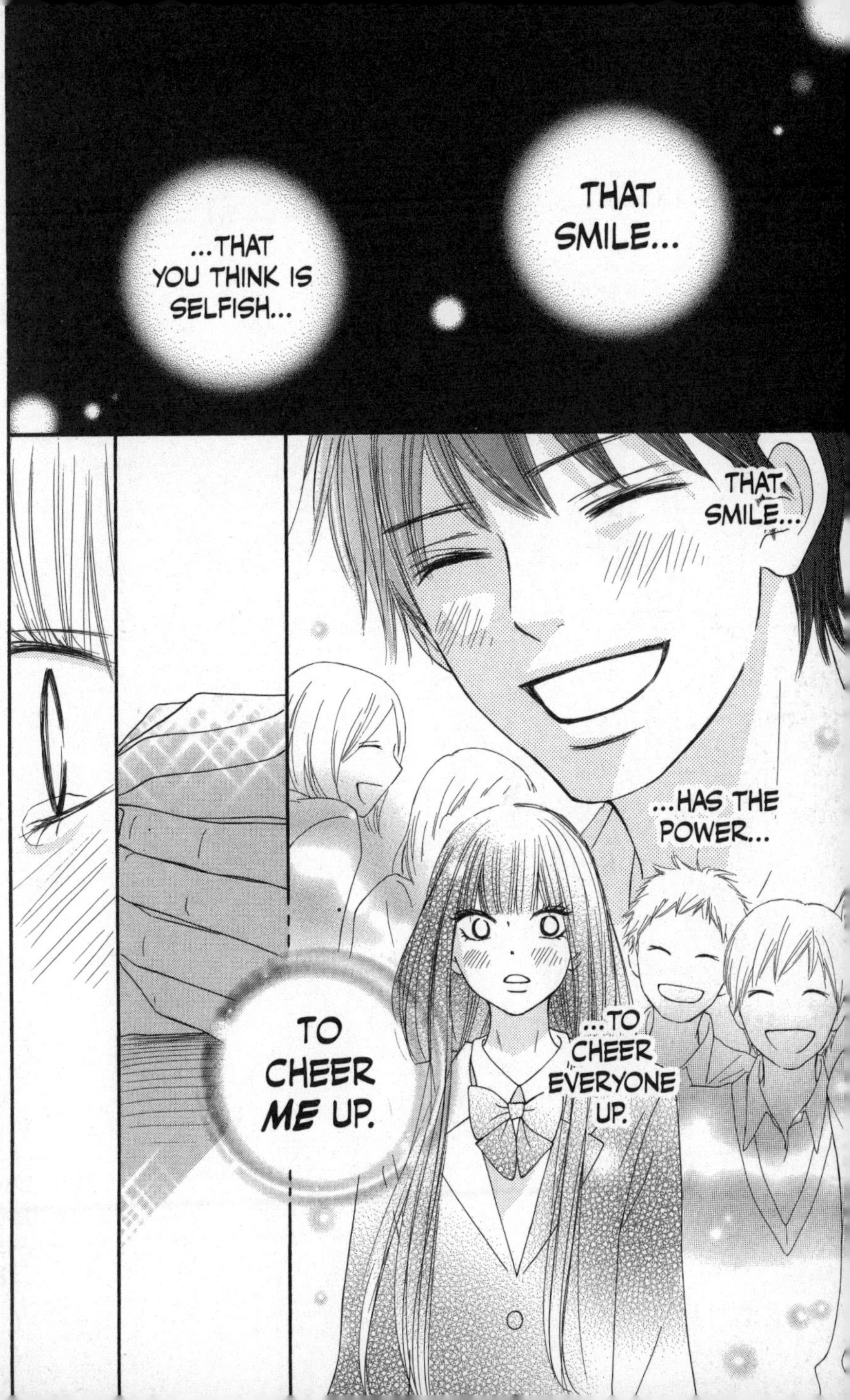
THAT SMILE...
...THAT YOU THINK IS SELFISH...
THAT SMILE...
...HAS THE POWER...
...TO CHEER EVERYONE UP.
TO CHEER *ME* UP.

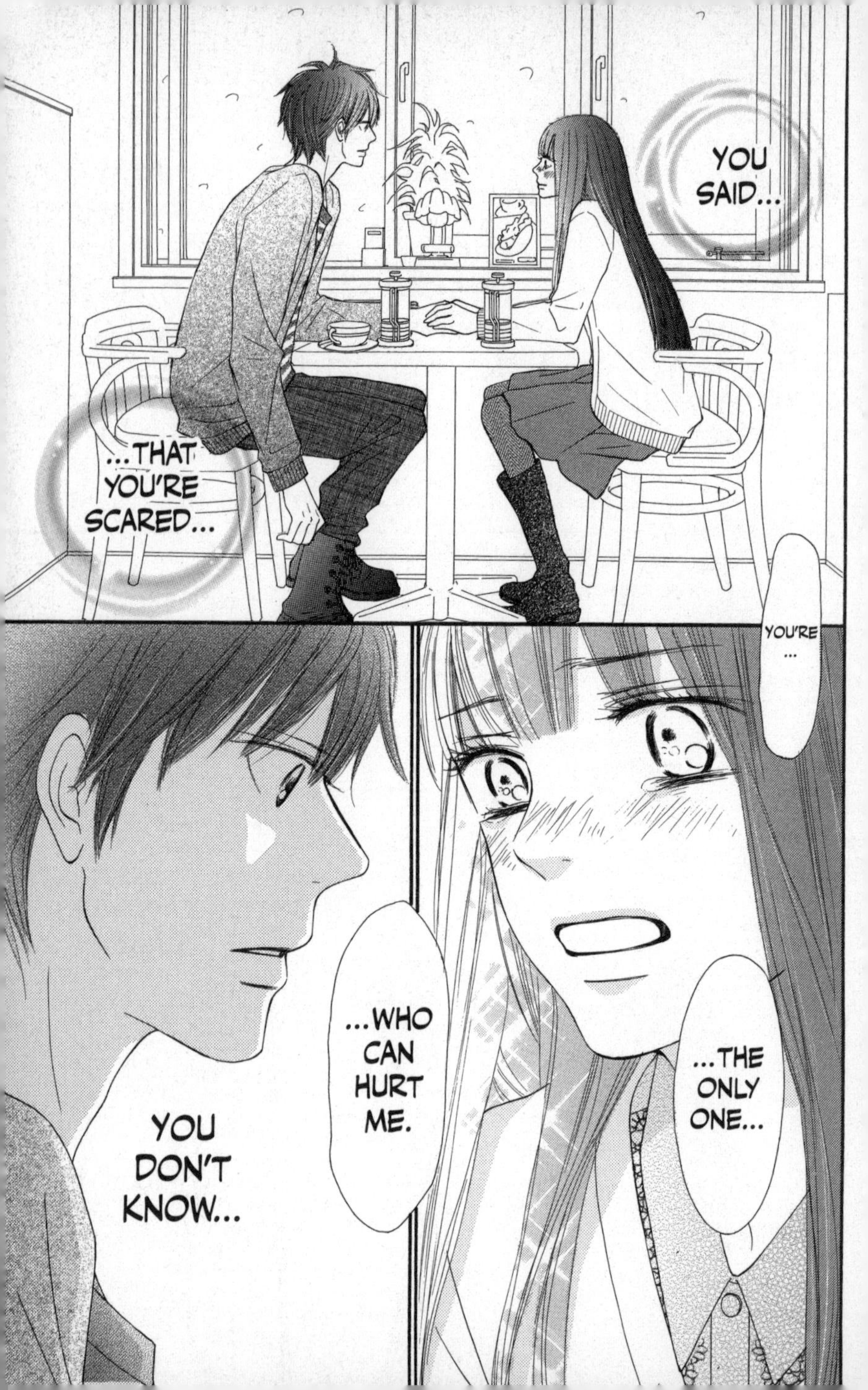
YOU SAID...
...THAT YOU'RE SCARED...
YOU'RE ...
...THE ONLY ONE...
...WHO CAN HURT ME.
YOU DON'T KNOW...

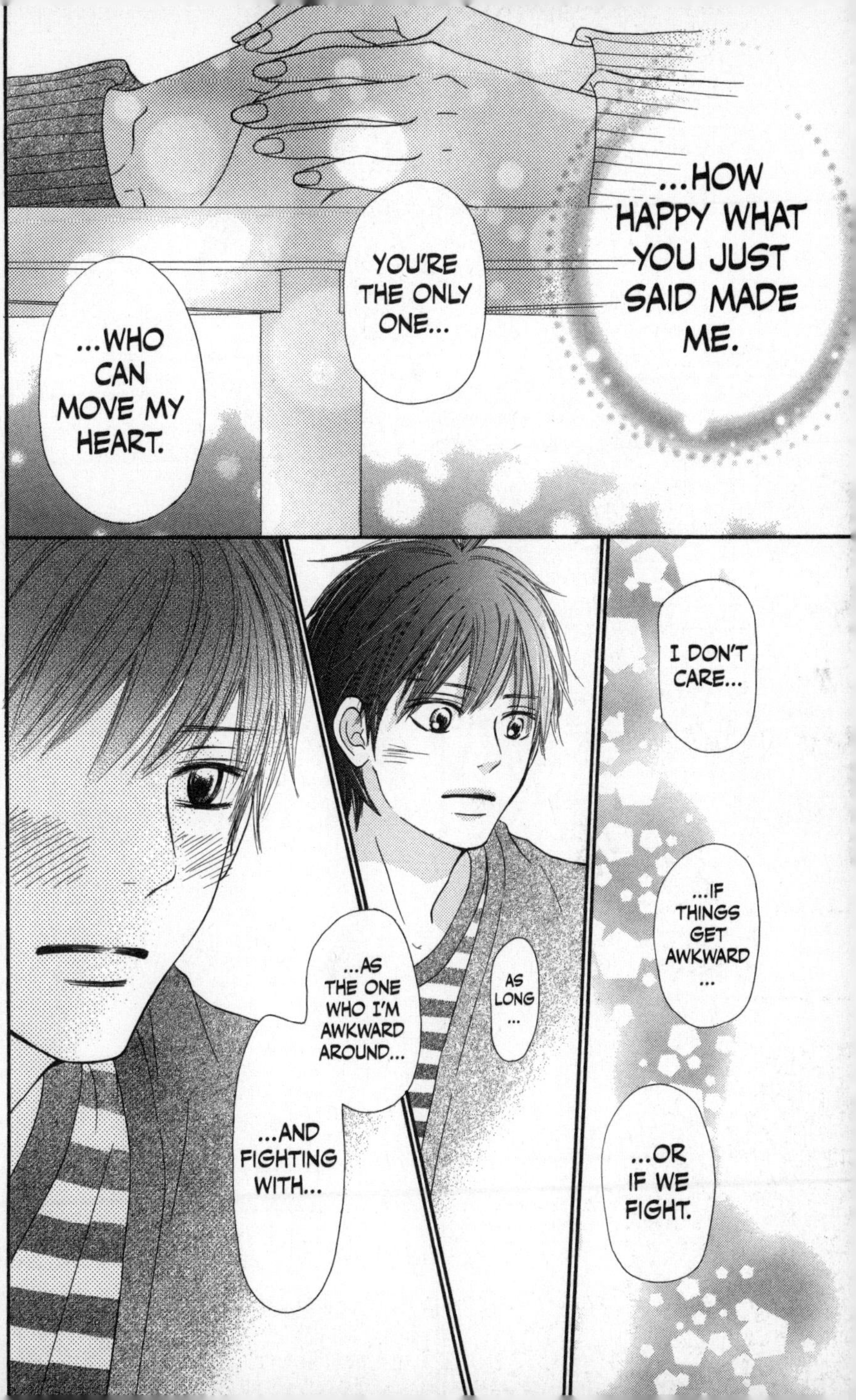
...HOW HAPPY WHAT YOU JUST SAID MADE ME.
YOU'RE THE ONLY ONE...
...WHO CAN MOVE MY HEART.
I DON'T CARE...
...IF THINGS GET AWKWARD...
...OR IF WE FIGHT.
AS LONG...
...AS THE ONE WHO I'M AWKWARD AROUND...
...AND FIGHTING WITH...

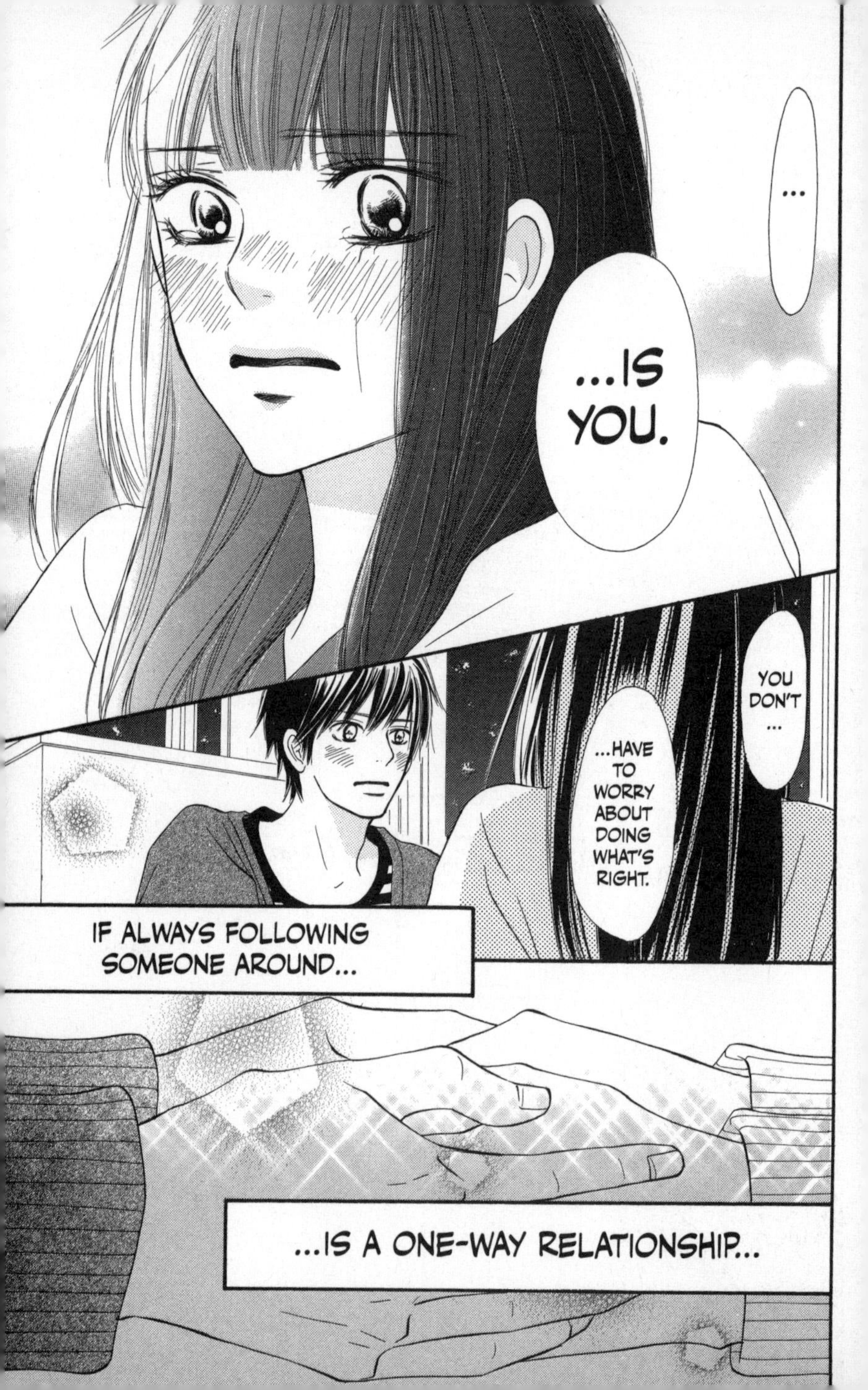
...
...IS YOU.
YOU DON'T ...
...HAVE TO WORRY ABOUT DOING WHAT'S RIGHT.
IF ALWAYS FOLLOWING SOMEONE AROUND...
...IS A ONE-WAY RELATIONSHIP...

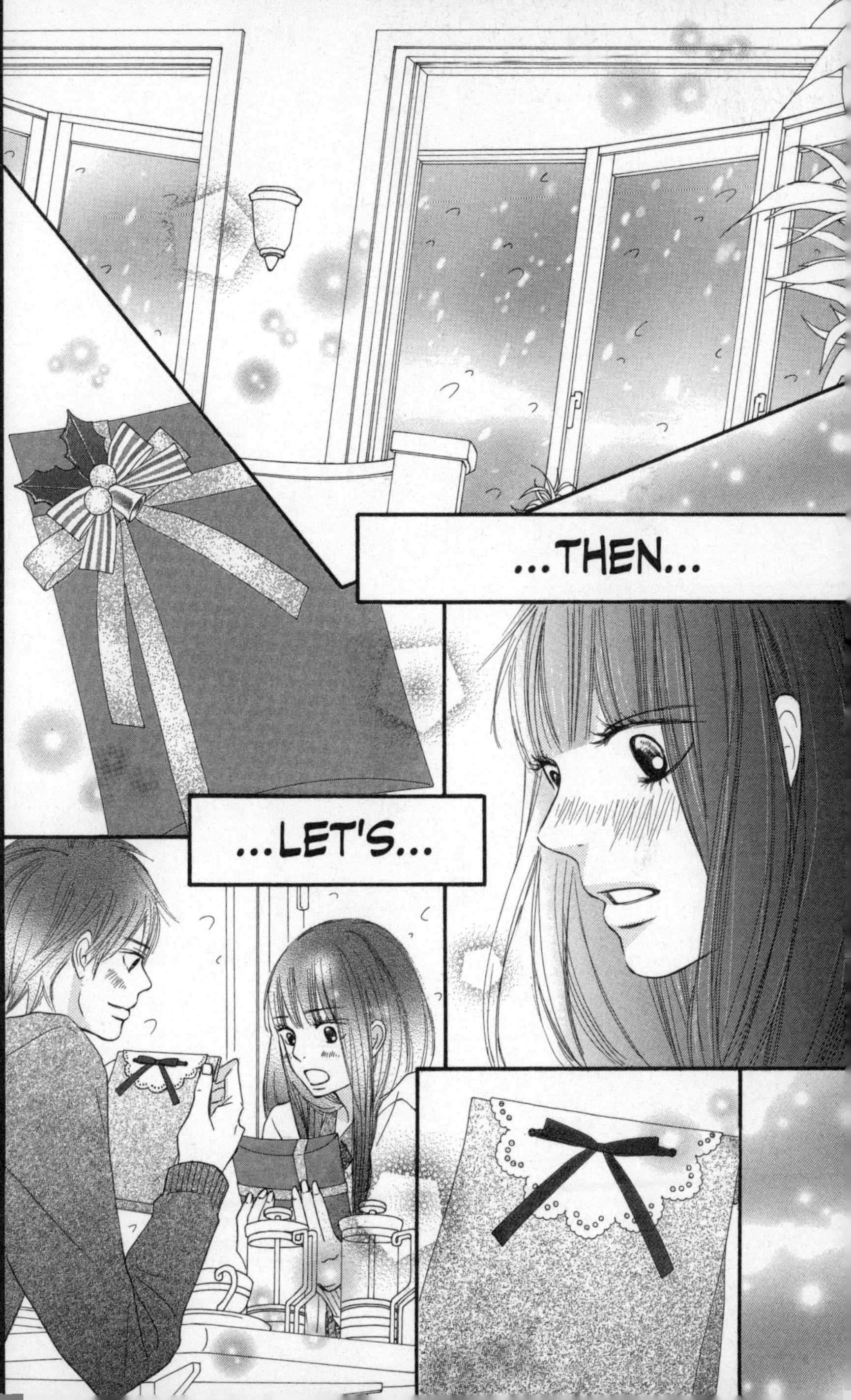
...THEN...
...LET'S...

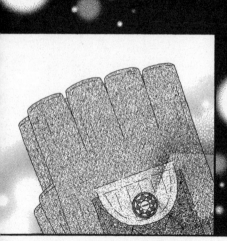

...LOOK AT...

The same present...

...EACH OTHER...

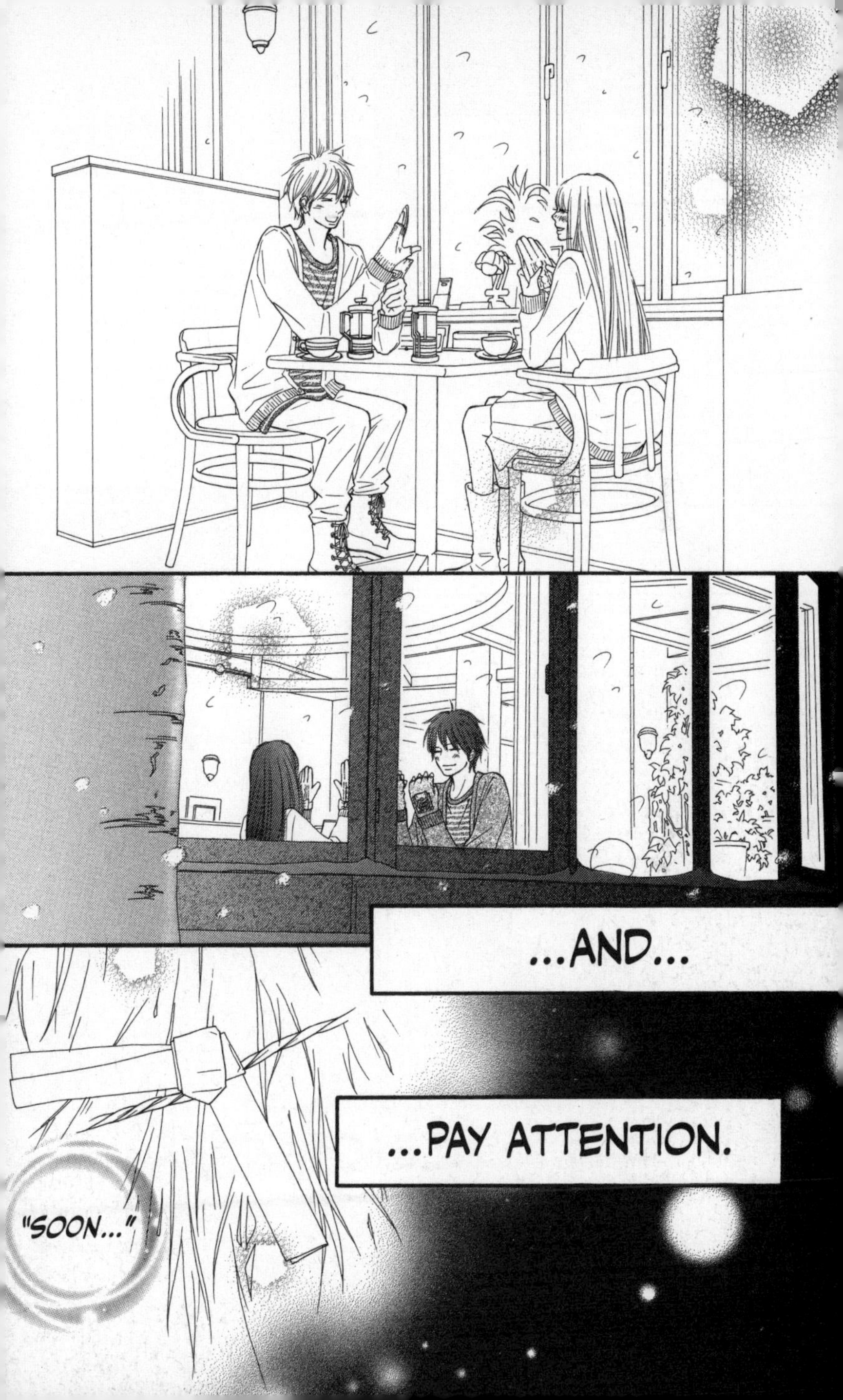
...AND...
...PAY ATTENTION.
"SOON..."

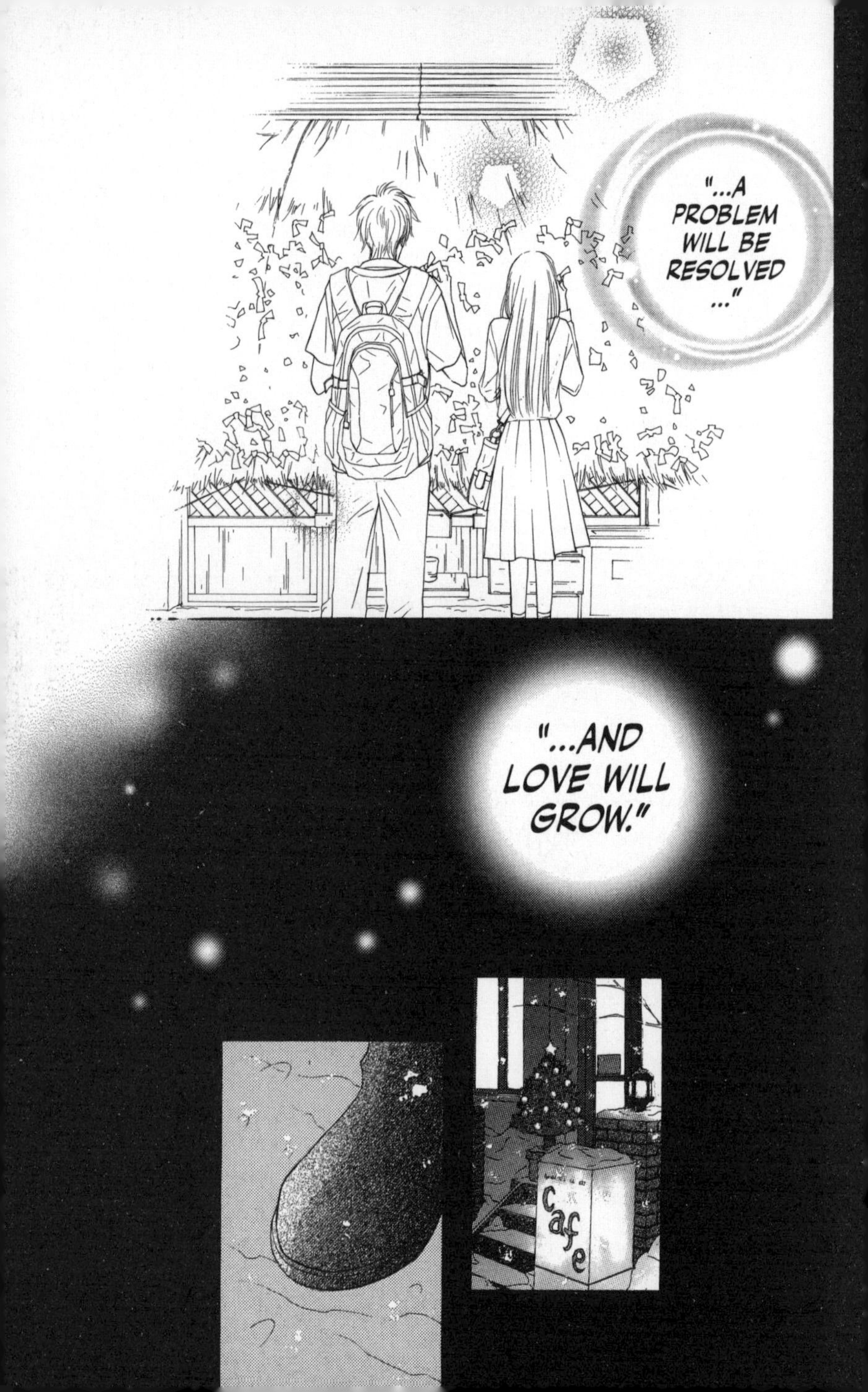
"...A PROBLEM WILL BE RESOLVED ..."
"...AND LOVE WILL GROW."
cafe

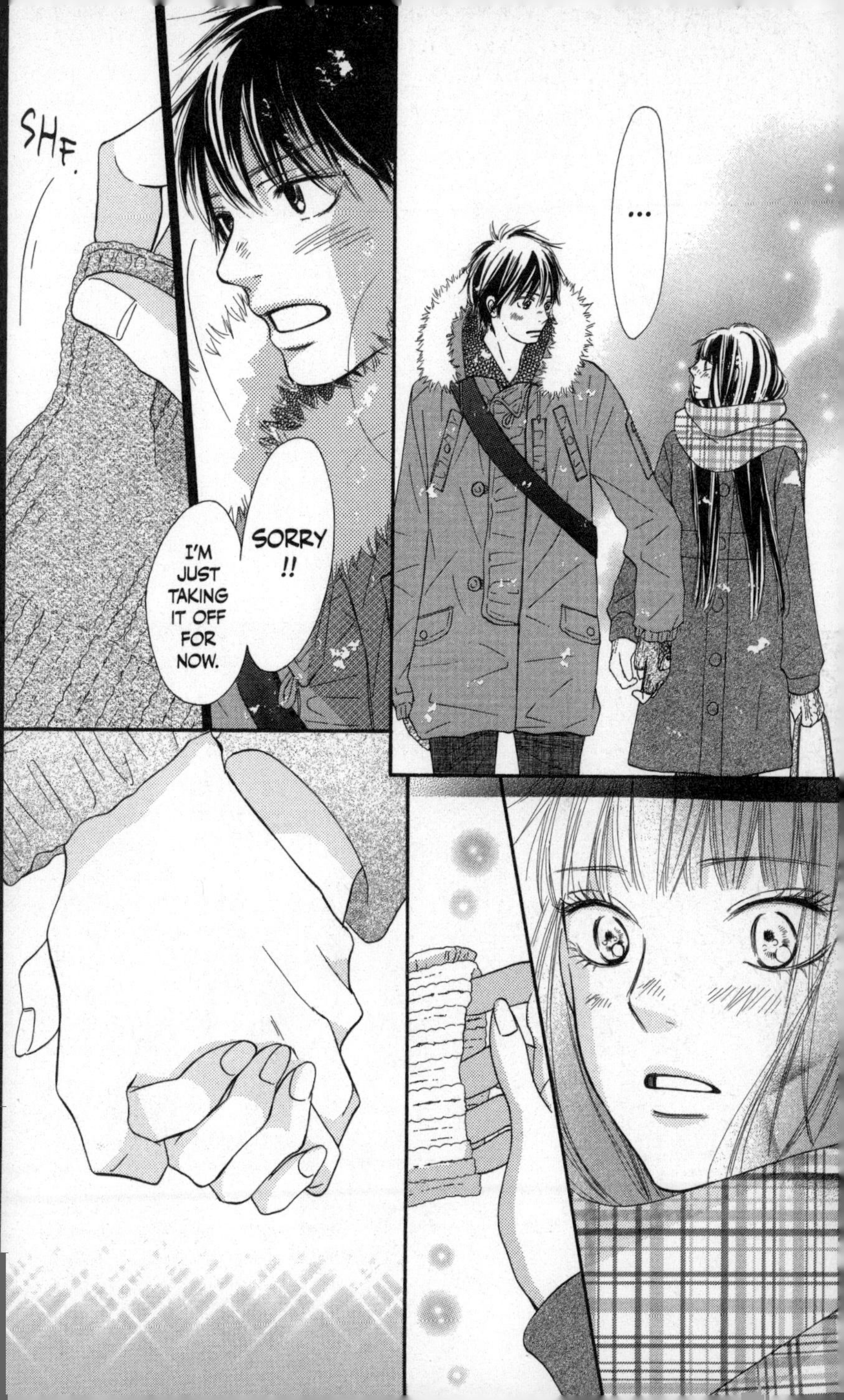
...
SHF.
SORRY!!
I'M JUST TAKING IT OFF FOR NOW.

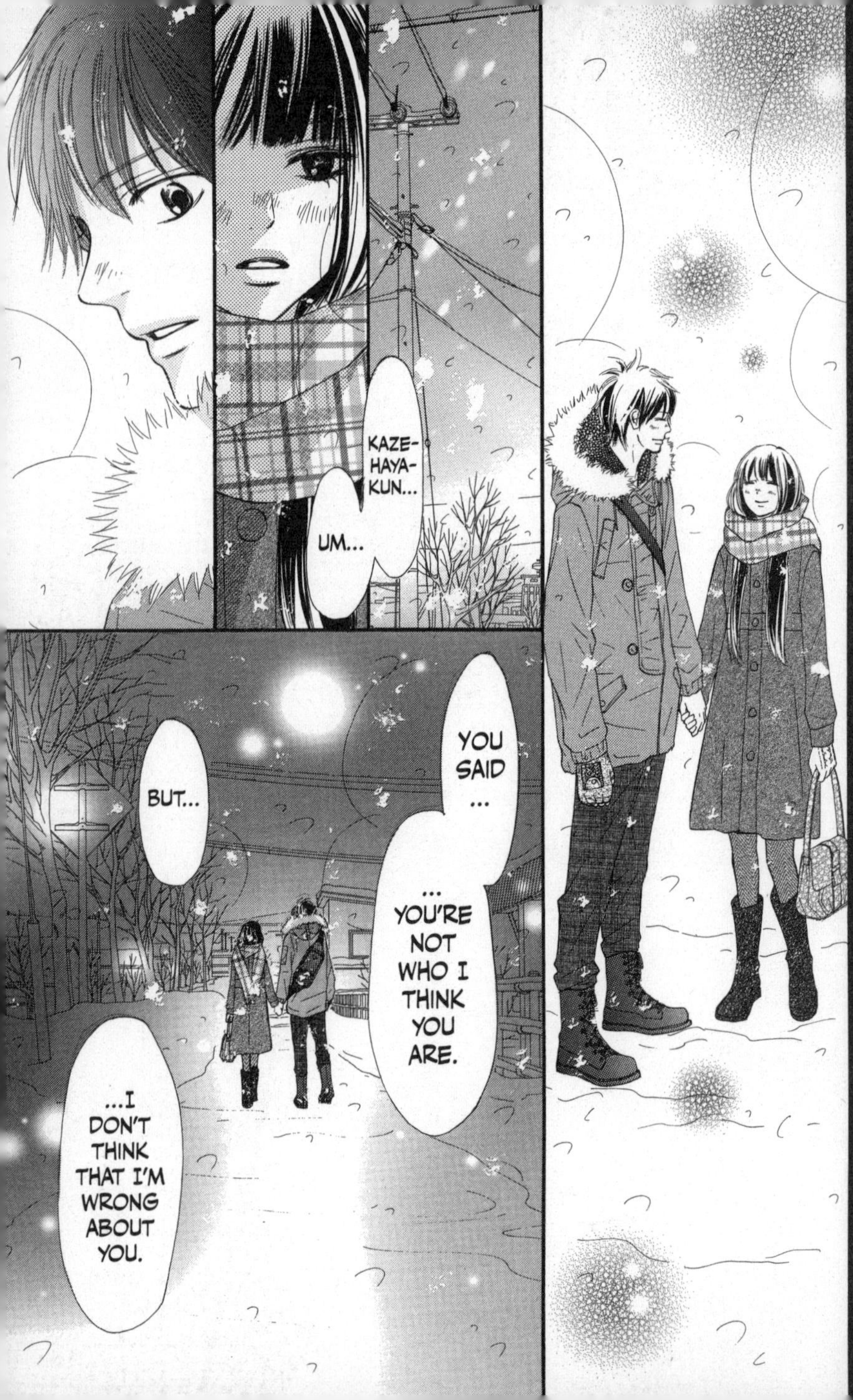
KAZE-HAYA-KUN...
UM...
YOU SAID ...
... YOU'RE NOT WHO I THINK YOU ARE.
BUT...
...I DON'T THINK THAT I'M WRONG ABOUT YOU.

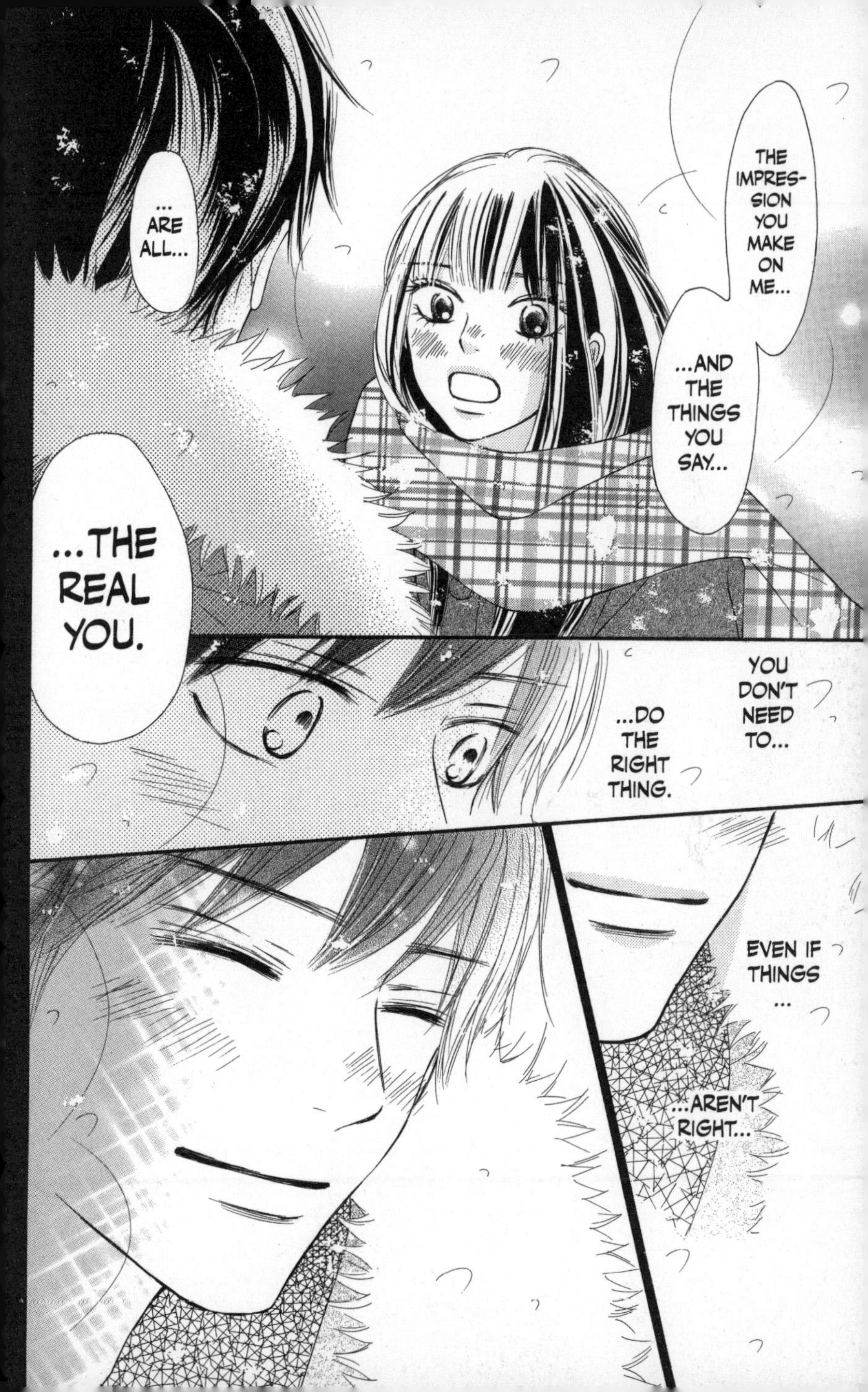
THE IMPRESSION YOU MAKE ON ME...
...AND THE THINGS YOU SAY...
...ARE ALL...
...THE REAL YOU.
YOU DON'T NEED TO...
...DO THE RIGHT THING.
EVEN IF THINGS...
...AREN'T RIGHT...

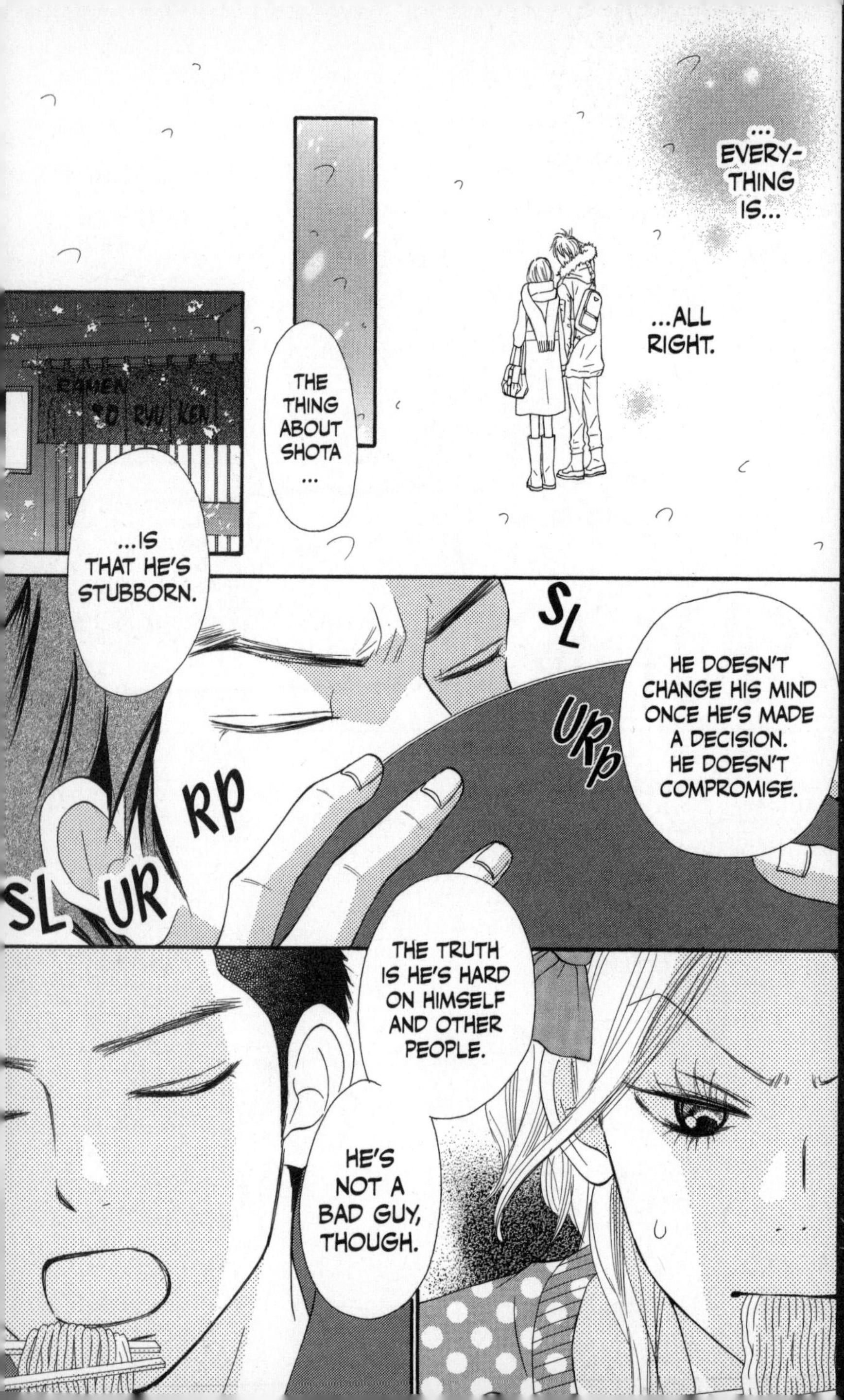

...EVERY-THING IS...
...ALL RIGHT.
THE THING ABOUT SHOTA...
...IS THAT HE'S STUBBORN.
SLURP
HE DOESN'T CHANGE HIS MIND ONCE HE'S MADE A DECISION. HE DOESN'T COMPROMISE.
SLURRP
THE TRUTH IS HE'S HARD ON HIMSELF AND OTHER PEOPLE.
HE'S NOT A BAD GUY, THOUGH.

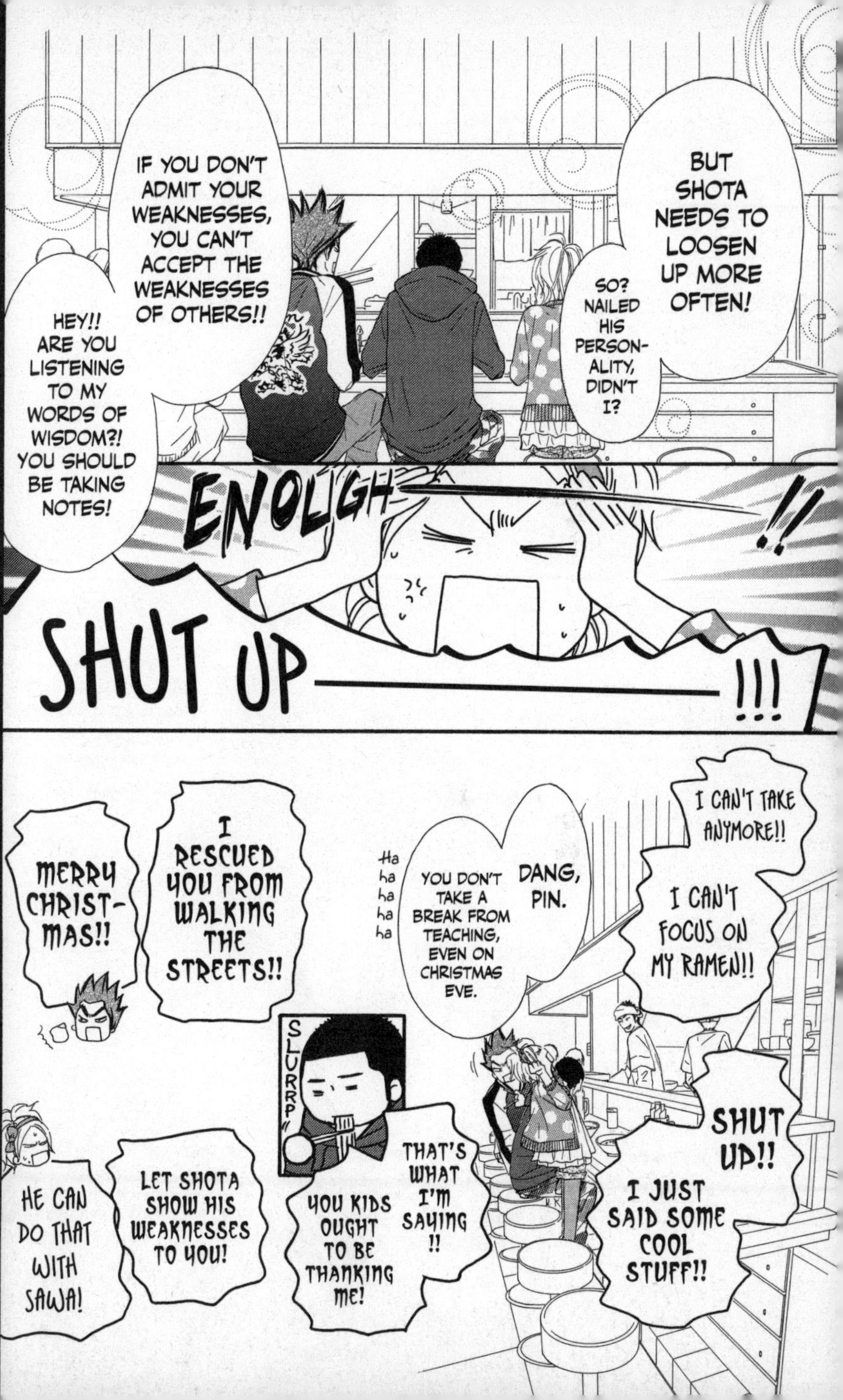
BUT SHOTA NEEDS TO LOOSEN UP MORE OFTEN!
SO? NAILED HIS PERSON-ALITY, DIDN'T I?
IF YOU DON'T ADMIT YOUR WEAKNESSES, YOU CAN'T ACCEPT THE WEAKNESSES OF OTHERS!!
HEY!! ARE YOU LISTENING TO MY WORDS OF WISDOM?! YOU SHOULD BE TAKING NOTES!
ENOUGH!!
SHUT UP———!!!
I CAN'T TAKE ANYMORE!!
I CAN'T FOCUS ON MY RAMEN!!
DANG, PIN.
YOU DON'T TAKE A BREAK FROM TEACHING, EVEN ON CHRISTMAS EVE.
Ha ha ha ha ha
I RESCUED YOU FROM WALKING THE STREETS!!
MERRY CHRIST-MAS!!
SHUT UP!!
I JUST SAID SOME COOL STUFF!!
SLURRP
THAT'S WHAT I'M SAYING!!
YOU KIDS OUGHT TO BE THANKING ME!
LET SHOTA SHOW HIS WEAKNESSES TO YOU!
HE CAN DO THAT WITH SAWA!

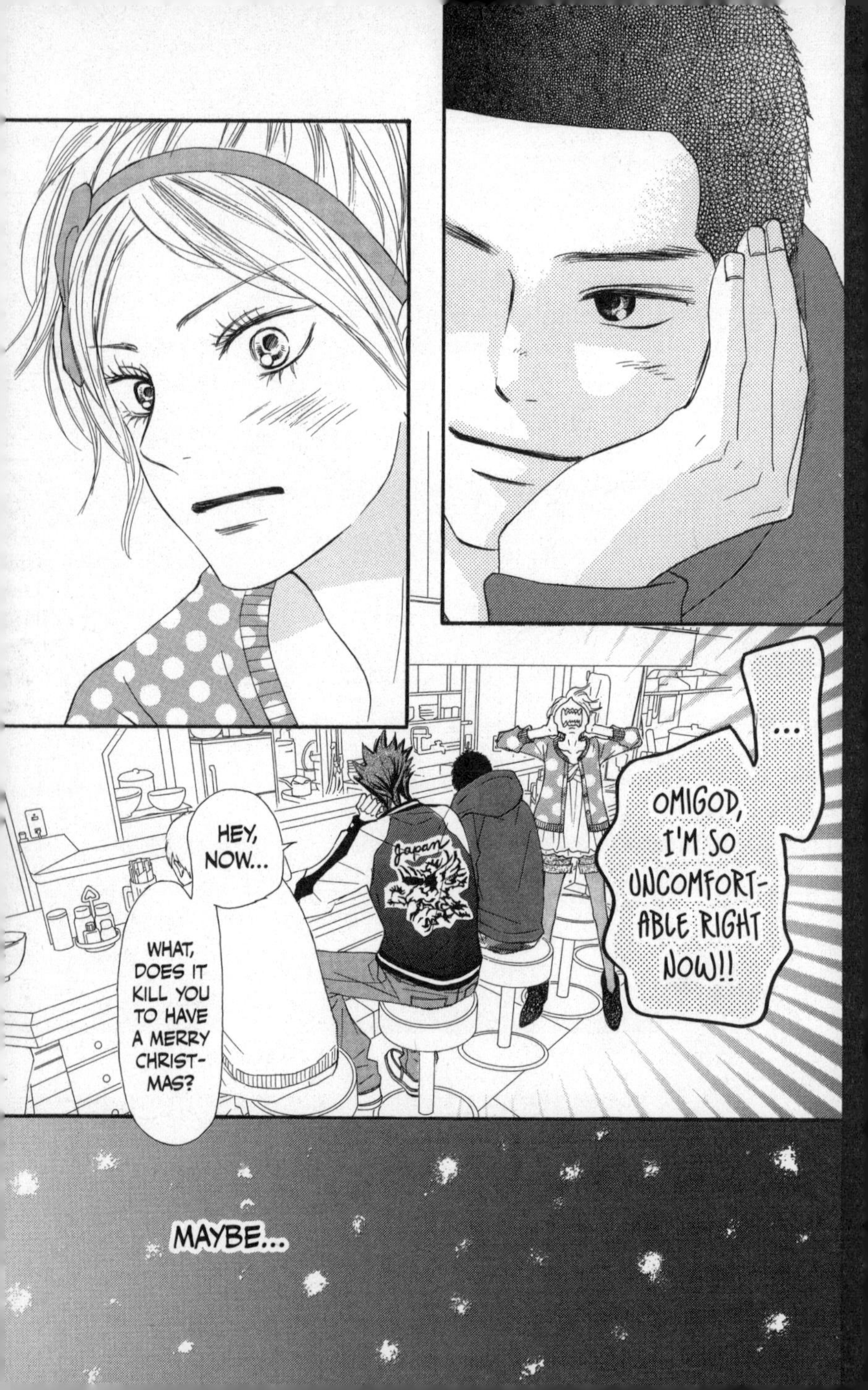
...
OMIGOD, I'M SO UNCOMFORT-ABLE RIGHT NOW!!
HEY, NOW...
WHAT, DOES IT KILL YOU TO HAVE A MERRY CHRIST-MAS?
Japan
MAYBE...

...I ADMIRE HIM MORE THAN I SHOULD.

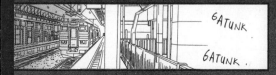

GATUNK.

GATUNK.

KITAHORO

Train ...

...now depart-ing...

GATUNK

GATUNK...

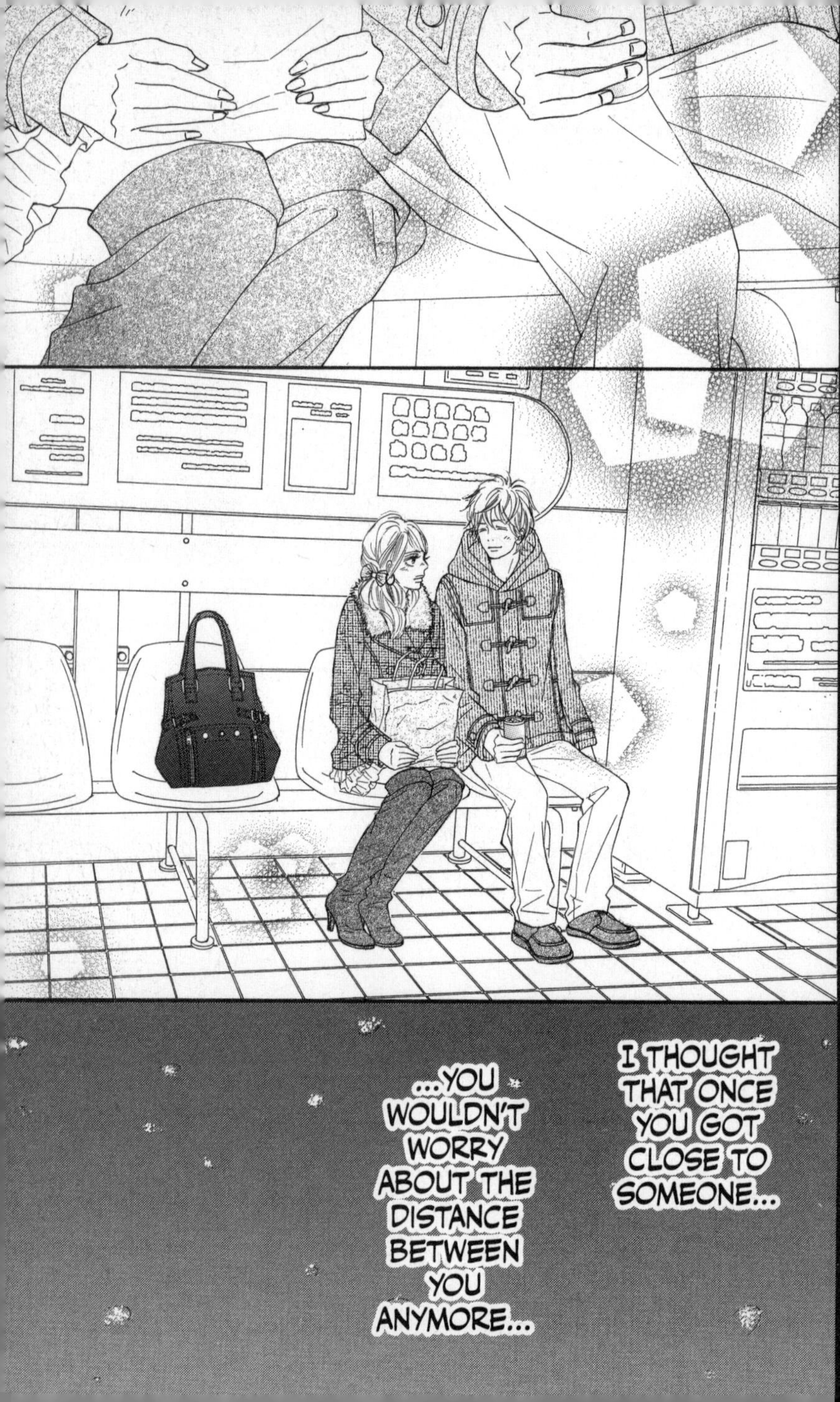
I THOUGHT THAT ONCE YOU GOT CLOSE TO SOMEONE...
...YOU WOULDN'T WORRY ABOUT THE DISTANCE BETWEEN YOU ANYMORE...

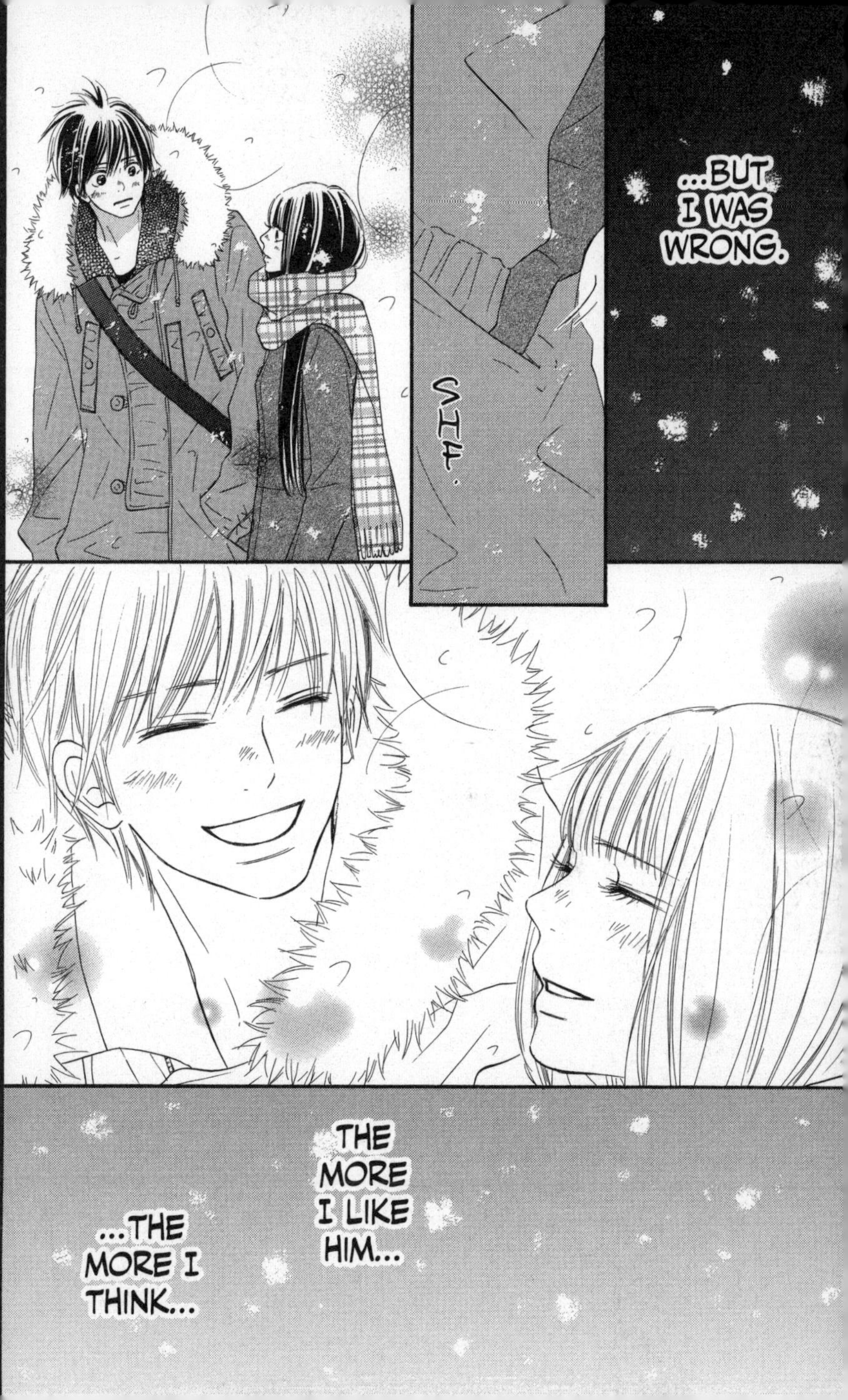
...BUT I WAS WRONG.
SIFT.
THE MORE I LIKE HIM...
...THE MORE I THINK...

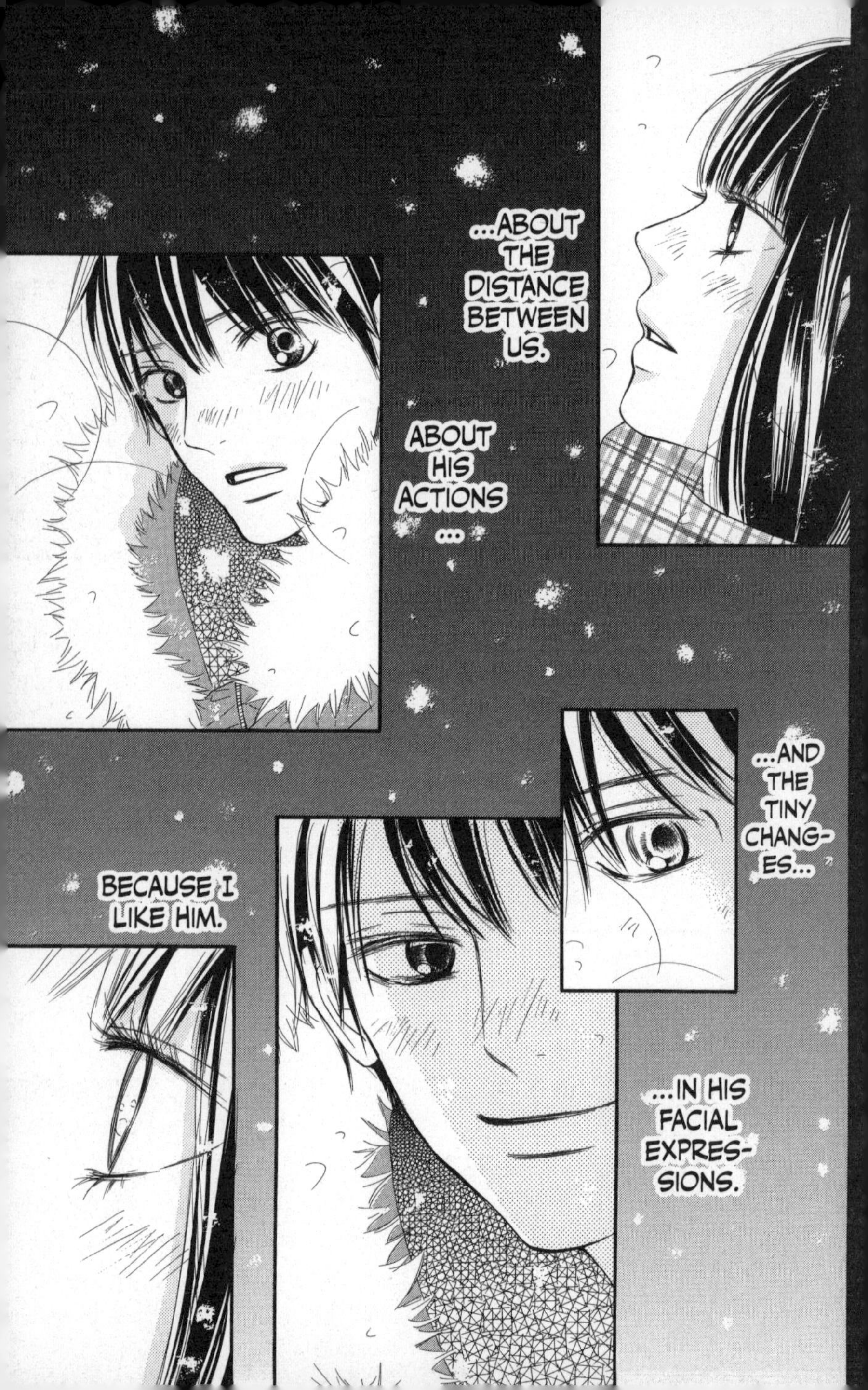
...ABOUT THE DISTANCE BETWEEN US.
ABOUT HIS ACTIONS...
...AND THE TINY CHANG-ES...
...IN HIS FACIAL EXPRES-SIONS.
BECAUSE I LIKE HIM.

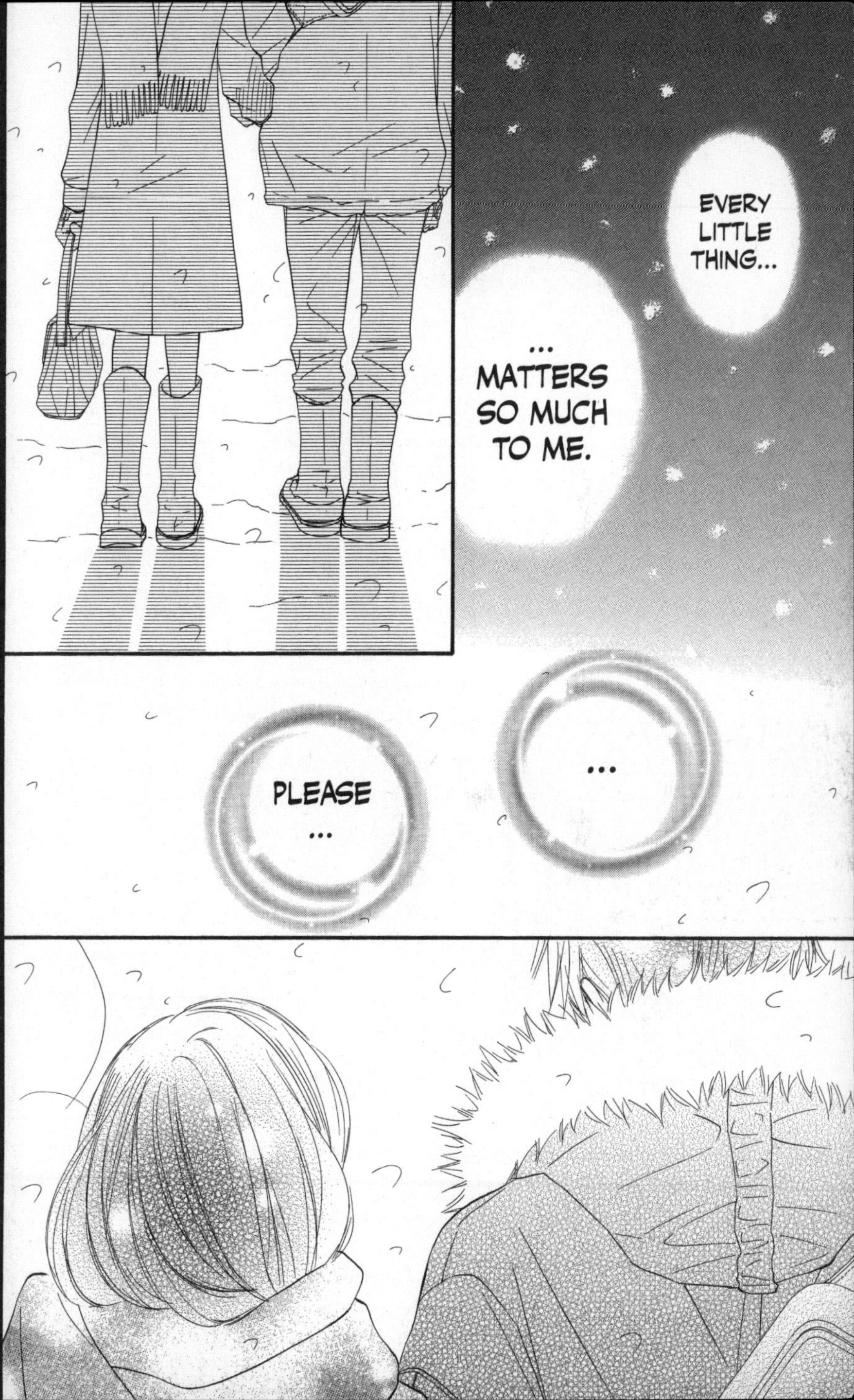
EVERY LITTLE THING...
...MATTERS SO MUCH TO ME.
...
PLEASE ...

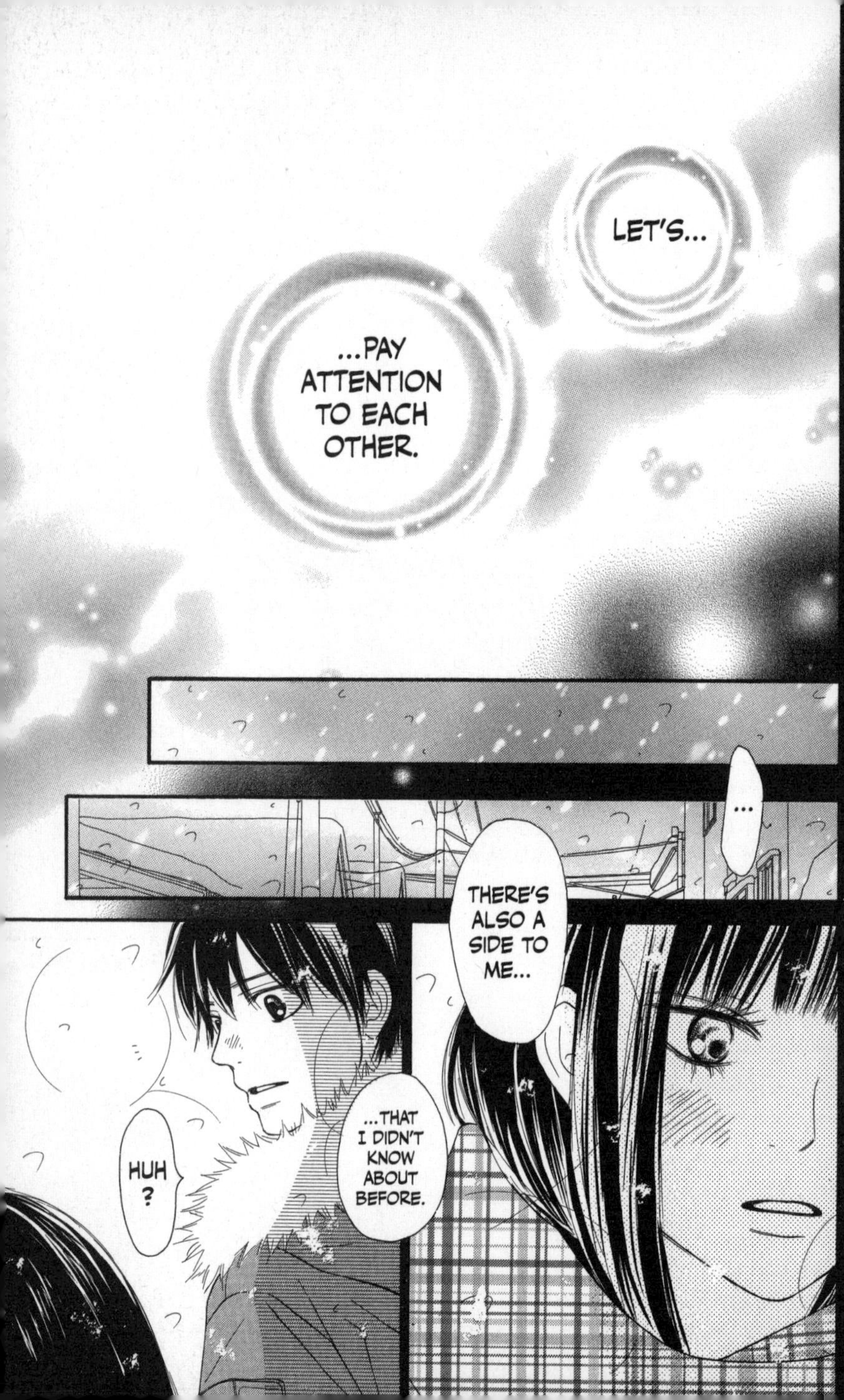
LET'S...
...PAY ATTENTION TO EACH OTHER.
...
THERE'S ALSO A SIDE TO ME...
...THAT I DIDN'T KNOW ABOUT BEFORE.
HUH ?

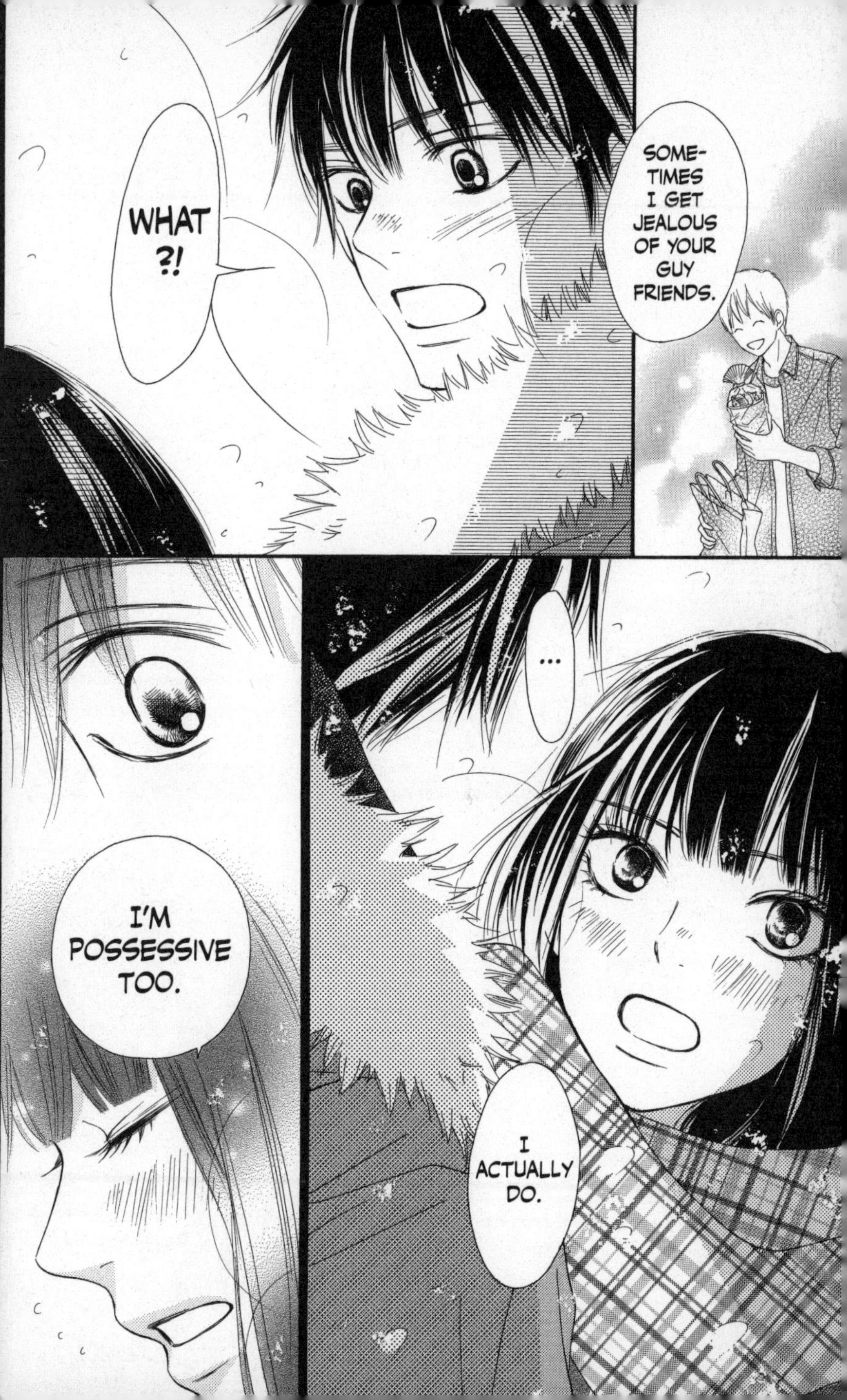
SOME-TIMES I GET JEALOUS OF YOUR GUY FRIENDS.
WHAT?!
...
I ACTUALLY DO.
I'M POSSESSIVE TOO.

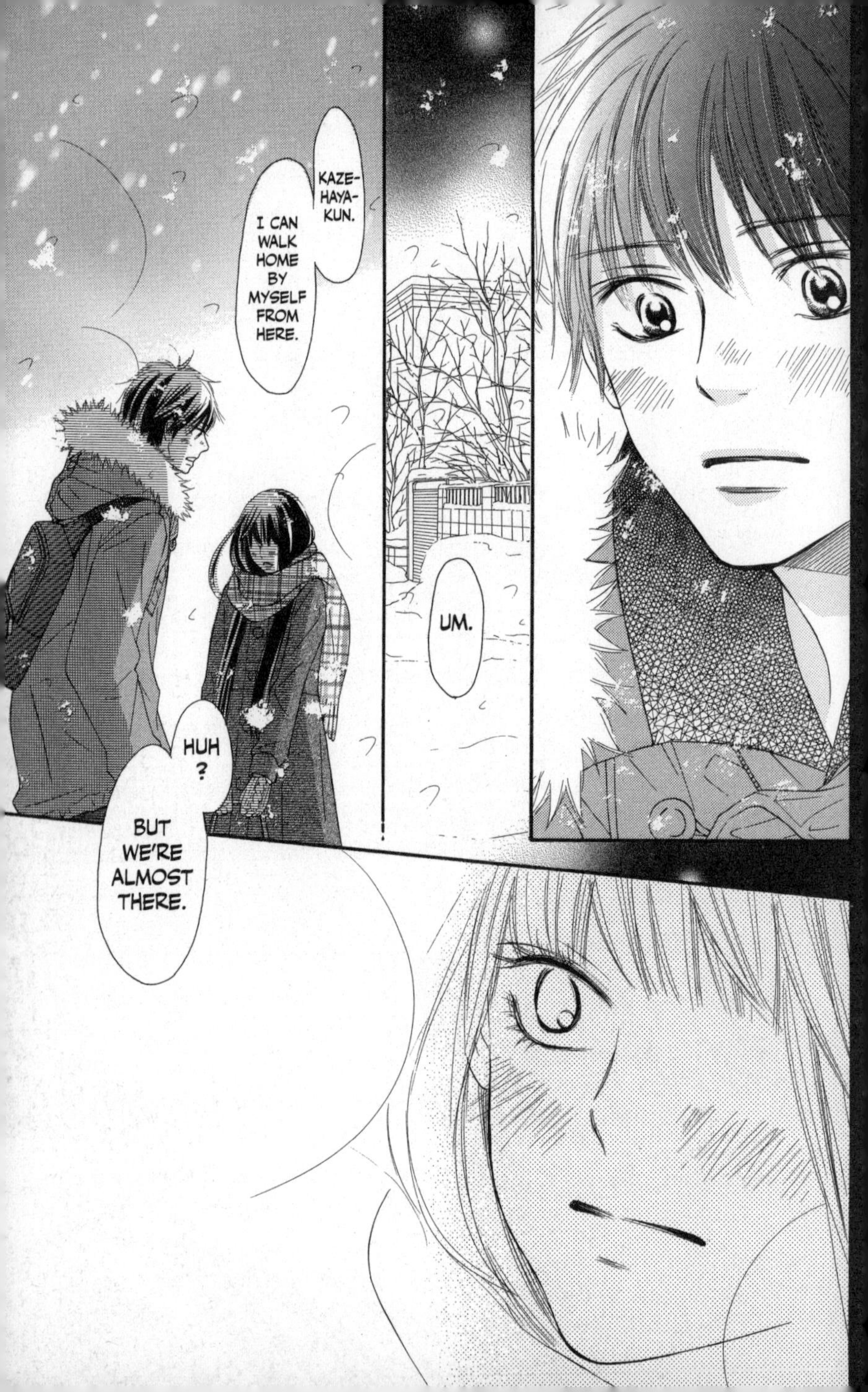
UM.
KAZE-HAYA-KUN.
I CAN WALK HOME BY MYSELF FROM HERE.
HUH?
BUT WE'RE ALMOST THERE.

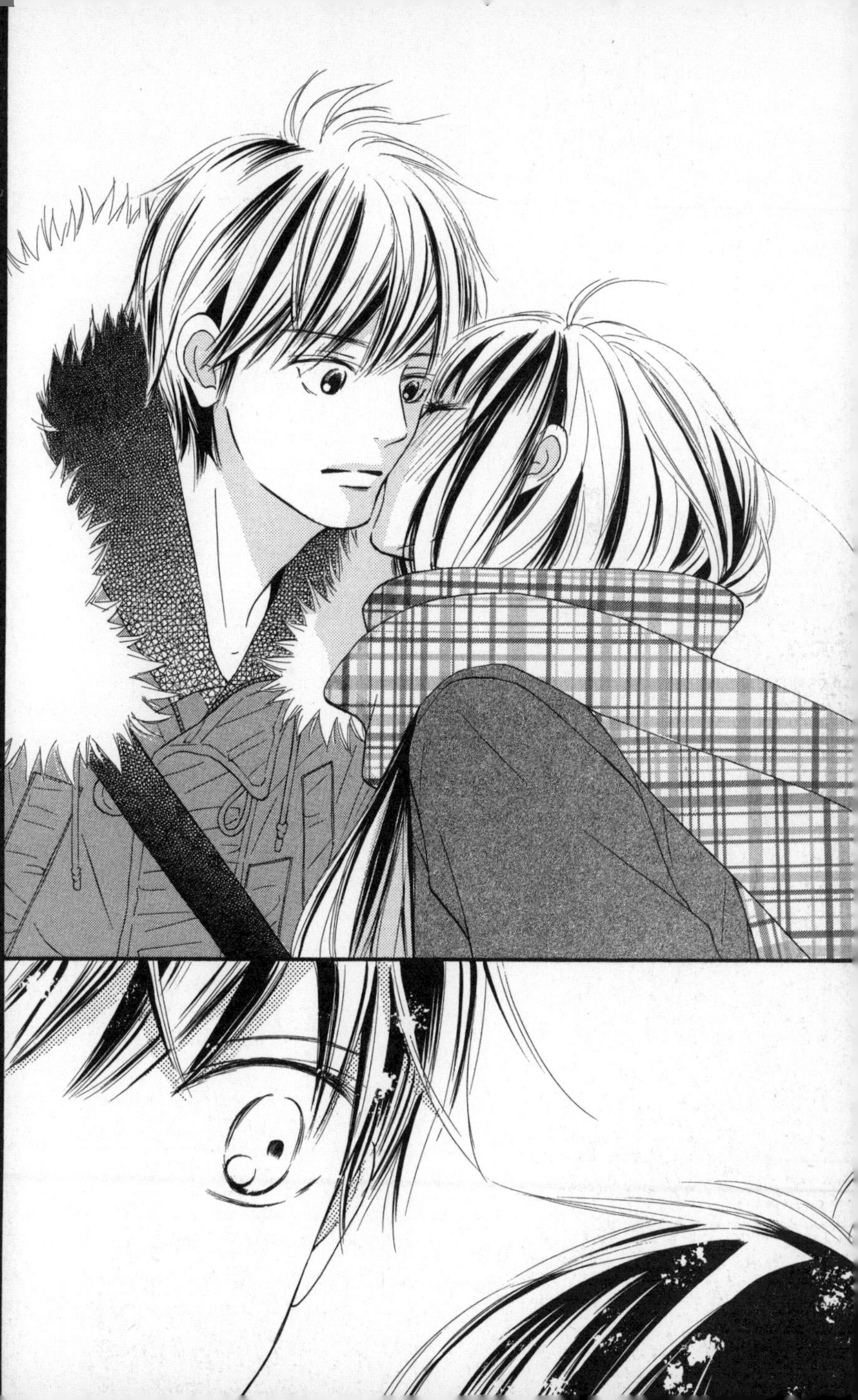

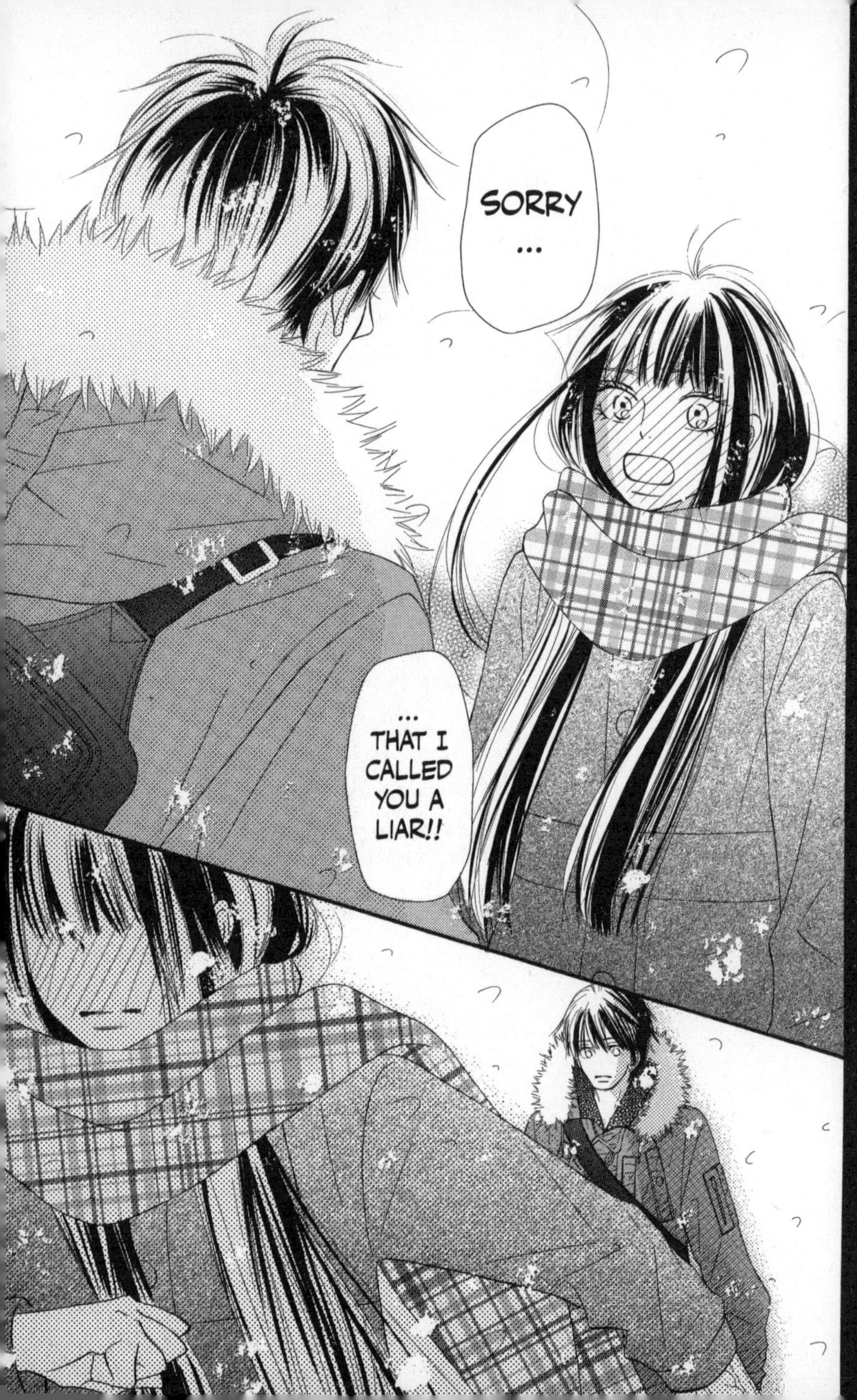
SORRY ...
... THAT I CALLED YOU A LIAR!!

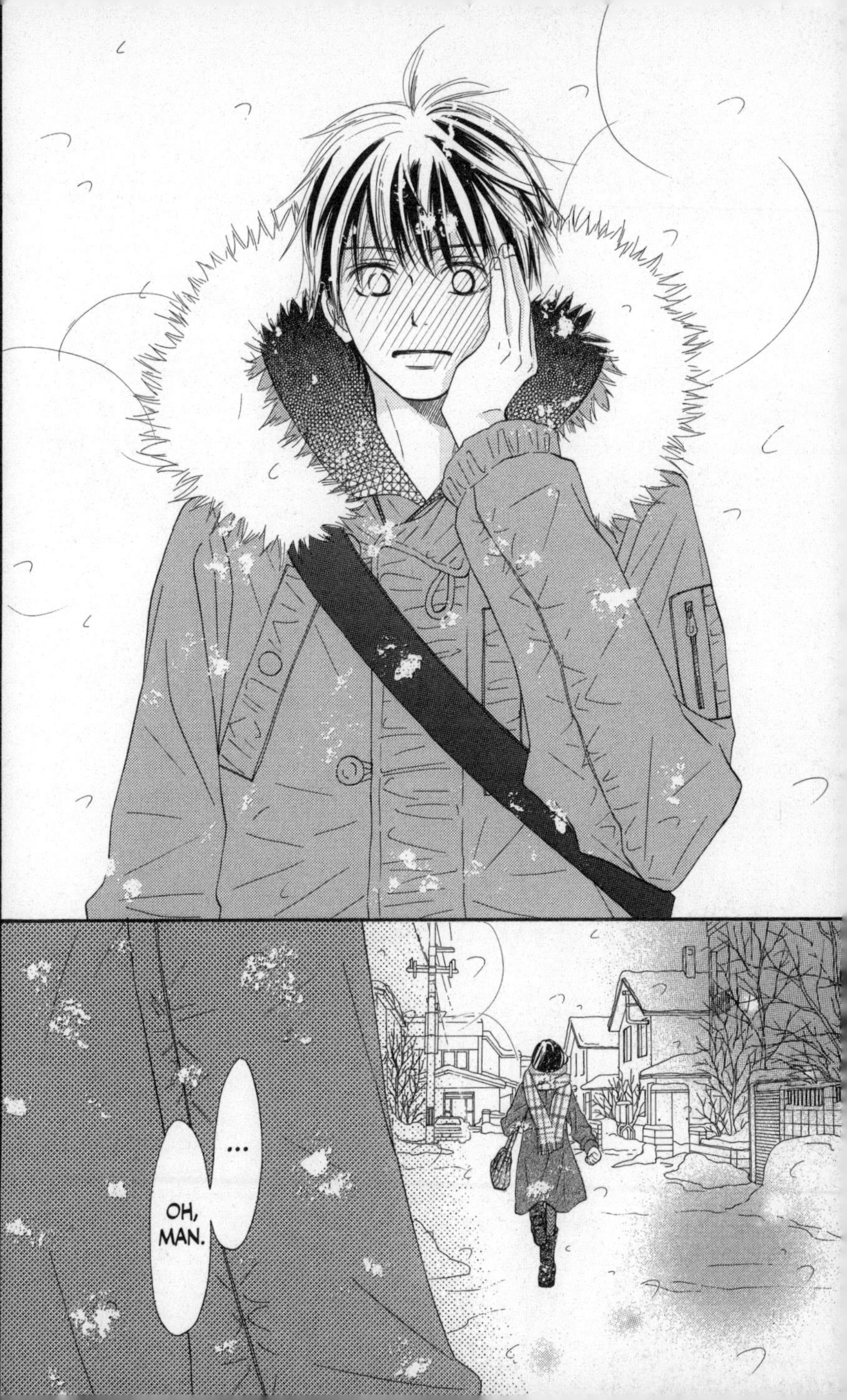
...
OH, MAN.

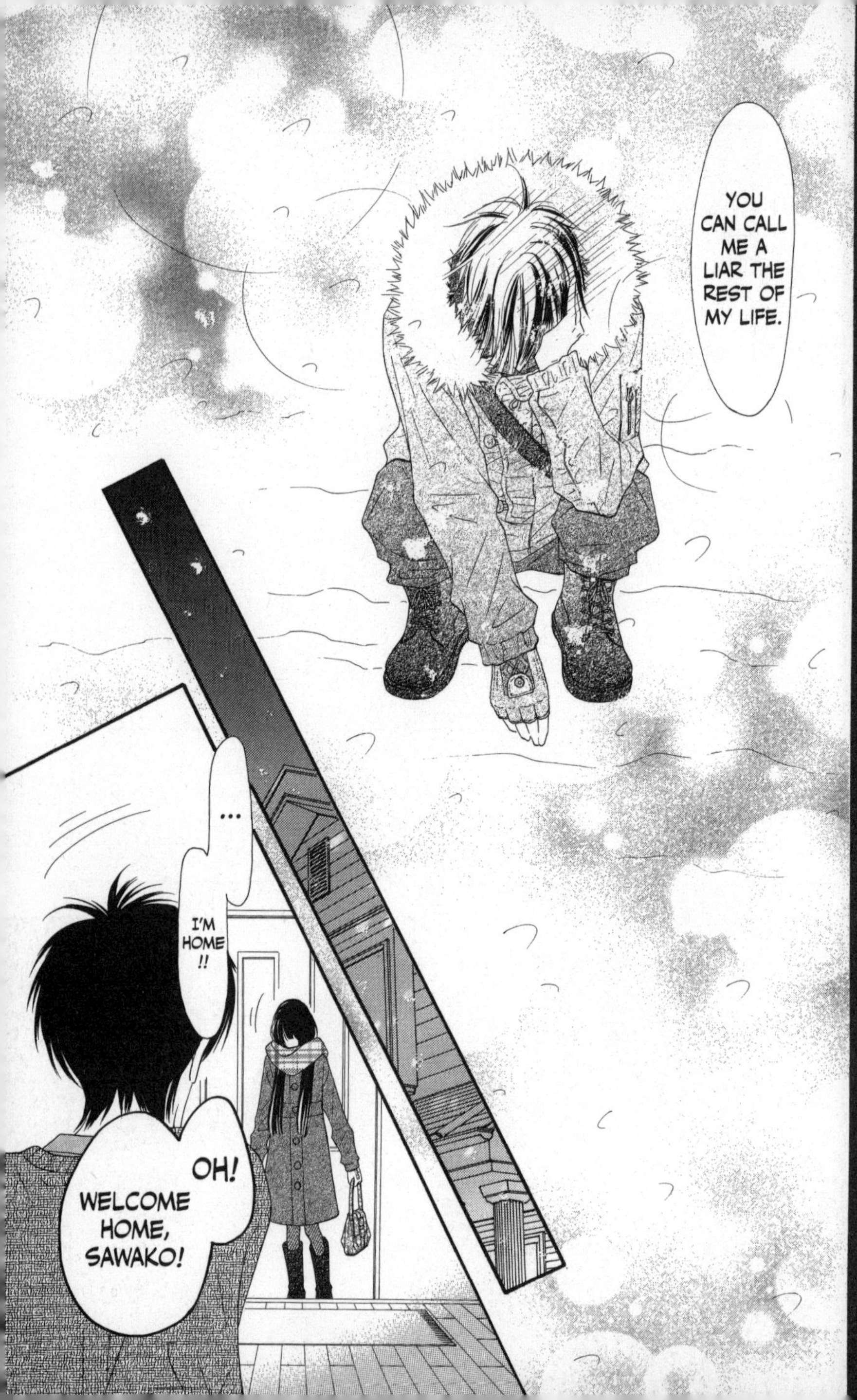
YOU CAN CALL ME A LIAR THE REST OF MY LIFE.
...
I'M HOME !!
OH! WELCOME HOME, SAWAKO!

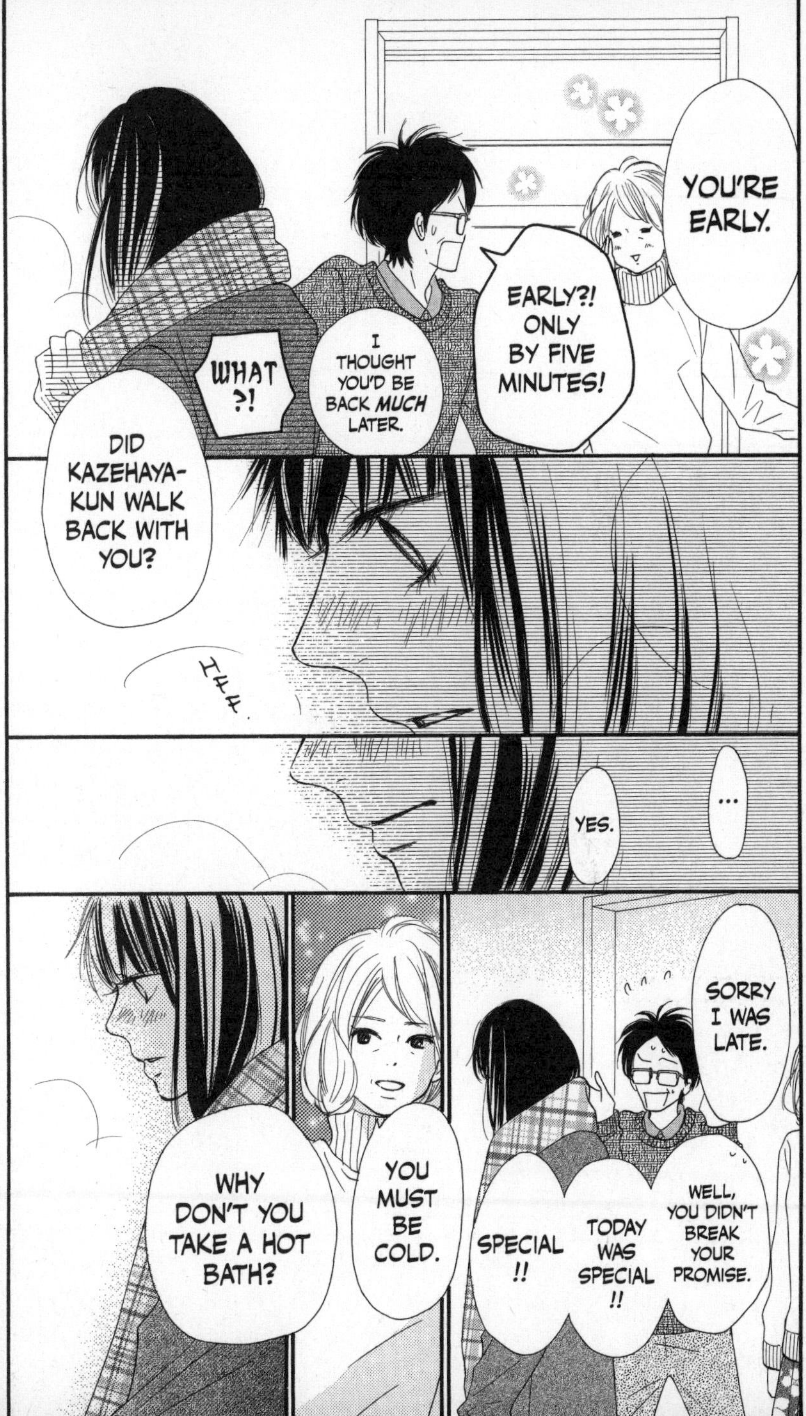
YOU'RE EARLY.
EARLY?! ONLY BY FIVE MINUTES!
I THOUGHT YOU'D BE BACK MUCH LATER.
WHAT ?!
DID KAZEHAYA-KUN WALK BACK WITH YOU?
...
YES.
SORRY I WAS LATE.
WELL, YOU DIDN'T BREAK YOUR PROMISE.
TODAY WAS SPECIAL !!
SPECIAL !!
YOU MUST BE COLD.
WHY DON'T YOU TAKE A HOT BATH?

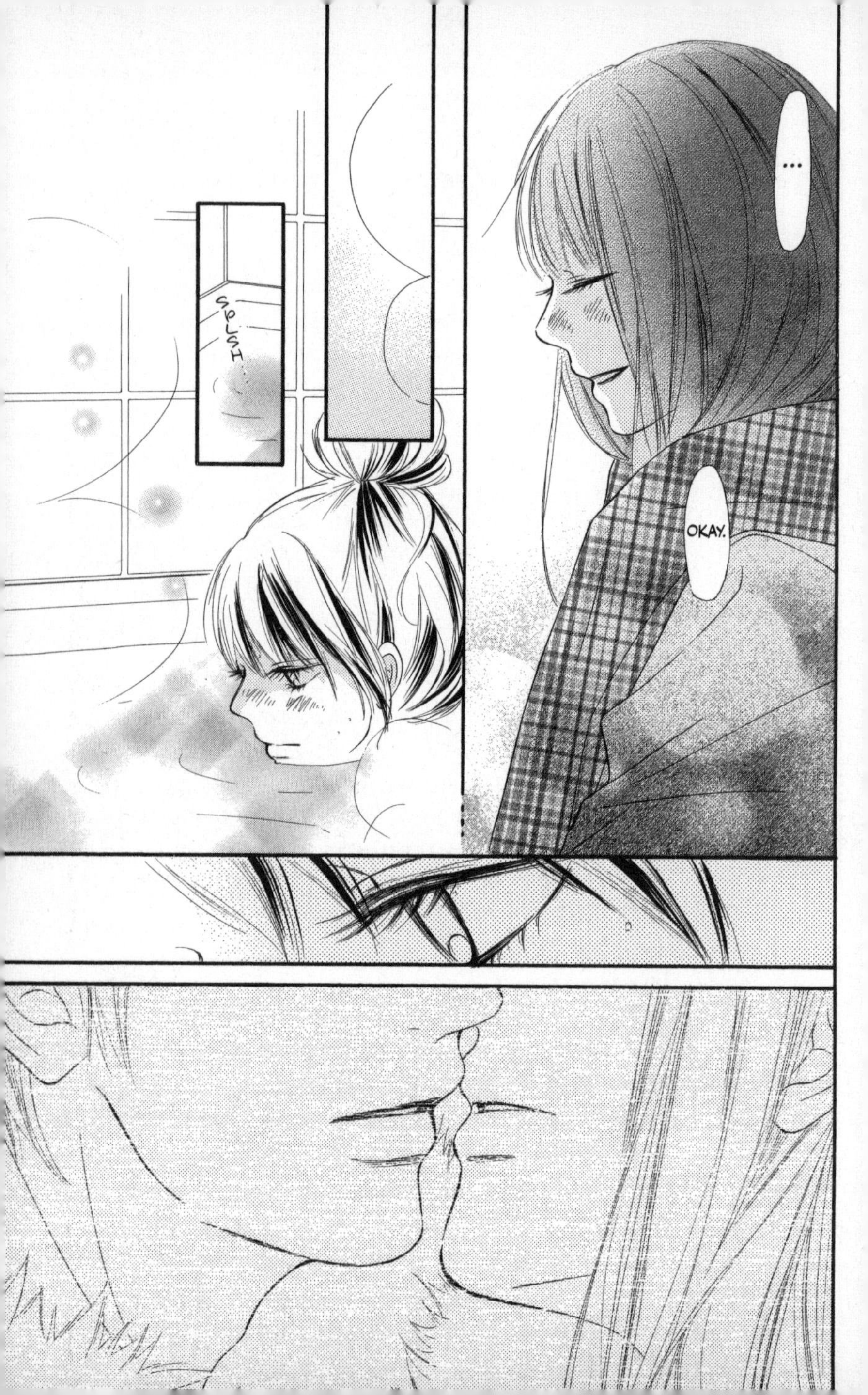
...
OKAY.
SPLASH...

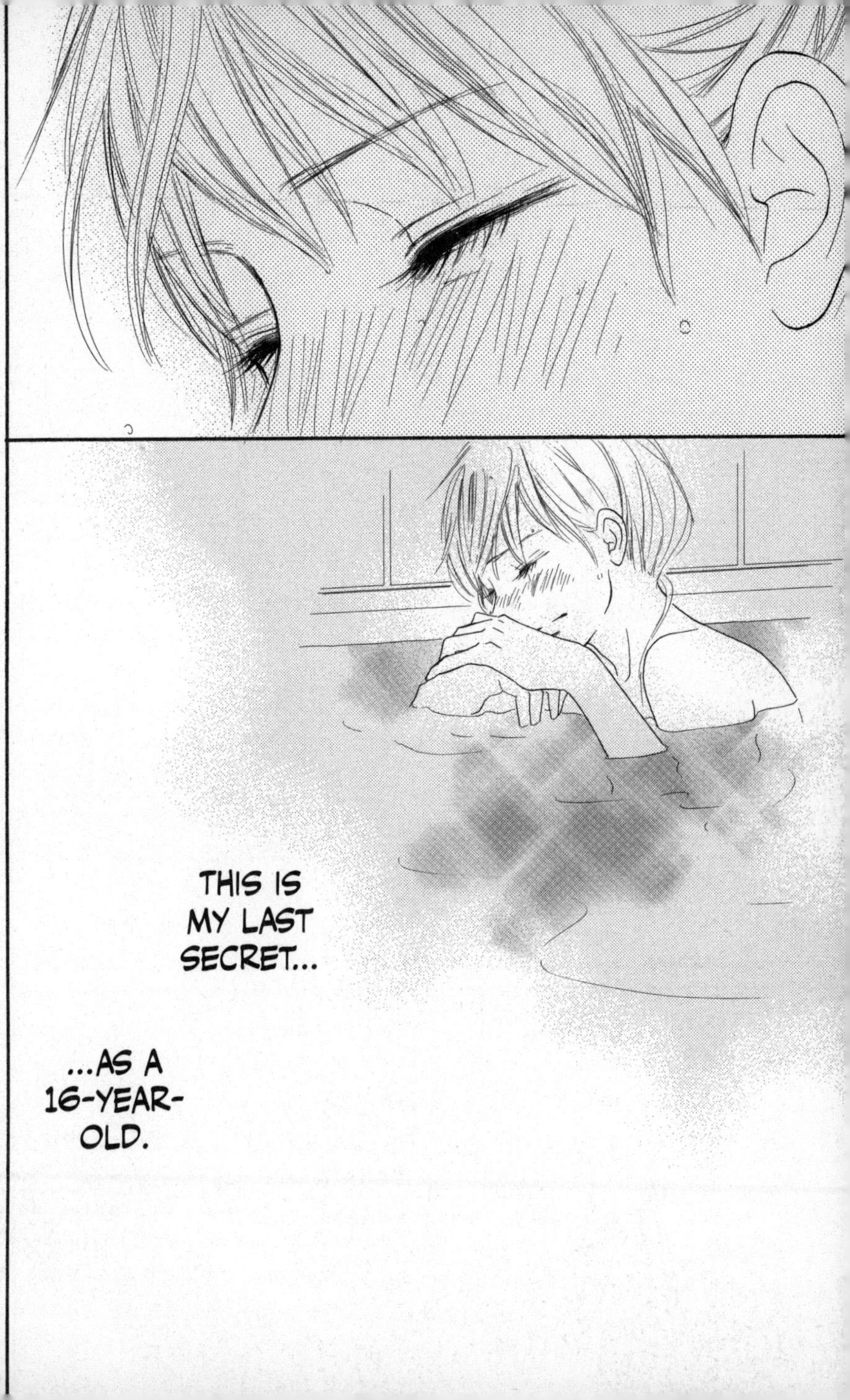
THIS IS MY LAST SECRET...
...AS A 16-YEAR-OLD.

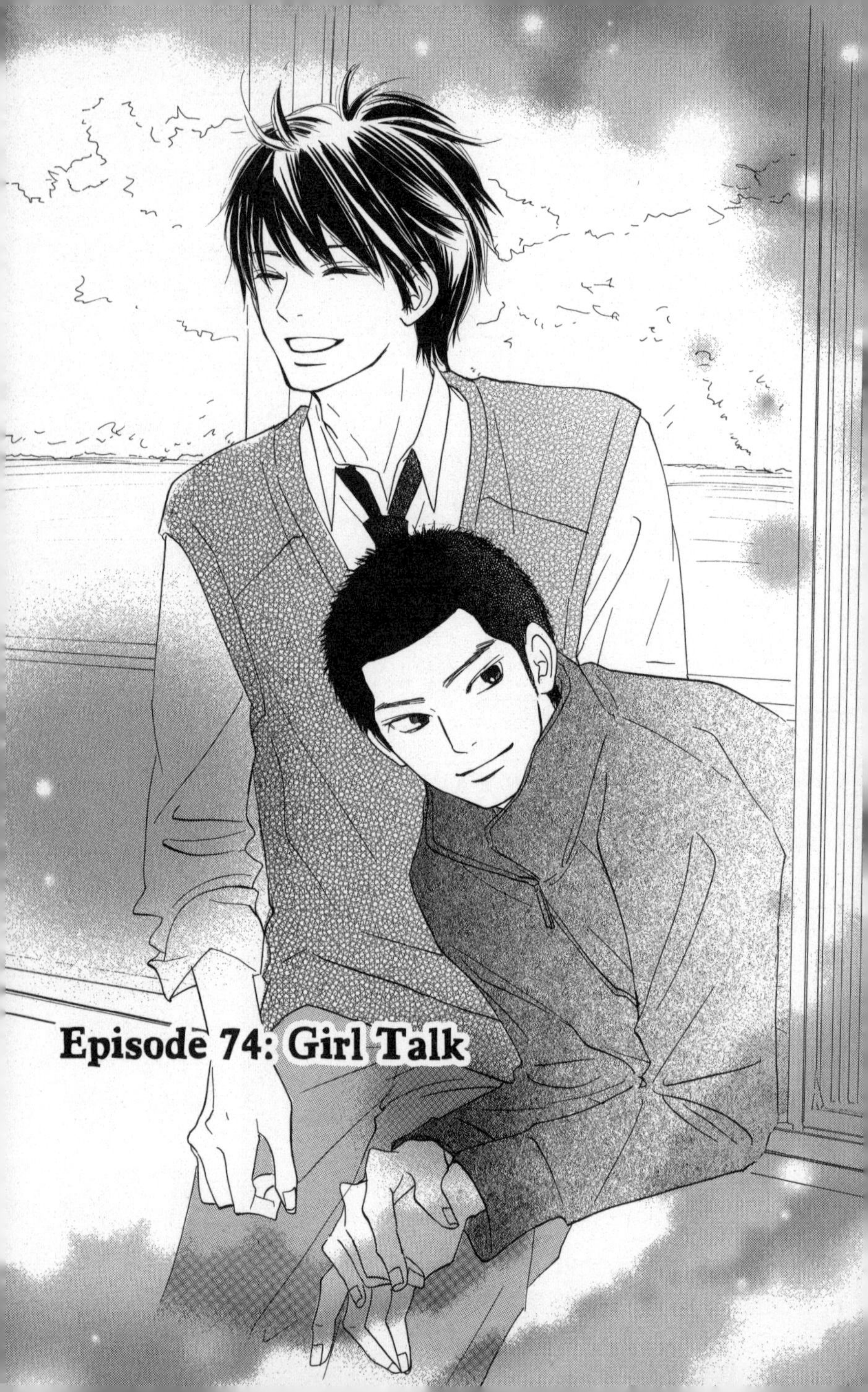
Episode 74: Girl Talk

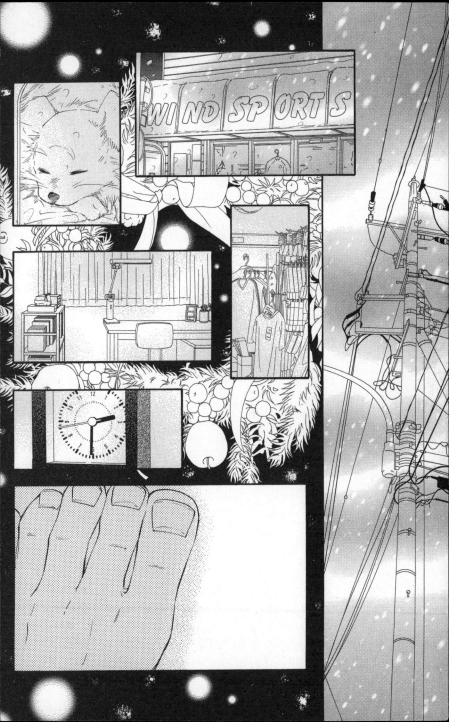

WIND SPORTS

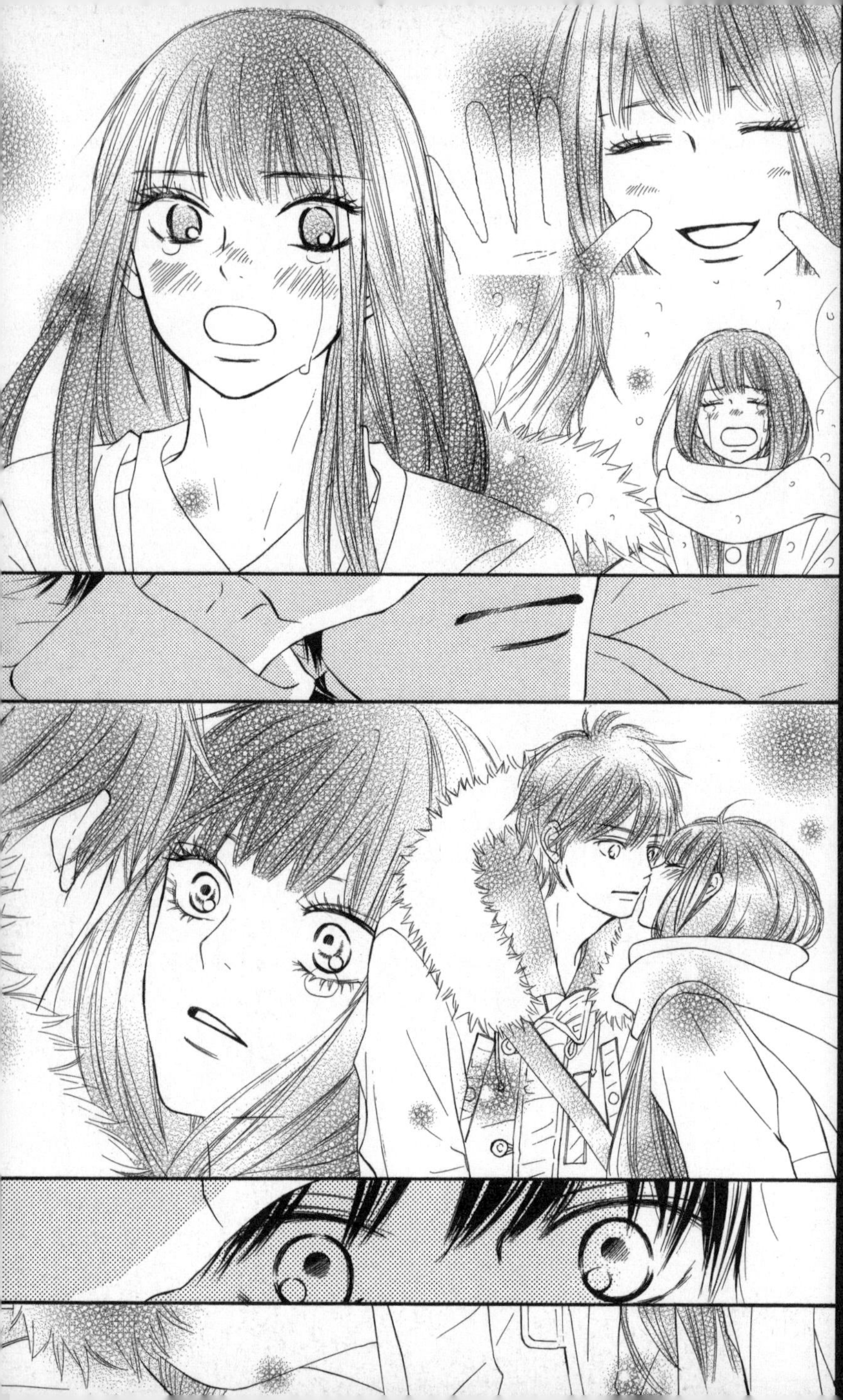

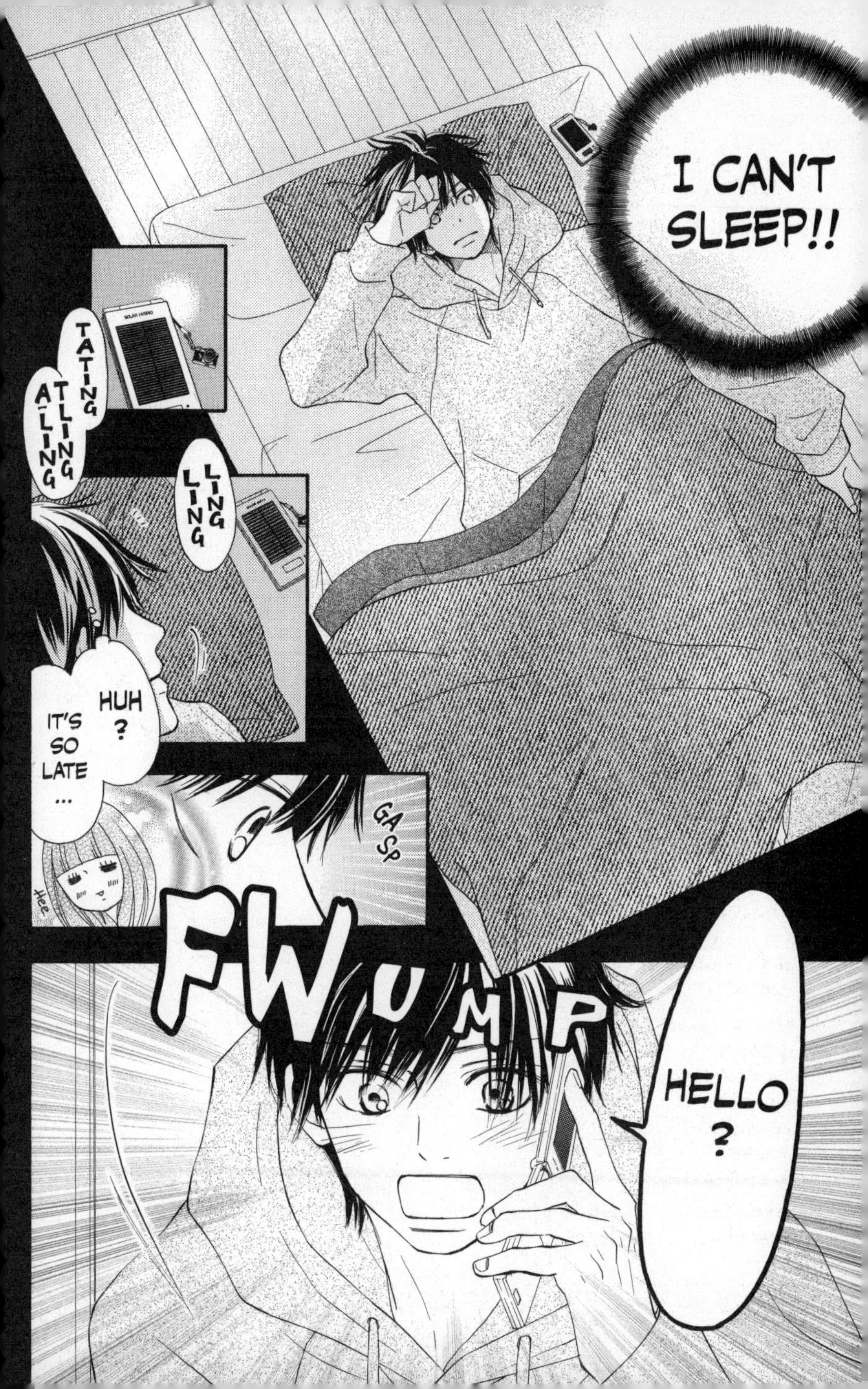
I CAN'T SLEEP!!
TATING TLING A-LING
LING LING
HUH?
IT'S SO LATE...
GASP
Hee
FWUMP
HELLO?

KARUPIN on JAPAN 1

Hi, how are you? I'm Shiina. I'm the author.

This volume comes out in January, so I thought about changing the picture on the back cover* from a flower to a New Year's decorative pine branch, but this will be in stores as soon as the end of the month and the story is about Christmas, so I decided to draw a Christmas wreath. I enjoy drawing flowers.

But it's getting old!

Someday I want to draw pine branches! They're not flowers, though...

Right now, as I'm writing this, it is the middle of December 2012!

Every year passes so quickly, but around December, I can't remember what happened back around January or New Year's. Time keeps marching on... Obviously...

*Spine in the VIZ edition

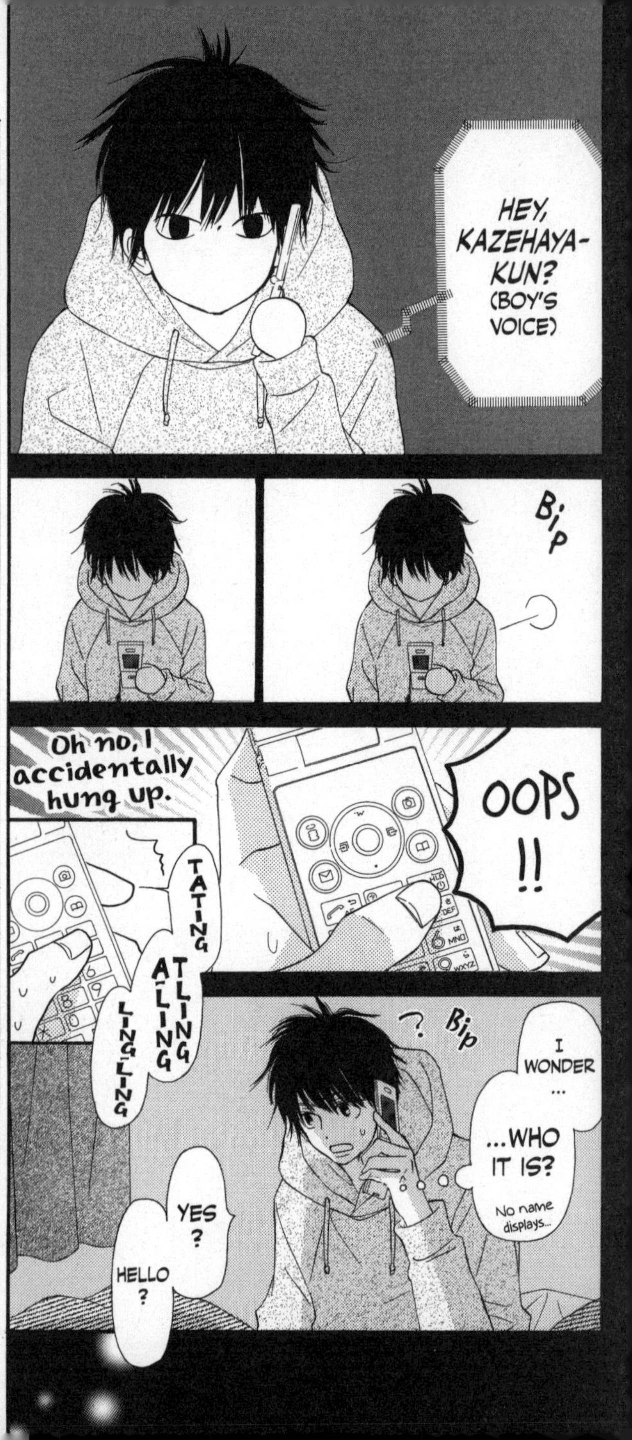
HEY, KAZEHAYA-KUN? (BOY'S VOICE)
Bip
OOPS !!
Oh no, I accidentally hung up.
TATING
TLING
A-LING
LING-LING
Bip
?
I WONDER...
...WHO IT IS?
No name displays...
YES?
HELLO?

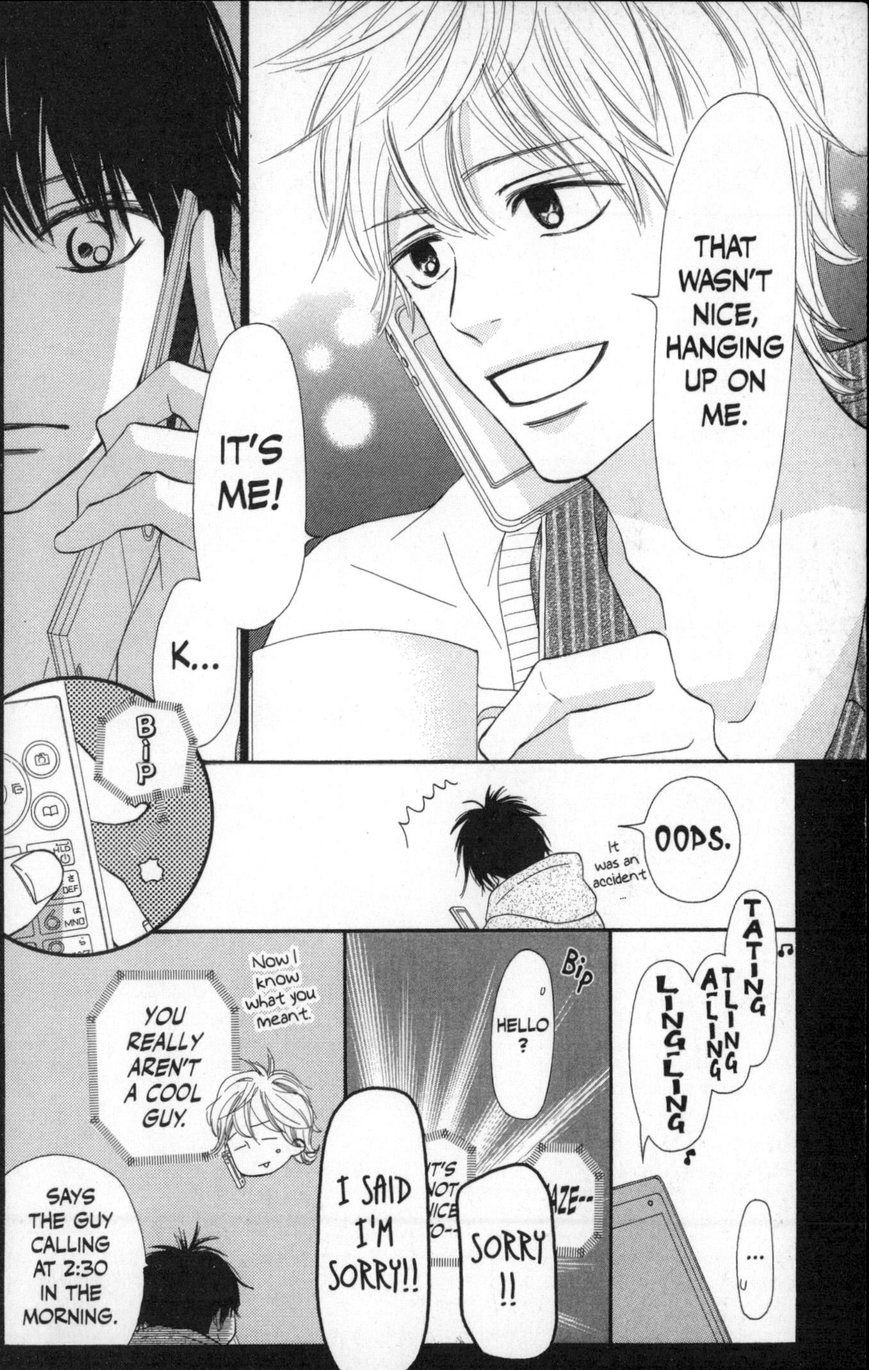
THAT WASN'T NICE, HANGING UP ON ME.
IT'S ME!
K...
BIP
OOPS.
It was an accident...
TATING
TLING
A-LING
LING-LING
...
Bip
HELLO?
AZE--
IT'S NOT NICE TO--
SORRY!!
I SAID I'M SORRY!!
Now I know what you meant.
YOU REALLY AREN'T A COOL GUY.
SAYS THE GUY CALLING AT 2:30 IN THE MORNING.

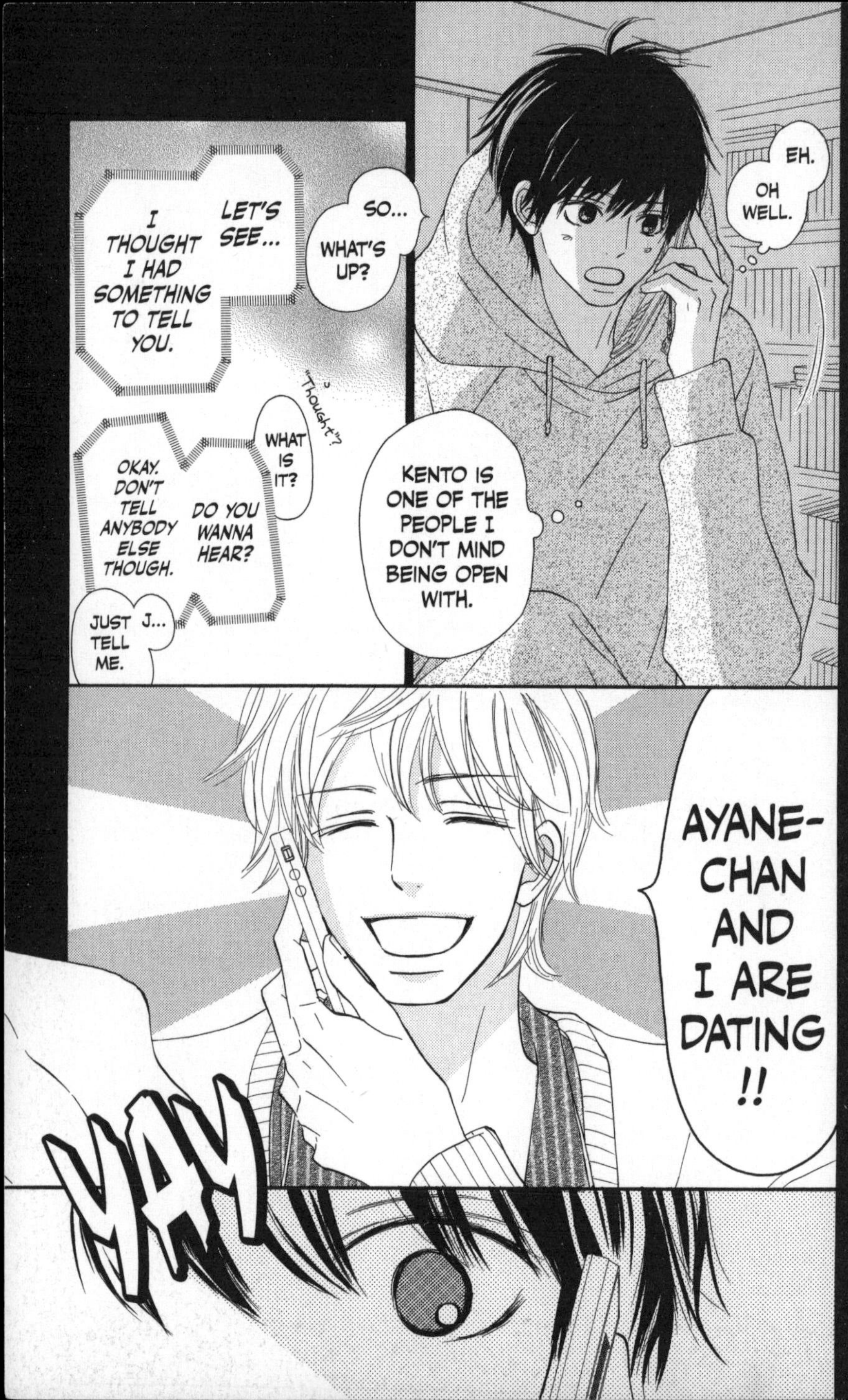
EH.
OH WELL.
KENTO IS ONE OF THE PEOPLE I DON'T MIND BEING OPEN WITH.
SO... WHAT'S UP?
LET'S SEE...
I THOUGHT I HAD SOMETHING TO TELL YOU.
"Thought"?
WHAT IS IT?
DO YOU WANNA HEAR?
OKAY. DON'T TELL ANYBODY ELSE THOUGH.
J...
JUST TELL ME.
AYANE-CHAN AND I ARE DATING!!
YAY

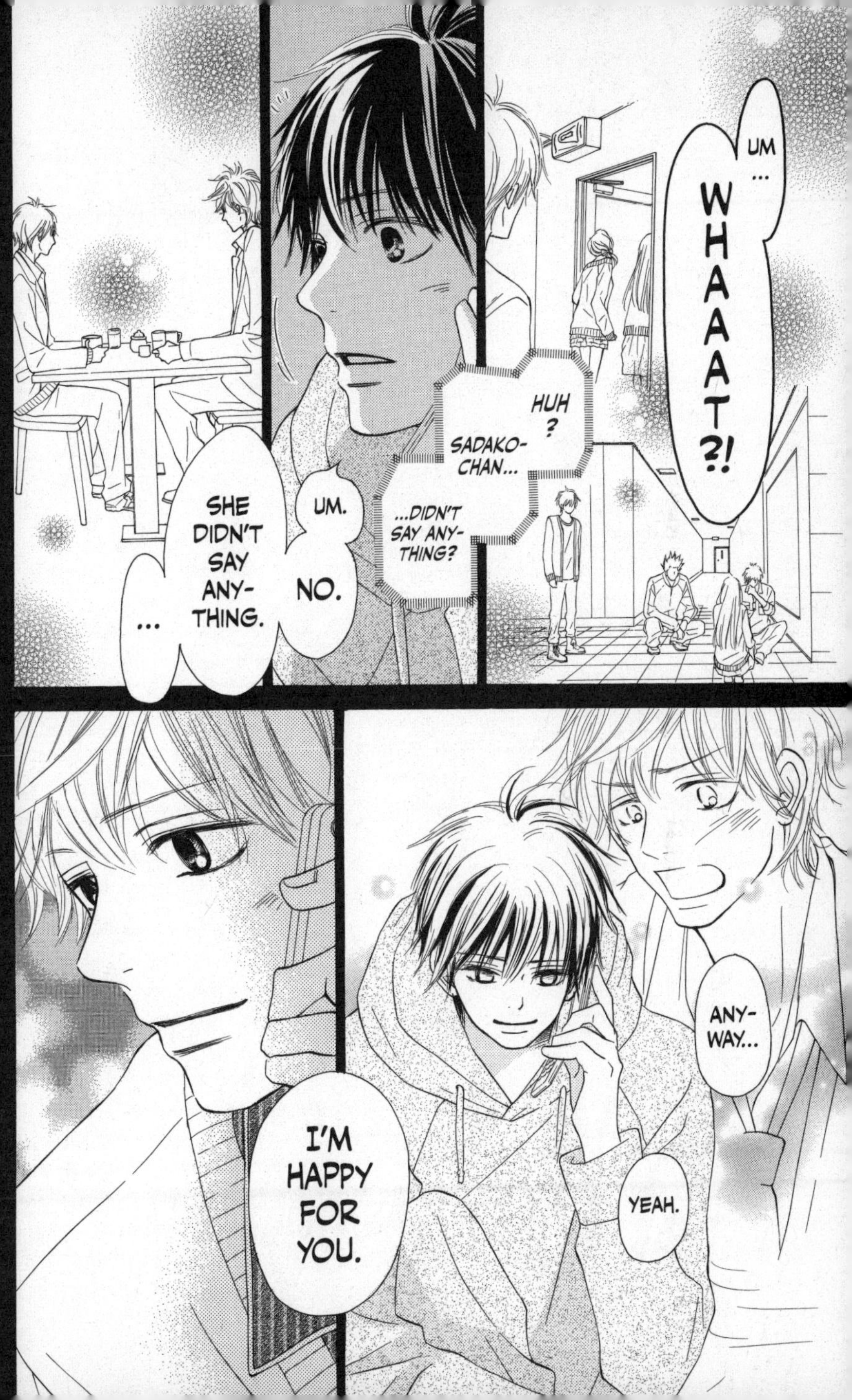
UM ... WHAAAAT?!
HUH? SADAKO-CHAN...
...DIDN'T SAY ANY-THING?
UM.
NO.
SHE DIDN'T SAY ANY-THING.
...
ANY-WAY...
YEAH.
I'M HAPPY FOR YOU.

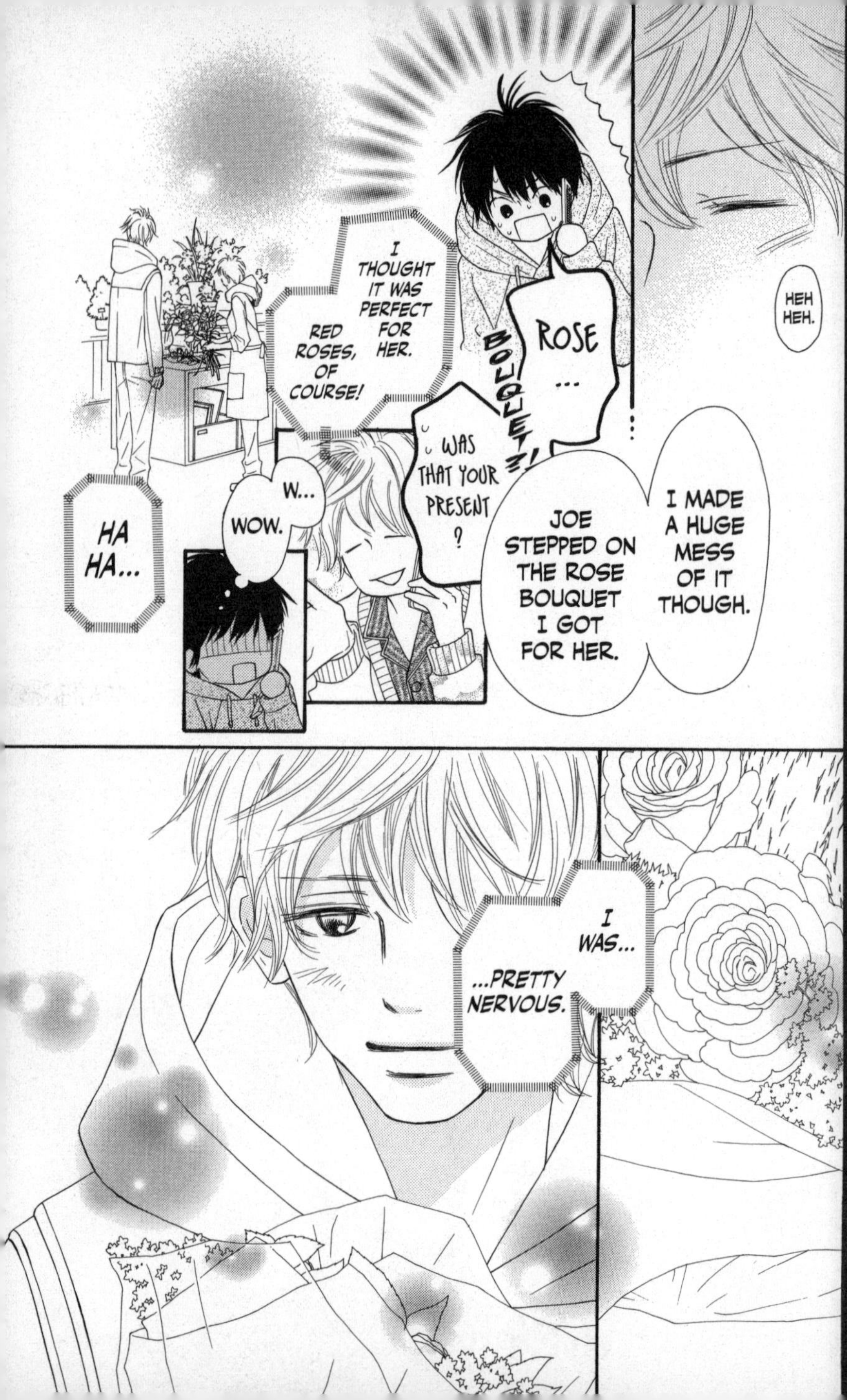
HEH HEH.
...
I MADE A HUGE MESS OF IT THOUGH.
JOE STEPPED ON THE ROSE BOUQUET I GOT FOR HER.
ROSE ...
BOUQUET!!
I THOUGHT IT WAS PERFECT FOR HER.
RED ROSES, OF COURSE!
WAS THAT YOUR PRESENT?
W... WOW.
HA HA...
I WAS...
...PRETTY NERVOUS.

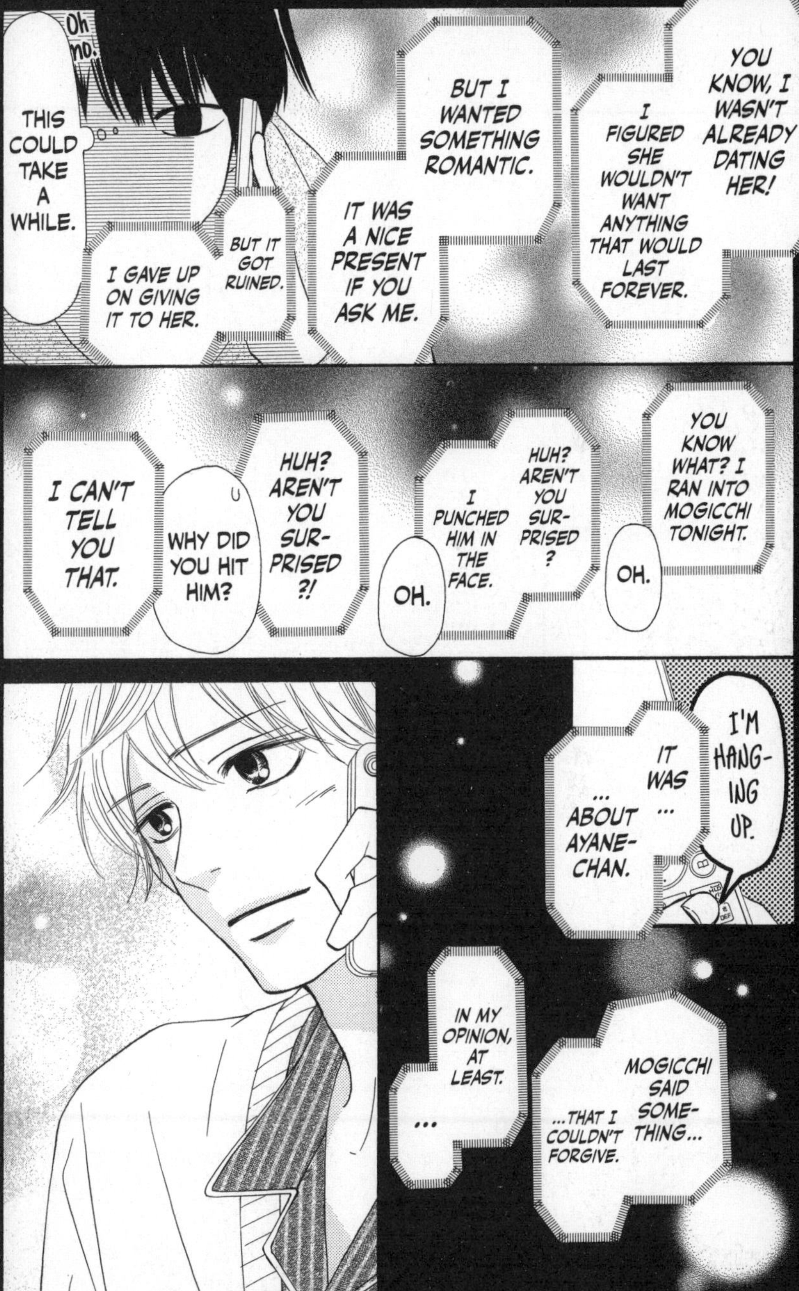
YOU KNOW, I WASN'T ALREADY DATING HER!
I FIGURED SHE WOULDN'T WANT ANYTHING THAT WOULD LAST FOREVER.
BUT I WANTED SOMETHING ROMANTIC.
IT WAS A NICE PRESENT IF YOU ASK ME.
BUT IT GOT RUINED.
I GAVE UP ON GIVING IT TO HER.
Oh no.
THIS COULD TAKE A WHILE.
YOU KNOW WHAT? I RAN INTO MOGICCHI TONIGHT.
OH.
HUH? AREN'T YOU SURPRISED?
I PUNCHED HIM IN THE FACE.
OH.
HUH? AREN'T YOU SURPRISED?!
WHY DID YOU HIT HIM?
I CAN'T TELL YOU THAT.
I'M HANGING UP.
IT WAS...
...ABOUT AYANE-CHAN.
MOGICCHI SAID SOMETHING...
...THAT I COULDN'T FORGIVE.
IN MY OPINION, AT LEAST.
...

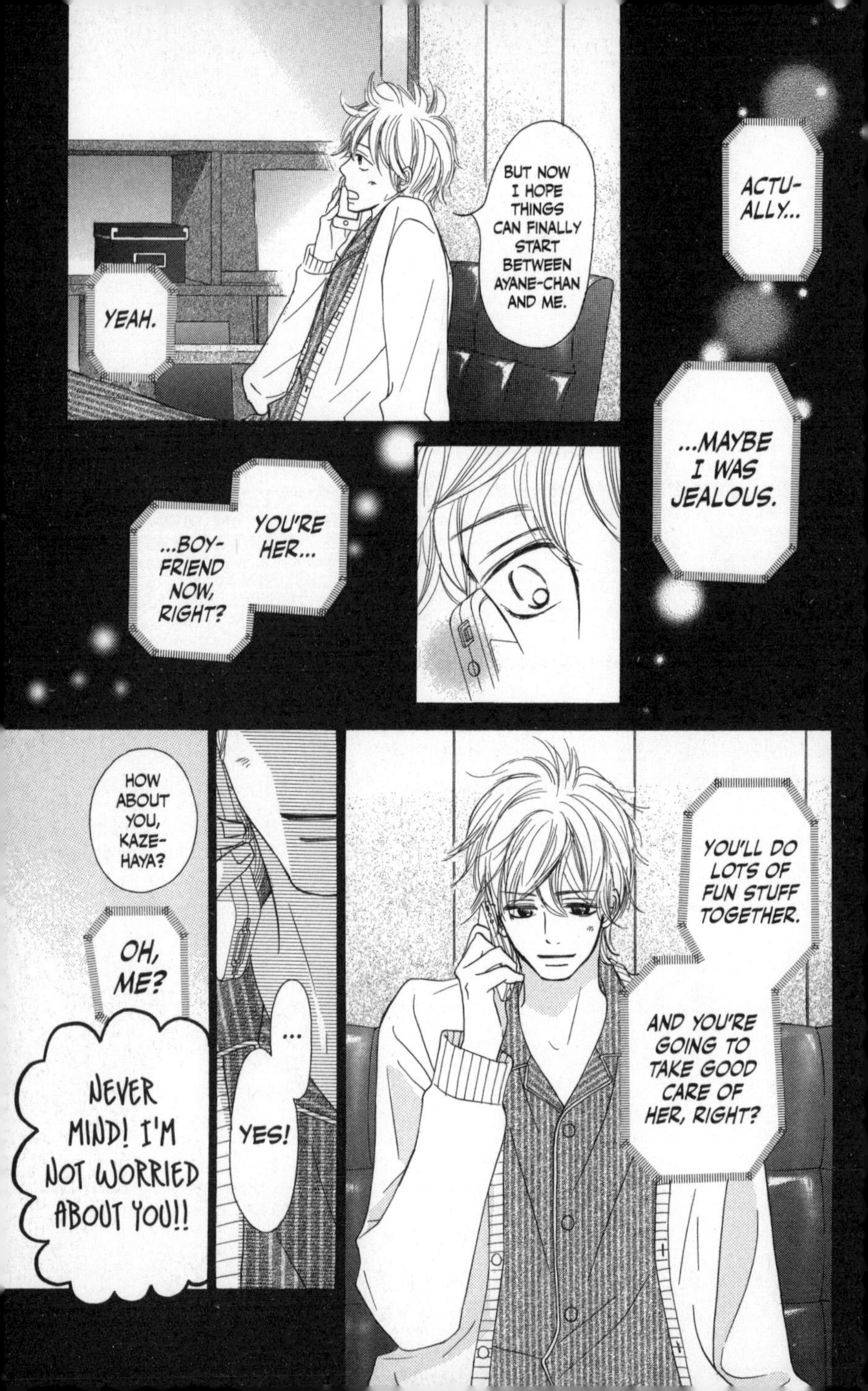
ACTU-ALLY...
...MAYBE I WAS JEALOUS.
BUT NOW I HOPE THINGS CAN FINALLY START BETWEEN AYANE-CHAN AND ME.
YEAH.
YOU'RE HER...
...BOY-FRIEND NOW, RIGHT?
YOU'LL DO LOTS OF FUN STUFF TOGETHER.
AND YOU'RE GOING TO TAKE GOOD CARE OF HER, RIGHT?
...
YES!
HOW ABOUT YOU, KAZE-HAYA?
OH, ME?
NEVER MIND! I'M NOT WORRIED ABOUT YOU!!

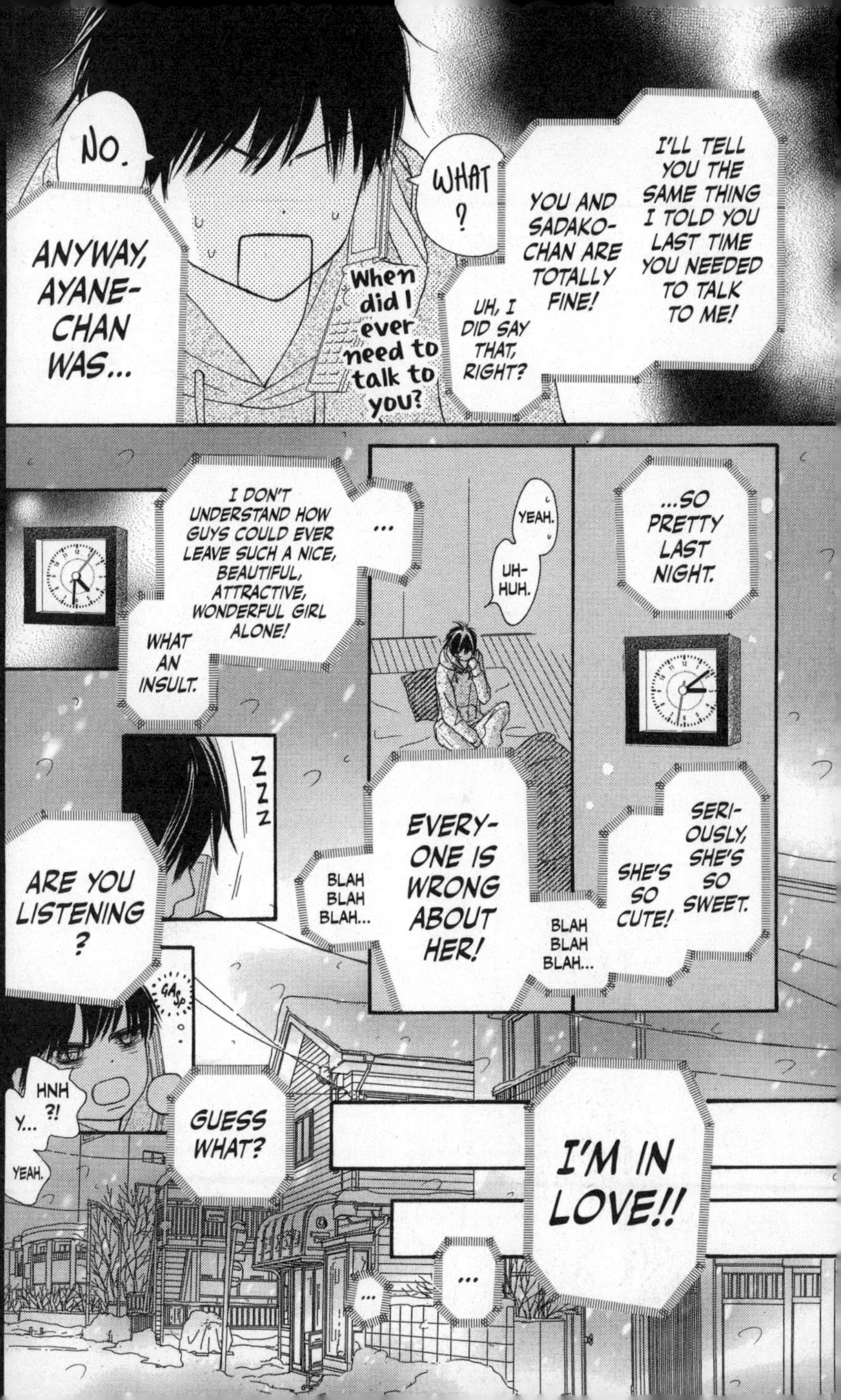
I'LL TELL YOU THE SAME THING I TOLD YOU LAST TIME YOU NEEDED TO TALK TO ME!
YOU AND SADAKO-CHAN ARE TOTALLY FINE!
UH, I DID SAY THAT, RIGHT?
WHAT?
When did I ever need to talk to you?
NO.
ANYWAY, AYANE-CHAN WAS...
...SO PRETTY LAST NIGHT.
SERIOUSLY, SHE'S SO SWEET.
SHE'S SO CUTE!
BLAH BLAH BLAH...
YEAH.
UH-HUH.
EVERYONE IS WRONG ABOUT HER!
BLAH BLAH BLAH...
...
I DON'T UNDERSTAND HOW GUYS COULD EVER LEAVE SUCH A NICE, BEAUTIFUL, ATTRACTIVE, WONDERFUL GIRL ALONE!
WHAT AN INSULT.
ZZZ
ARE YOU LISTENING?
GASP
HNH?!
Y... YEAH.
I'M IN LOVE!!
GUESS WHAT?
...
...

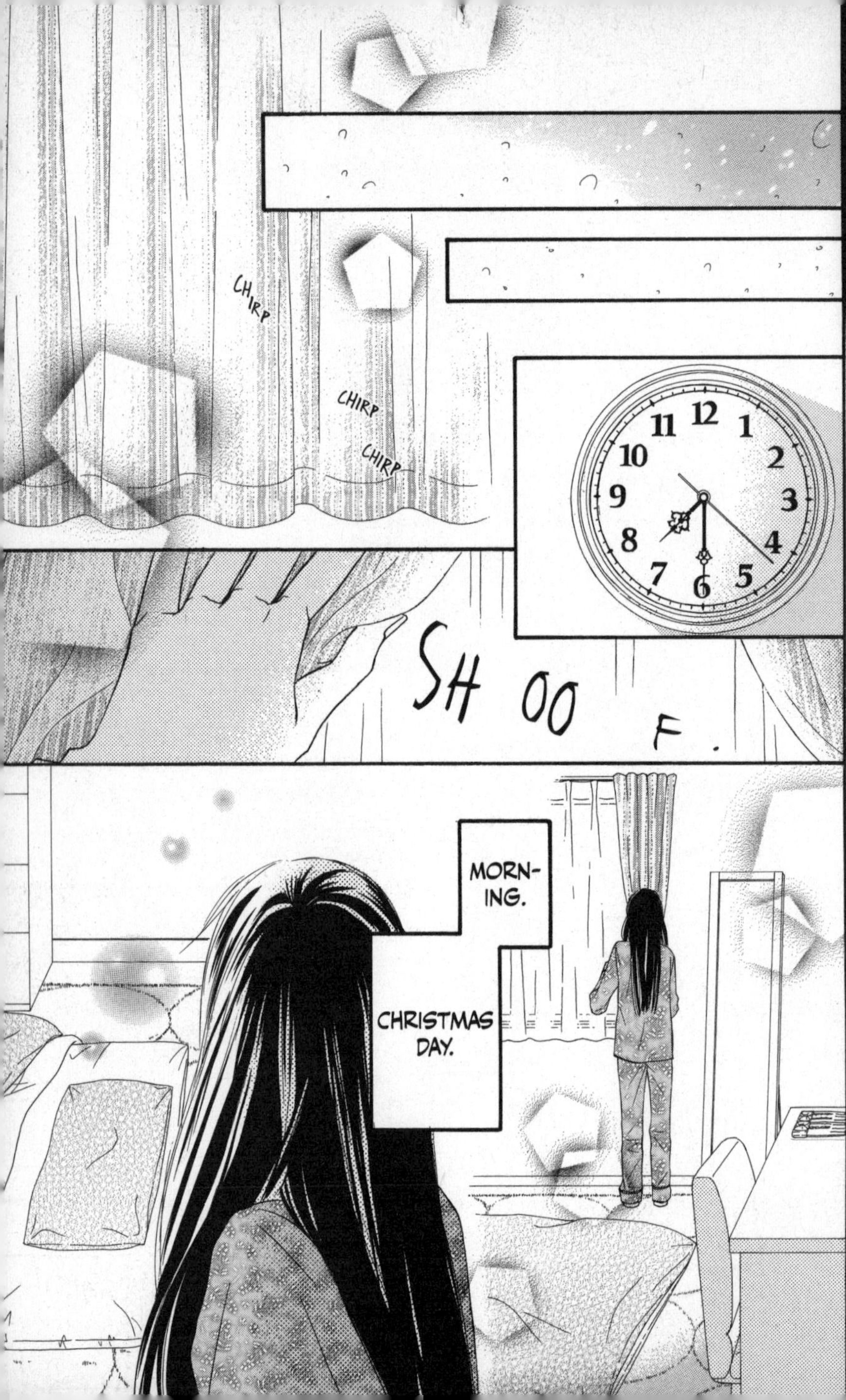
12
1
2
3
4
5
6
7
8
9
10
11
CHIRP
CHIRP
CHIRP
SHOOF.
MORNING.
CHRISTMAS DAY.

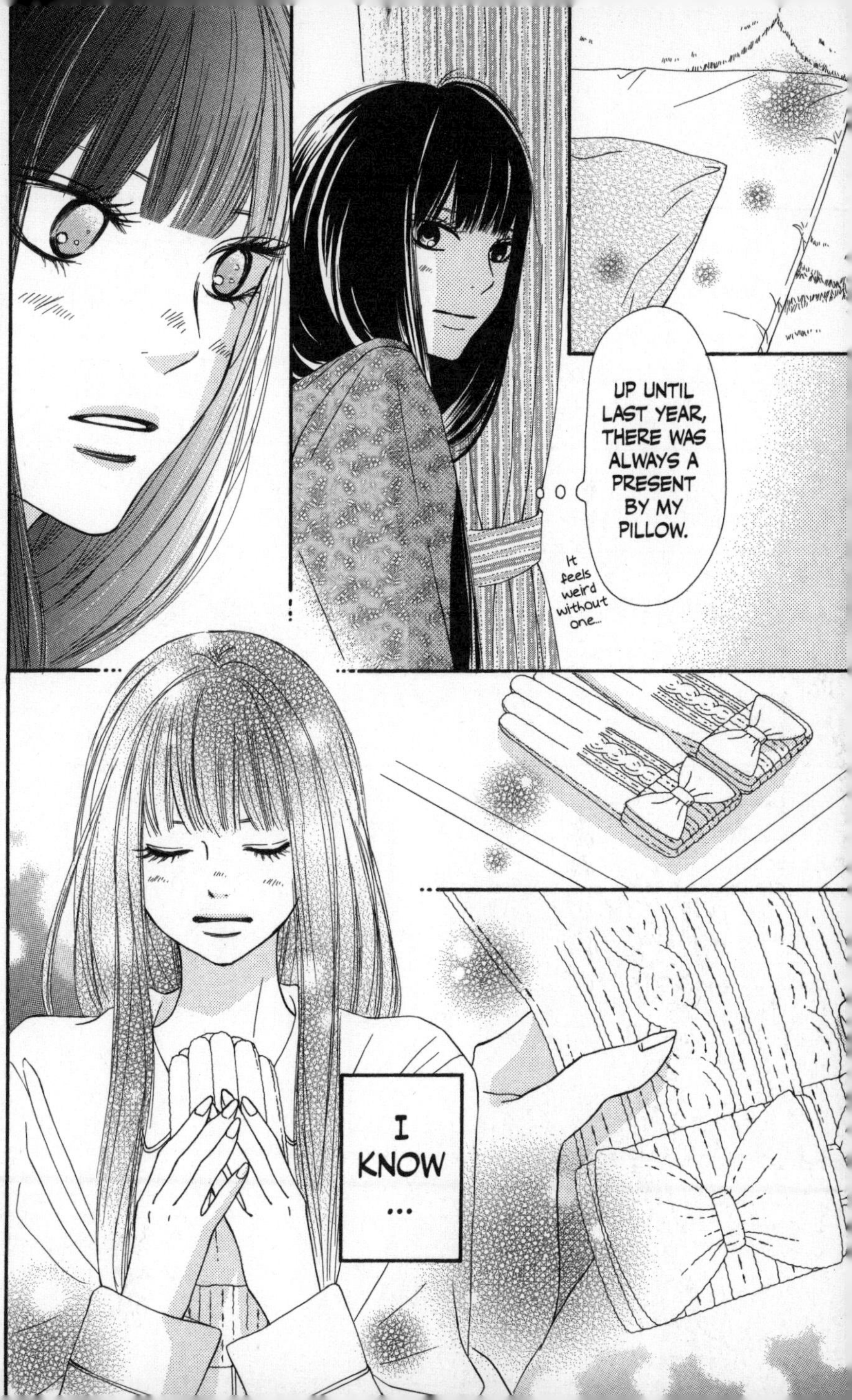
UP UNTIL LAST YEAR, THERE WAS ALWAYS A PRESENT BY MY PILLOW.
It feels weird without one...
I KNOW ...

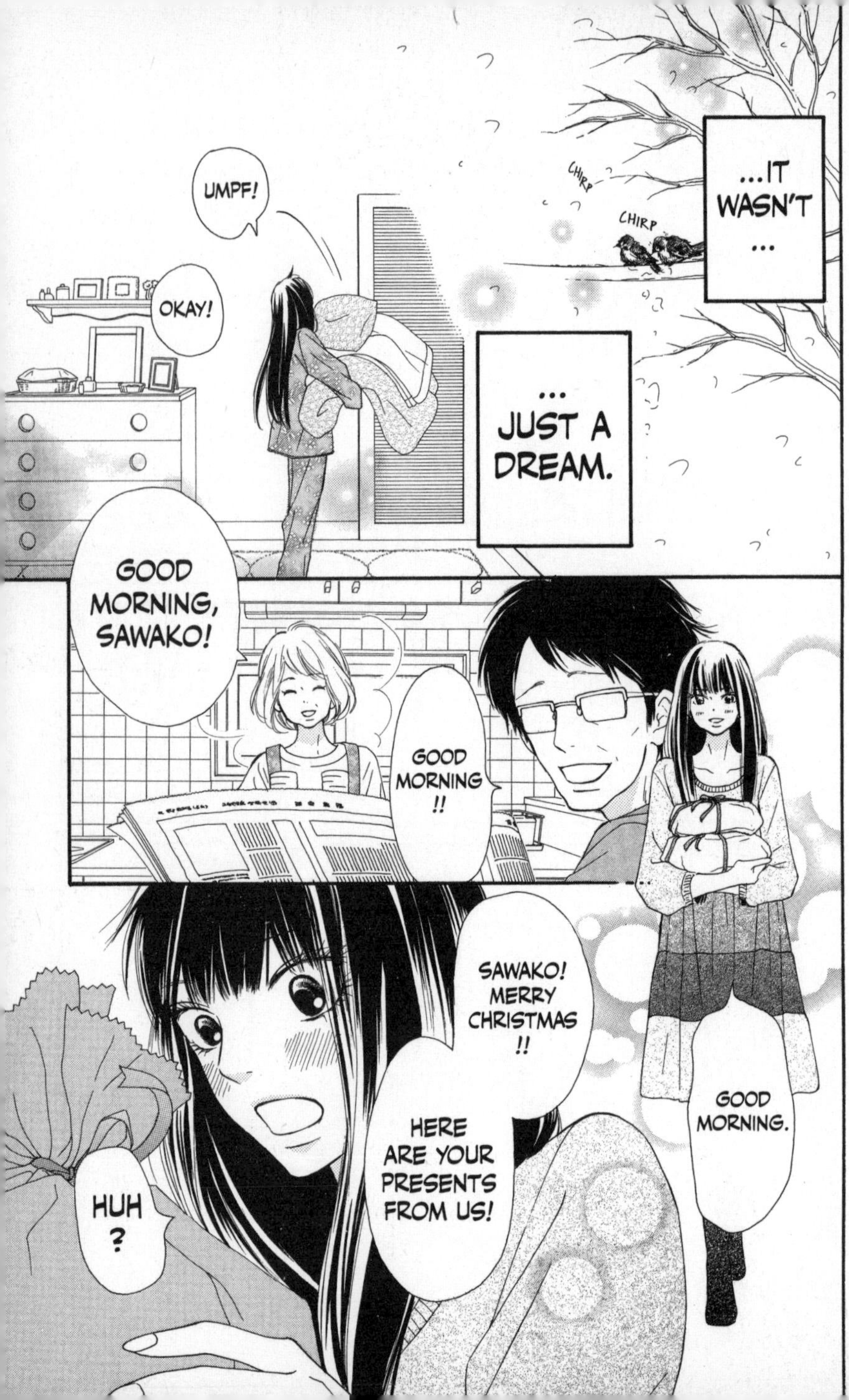
CHIRP
...IT WASN'T ...
CHIRP
... JUST A DREAM.
UMPF!
OKAY!
GOOD MORNING.
GOOD MORNING, SAWAKO!
GOOD MORNING !!
SAWAKO! MERRY CHRISTMAS !!
HERE ARE YOUR PRESENTS FROM US!
HUH ?

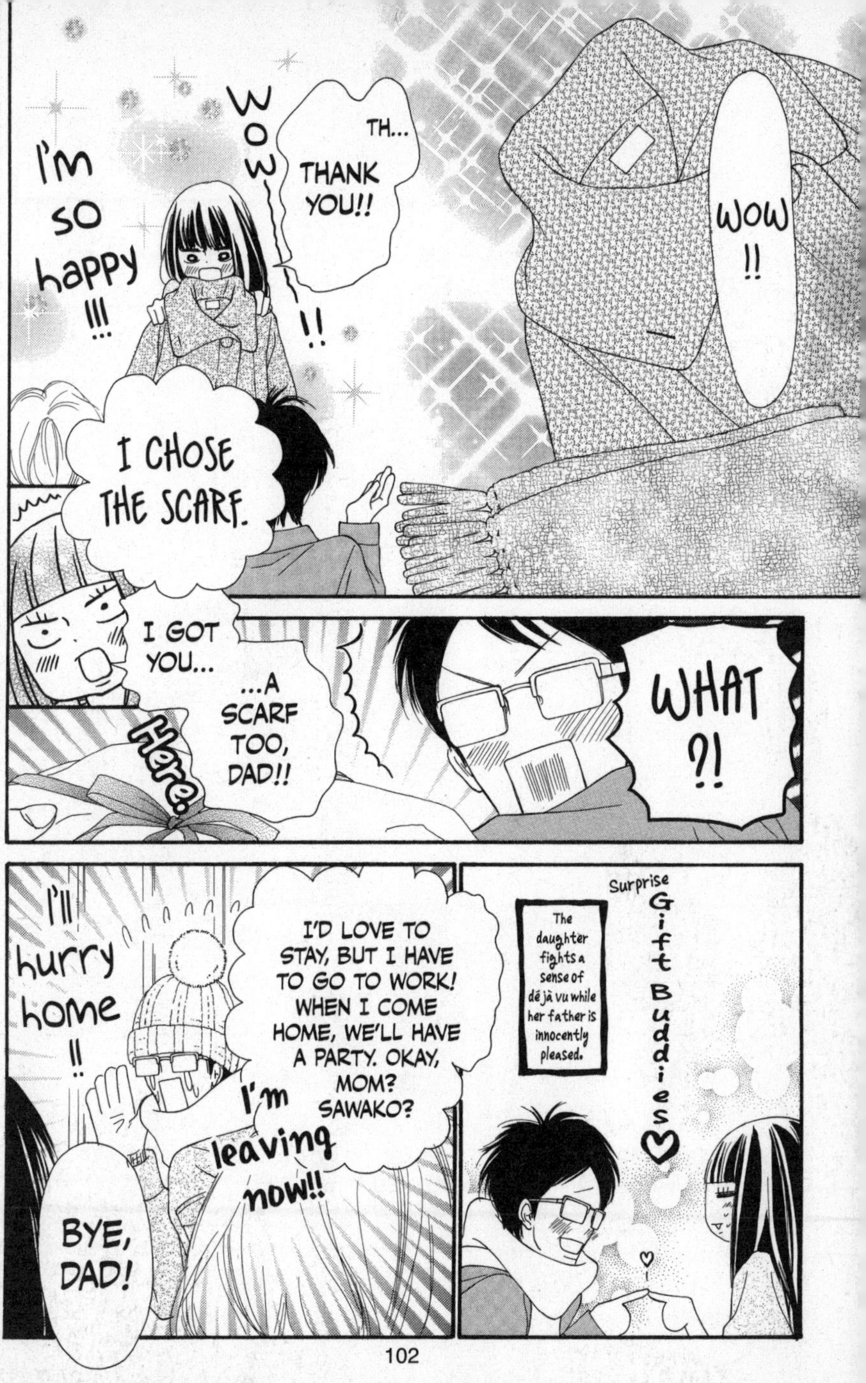
WOW!!
TH... THANK YOU!!
WOW!!
I'm so happy!!!
I CHOSE THE SCARF.
I GOT YOU...
...A SCARF TOO, DAD!!
Here.
WHAT?!
Surprise Gift Buddies♥
The daughter fights a sense of déjà vu while her father is innocently pleased.
I'D LOVE TO STAY, BUT I HAVE TO GO TO WORK! WHEN I COME HOME, WE'LL HAVE A PARTY. OKAY, MOM? SAWAKO?
I'm leaving now!!
I'll hurry home!!
BYE, DAD!

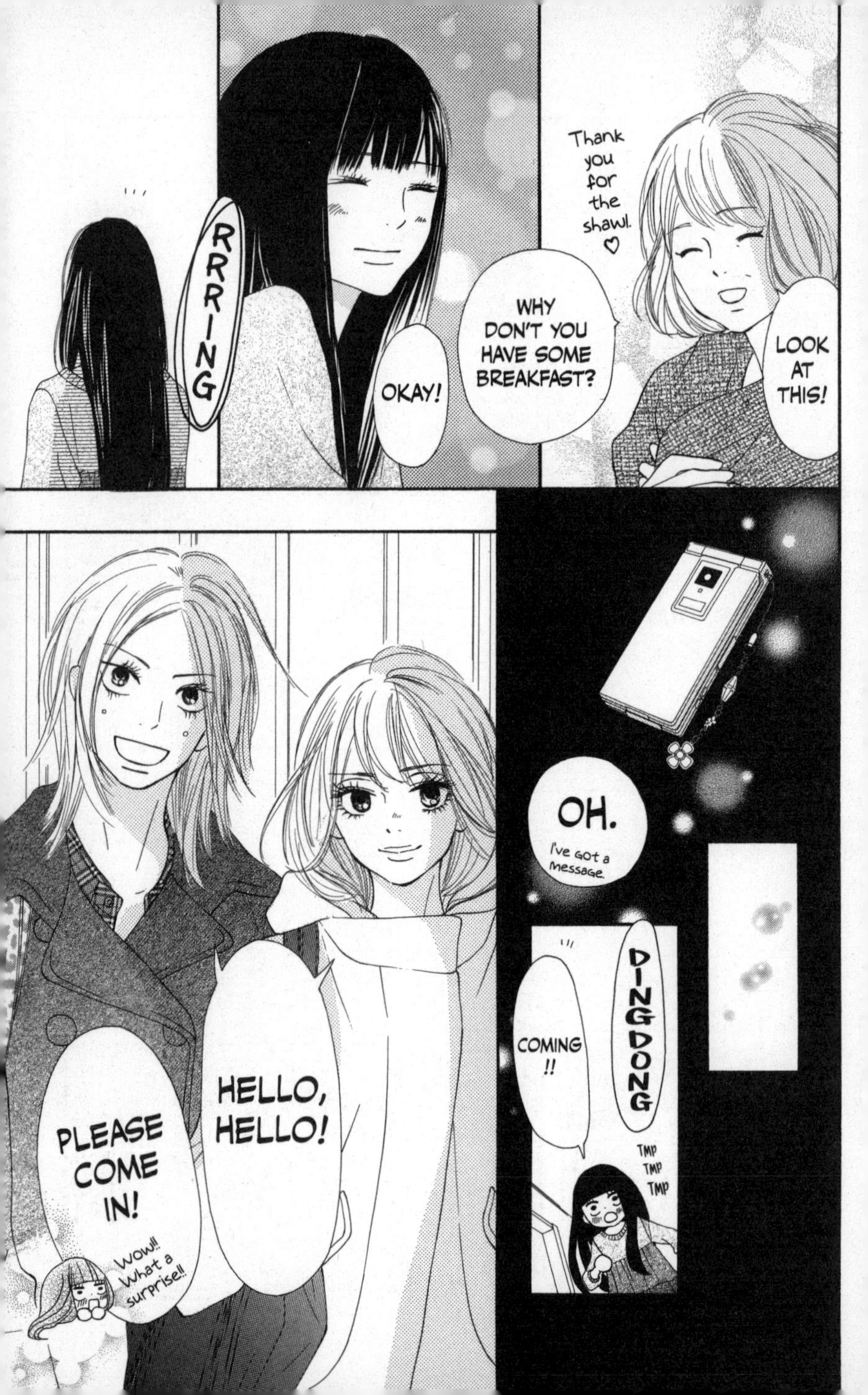
LOOK AT THIS!
Thank you for the shawl. ♡
WHY DON'T YOU HAVE SOME BREAKFAST?
OKAY!
RRRING
OH.
I've got a message.
DING DONG
COMING!!
TMP TMP TMP
HELLO, HELLO!
PLEASE COME IN!
Wow!! What a surprise!!

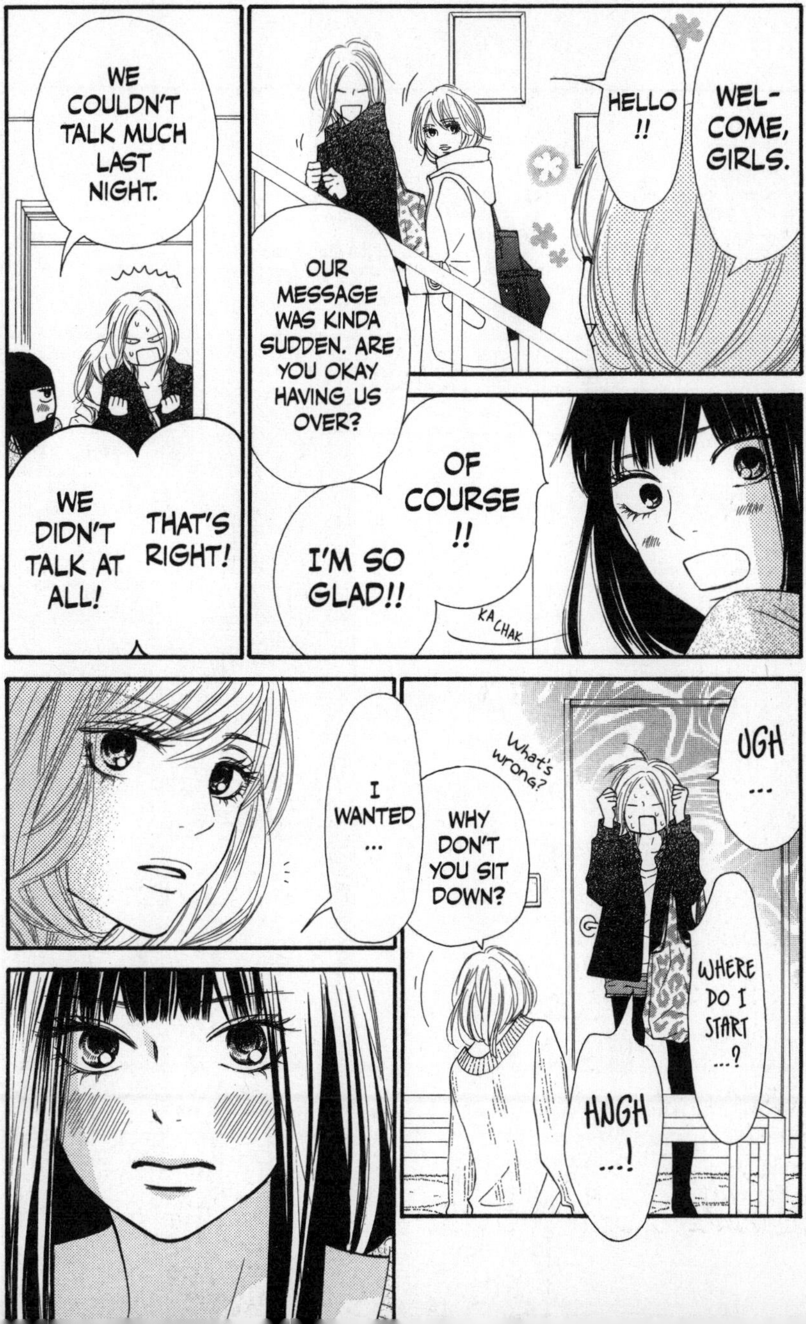
WEL-COME, GIRLS.
HELLO!!
OUR MESSAGE WAS KINDA SUDDEN. ARE YOU OKAY HAVING US OVER?
OF COURSE!!
I'M SO GLAD!!
KA CHAK
WE COULDN'T TALK MUCH LAST NIGHT.
THAT'S RIGHT!
WE DIDN'T TALK AT ALL!
UGH...
What's wrong?
WHY DON'T YOU SIT DOWN?
WHERE DO I START...?
HNGH...!
I WANTED...

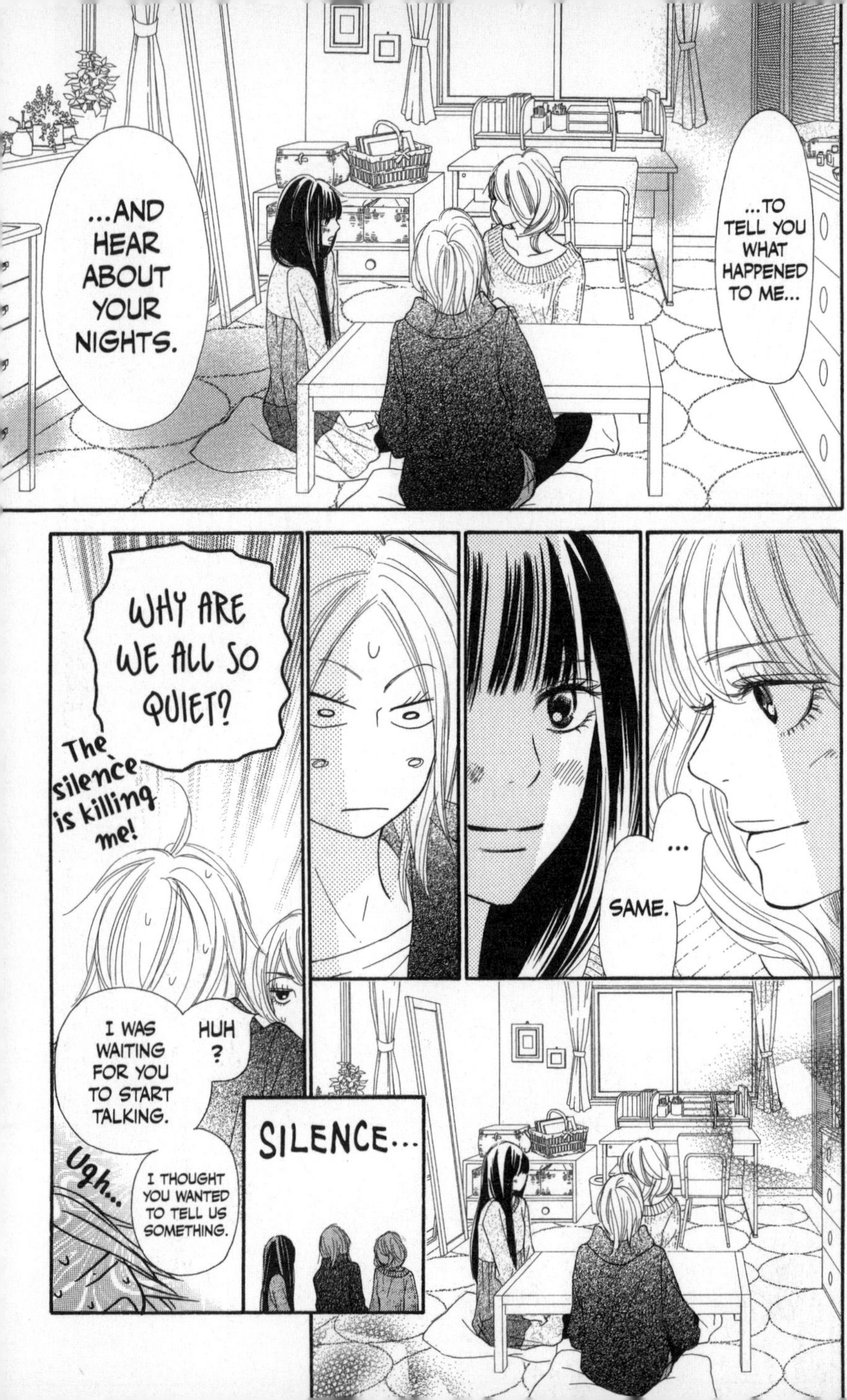
...TO TELL YOU WHAT HAPPENED TO ME...
...AND HEAR ABOUT YOUR NIGHTS.
...
SAME.
SILENCE...
WHY ARE WE ALL SO QUIET?
The silence is killing me!
HUH?
I WAS WAITING FOR YOU TO START TALKING.
I THOUGHT YOU WANTED TO TELL US SOMETHING.
Ugh...

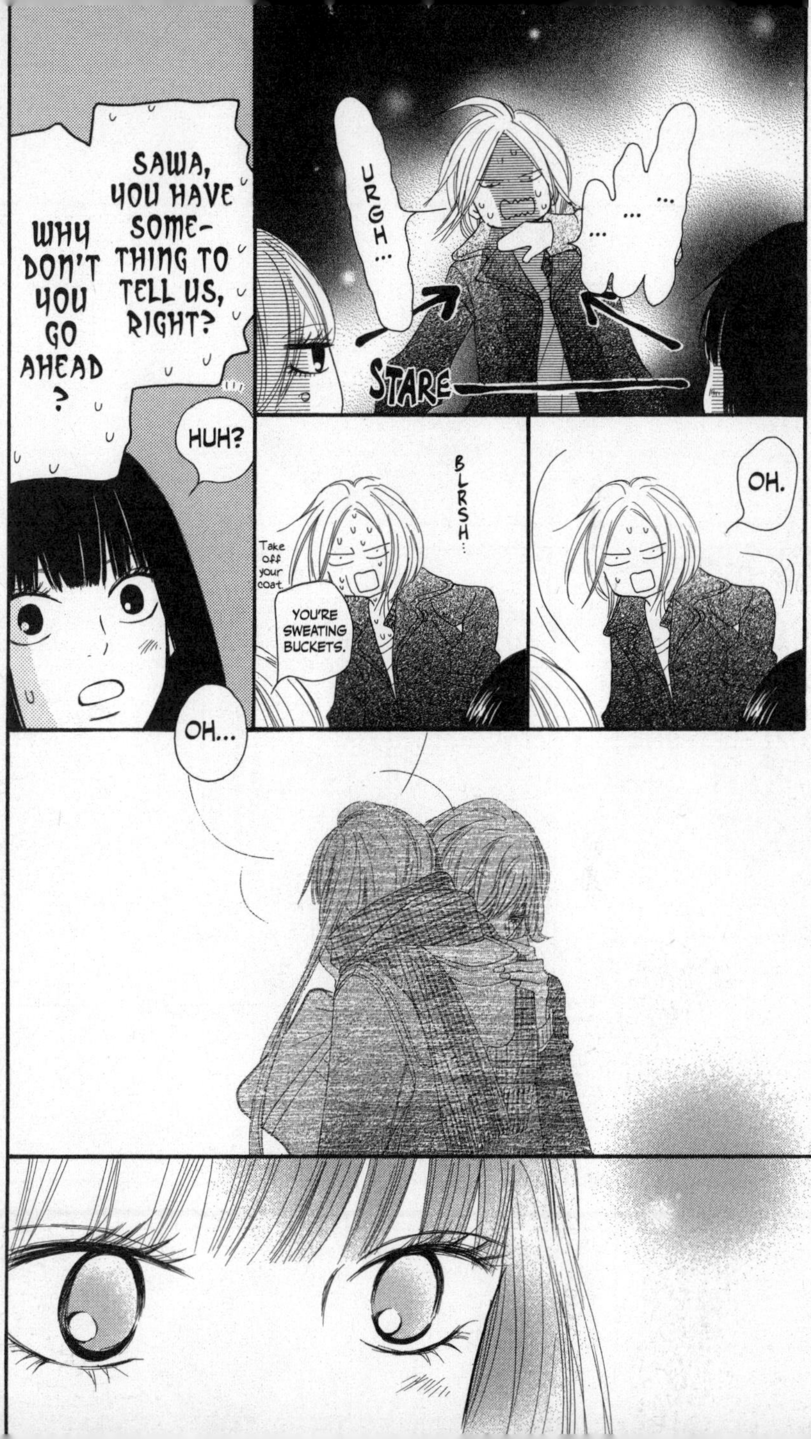
URGH...
... ...
STARE
OH.
BLRSH...
Take off your coat.
YOU'RE SWEATING BUCKETS.
SAWA, YOU HAVE SOME-THING TO TELL US, RIGHT?
WHY DON'T YOU GO AHEAD?
HUH?
OH...

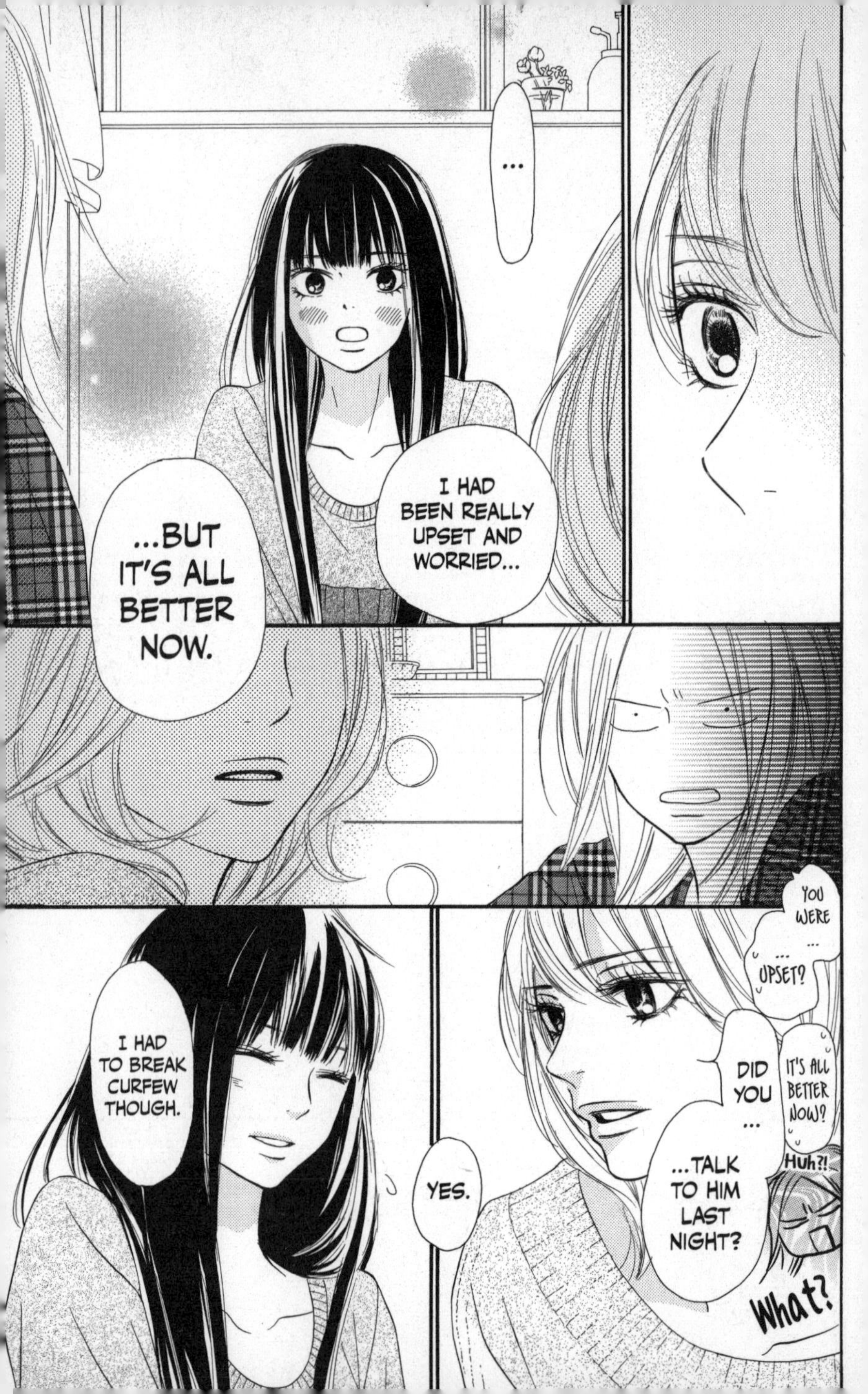
...
I HAD BEEN REALLY UPSET AND WORRIED...
...BUT IT'S ALL BETTER NOW.
YOU WERE... ...UPSET?
IT'S ALL BETTER NOW?
DID YOU... ...TALK TO HIM LAST NIGHT?
Huh?!
What?
YES.
I HAD TO BREAK CURFEW THOUGH.

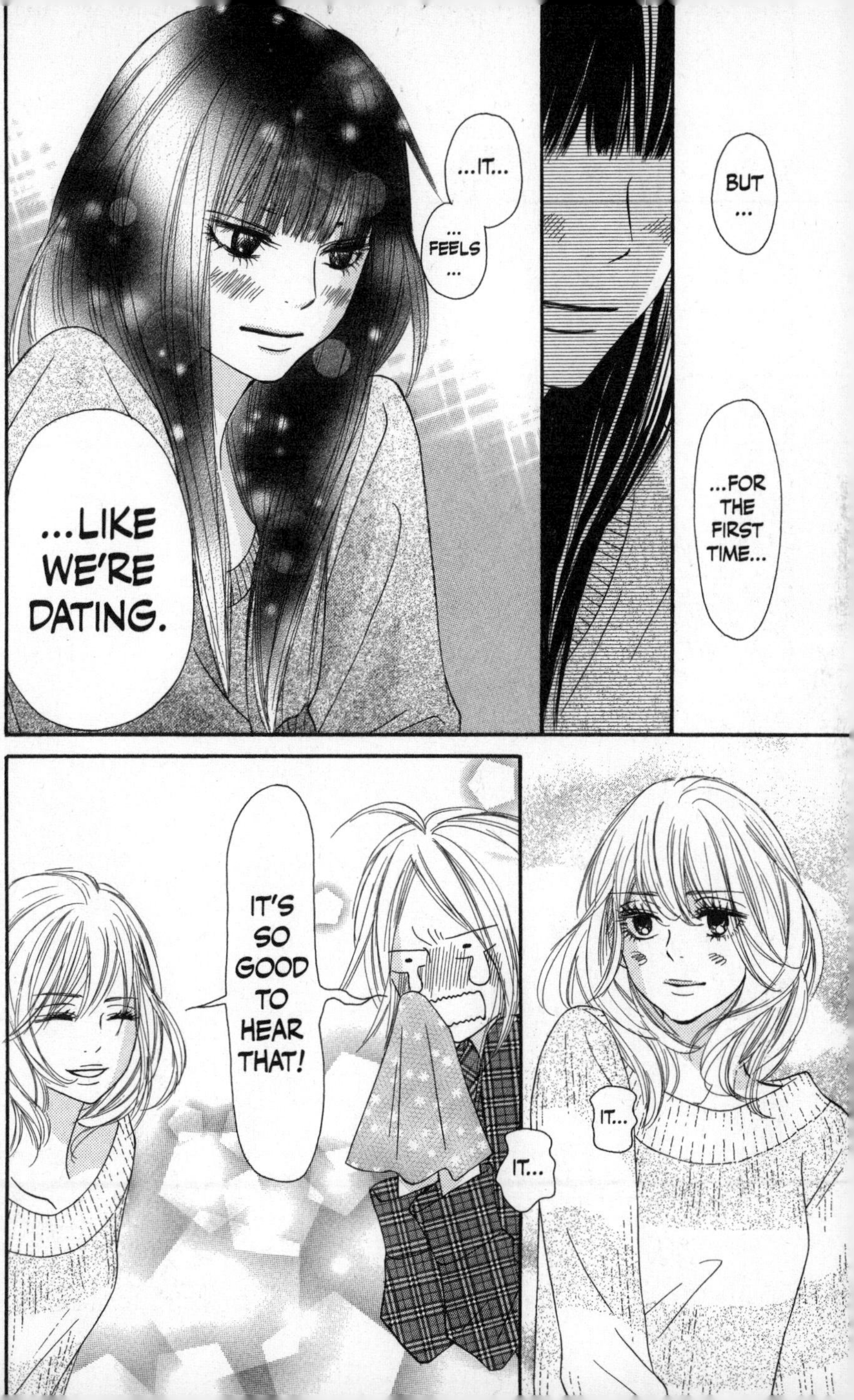
BUT...
...FOR THE FIRST TIME...
...IT...
...FEELS...
...LIKE WE'RE DATING.
IT...
IT...
IT'S SO GOOD TO HEAR THAT!

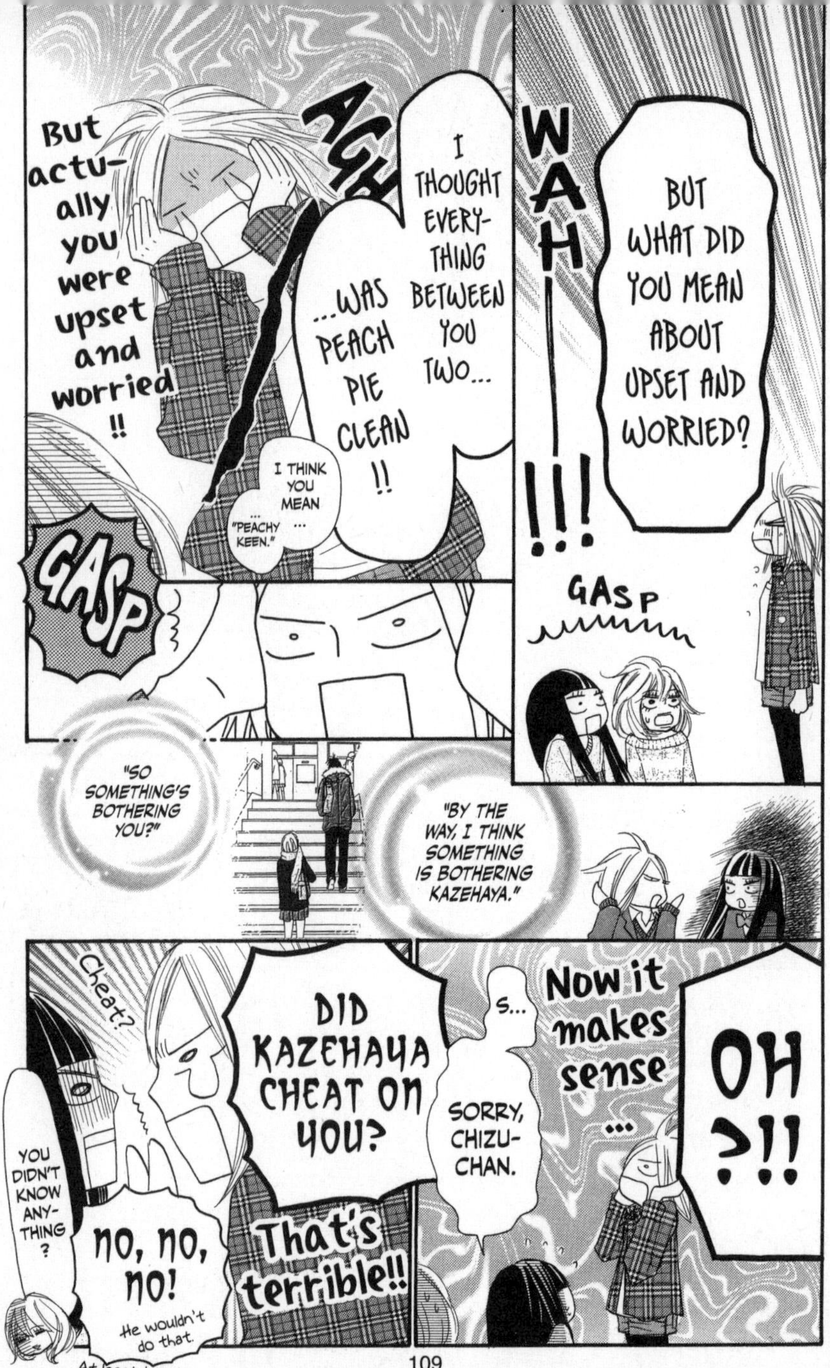
WAH!!!
BUT WHAT DID YOU MEAN ABOUT UPSET AND WORRIED?
GASP
ACH
I THOUGHT EVERYTHING BETWEEN YOU TWO...
...WAS PEACH PIE CLEAN!!
I THINK YOU MEAN ... "PEACHY KEEN."
But actually you were upset and worried!!
GASP
"BY THE WAY, I THINK SOMETHING IS BOTHERING KAZEHAYA."
"SO SOMETHING'S BOTHERING YOU?"
OH?!!
Now it makes sense...
S... SORRY, CHIZU-CHAN.
DID KAZEHAYA CHEAT ON YOU?
Cheat?
That's terrible!!
YOU DIDN'T KNOW ANYTHING?
no, no, no! He wouldn't do that.
At least, I don't think so...

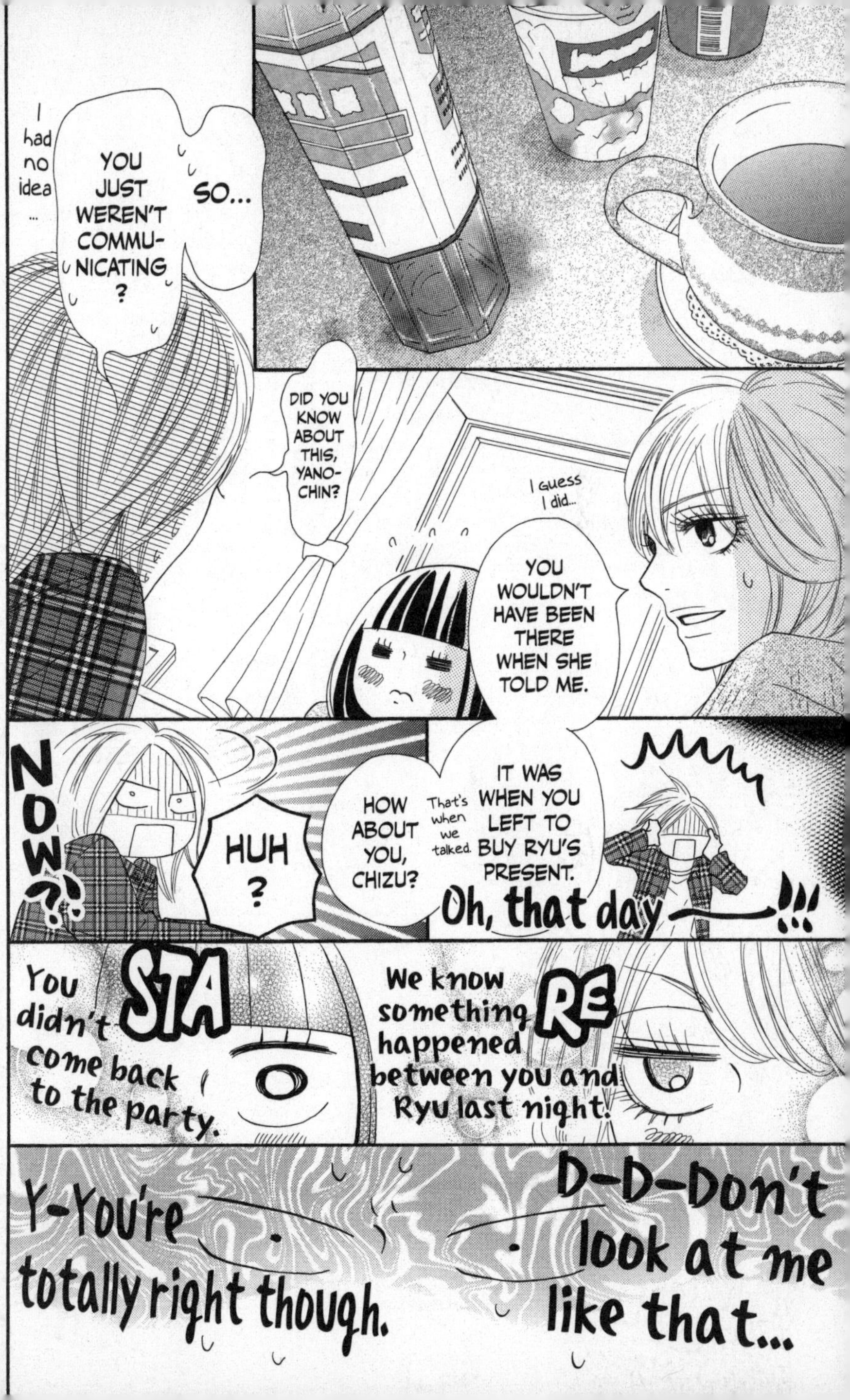
SO...
YOU JUST WEREN'T COMMUNICATING?
I had no idea...
DID YOU KNOW ABOUT THIS, YANO-CHIN?
I guess I did...
YOU WOULDN'T HAVE BEEN THERE WHEN SHE TOLD ME.
IT WAS WHEN YOU LEFT TO BUY RYU'S PRESENT.
That's when we talked.
HOW ABOUT YOU, CHIZU?
Oh, that day—!!!
HUH?
NOW?!
We know something happened between you and Ryu last night.
RE
STA
You didn't come back to the party.
D-D-Don't look at me like that...
Y-You're totally right though.

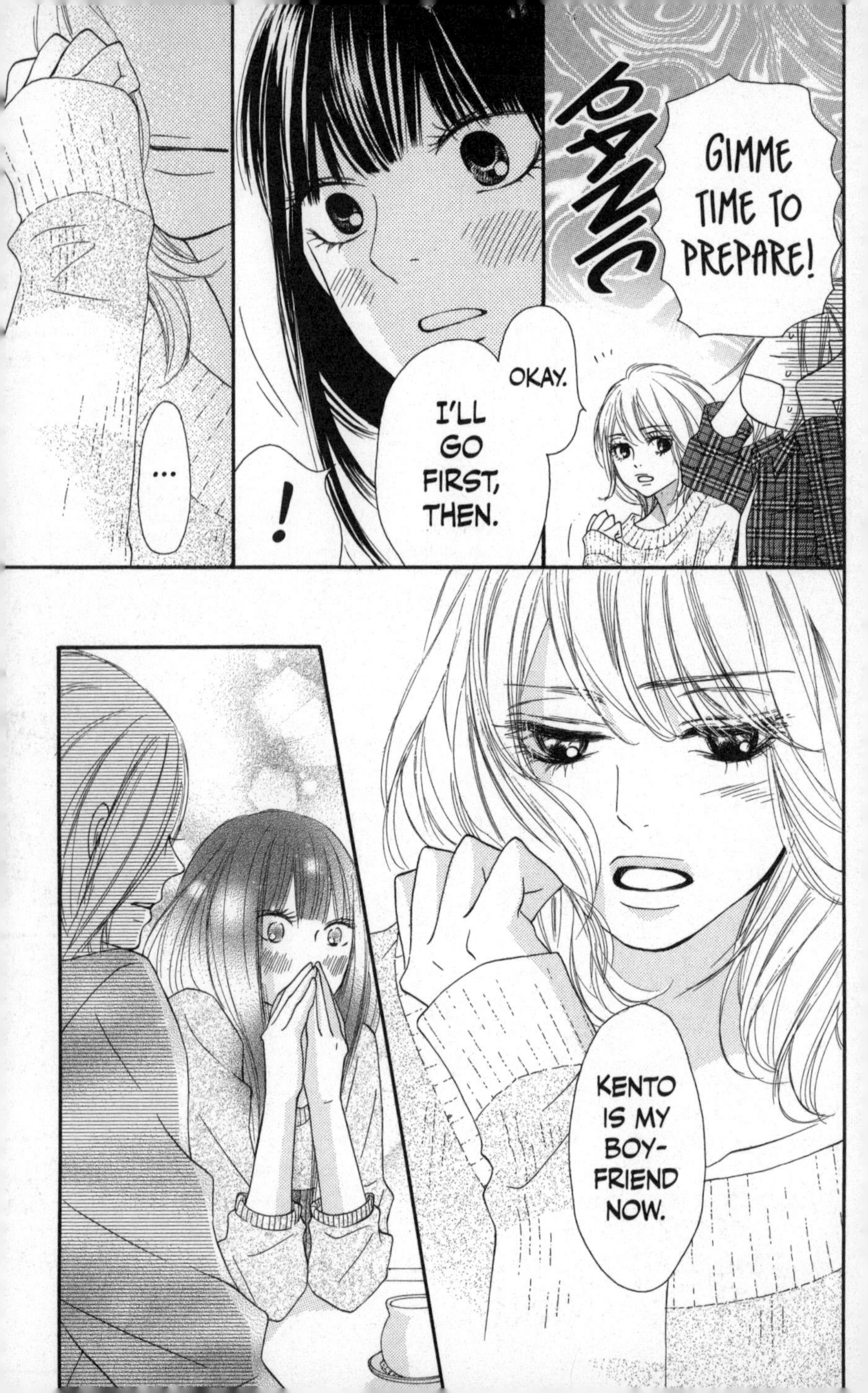
PANIC
GIMME TIME TO PREPARE!
OKAY. I'LL GO FIRST, THEN.
!
...
KENTO IS MY BOYFRIEND NOW.

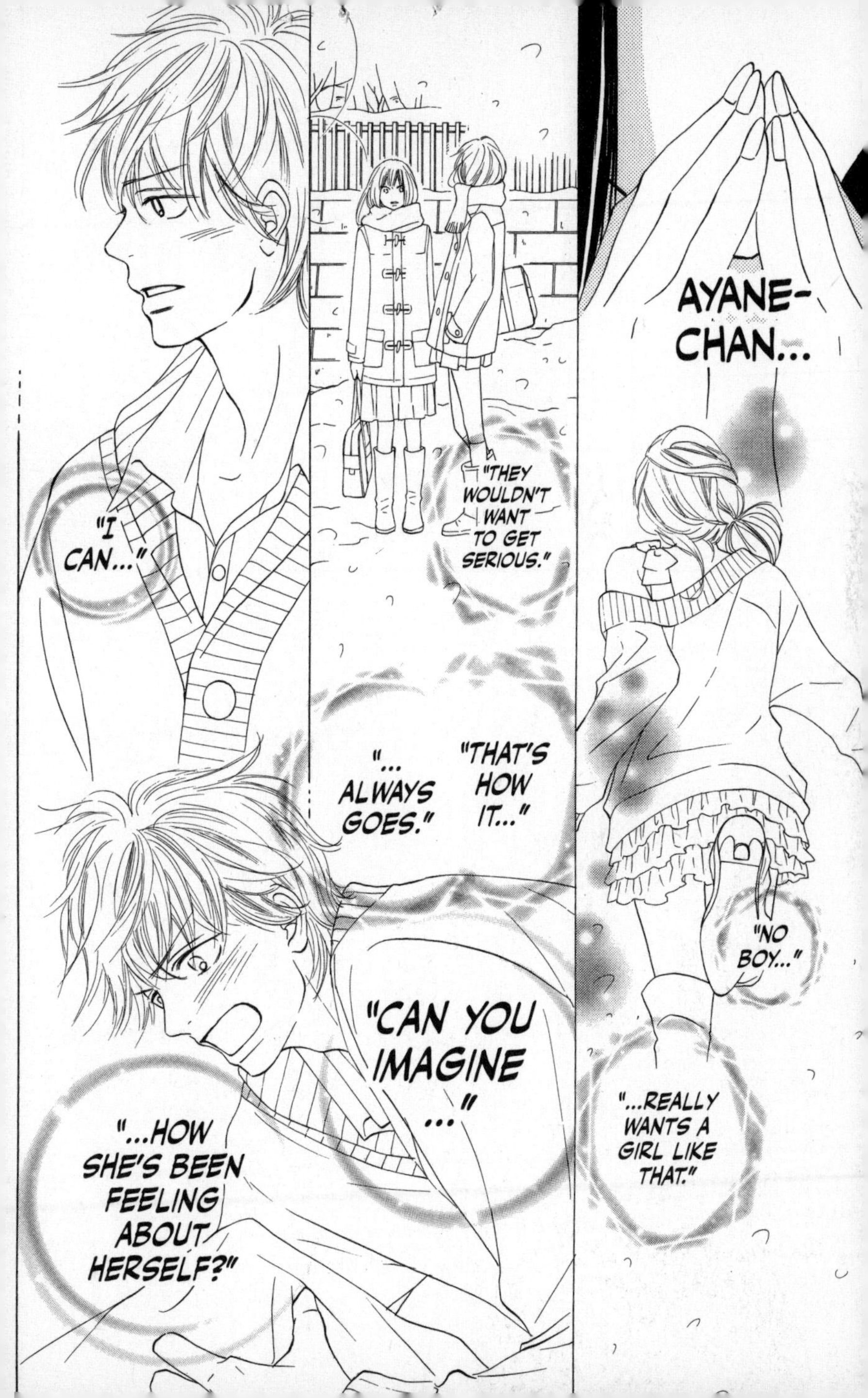
AYANE-CHAN...
"NO BOY..."
"...REALLY WANTS A GIRL LIKE THAT."
"THEY WOULDN'T WANT TO GET SERIOUS."
"THAT'S HOW IT..."
"...ALWAYS GOES."
"I CAN..."
"CAN YOU IMAGINE..."
"...HOW SHE'S BEEN FEELING ABOUT HERSELF?"

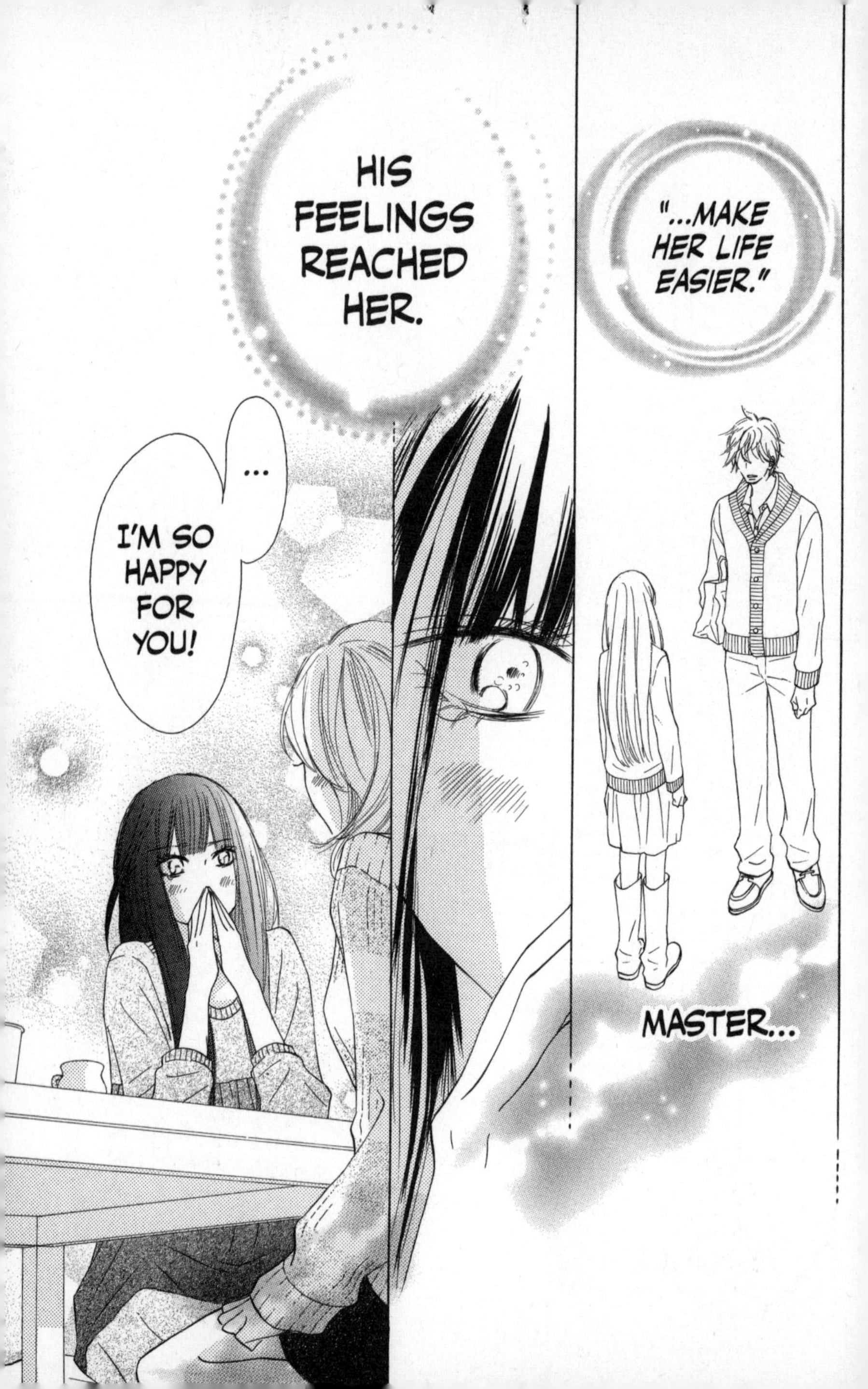
"...MAKE HER LIFE EASIER."
MASTER...
HIS FEELINGS REACHED HER.
...
I'M SO HAPPY FOR YOU!

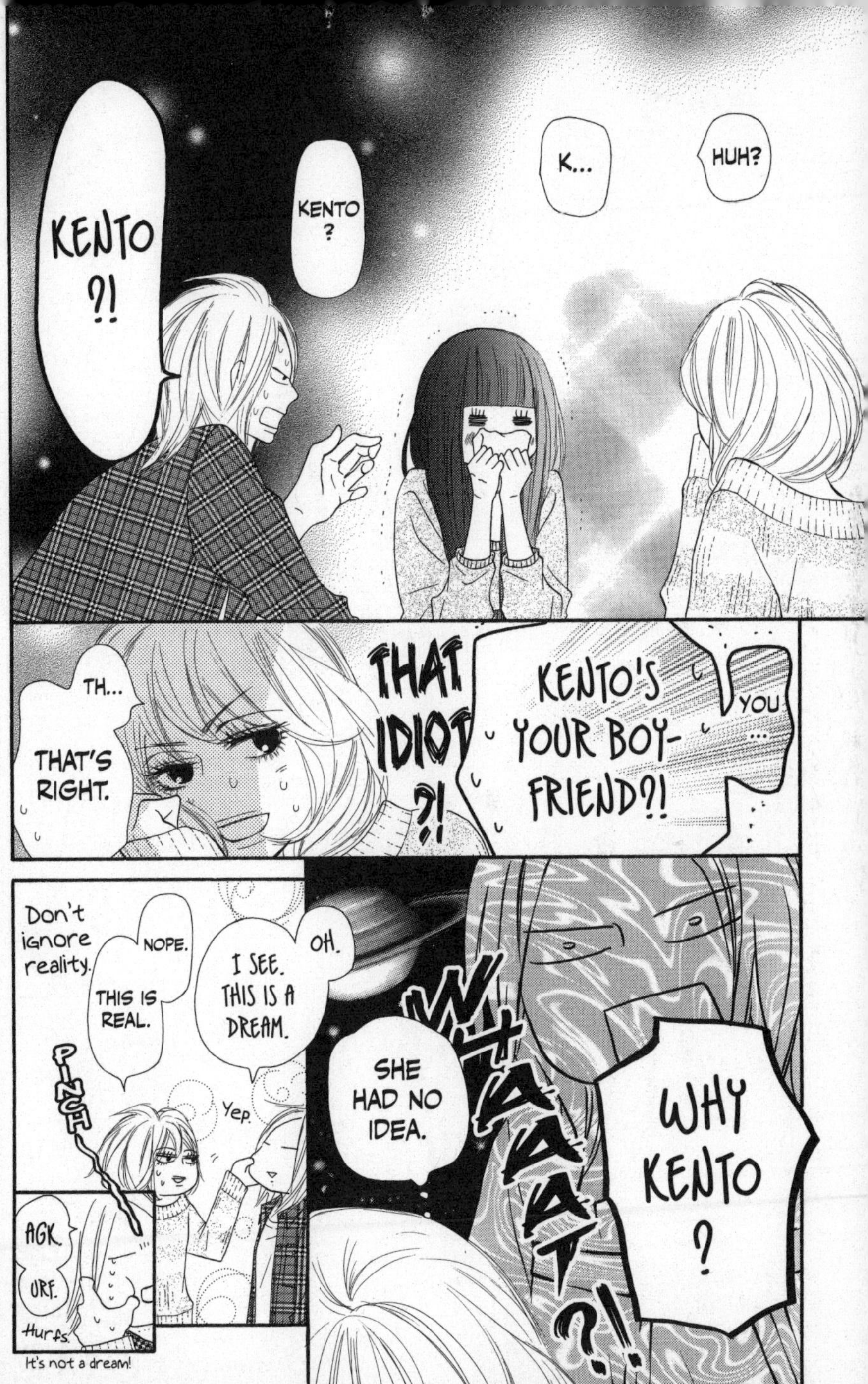
HUH?
K...
KENTO?
KENTO?!
YOU...
KENTO'S YOUR BOY-FRIEND?!
THAT IDIOT?!
TH...
THAT'S RIGHT.
WHY KENTO?
WHAAAT?!
SHE HAD NO IDEA.
OH.
I SEE. THIS IS A DREAM.
NOPE.
THIS IS REAL.
Don't ignore reality.
PINCH
Yep.
AGK.
URF.
Hurfs.
It's not a dream!

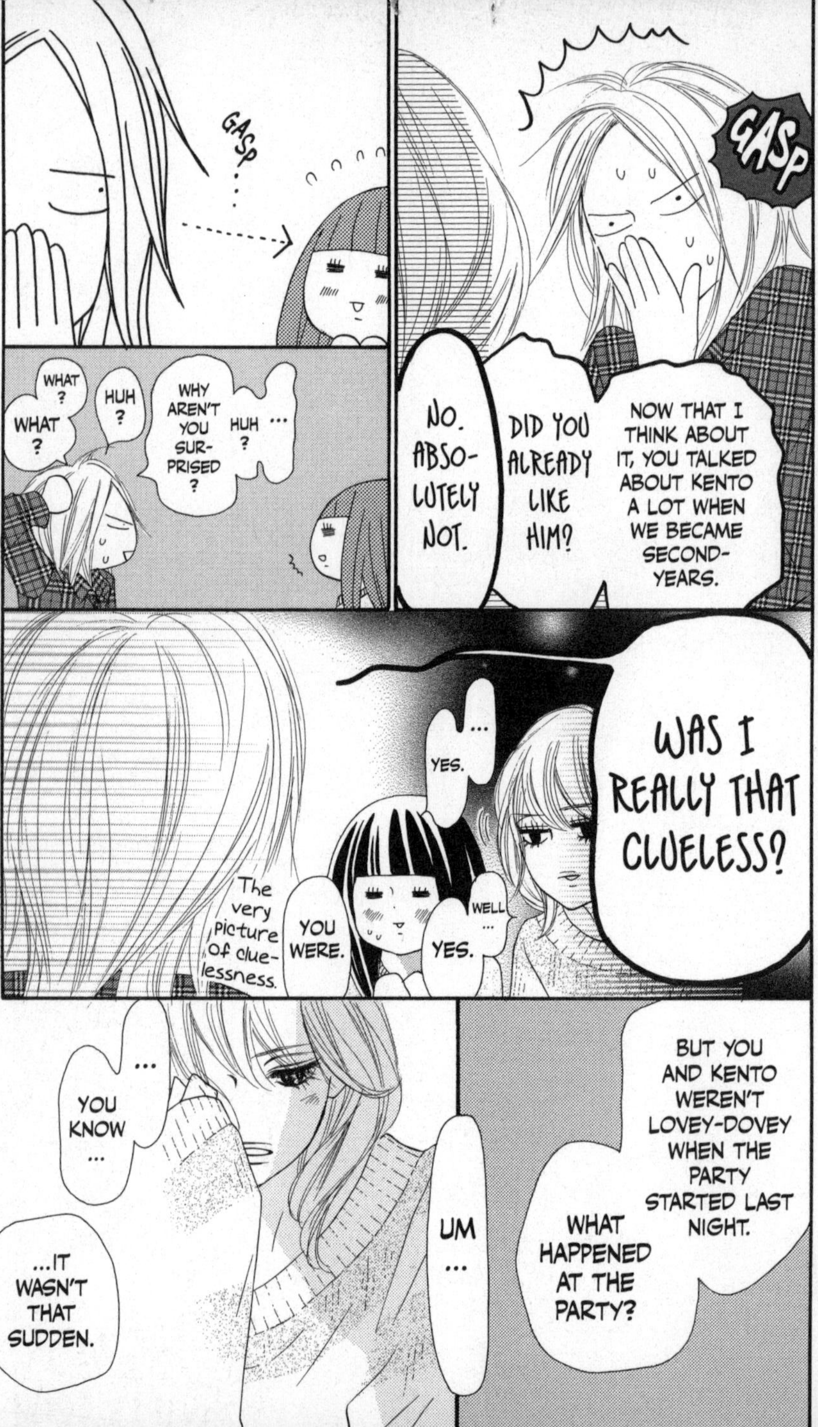
GASP
NOW THAT I THINK ABOUT IT, YOU TALKED ABOUT KENTO A LOT WHEN WE BECAME SECOND-YEARS.
DID YOU ALREADY LIKE HIM?
NO. ABSOLUTELY NOT.
GASP...
WHAT? WHAT?
HUH?
WHY AREN'T YOU SURPRISED?
HUH?...
WAS I REALLY THAT CLUELESS?
...YES.
WELL... YES.
YOU WERE.
The very picture of cluelessness.
BUT YOU AND KENTO WEREN'T LOVEY-DOVEY WHEN THE PARTY STARTED LAST NIGHT.
WHAT HAPPENED AT THE PARTY?
UM...
...YOU KNOW...
...IT WASN'T THAT SUDDEN.

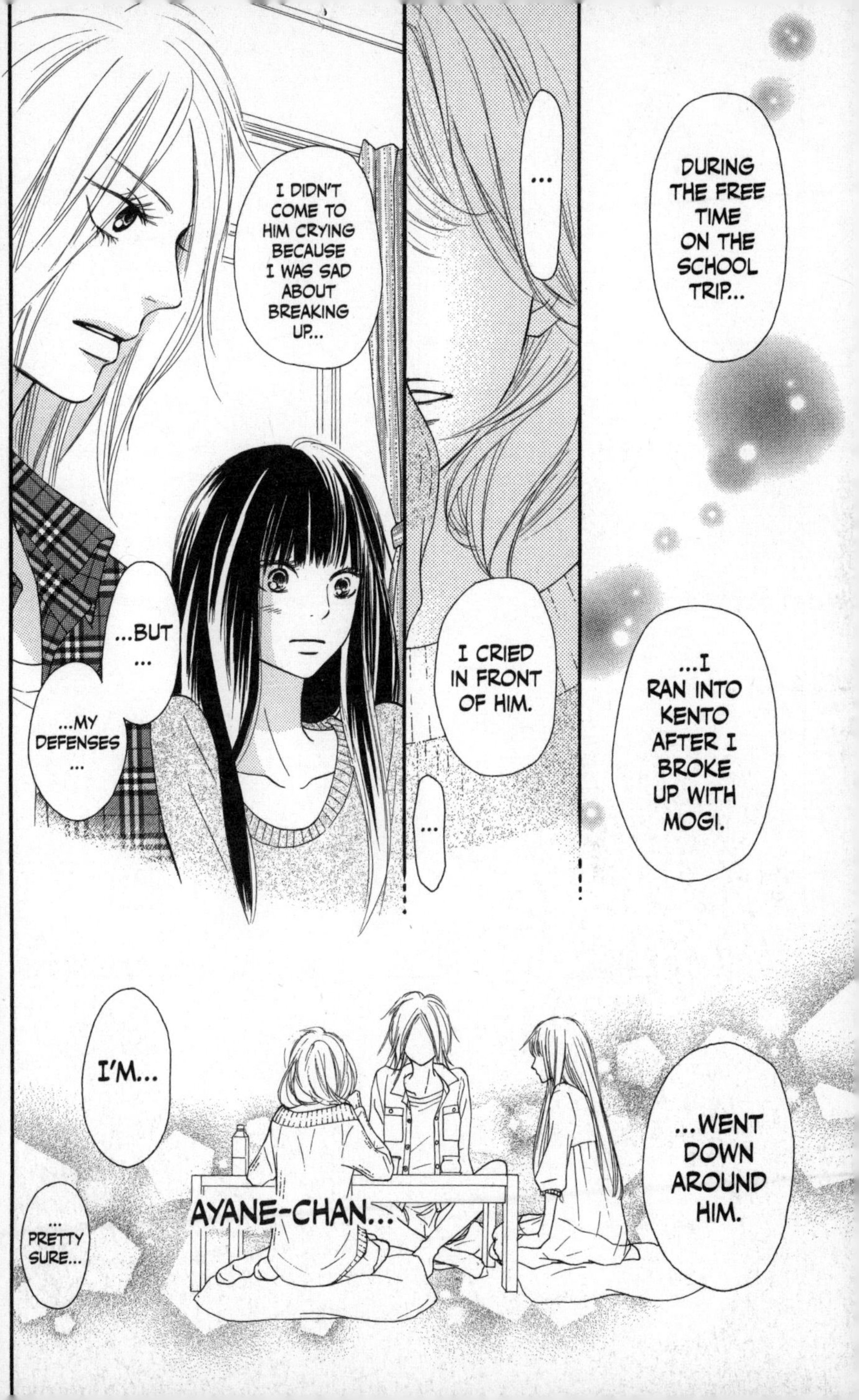
DURING THE FREE TIME ON THE SCHOOL TRIP...
...I RAN INTO KENTO AFTER I BROKE UP WITH MOGI.
...
I CRIED IN FRONT OF HIM.
...
I DIDN'T COME TO HIM CRYING BECAUSE I WAS SAD ABOUT BREAKING UP...
...BUT ...
...MY DEFENSES ...
...WENT DOWN AROUND HIM.
AYANE-CHAN...
I'M...
... PRETTY SURE...

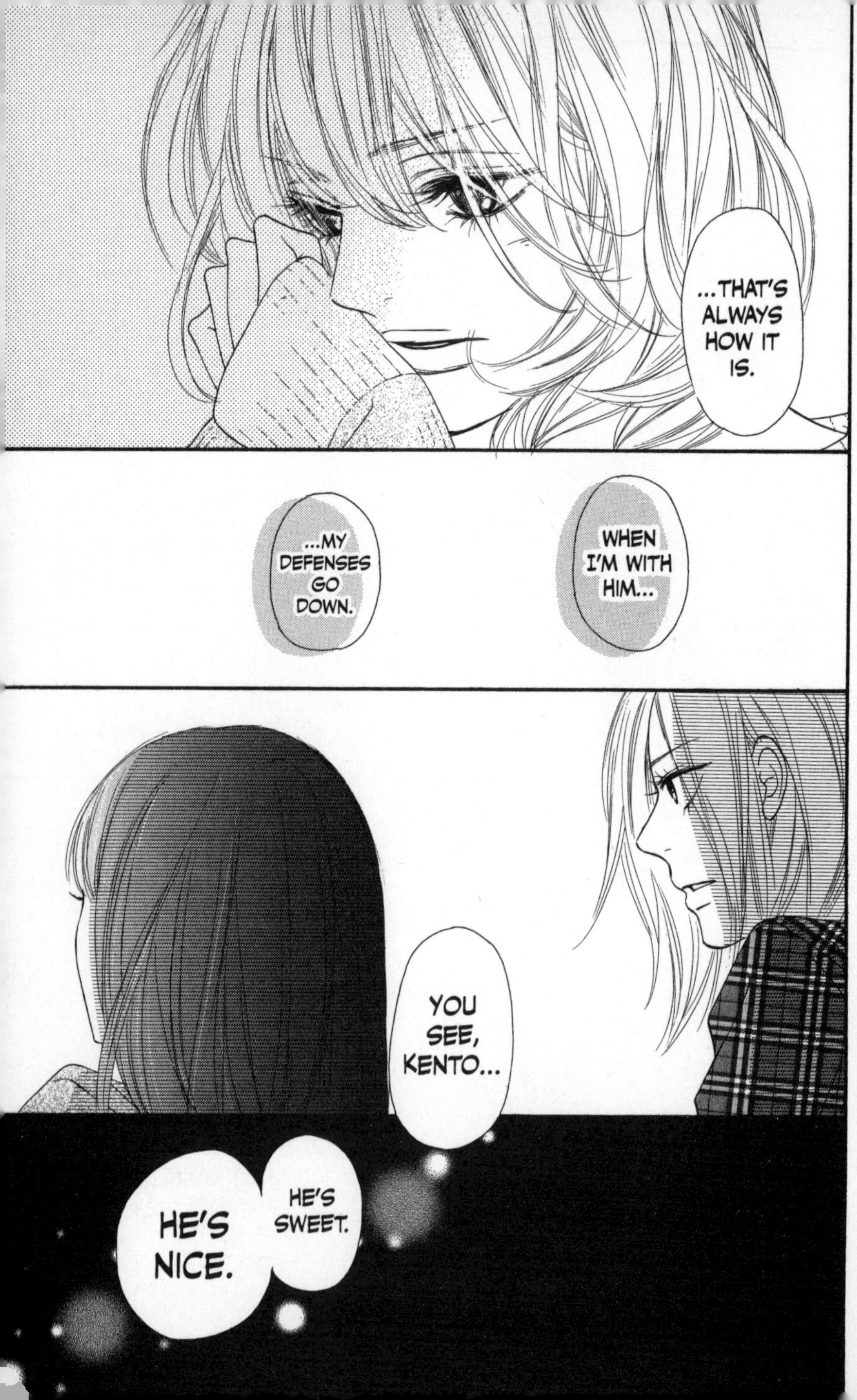
...THAT'S ALWAYS HOW IT IS.
WHEN I'M WITH HIM...
...MY DEFENSES GO DOWN.
YOU SEE, KENTO...
HE'S SWEET.
HE'S NICE.

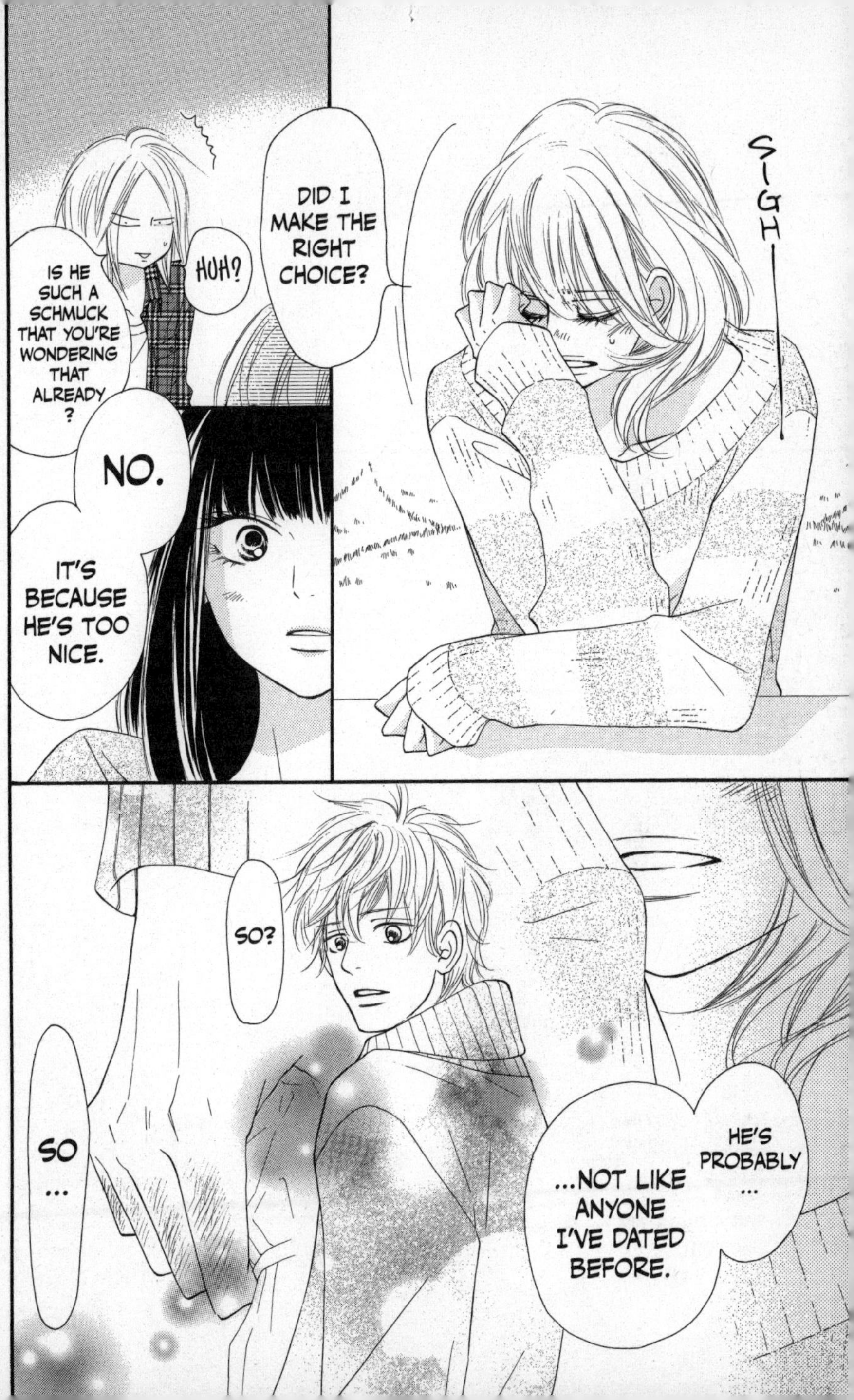
SIGH
DID I MAKE THE RIGHT CHOICE?
HUH?
IS HE SUCH A SCHMUCK THAT YOU'RE WONDERING THAT ALREADY ?
NO.
IT'S BECAUSE HE'S TOO NICE.
HE'S PROBABLY ...
...NOT LIKE ANYONE I'VE DATED BEFORE.
SO?
SO ...

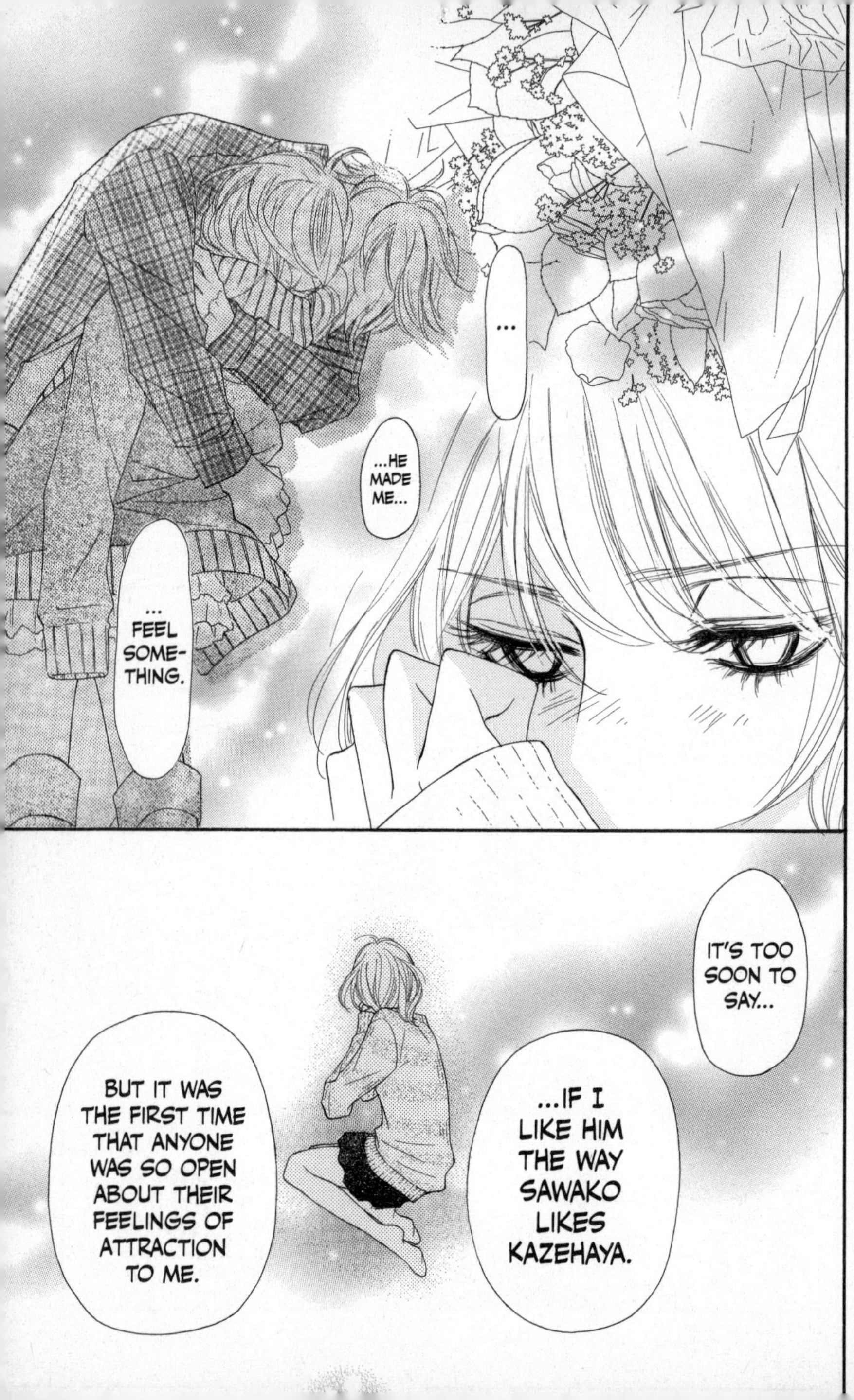
...
...HE MADE ME...
... FEEL SOME-THING.
IT'S TOO SOON TO SAY...
...IF I LIKE HIM THE WAY SAWAKO LIKES KAZEHAYA.
BUT IT WAS THE FIRST TIME THAT ANYONE WAS SO OPEN ABOUT THEIR FEELINGS OF ATTRACTION TO ME.

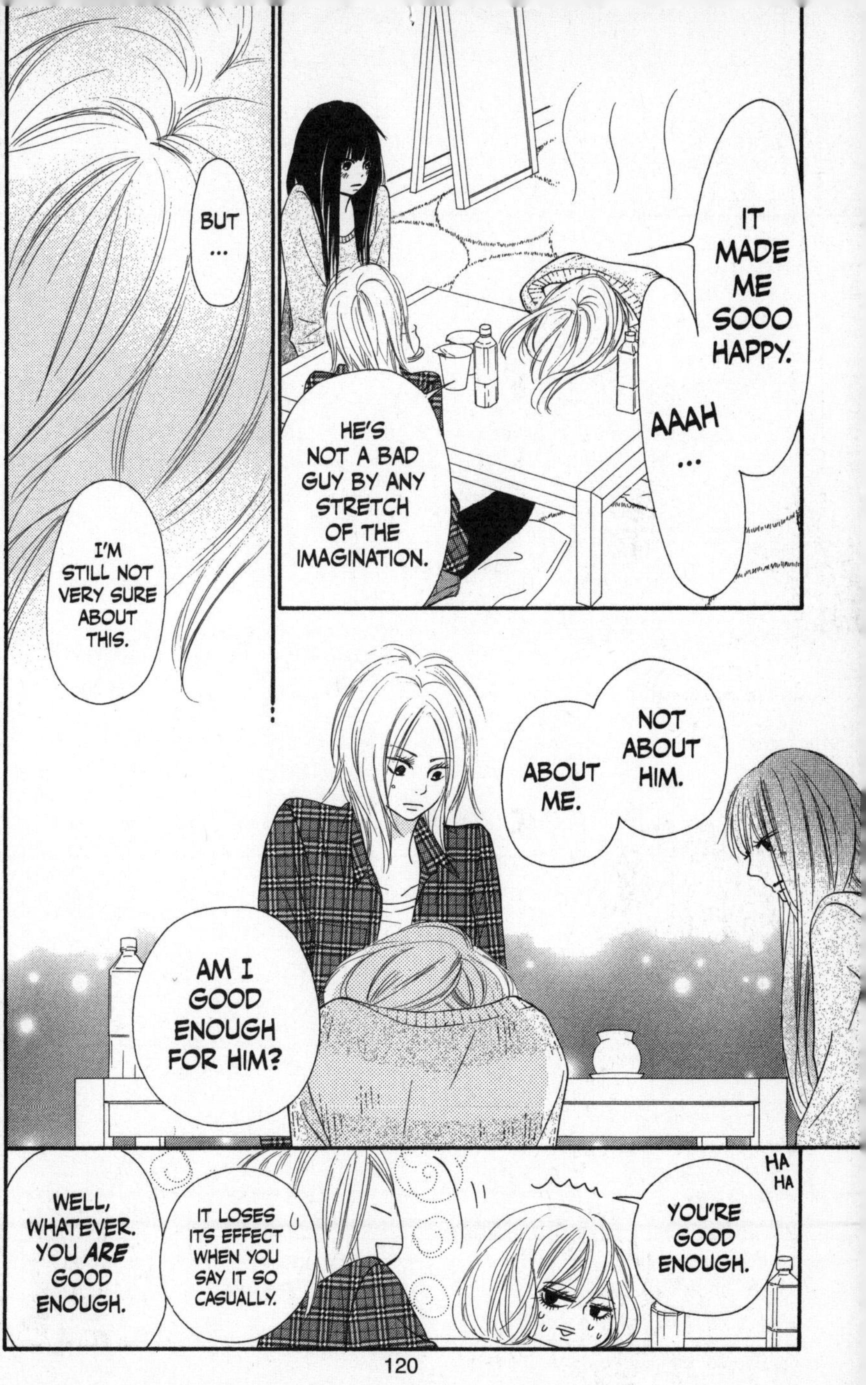
IT MADE ME SOOO HAPPY.
AAAH ...
HE'S NOT A BAD GUY BY ANY STRETCH OF THE IMAGINATION.
BUT ...
I'M STILL NOT VERY SURE ABOUT THIS.
NOT ABOUT HIM.
ABOUT ME.
AM I GOOD ENOUGH FOR HIM?
HA HA
YOU'RE GOOD ENOUGH.
IT LOSES ITS EFFECT WHEN YOU SAY IT SO CASUALLY.
WELL, WHATEVER. YOU *ARE* GOOD ENOUGH.

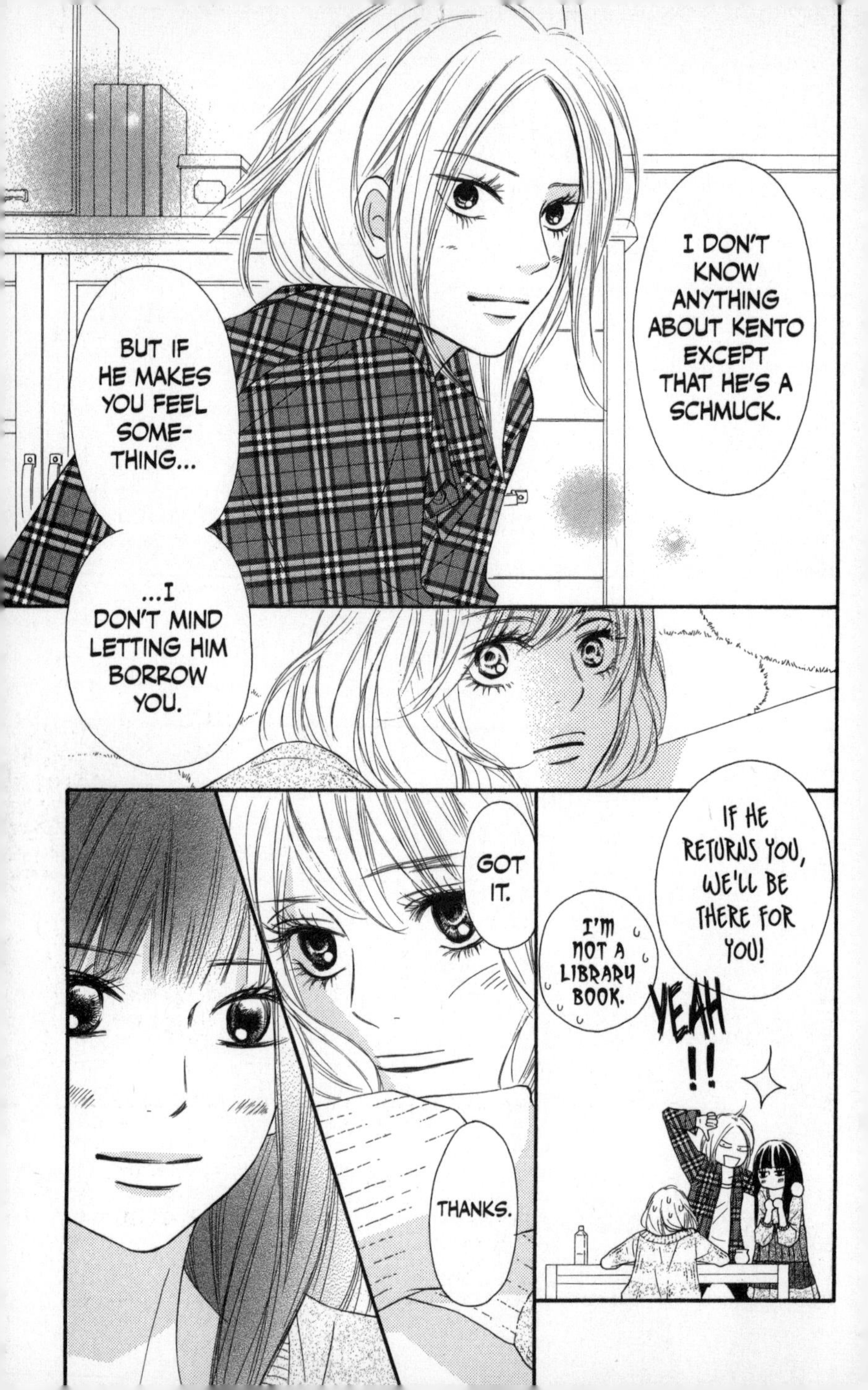
I DON'T KNOW ANYTHING ABOUT KENTO EXCEPT THAT HE'S A SCHMUCK.
BUT IF HE MAKES YOU FEEL SOME-THING...
...I DON'T MIND LETTING HIM BORROW YOU.
IF HE RETURNS YOU, WE'LL BE THERE FOR YOU!
I'M NOT A LIBRARY BOOK.
YEAH !!
GOT IT.
THANKS.

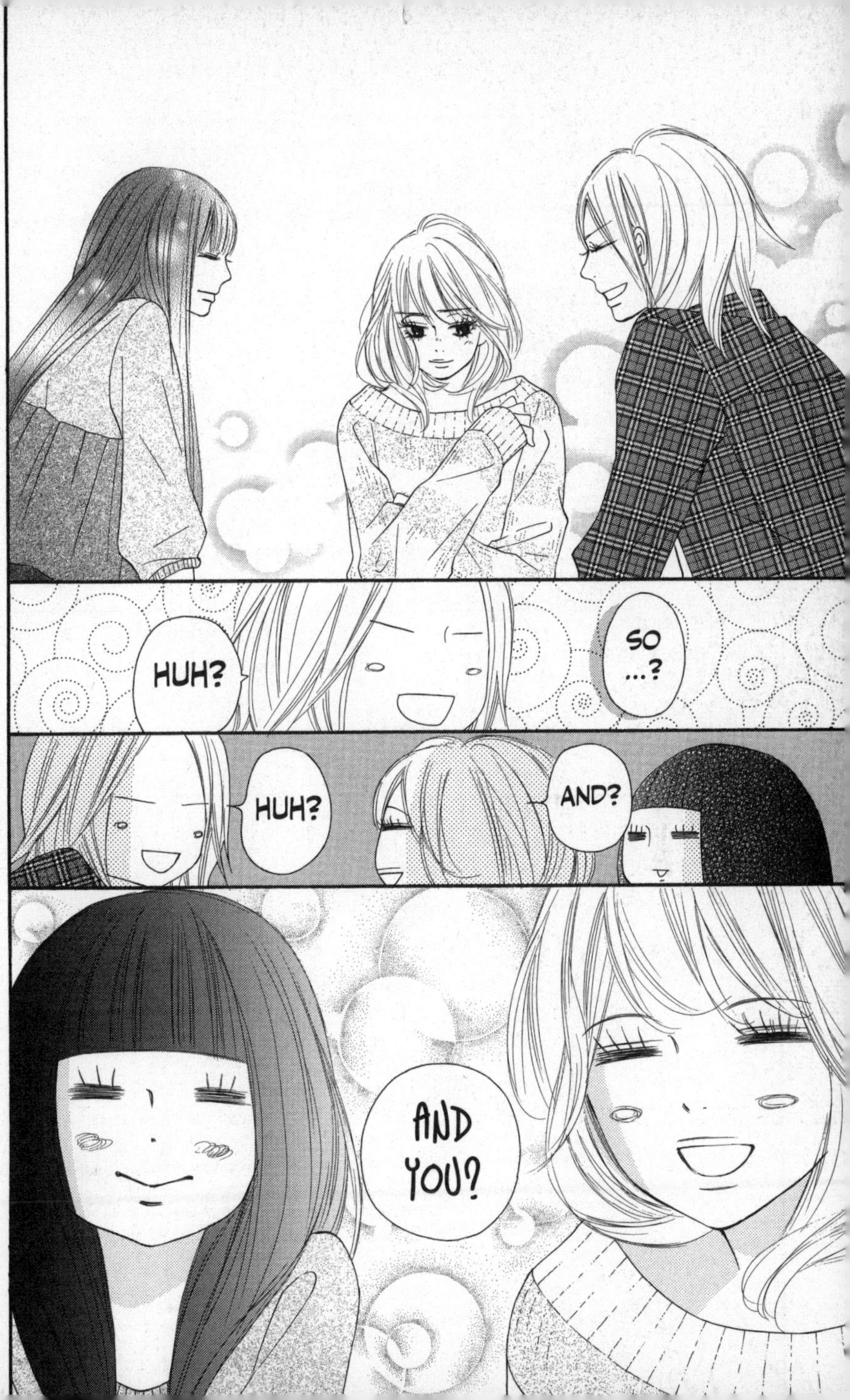
SO ...?
HUH?
AND?
HUH?
AND YOU?

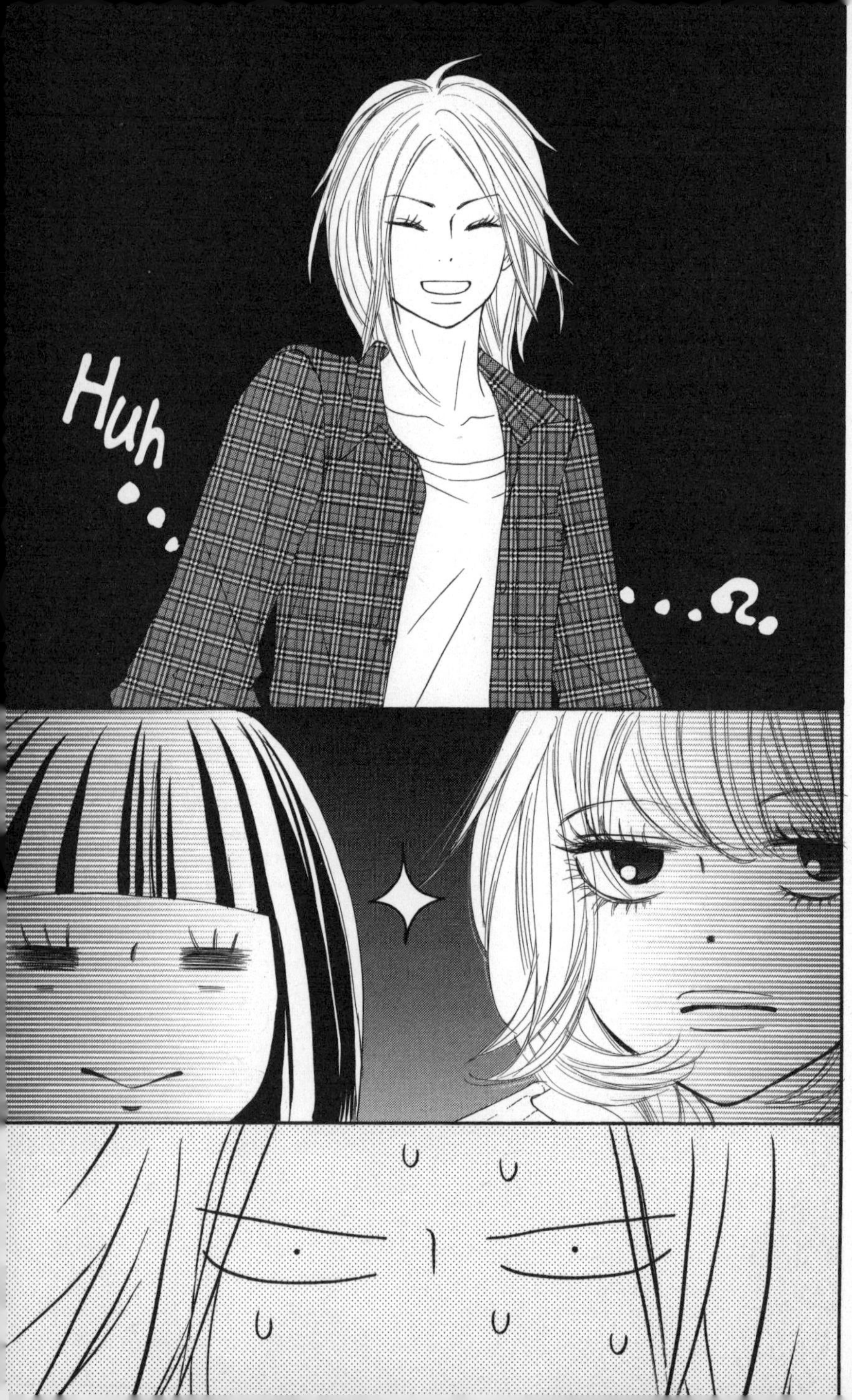

Huh...
...?

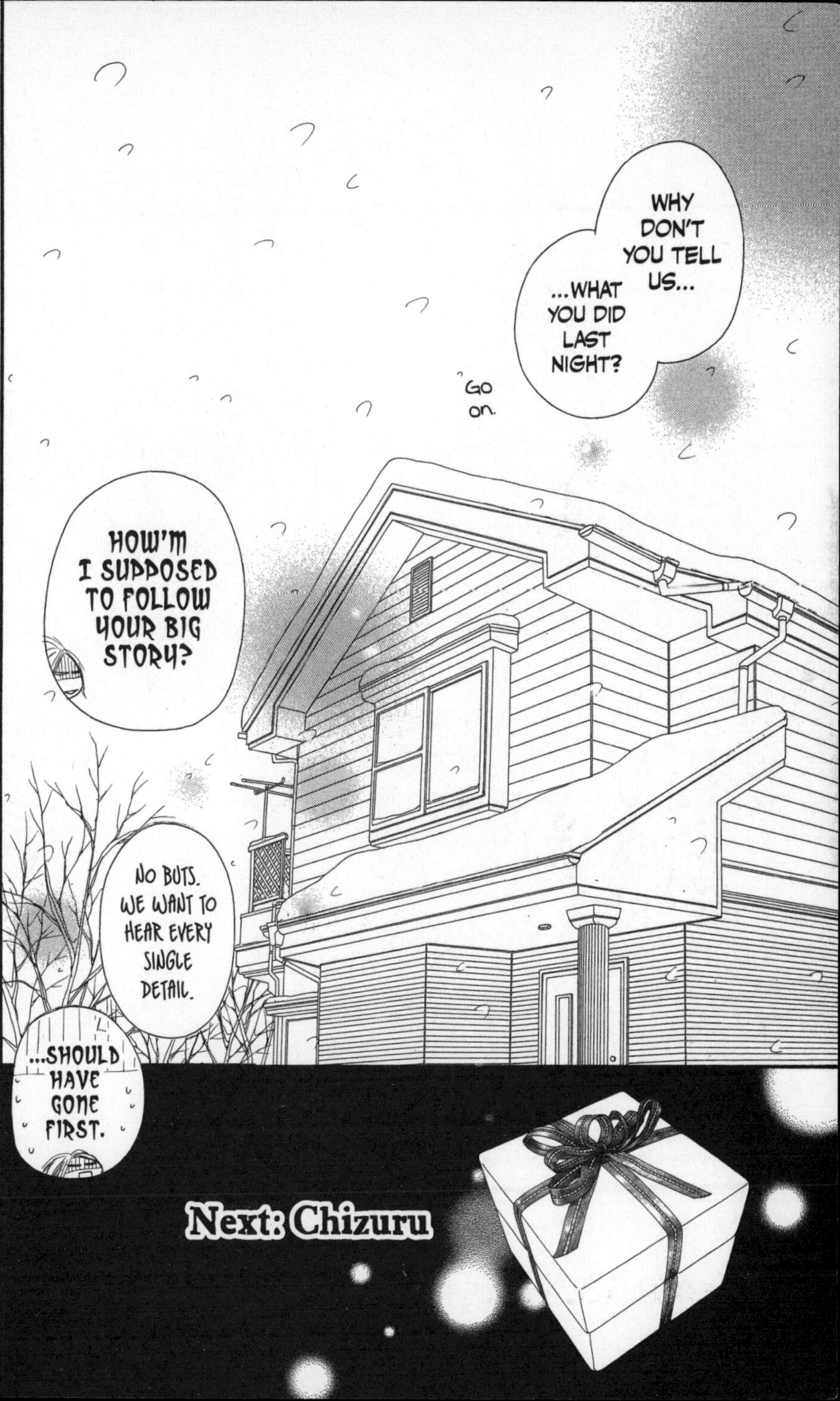
WHY DON'T YOU TELL US...
...WHAT YOU DID LAST NIGHT?
GO ON.
HOW'M I SUPPOSED TO FOLLOW YOUR BIG STORY?
NO BUTS. WE WANT TO HEAR EVERY SINGLE DETAIL.
...SHOULD HAVE GONE FIRST.
Next: Chizuru

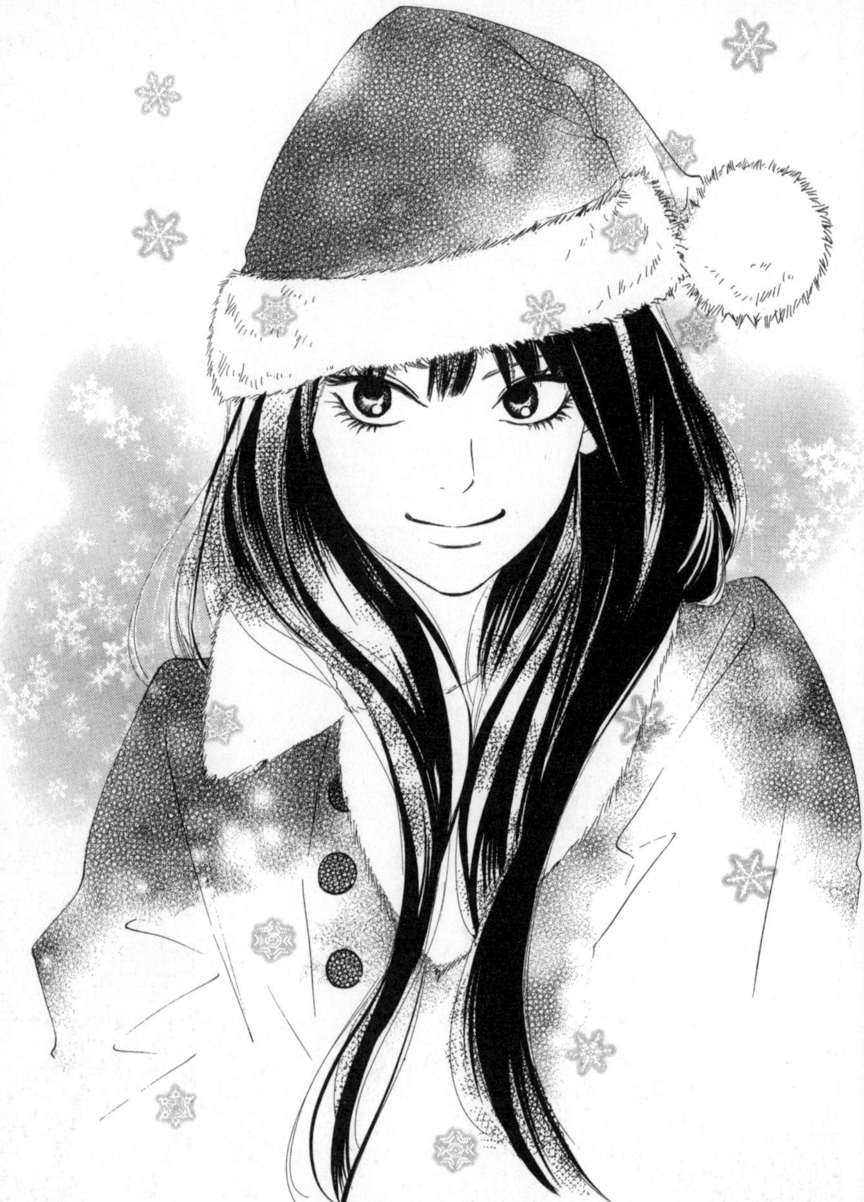

Episode 75: Happy Moment

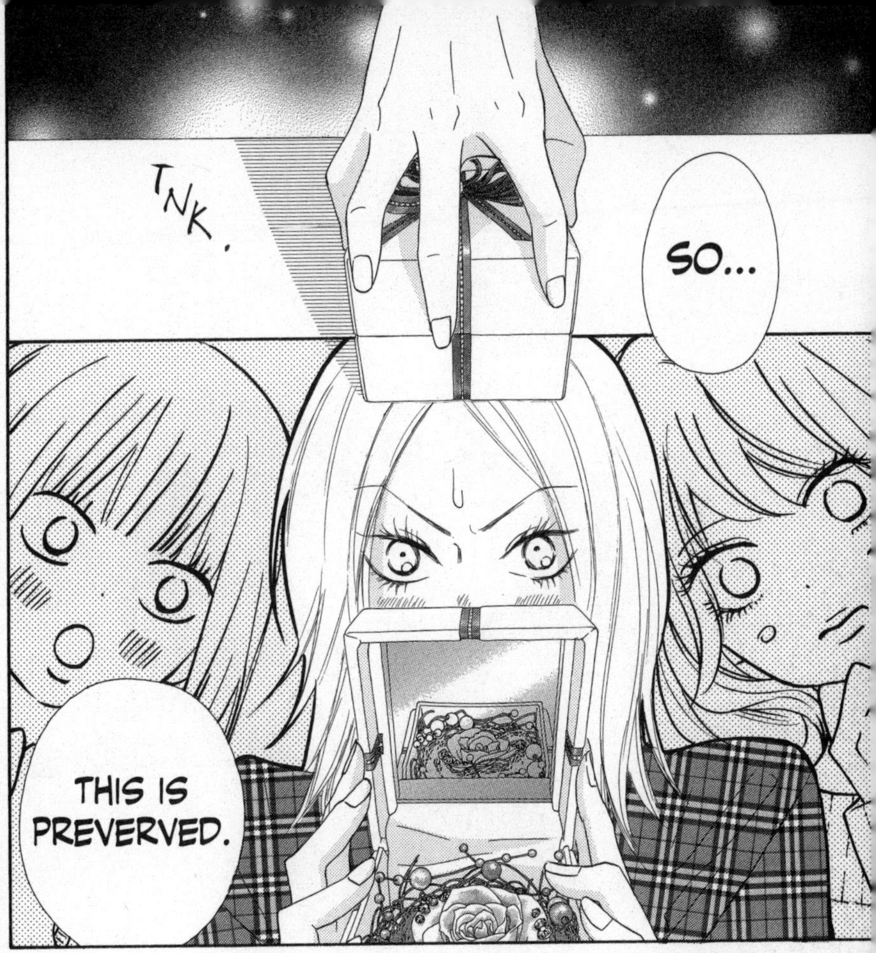
SO...
TNK.
THIS IS PREVERVED.

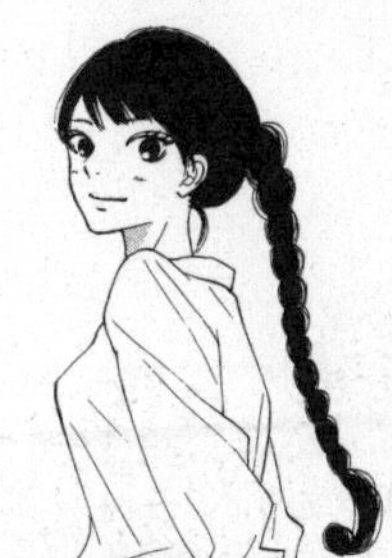

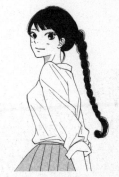

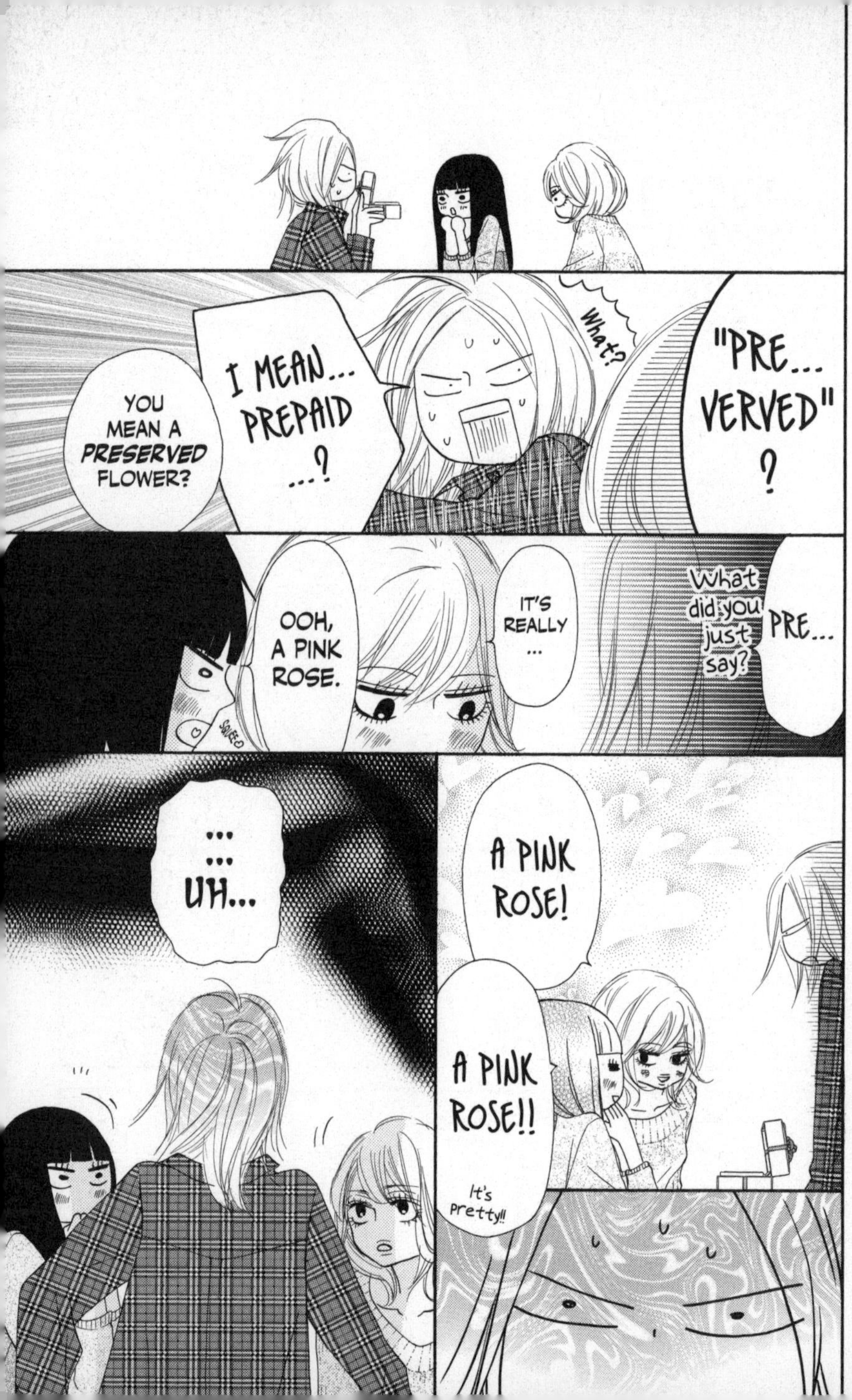
"PRE... VERVED"?
What?
I MEAN... PREPAID ...?
YOU MEAN A PRESERVED FLOWER?
PRE...
What did you just say?
IT'S REALLY ...
OOH, A PINK ROSE.
A PINK ROSE!
A PINK ROSE!!
It's pretty!!
... ... UH...

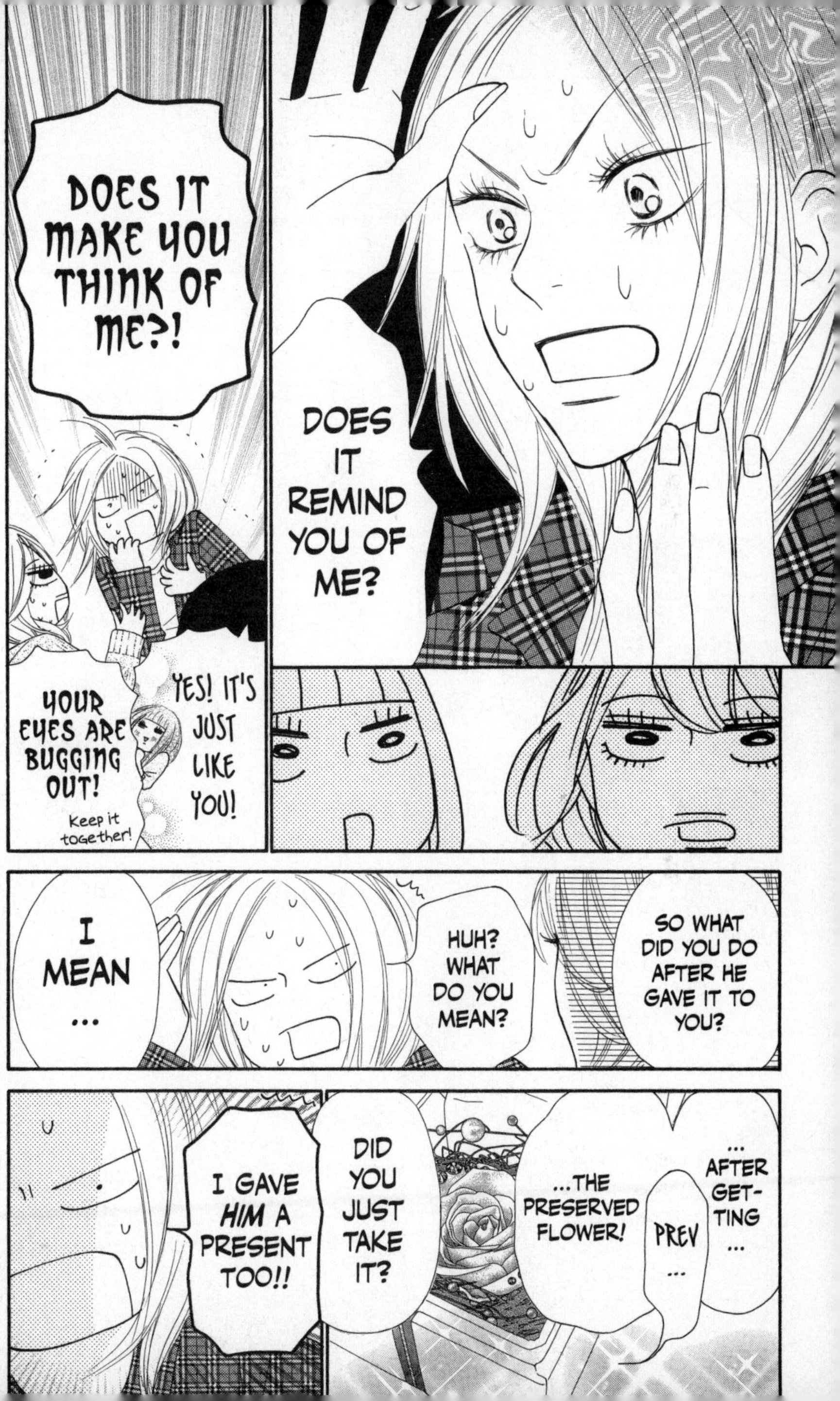
DOES IT REMIND YOU OF ME?
DOES IT MAKE YOU THINK OF ME?!
YES! IT'S JUST LIKE YOU!
YOUR EYES ARE BUGGING OUT!
Keep it together!
SO WHAT DID YOU DO AFTER HE GAVE IT TO YOU?
HUH? WHAT DO YOU MEAN?
I MEAN...
...AFTER GETTING...
PREV...
...THE PRESERVED FLOWER!
DID YOU JUST TAKE IT?
I GAVE *HIM* A PRESENT TOO!!

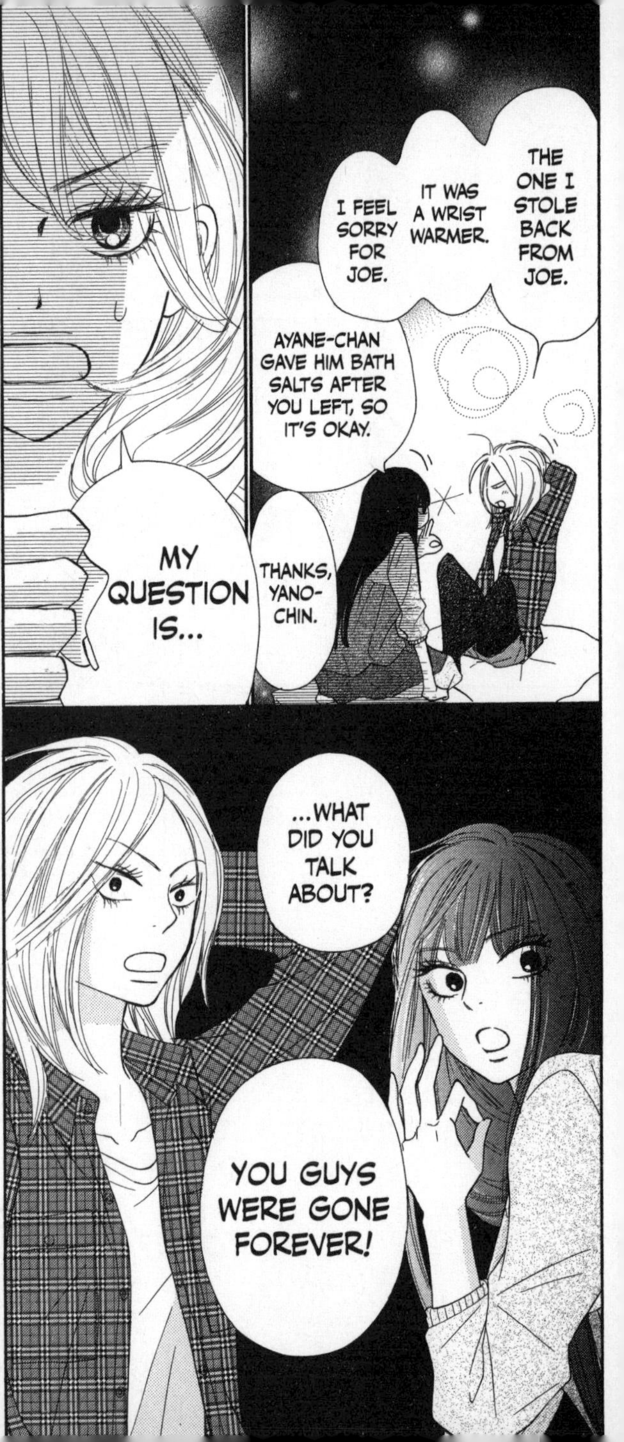
THE ONE I STOLE BACK FROM JOE.
IT WAS A WRIST WARMER.
I FEEL SORRY FOR JOE.
AYANE-CHAN GAVE HIM BATH SALTS AFTER YOU LEFT, SO IT'S OKAY.
THANKS, YANO-CHIN.
MY QUESTION IS...
...WHAT DID YOU TALK ABOUT?
YOU GUYS WERE GONE FOREVER!

KARUPIN on JAPAN 2

When I'm drawing manga for a monthly magazine, the year feels divided into twelve parts, so I feel like time flies by.

But after walking three steps, I forget about January and February--I mean, even after one step! I forget all kinds of stuff with just the slightest movement... so no wonder I forget such things.

(I'm worried about myself.)

This will be in stores in January.

(The graphic novel)

By then, I'll forget what I wrote...in the sidebars, at least. As for the story of the manga, I'm working hard at reading it back over from volume 1.

(I fall asleep!)

Reading just thirteen pages of my manga makes me sleepy.

Anyway... To those of you who read volume 19, see you then!

Karuho Shiina

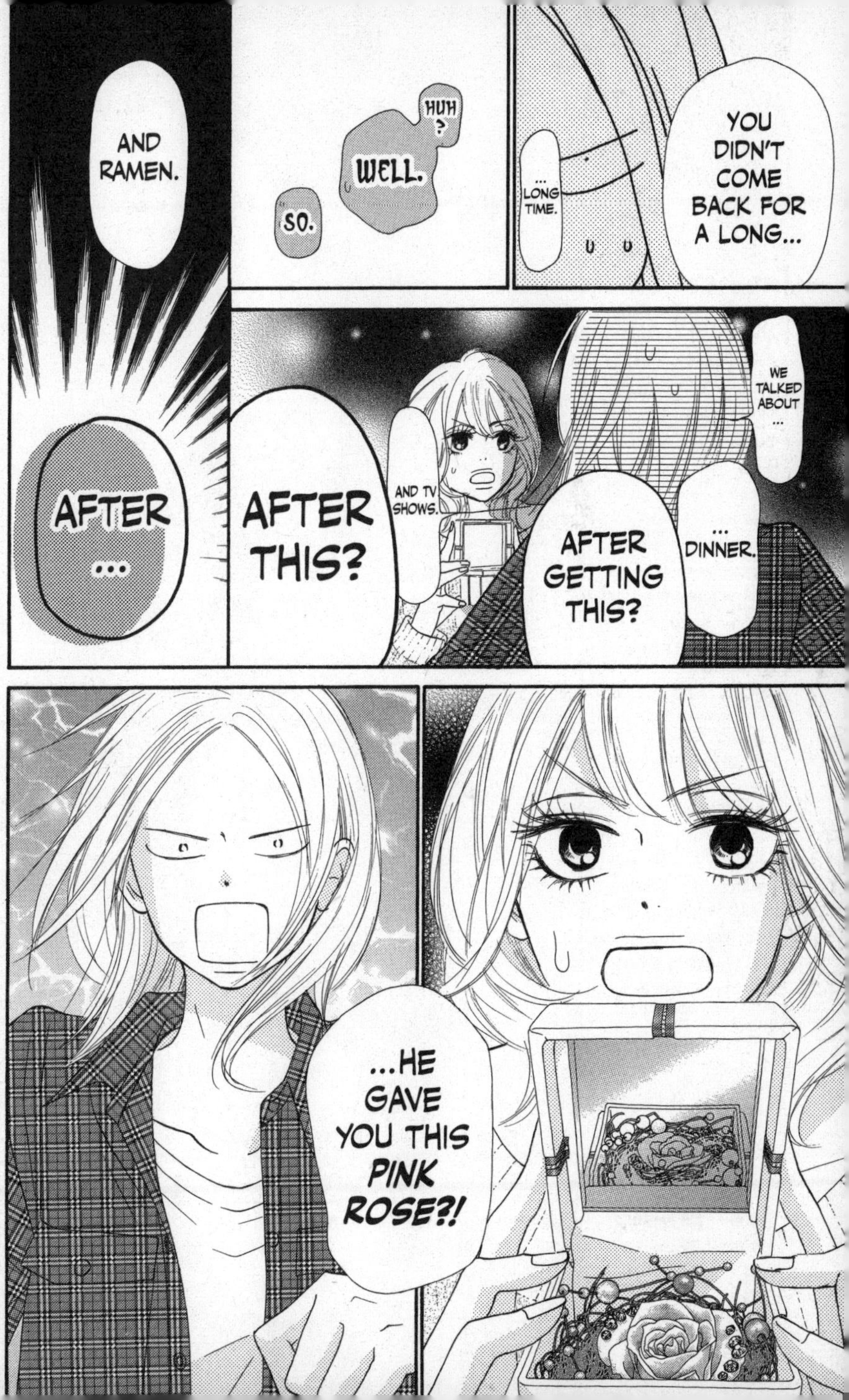
YOU DIDN'T COME BACK FOR A LONG...
...LONG TIME.
HUH?
WELL.
SO.
WE TALKED ABOUT...
...DINNER.
AND TV SHOWS.
AFTER GETTING THIS?
AFTER THIS?
AND RAMEN.
AFTER...
...HE GAVE YOU THIS PINK ROSE?!

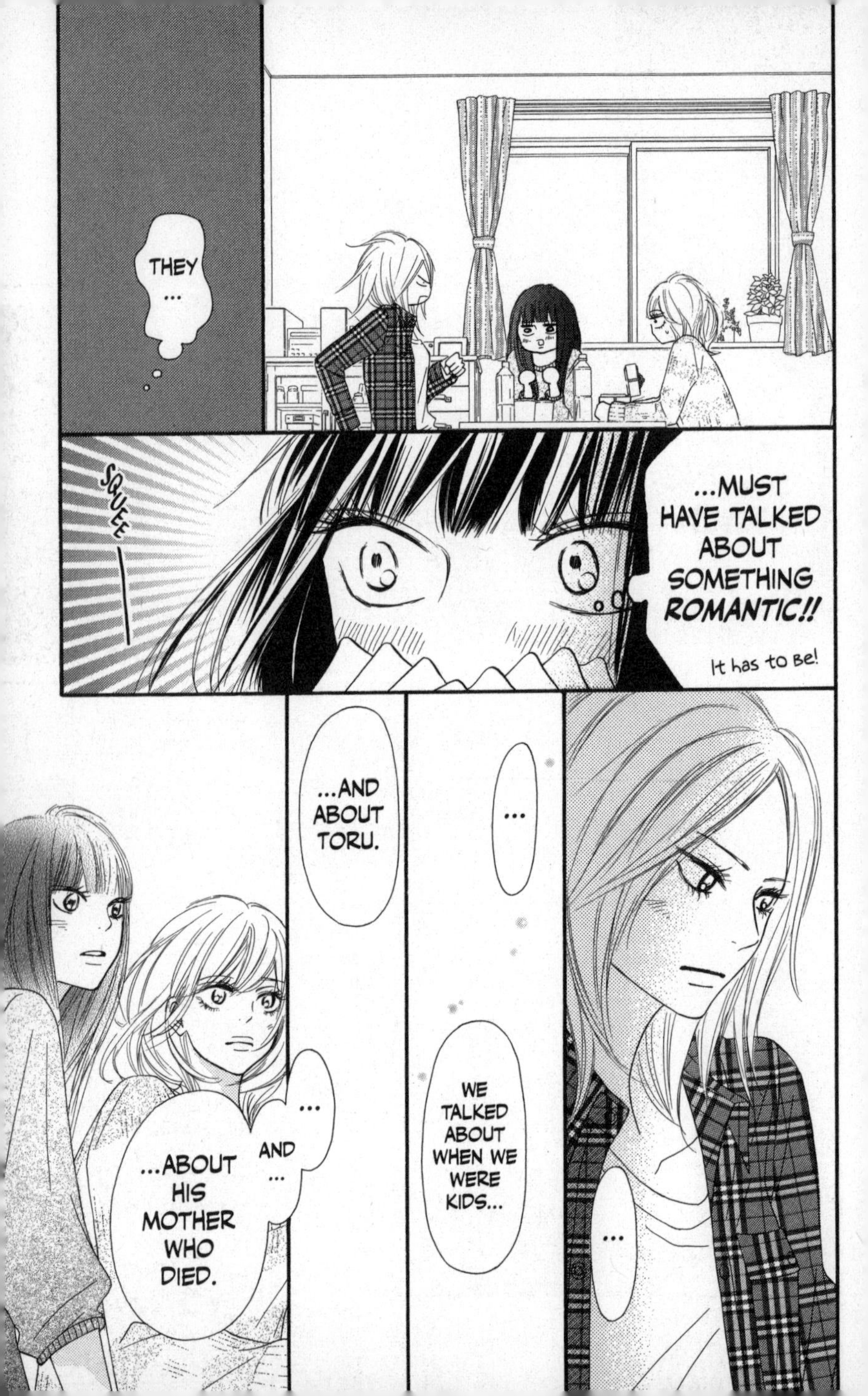
THEY ...
...MUST HAVE TALKED ABOUT SOMETHING ROMANTIC!!
SQUEEE—
It has to be!
...
...
WE TALKED ABOUT WHEN WE WERE KIDS...
...AND ABOUT TORU.
...
AND ...
...ABOUT HIS MOTHER WHO DIED.

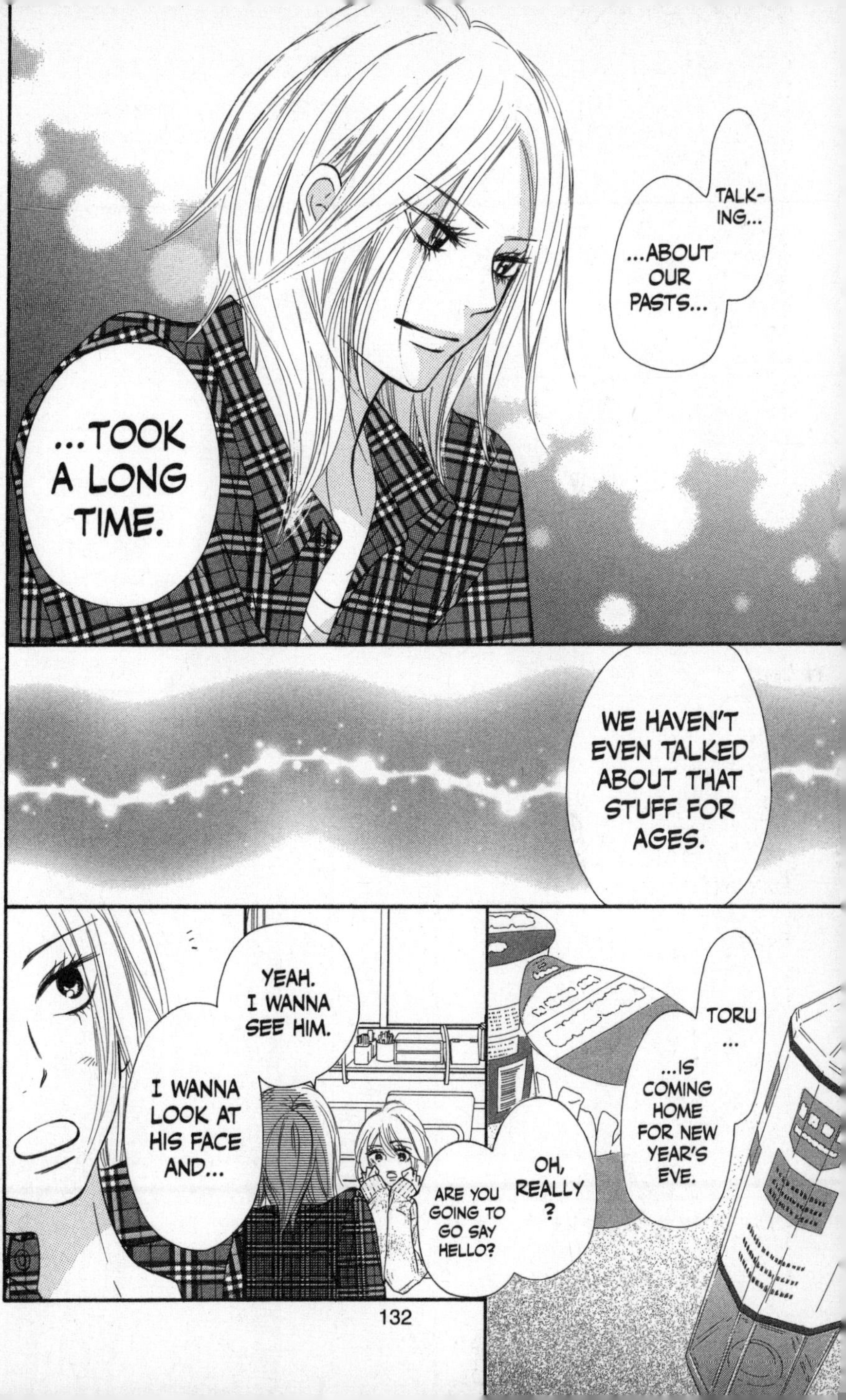
TALK-ING...
...ABOUT OUR PASTS...
...TOOK A LONG TIME.
WE HAVEN'T EVEN TALKED ABOUT THAT STUFF FOR AGES.
TORU ...
...IS COMING HOME FOR NEW YEAR'S EVE.
OH, REALLY ?
ARE YOU GOING TO GO SAY HELLO?
YEAH. I WANNA SEE HIM.
I WANNA LOOK AT HIS FACE AND...

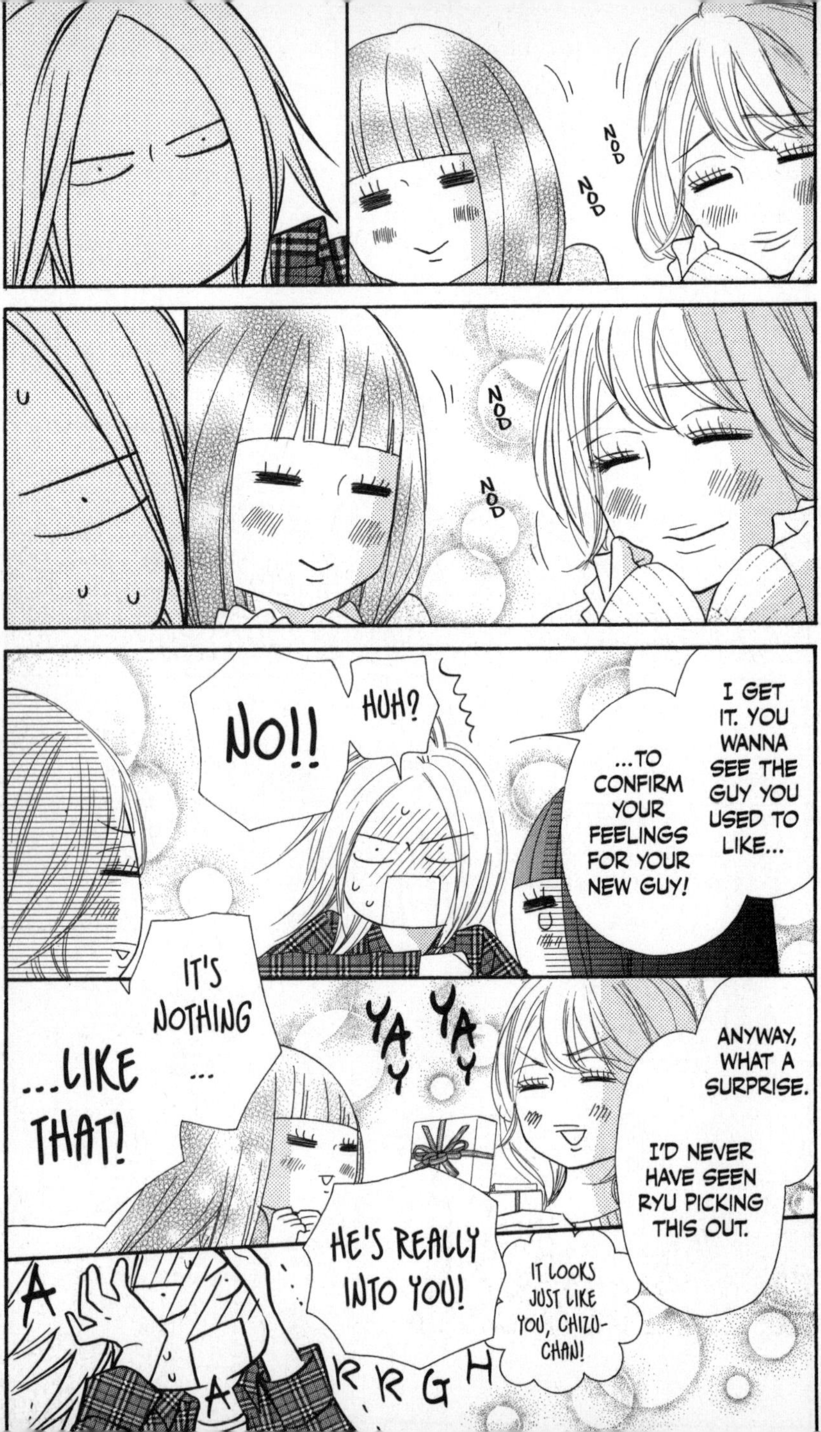
NOD NOD
NOD NOD
I GET IT. YOU WANNA SEE THE GUY YOU USED TO LIKE...
...TO CONFIRM YOUR FEELINGS FOR YOUR NEW GUY!
HUH?
NO!!
ANYWAY, WHAT A SURPRISE.
I'D NEVER HAVE SEEN RYU PICKING THIS OUT.
YAY YAY
IT'S NOTHING ...
...LIKE THAT!
IT LOOKS JUST LIKE YOU, CHIZU-CHAN!
HE'S REALLY INTO YOU!
AAARRGH

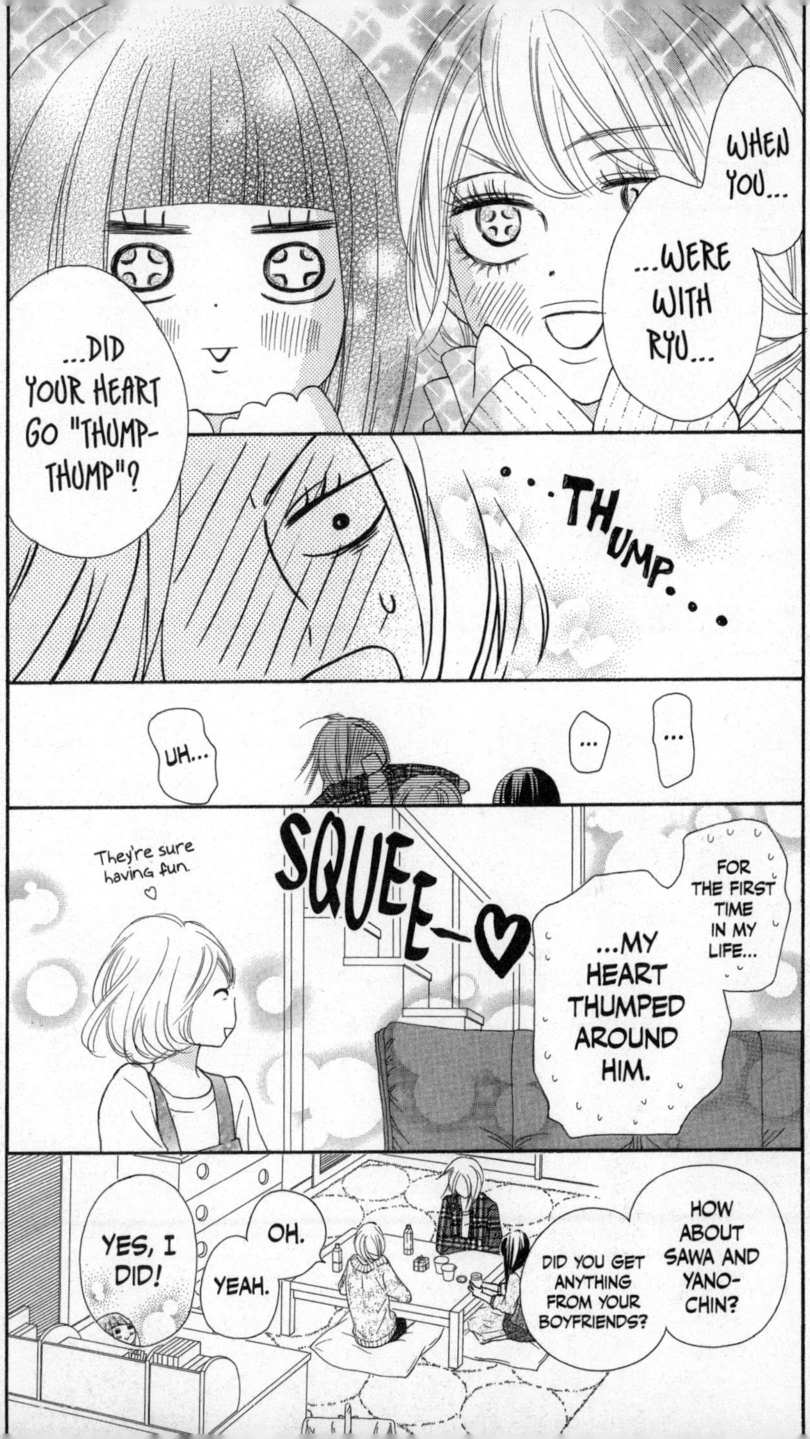
WHEN YOU...
...WERE WITH RYU...
...DID YOUR HEART GO "THUMP-THUMP"?
...THUMP...
...
...
UH...
FOR THE FIRST TIME IN MY LIFE...
...MY HEART THUMPED AROUND HIM.
SQUEE-♥
They're sure having fun. ♡
HOW ABOUT SAWA AND YANO-CHIN?
DID YOU GET ANYTHING FROM YOUR BOYFRIENDS?
OH.
YEAH.
YES, I DID!

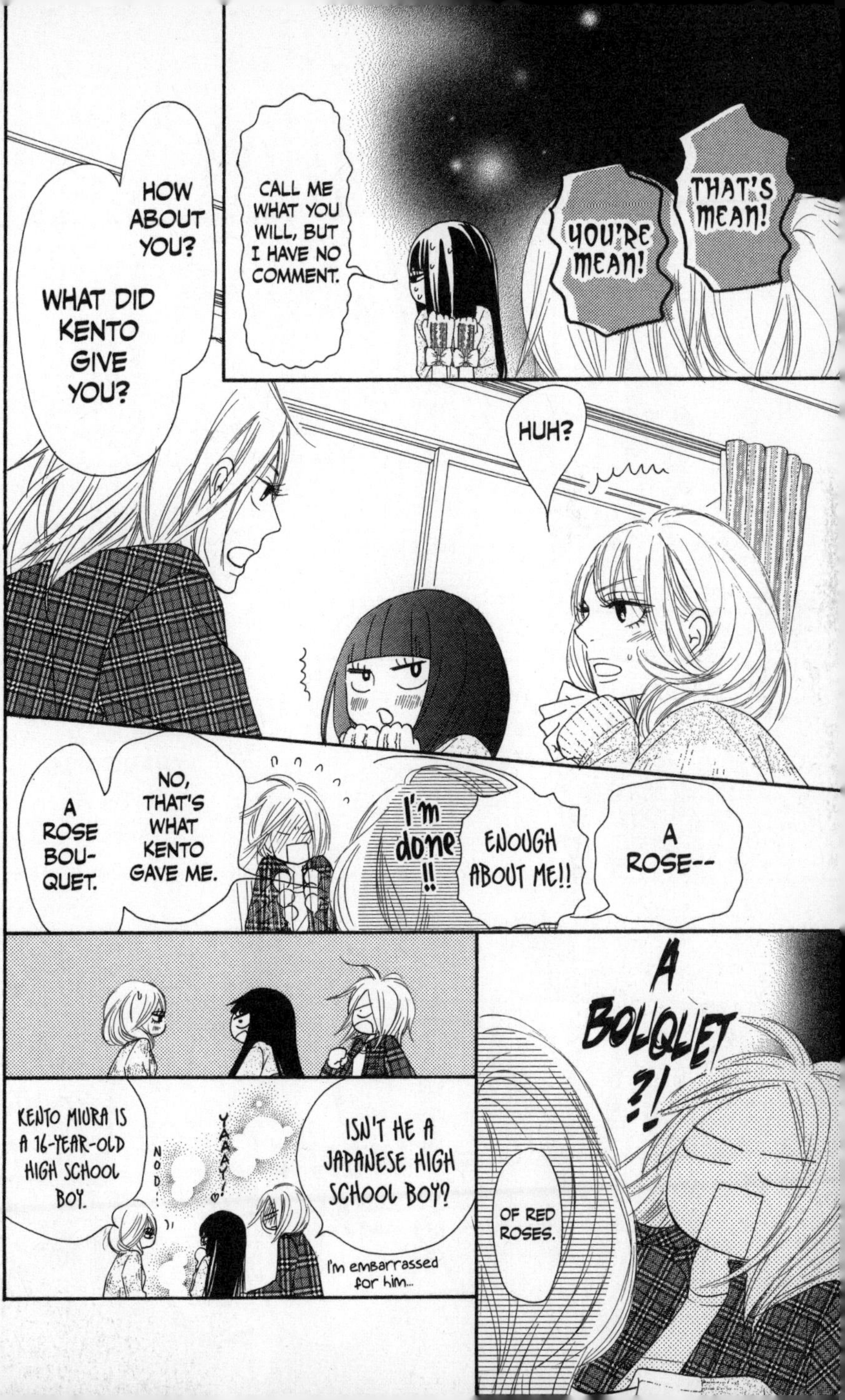
THAT'S MEAN!
YOU'RE MEAN!
CALL ME WHAT YOU WILL, BUT I HAVE NO COMMENT.
HOW ABOUT YOU?
WHAT DID KENTO GIVE YOU?
HUH?
A ROSE--
ENOUGH ABOUT ME!!
I'm done!!
NO, THAT'S WHAT KENTO GAVE ME.
A ROSE BOUQUET.
A BOUQUET ?!
OF RED ROSES.
ISN'T HE A JAPANESE HIGH SCHOOL BOY?
YAAAY!
NOD...
KENTO MIURA IS A 16-YEAR-OLD HIGH SCHOOL BOY.
I'm embarrassed for him...

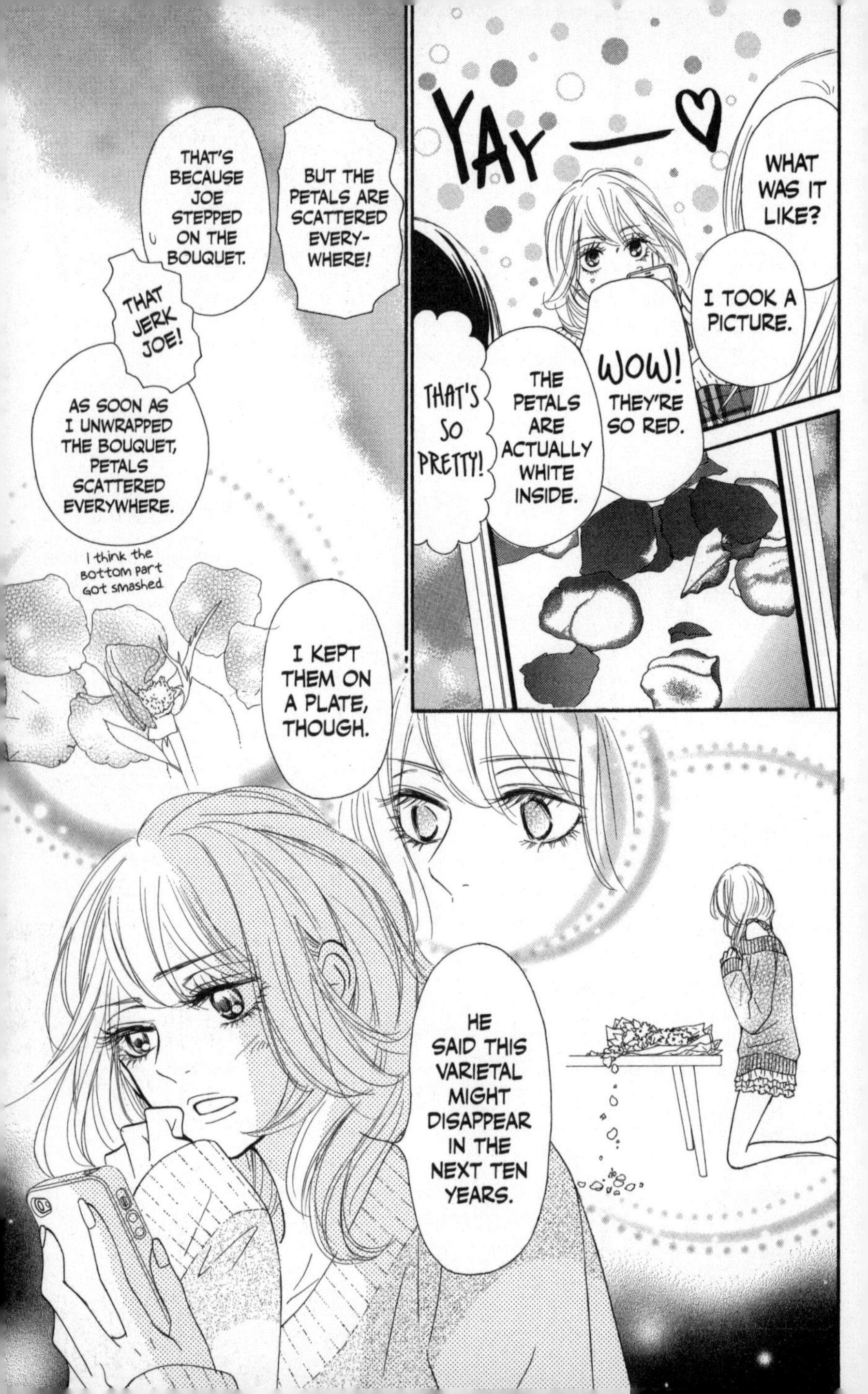
YAY—♥
WHAT WAS IT LIKE?
I TOOK A PICTURE.
WOW! THEY'RE SO RED.
THE PETALS ARE ACTUALLY WHITE INSIDE.
THAT'S SO PRETTY!
BUT THE PETALS ARE SCATTERED EVERYWHERE!
THAT'S BECAUSE JOE STEPPED ON THE BOUQUET.
THAT JERK JOE!
AS SOON AS I UNWRAPPED THE BOUQUET, PETALS SCATTERED EVERYWHERE.
I think the bottom part got smashed.
I KEPT THEM ON A PLATE, THOUGH.
HE SAID THIS VARIETAL MIGHT DISAPPEAR IN THE NEXT TEN YEARS.

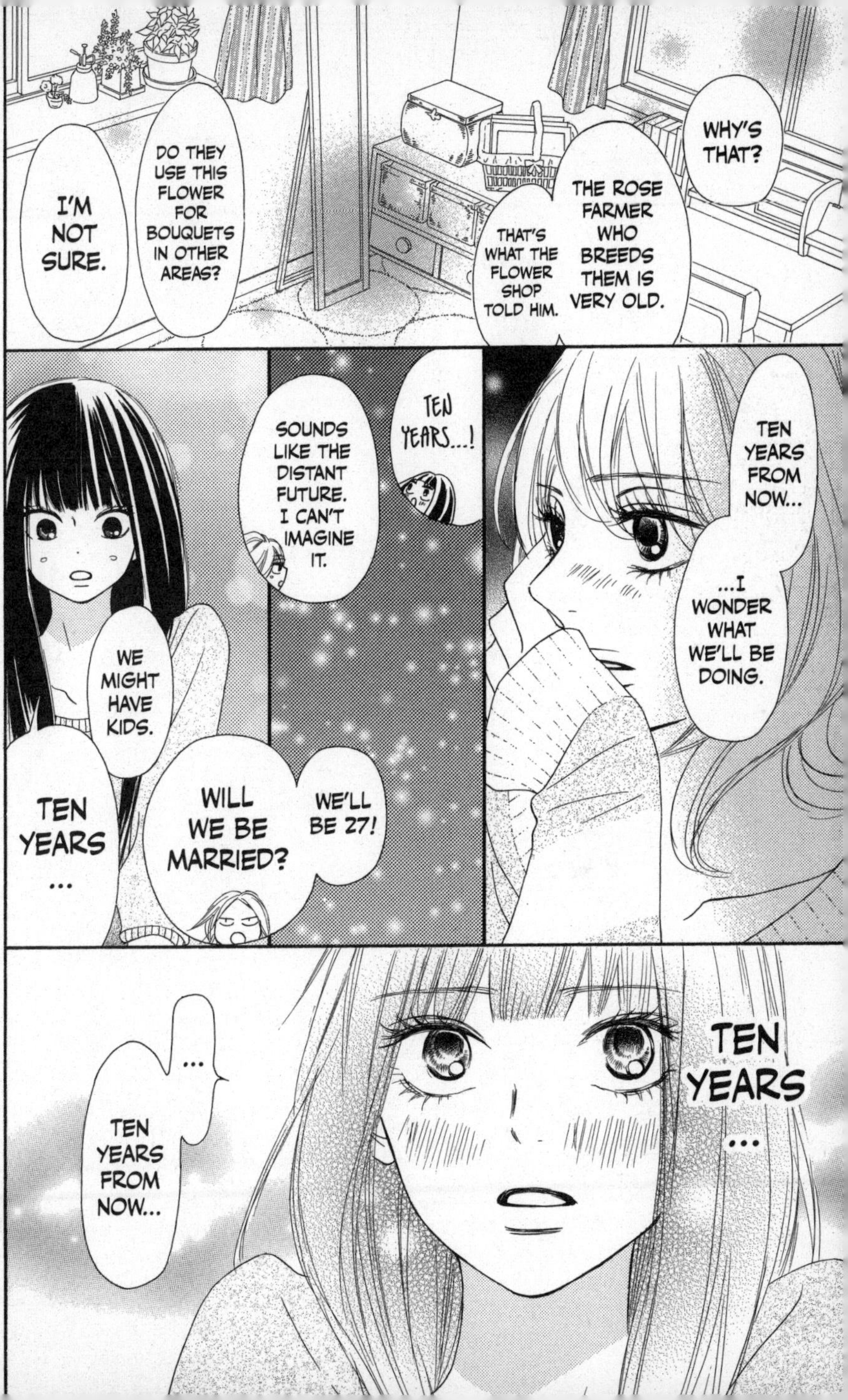
WHY'S THAT?
THE ROSE FARMER WHO BREEDS THEM IS VERY OLD.
THAT'S WHAT THE FLOWER SHOP TOLD HIM.
DO THEY USE THIS FLOWER FOR BOUQUETS IN OTHER AREAS?
I'M NOT SURE.
TEN YEARS FROM NOW...
...I WONDER WHAT WE'LL BE DOING.
TEN YEARS...!
SOUNDS LIKE THE DISTANT FUTURE. I CAN'T IMAGINE IT.
WE'LL BE 27!
WILL WE BE MARRIED?
WE MIGHT HAVE KIDS.
TEN YEARS...
TEN YEARS...
...
TEN YEARS FROM NOW...

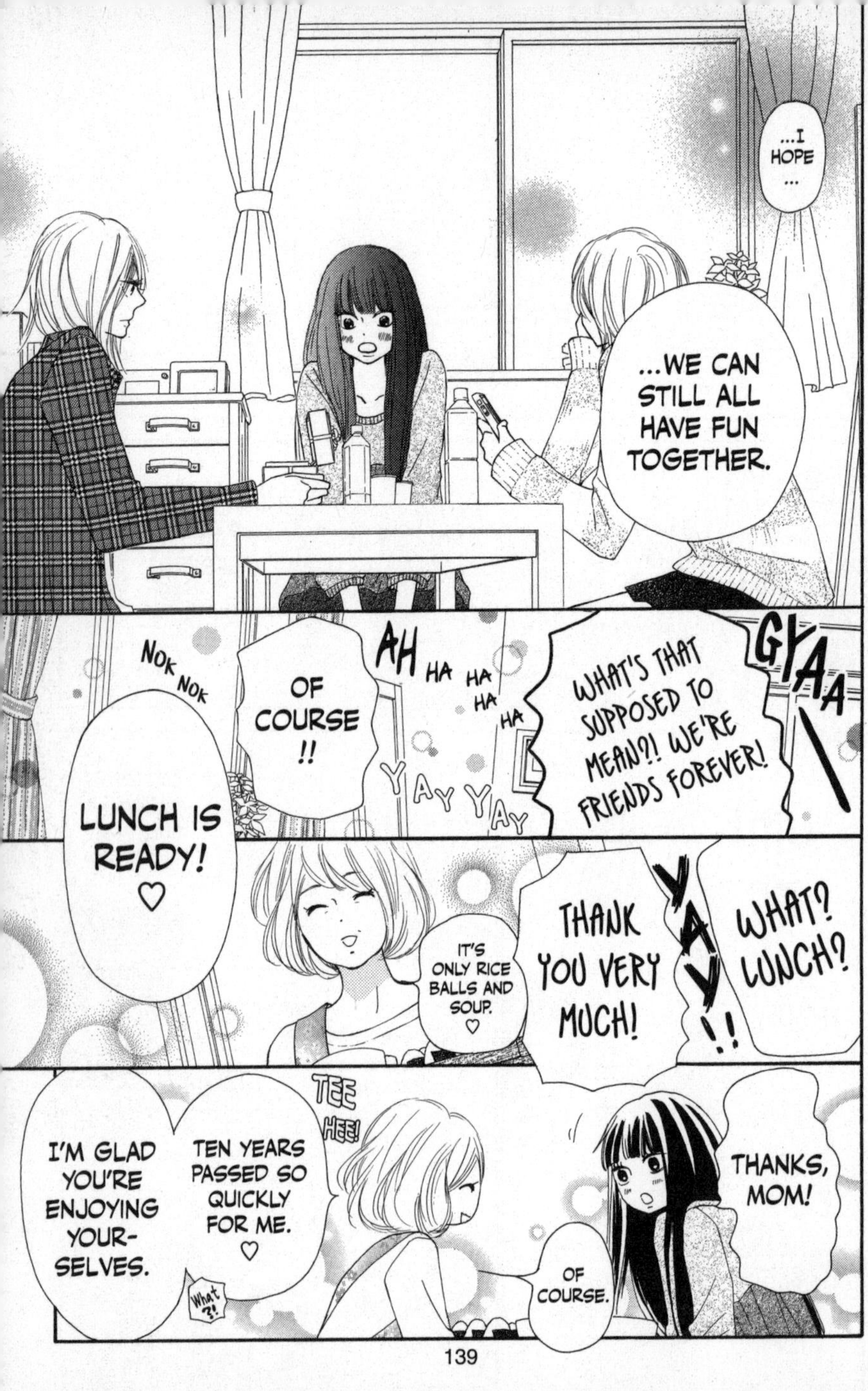
...I HOPE ...
...WE CAN STILL ALL HAVE FUN TOGETHER.
GYAAA
WHAT'S THAT SUPPOSED TO MEAN?! WE'RE FRIENDS FOREVER!
AH HA HA HA HA
YAY YAY
OF COURSE !!
NOK NOK
LUNCH IS READY! ♡
WHAT? LUNCH?
YAY!!
THANK YOU VERY MUCH!
IT'S ONLY RICE BALLS AND SOUP. ♡
THANKS, MOM!
OF COURSE.
TEE HEE!
TEN YEARS PASSED SO QUICKLY FOR ME. ♡
What?!
I'M GLAD YOU'RE ENJOYING YOUR-SELVES.

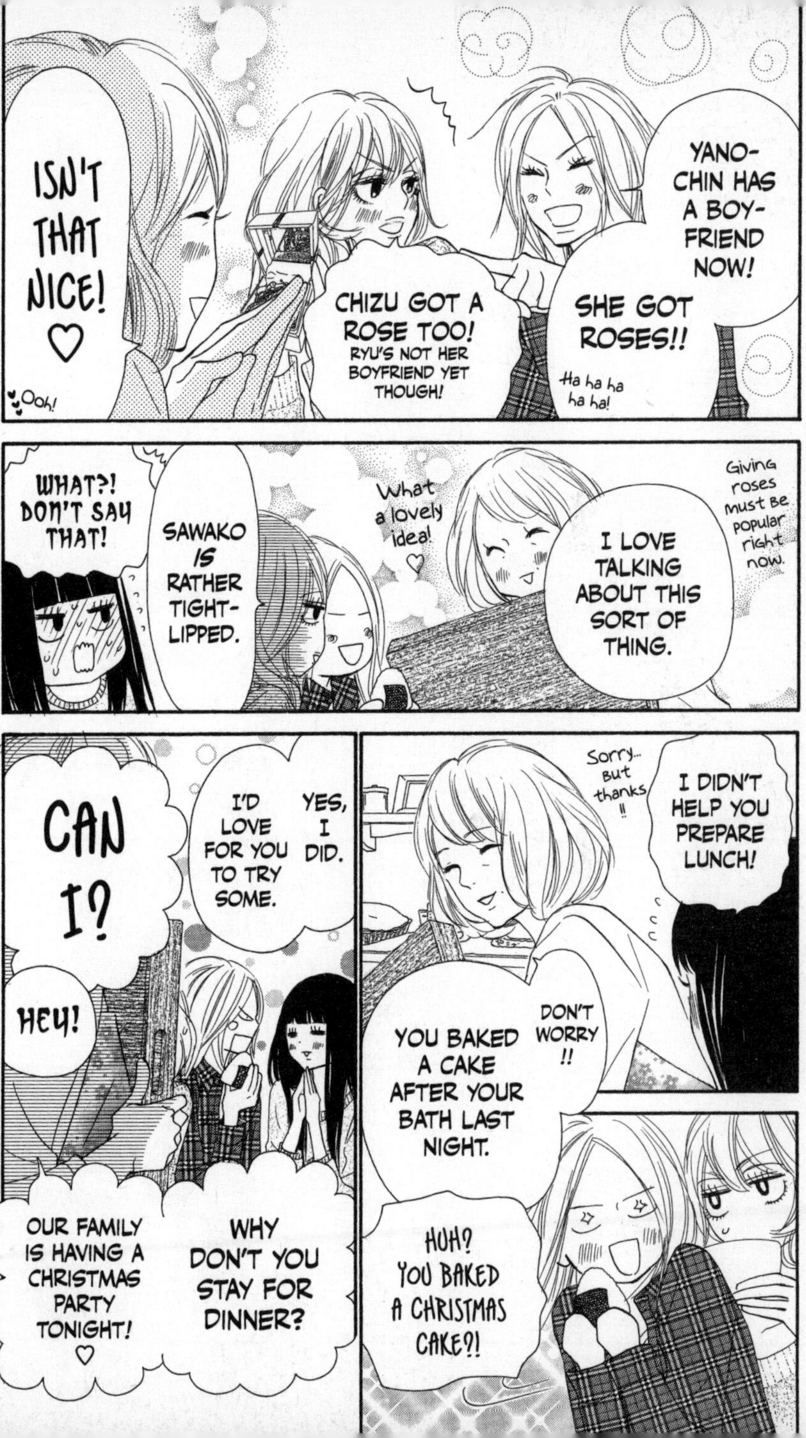
YANO-CHIN HAS A BOY-FRIEND NOW!
SHE GOT ROSES!!
Ha ha ha ha ha!
CHIZU GOT A ROSE TOO!
RYU'S NOT HER BOYFRIEND YET THOUGH!
ISN'T THAT NICE! ♡
Ooh!
Giving roses must be popular right now.
I LOVE TALKING ABOUT THIS SORT OF THING.
What a lovely idea! ♡
SAWAKO IS RATHER TIGHT-LIPPED.
WHAT?! DON'T SAY THAT!
I DIDN'T HELP YOU PREPARE LUNCH!
Sorry... but thanks!!
DON'T WORRY!!
YOU BAKED A CAKE AFTER YOUR BATH LAST NIGHT.
HUH? YOU BAKED A CHRISTMAS CAKE?!
YES, I DID.
I'D LOVE FOR YOU TO TRY SOME.
CAN I?
HEY!
WHY DON'T YOU STAY FOR DINNER?
OUR FAMILY IS HAVING A CHRISTMAS PARTY TONIGHT! ♡

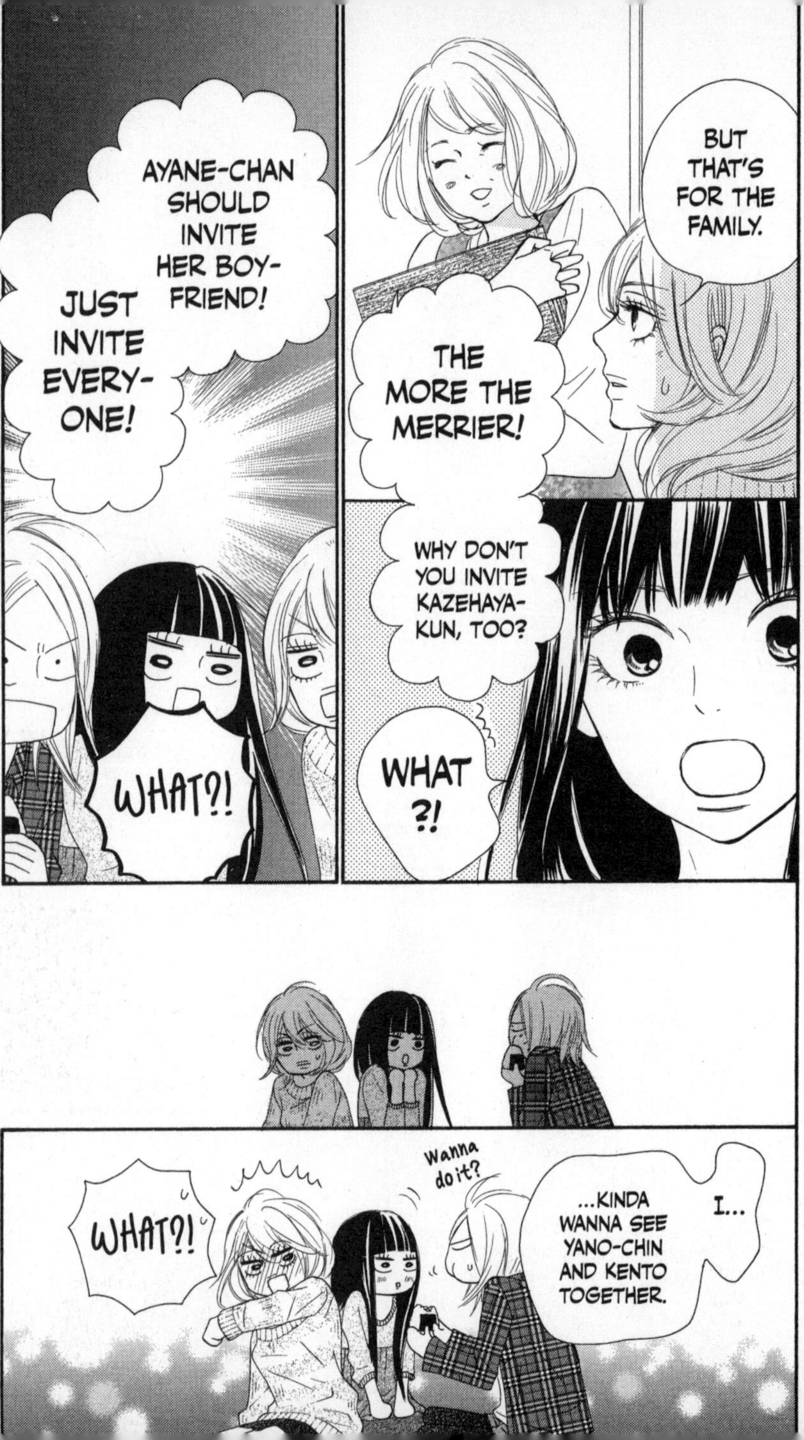
BUT THAT'S FOR THE FAMILY.
THE MORE THE MERRIER!
WHY DON'T YOU INVITE KAZEHAYA-KUN, TOO?
WHAT ?!
AYANE-CHAN SHOULD INVITE HER BOY-FRIEND!
JUST INVITE EVERY-ONE!
WHAT?!
I...
...KINDA WANNA SEE YANO-CHIN AND KENTO TOGETHER.
Wanna do it?
WHAT?!

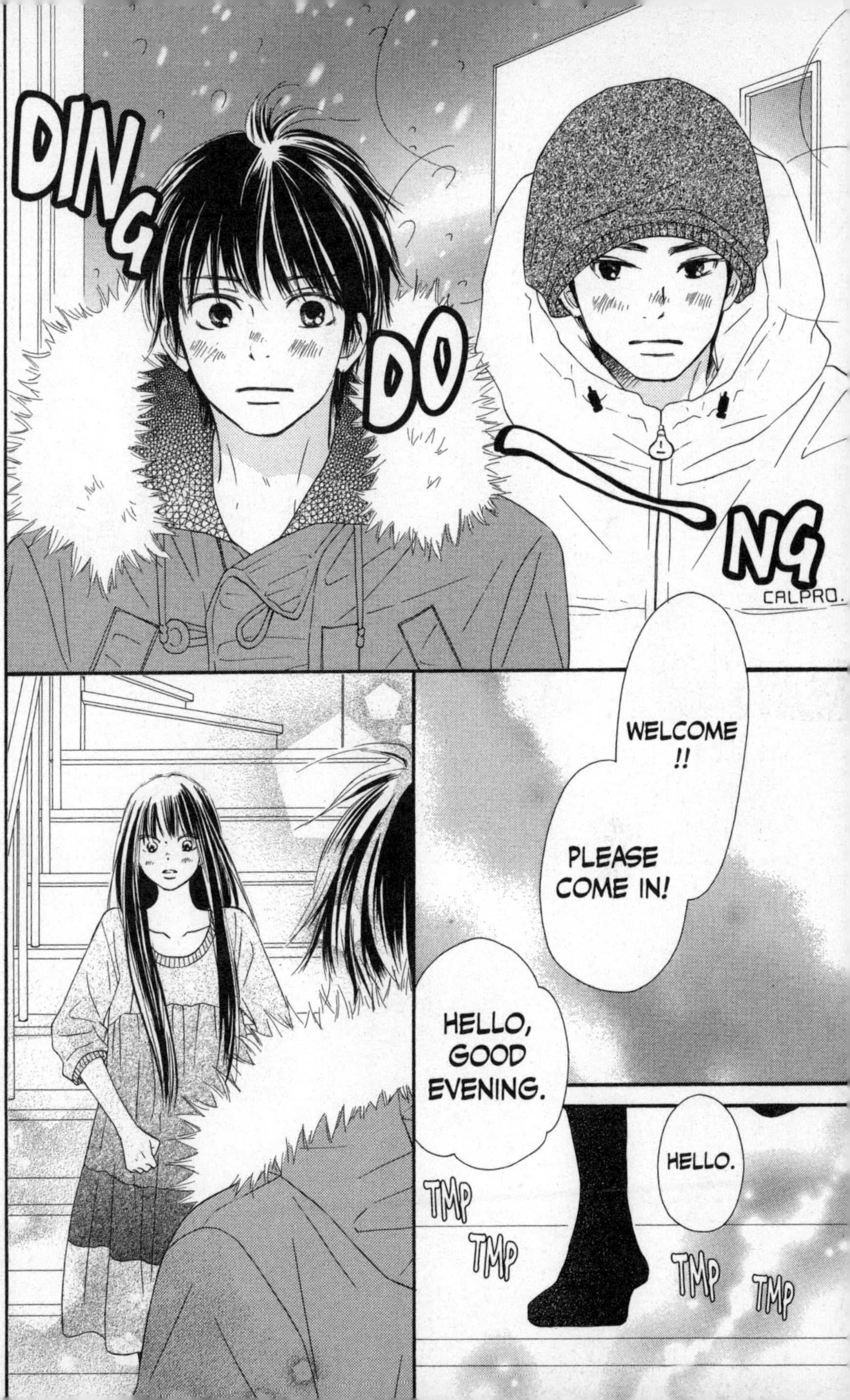
DING DO NG
CALPRO.
WELCOME !!
PLEASE COME IN!
HELLO.
TMP
TMP
HELLO, GOOD EVENING.
TMP
TMP

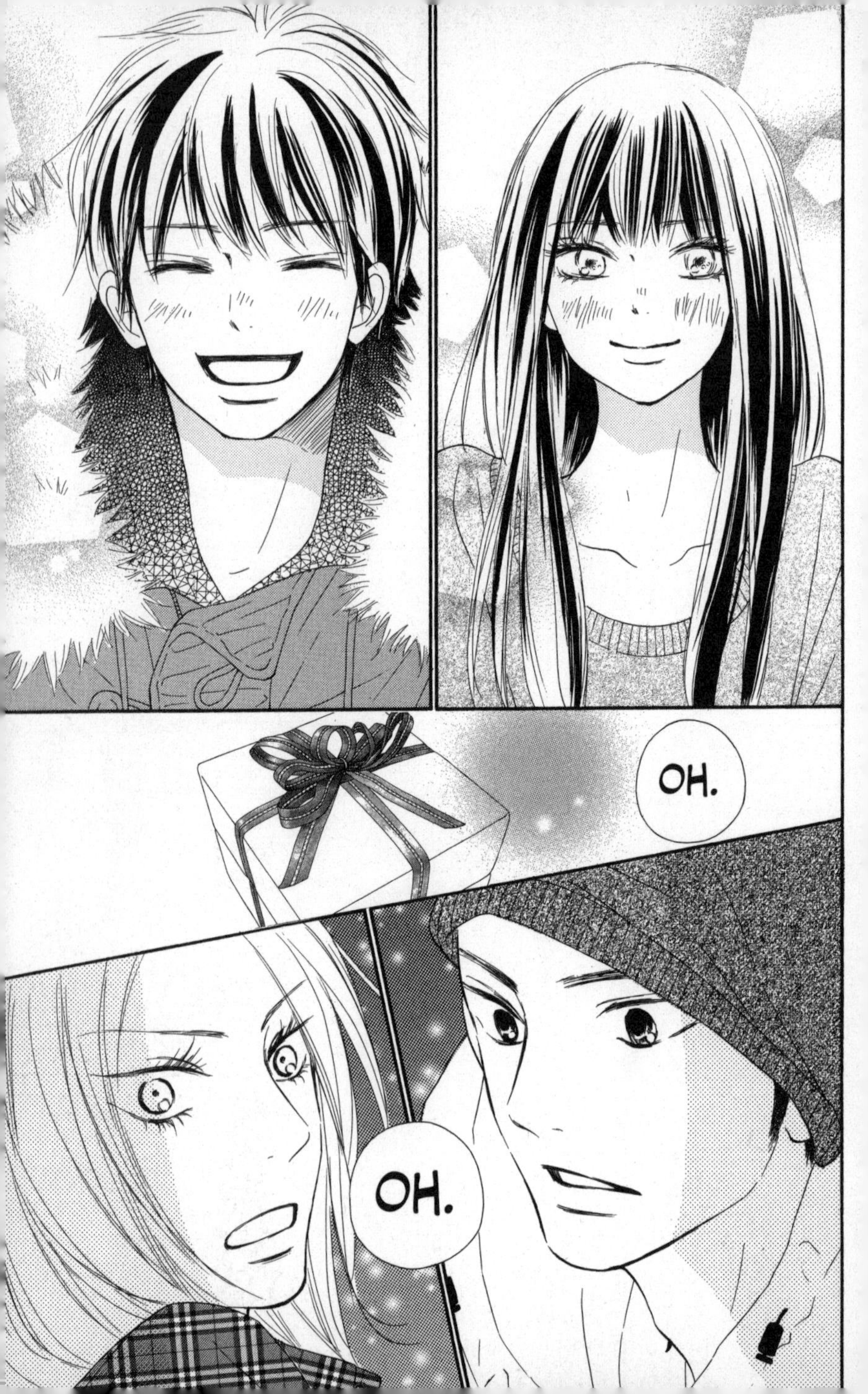
OH.
OH.

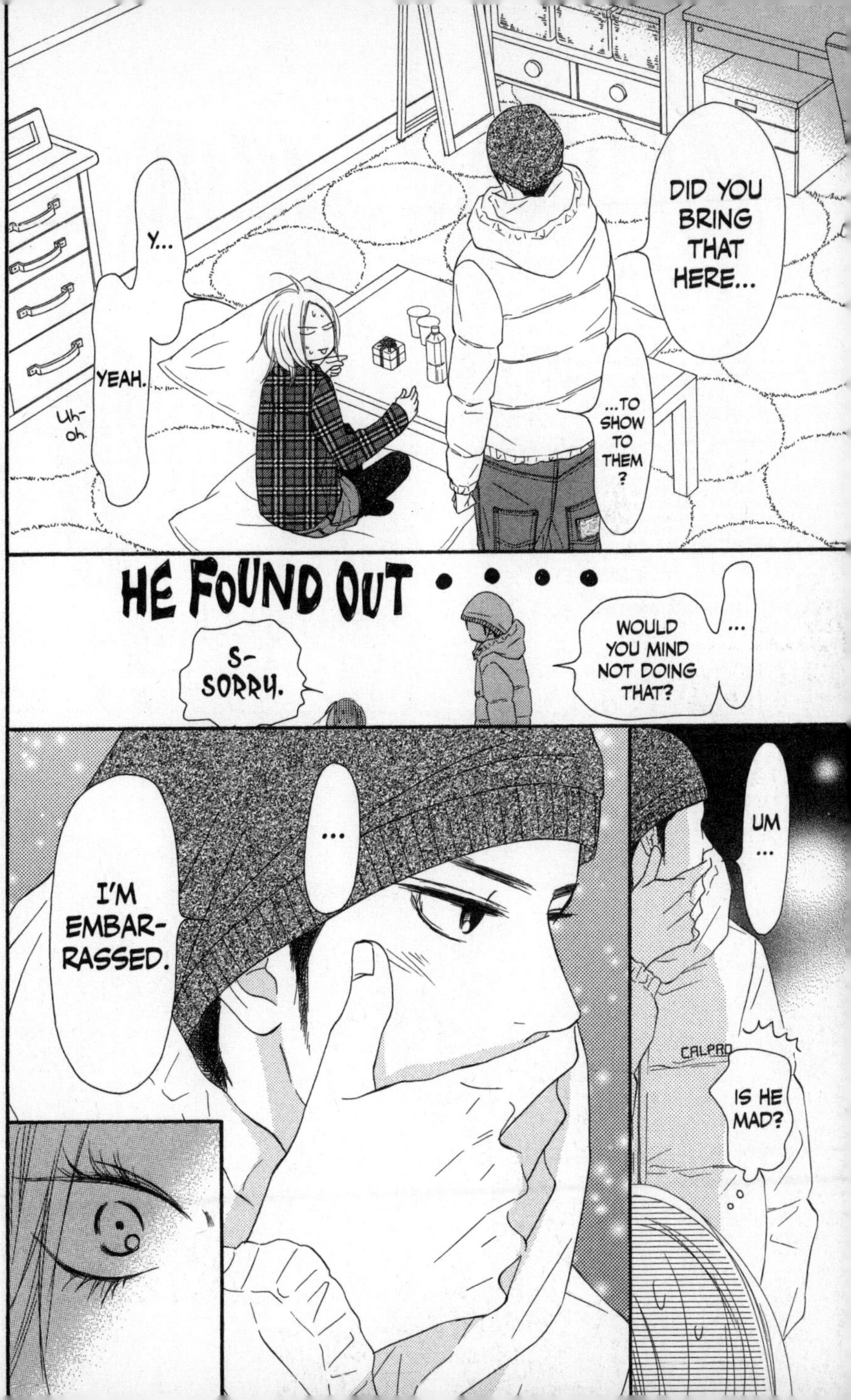
DID YOU BRING THAT HERE...
...TO SHOW TO THEM?
Y...
YEAH.
Uh-oh.
...
WOULD YOU MIND NOT DOING THAT?
HE FOUND OUT • • • •
S-SORRY.
UM ...
CALPRO
IS HE MAD?
...
I'M EMBARRASSED.

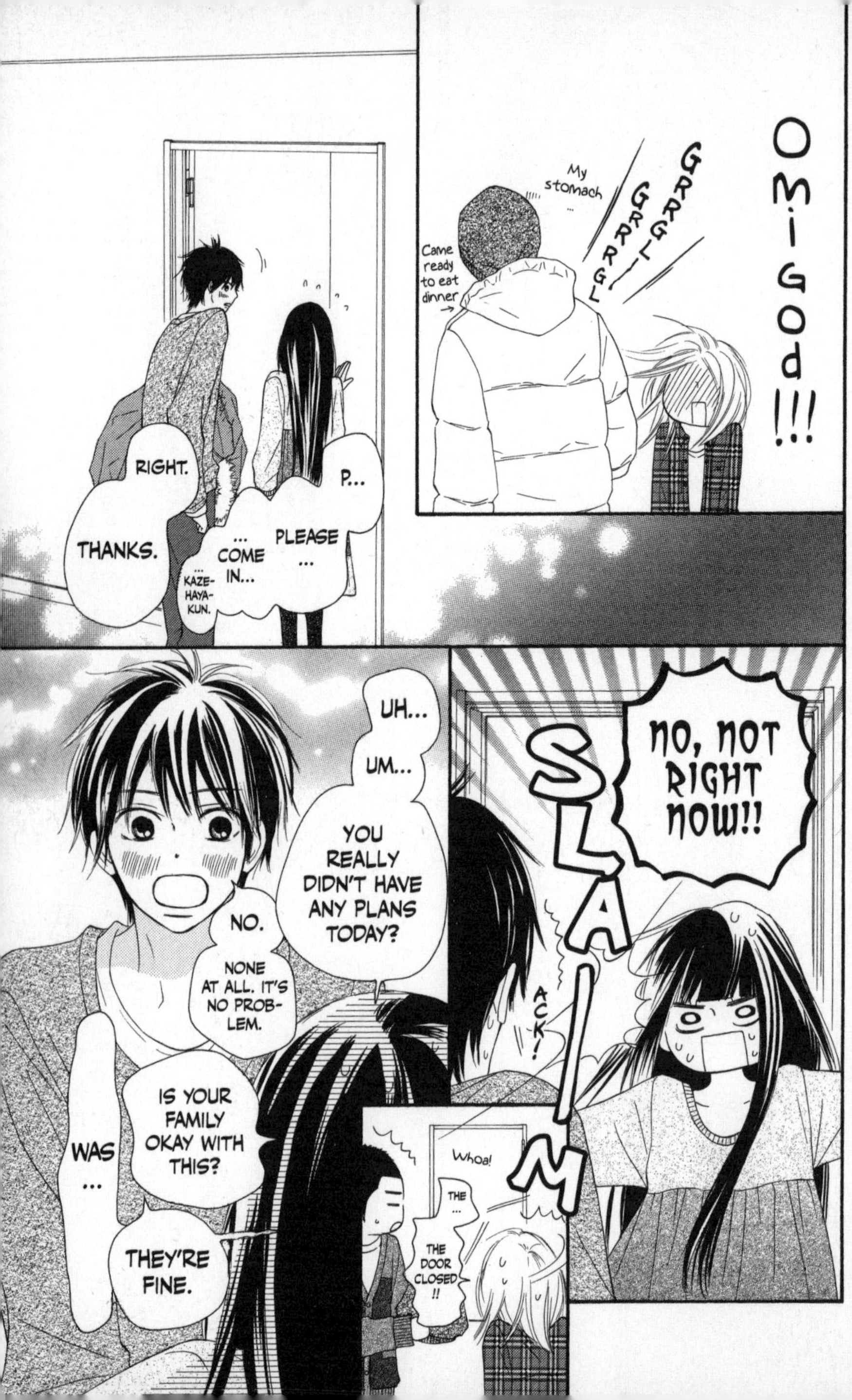
OMIGOD!!!
GRRRGL
GRRGL
My stomach...
Came ready to eat dinner
P...
PLEASE ...
... COME IN...
... KAZE-HAYA-KUN.
RIGHT.
THANKS.
NO, NOT RIGHT NOW!!
SLAM
ACK!
Whoa!
THE ...
THE DOOR CLOSED!!
UH...
UM...
YOU REALLY DIDN'T HAVE ANY PLANS TODAY?
NO.
NONE AT ALL. IT'S NO PROB-LEM.
IS YOUR FAMILY OKAY WITH THIS?
WAS ...
THEY'RE FINE.

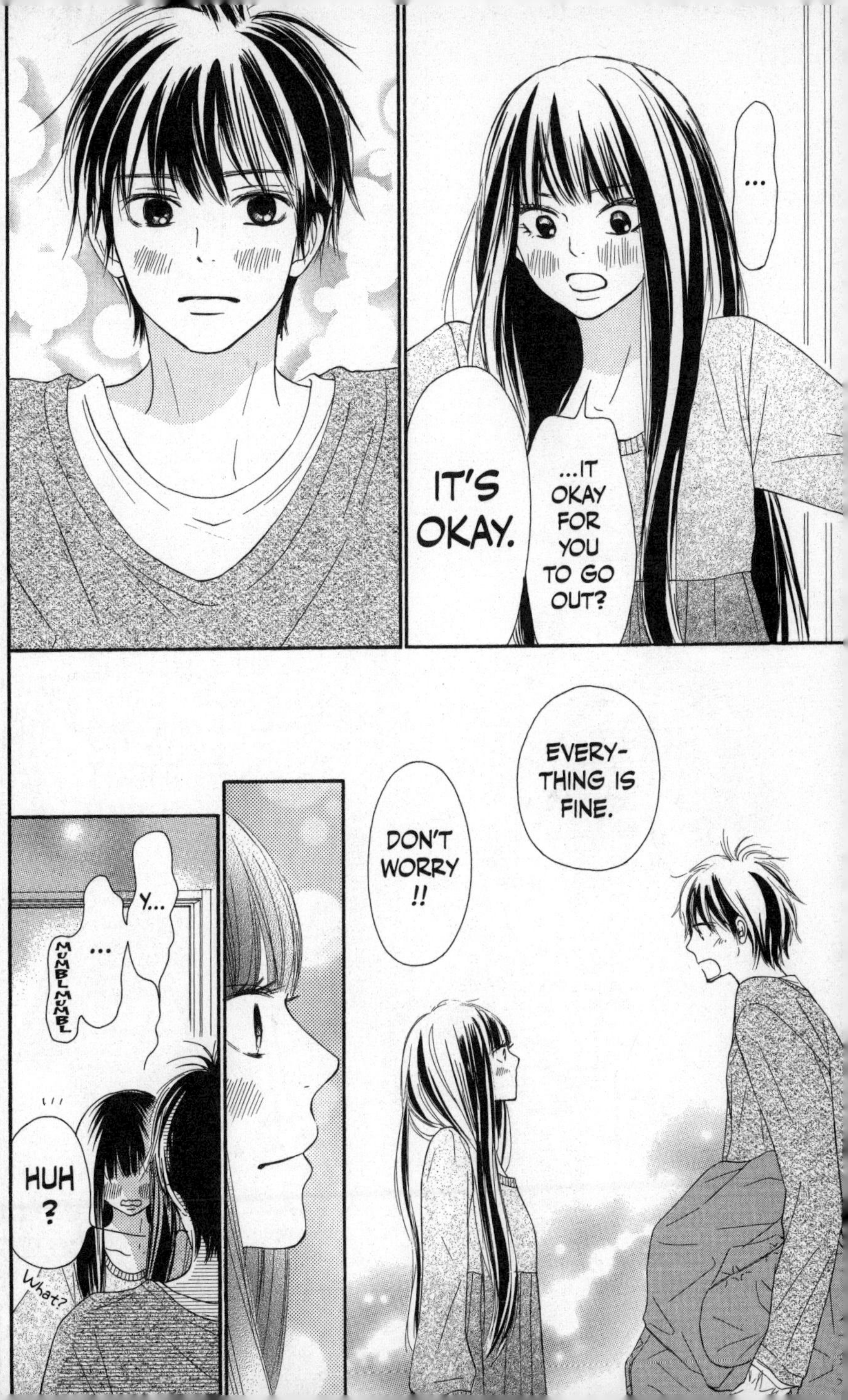
...
...IT OKAY FOR YOU TO GO OUT?
IT'S OKAY.
EVERY-THING IS FINE.
DON'T WORRY !!
Y...
...
MUMBL MUMBL
HUH ?
What?

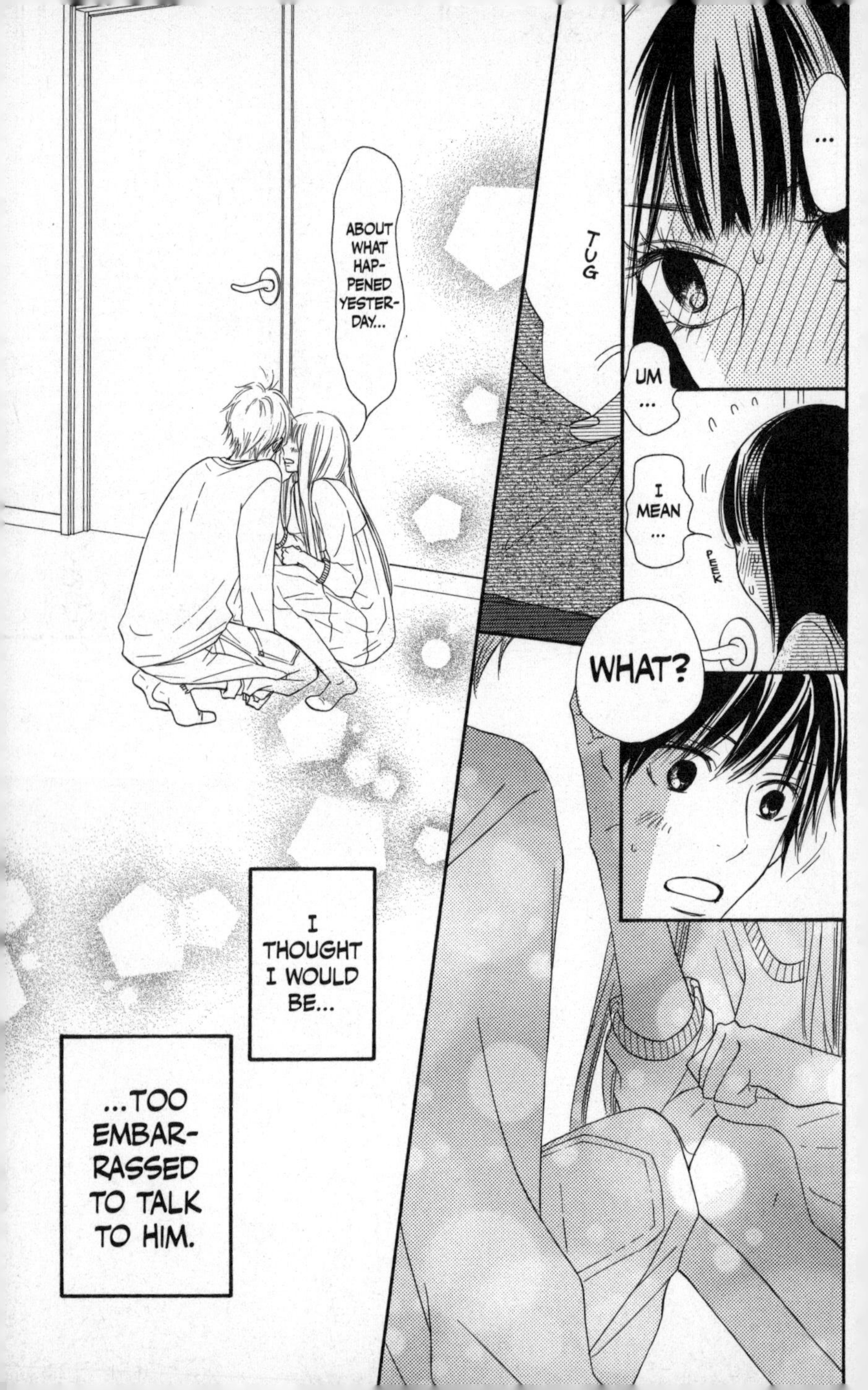
...
TUG
UM ...
I MEAN ...
PEEK
WHAT?
ABOUT WHAT HAPPENED YESTERDAY...
I THOUGHT I WOULD BE...
...TOO EMBARRASSED TO TALK TO HIM.

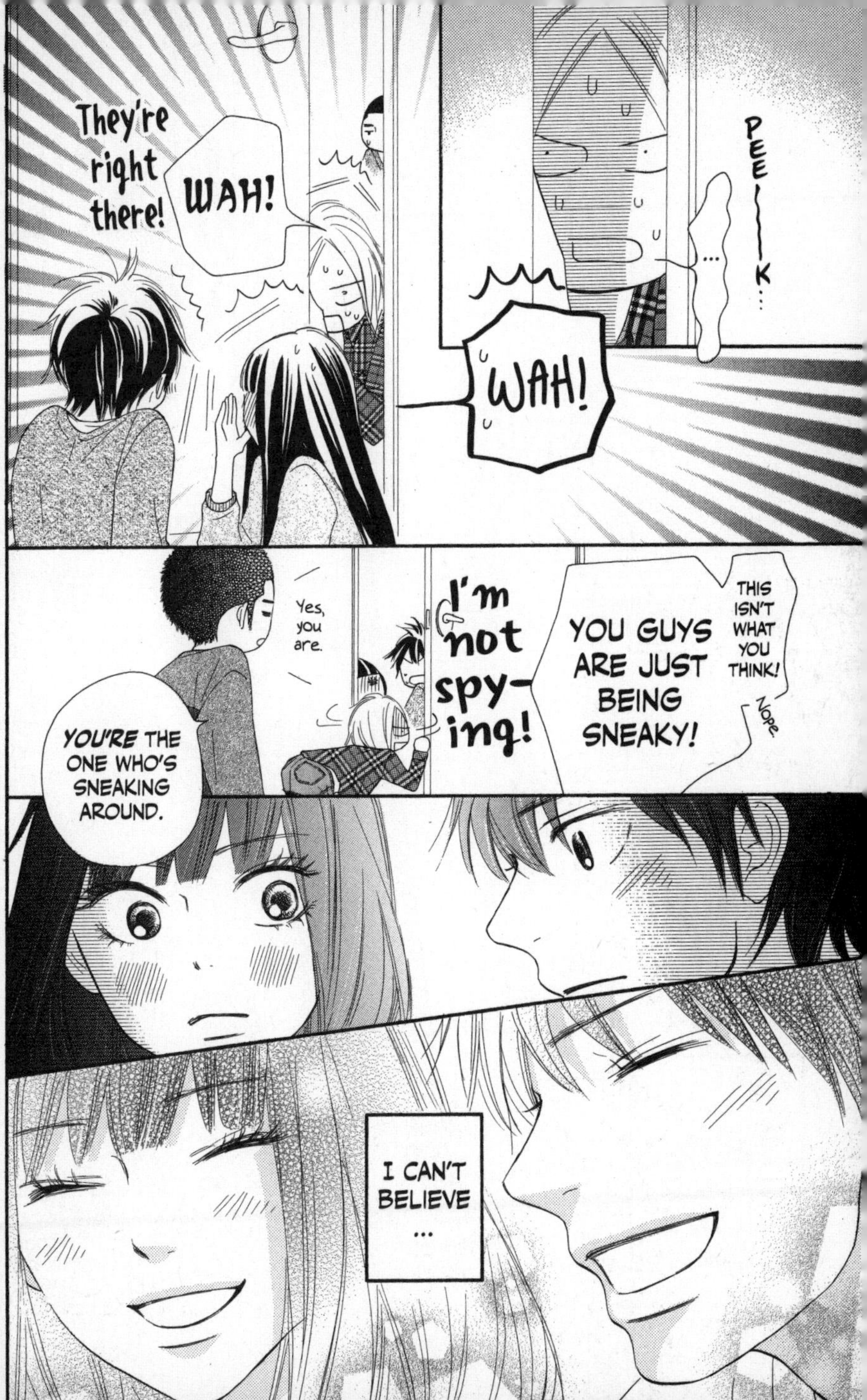
PEE--K...
...
WAH!
WAH!
They're right there!
THIS ISN'T WHAT YOU THINK!
Nope.
YOU GUYS ARE JUST BEING SNEAKY!
I'm not spying!
Yes, you are.
YOU'RE THE ONE WHO'S SNEAKING AROUND.
I CAN'T BELIEVE ...

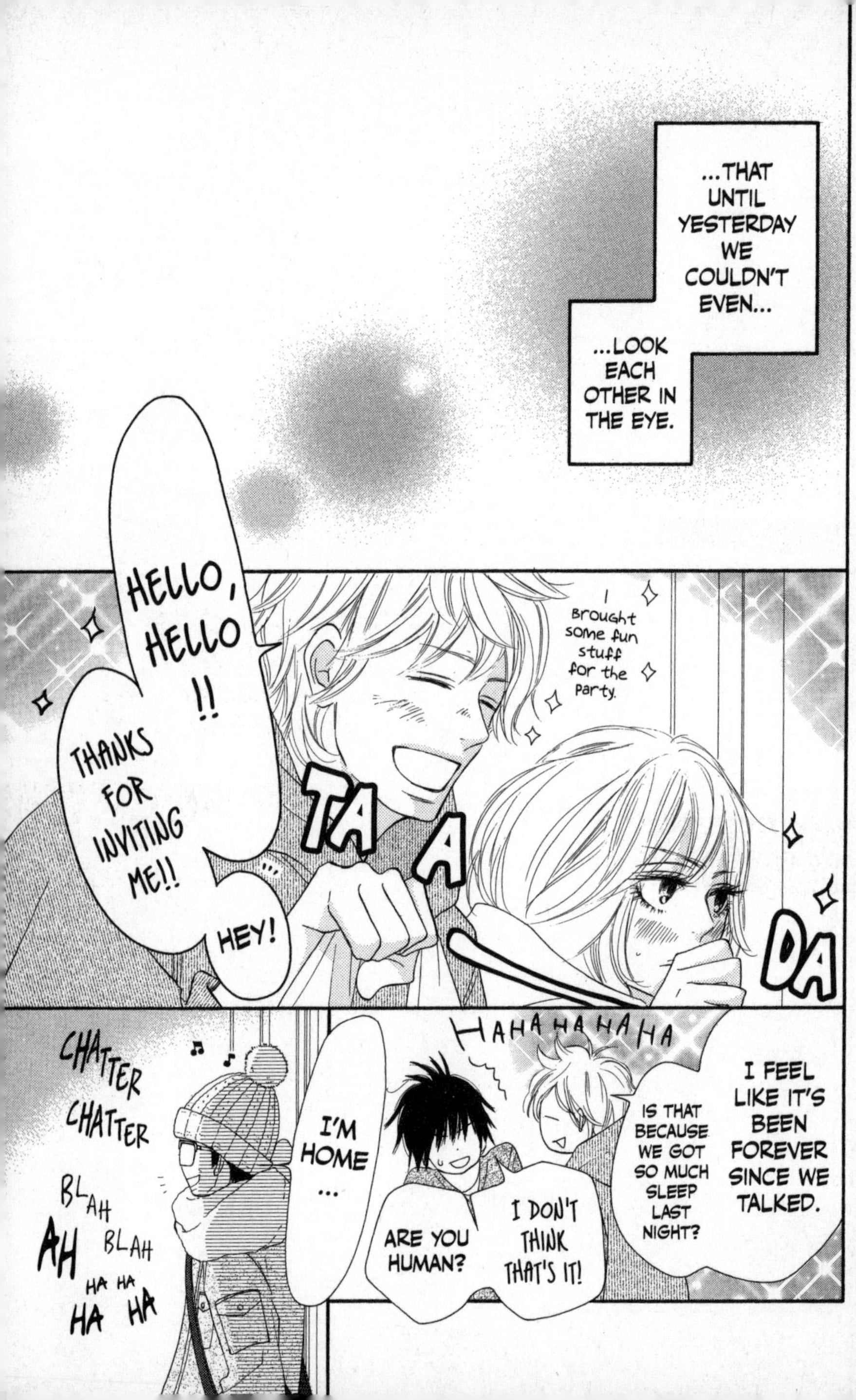
...THAT UNTIL YESTERDAY WE COULDN'T EVEN...
...LOOK EACH OTHER IN THE EYE.
I brought some fun stuff for the party.
TA A DA
HELLO, HELLO!!
THANKS FOR INVITING ME!!
...
HEY!
I FEEL LIKE IT'S BEEN FOREVER SINCE WE TALKED.
IS THAT BECAUSE WE GOT SO MUCH SLEEP LAST NIGHT?
HAHAHAHAHAHA
I DON'T THINK THAT'S IT!
ARE YOU HUMAN?
I'M HOME...
CHATTER CHATTER
BLAH BLAH
AH HA HA HA HA

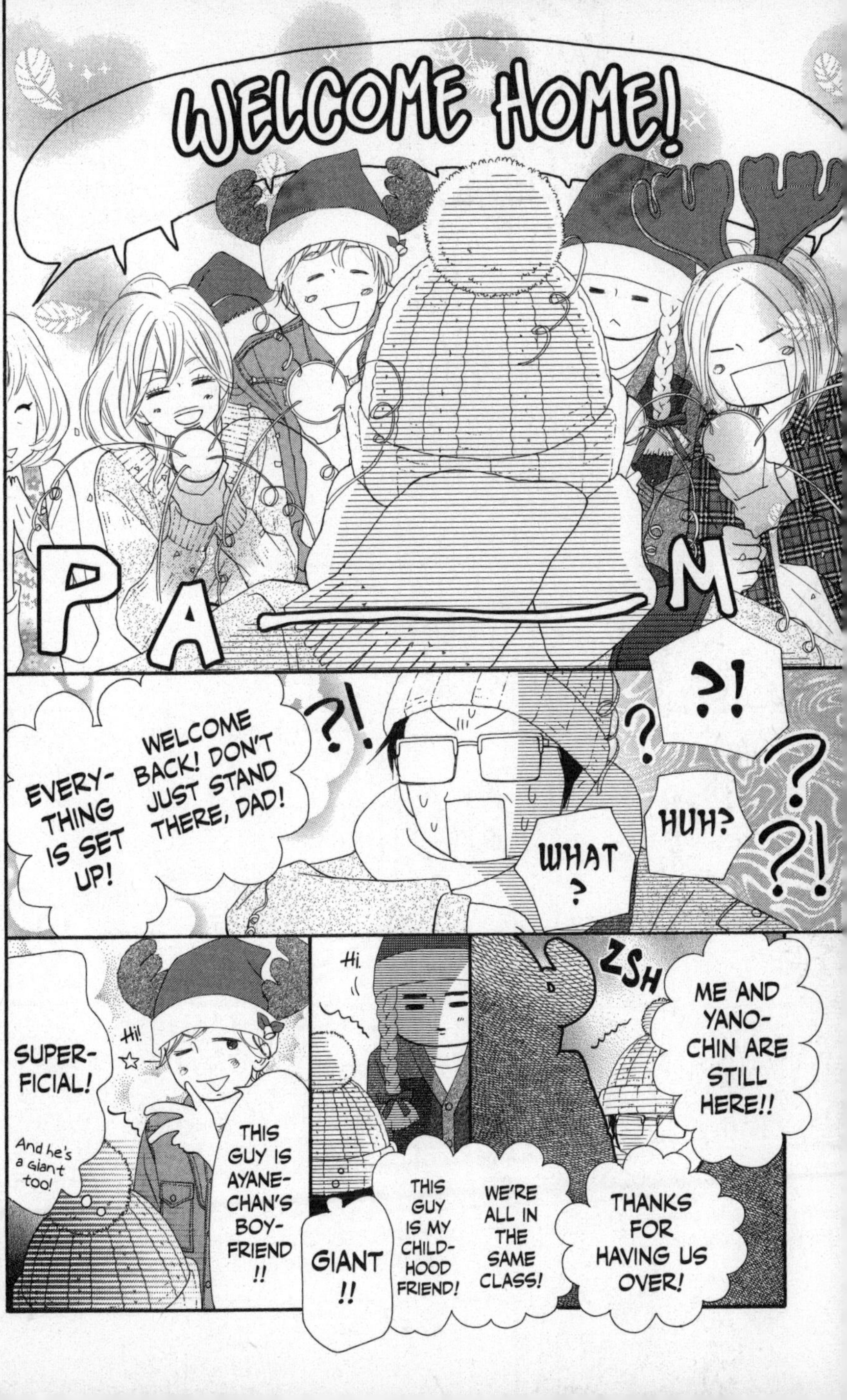
WELCOME HOME!
PAM
?!
HUH?
WHAT?
??!
?!
WELCOME BACK! DON'T JUST STAND THERE, DAD!
EVERY-THING IS SET UP!
ZSH
ME AND YANO-CHIN ARE STILL HERE!!
THANKS FOR HAVING US OVER!
Hi.
WE'RE ALL IN THE SAME CLASS!
THIS GUY IS MY CHILD-HOOD FRIEND!
GIANT!!
Hi!
THIS GUY IS AYANE-CHAN'S BOY-FRIEND!!
SUPER-FICIAL!
And he's a Giant too!

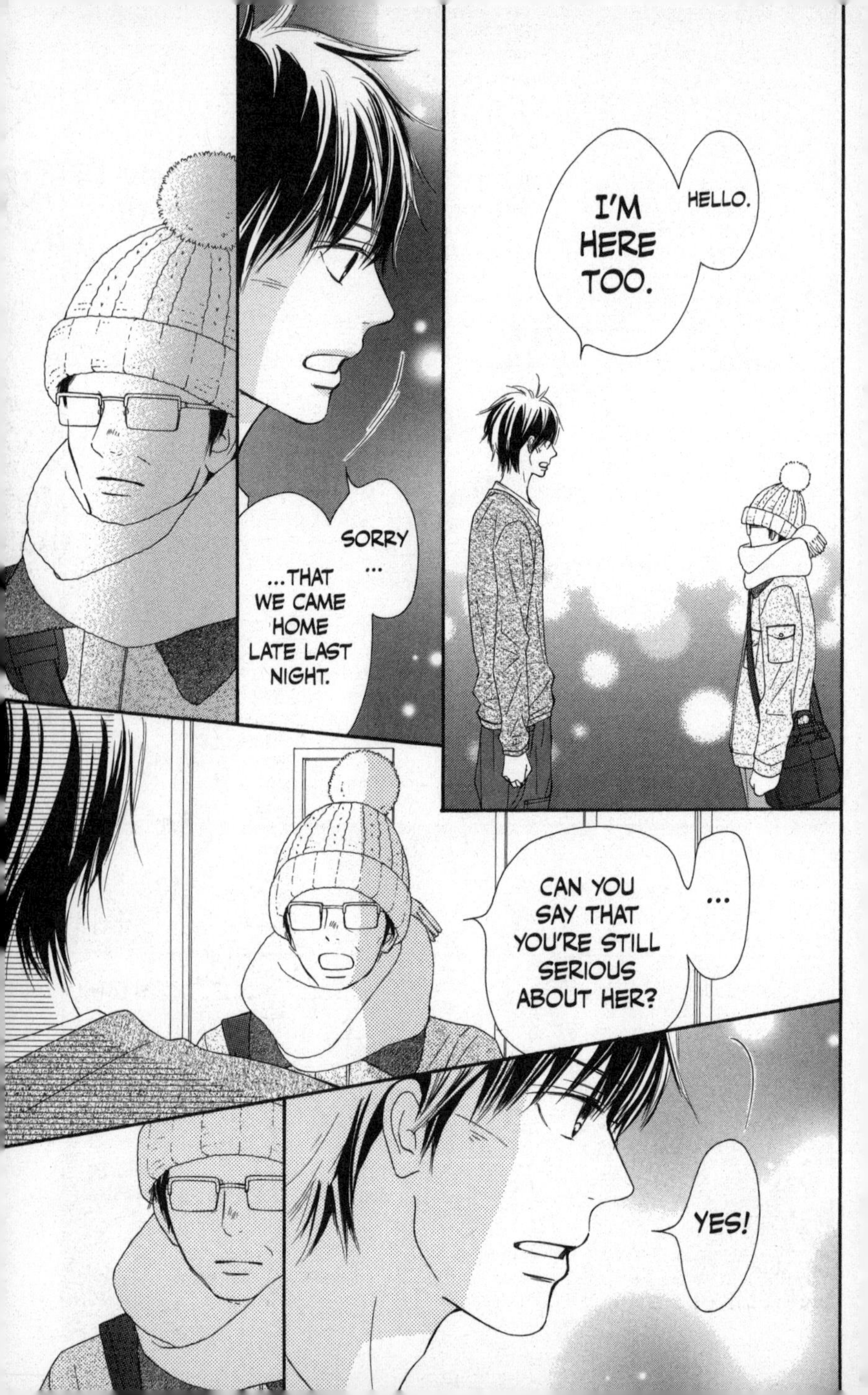
HELLO.
I'M HERE TOO.
SORRY...
...THAT WE CAME HOME LATE LAST NIGHT.
...
CAN YOU SAY THAT YOU'RE STILL SERIOUS ABOUT HER?
YES!

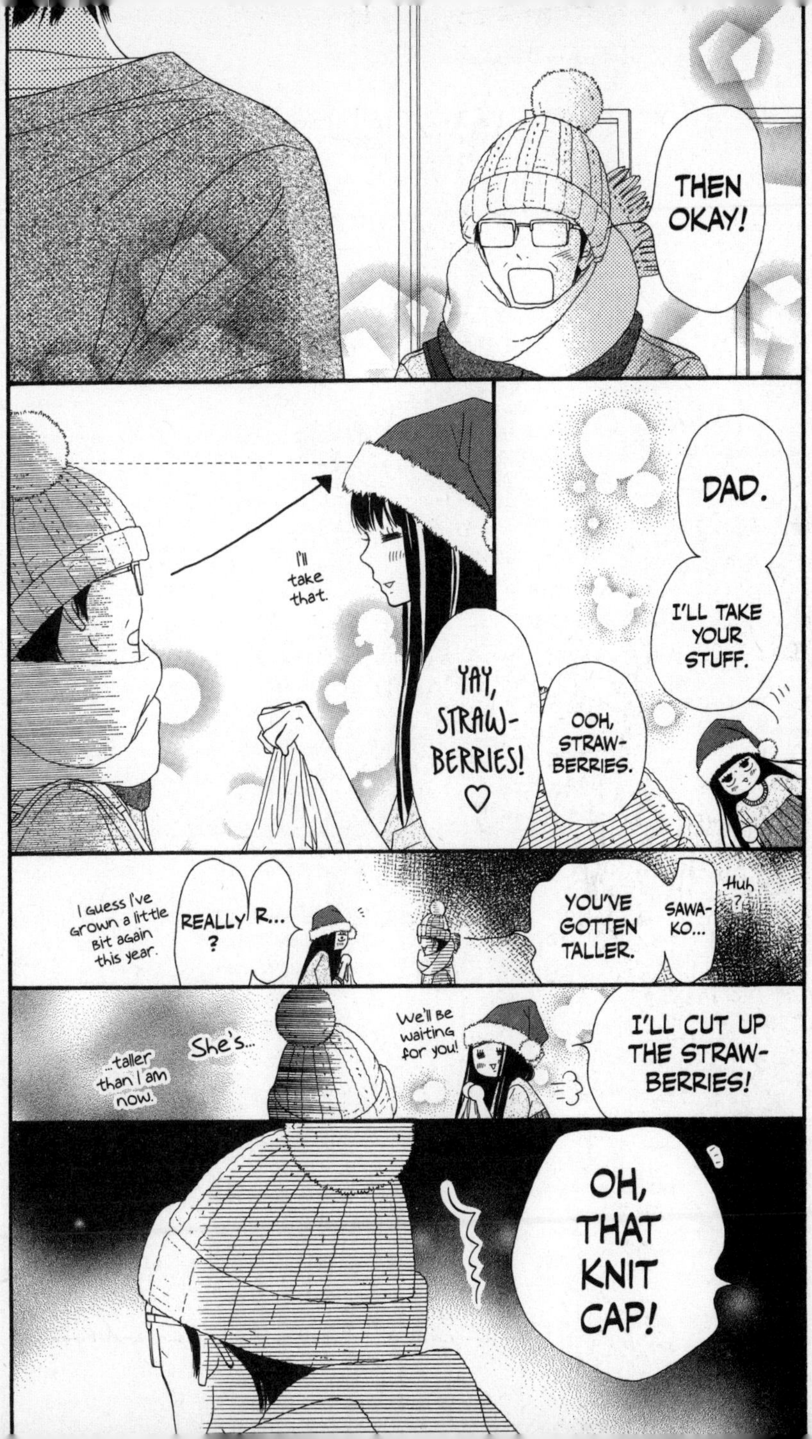
THEN OKAY!
DAD.
I'LL TAKE YOUR STUFF.
OOH, STRAW-BERRIES.
I'll take that.
YAY, STRAW-BERRIES! ♡
Huh?
SAWA-KO...
YOU'VE GOTTEN TALLER.
R...
REALLY?
I guess I've grown a little bit again this year.
I'LL CUT UP THE STRAW-BERRIES!
We'll be waiting for you!
She's...
...taller than I am now.
OH, THAT KNIT CAP!

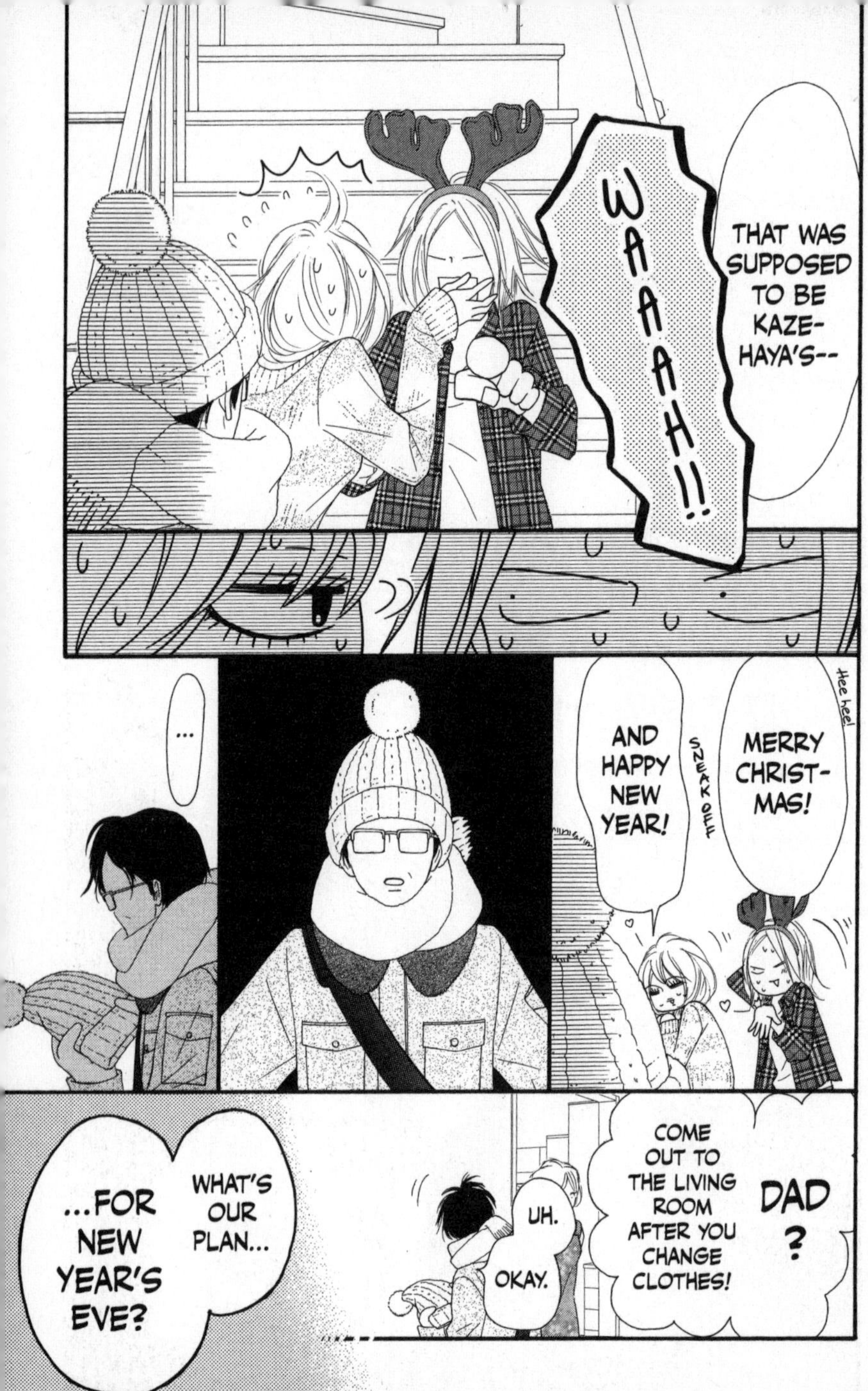
THAT WAS SUPPOSED TO BE KAZE-HAYA'S--
WAAAAH!!
Hee hee!
MERRY CHRIST-MAS!
SNEAK OFF
AND HAPPY NEW YEAR!
...
DAD?
COME OUT TO THE LIVING ROOM AFTER YOU CHANGE CLOTHES!
UH.
OKAY.
WHAT'S OUR PLAN...
...FOR NEW YEAR'S EVE?

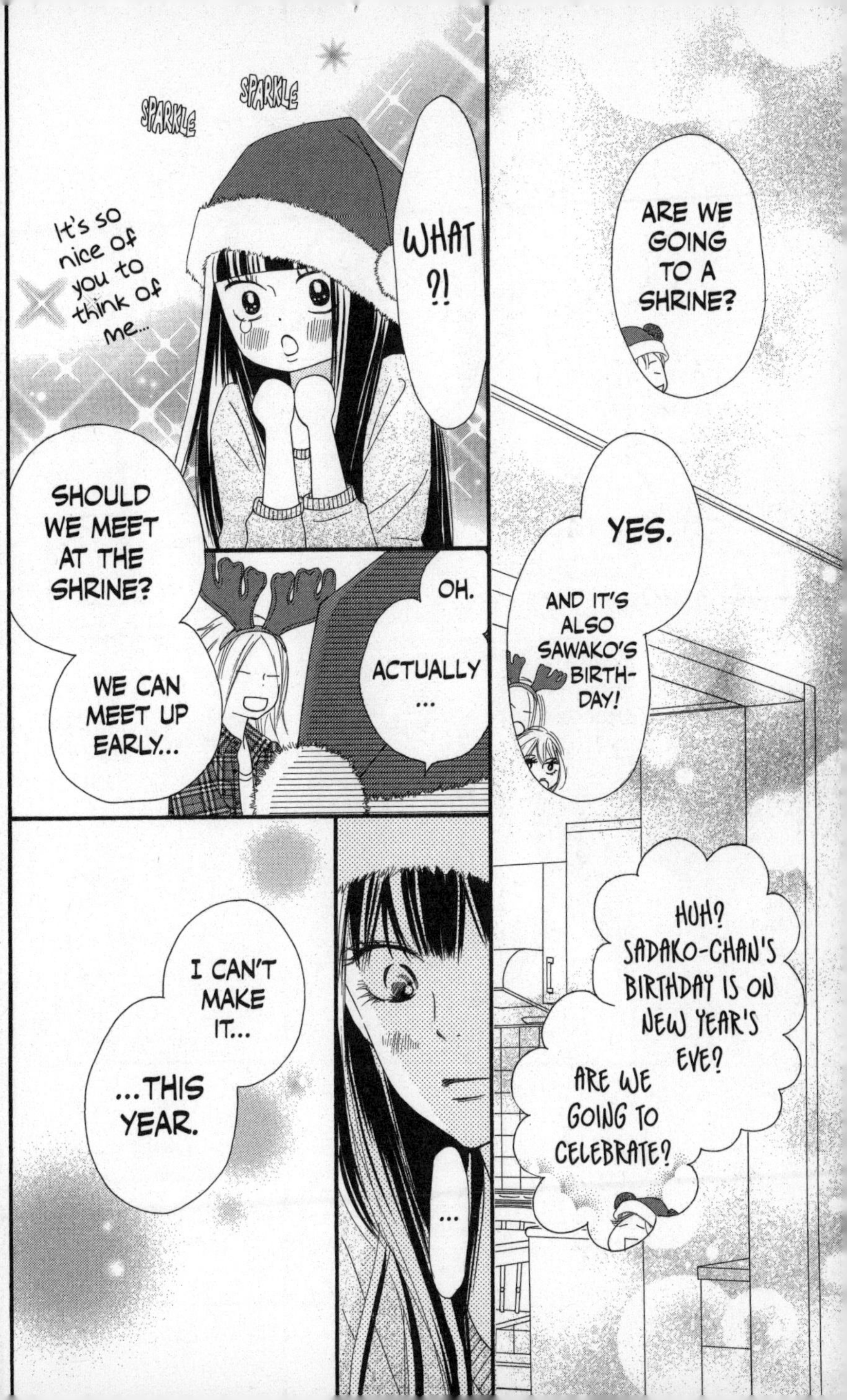
ARE WE GOING TO A SHRINE?
YES.
AND IT'S ALSO SAWAKO'S BIRTH-DAY!
HUH? SADAKO-CHAN'S BIRTHDAY IS ON NEW YEAR'S EVE?
ARE WE GOING TO CELEBRATE?
SPARKLE
SPARKLE
WHAT ?!
It's so nice of you to think of me...
SHOULD WE MEET AT THE SHRINE?
WE CAN MEET UP EARLY...
OH.
ACTUALLY ...
...
I CAN'T MAKE IT...
...THIS YEAR.

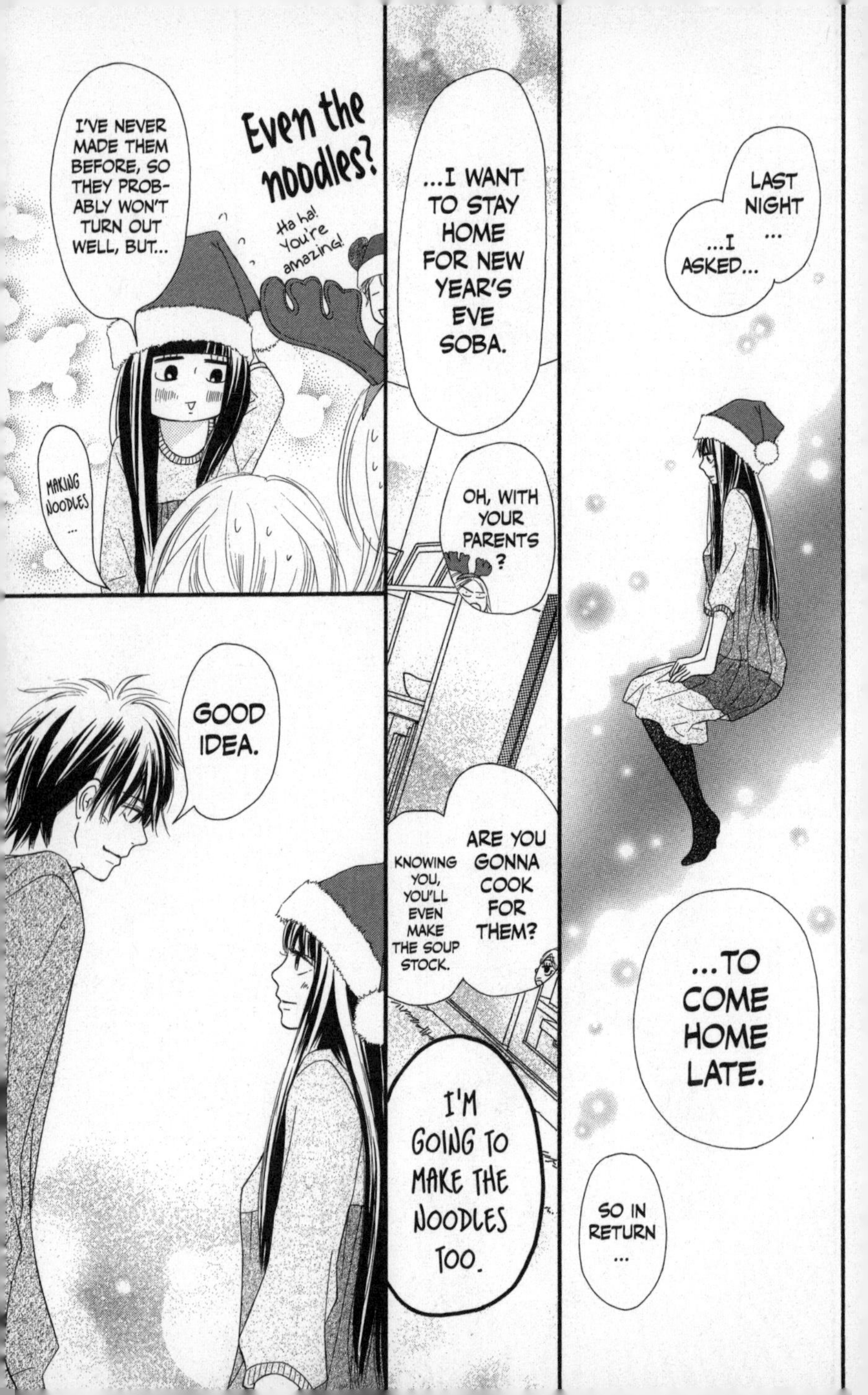
LAST NIGHT ...
...I ASKED...
...TO COME HOME LATE.
SO IN RETURN ...
...I WANT TO STAY HOME FOR NEW YEAR'S EVE SOBA.
OH, WITH YOUR PARENTS?
ARE YOU GONNA COOK FOR THEM?
KNOWING YOU, YOU'LL EVEN MAKE THE SOUP STOCK.
I'M GOING TO MAKE THE NOODLES TOO.
Even the noodles?
Ha ha! You're amazing!
I'VE NEVER MADE THEM BEFORE, SO THEY PROBABLY WON'T TURN OUT WELL, BUT...
MAKING NOODLES ...
GOOD IDEA.

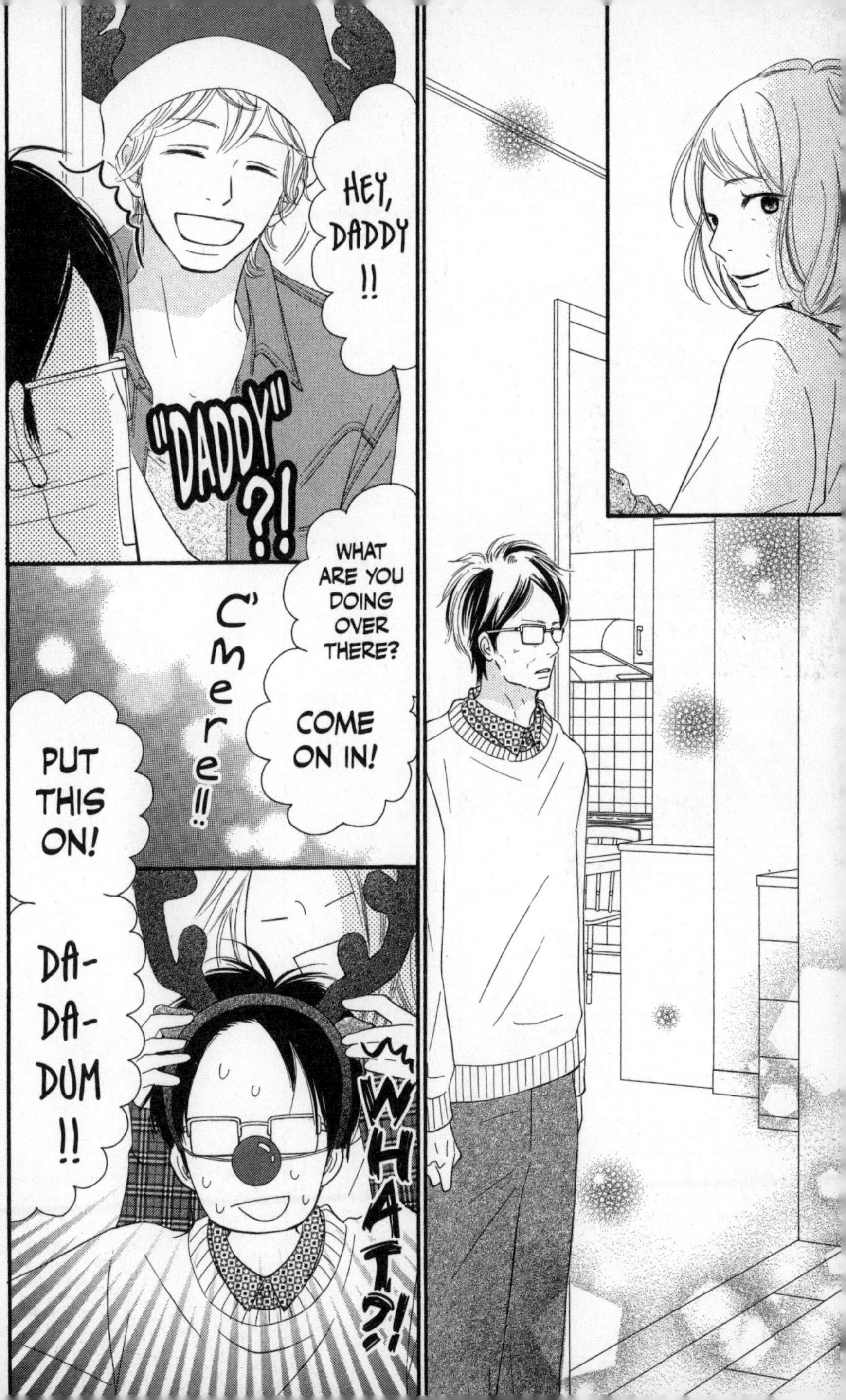
HEY, DADDY!!
"DADDY"?!
WHAT ARE YOU DOING OVER THERE?
COME ON IN!
C'mere!!
PUT THIS ON!
WHAT?!
DA-DA-DUM!!

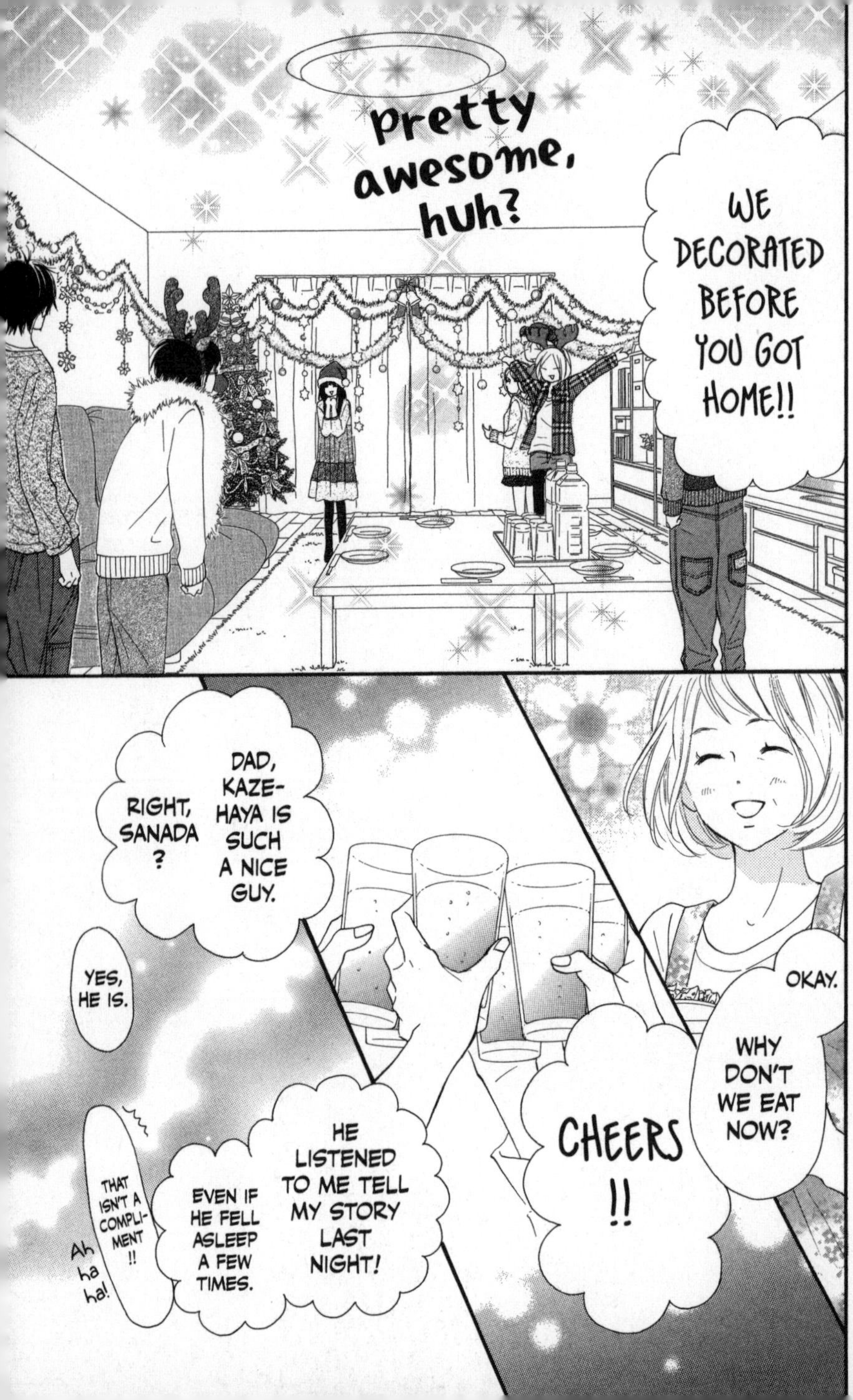
WE DECORATED BEFORE YOU GOT HOME!!
pretty awesome, huh?
OKAY.
WHY DON'T WE EAT NOW?
CHEERS!!
DAD, KAZE-HAYA IS SUCH A NICE GUY.
RIGHT, SANADA?
YES, HE IS.
HE LISTENED TO ME TELL MY STORY LAST NIGHT!
EVEN IF HE FELL ASLEEP A FEW TIMES.
THAT ISN'T A COMPLI-MENT!!
Ah ha ha!

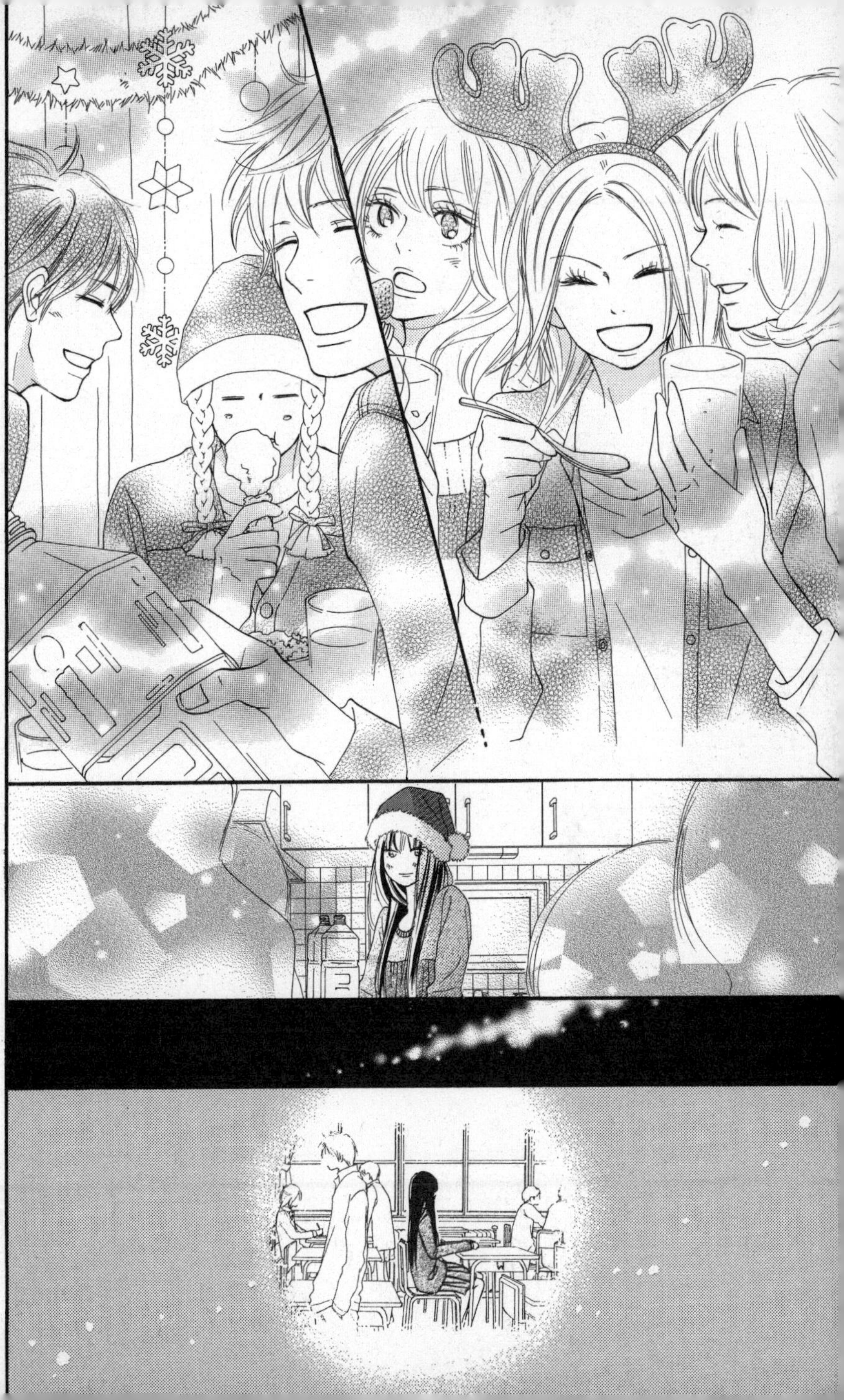

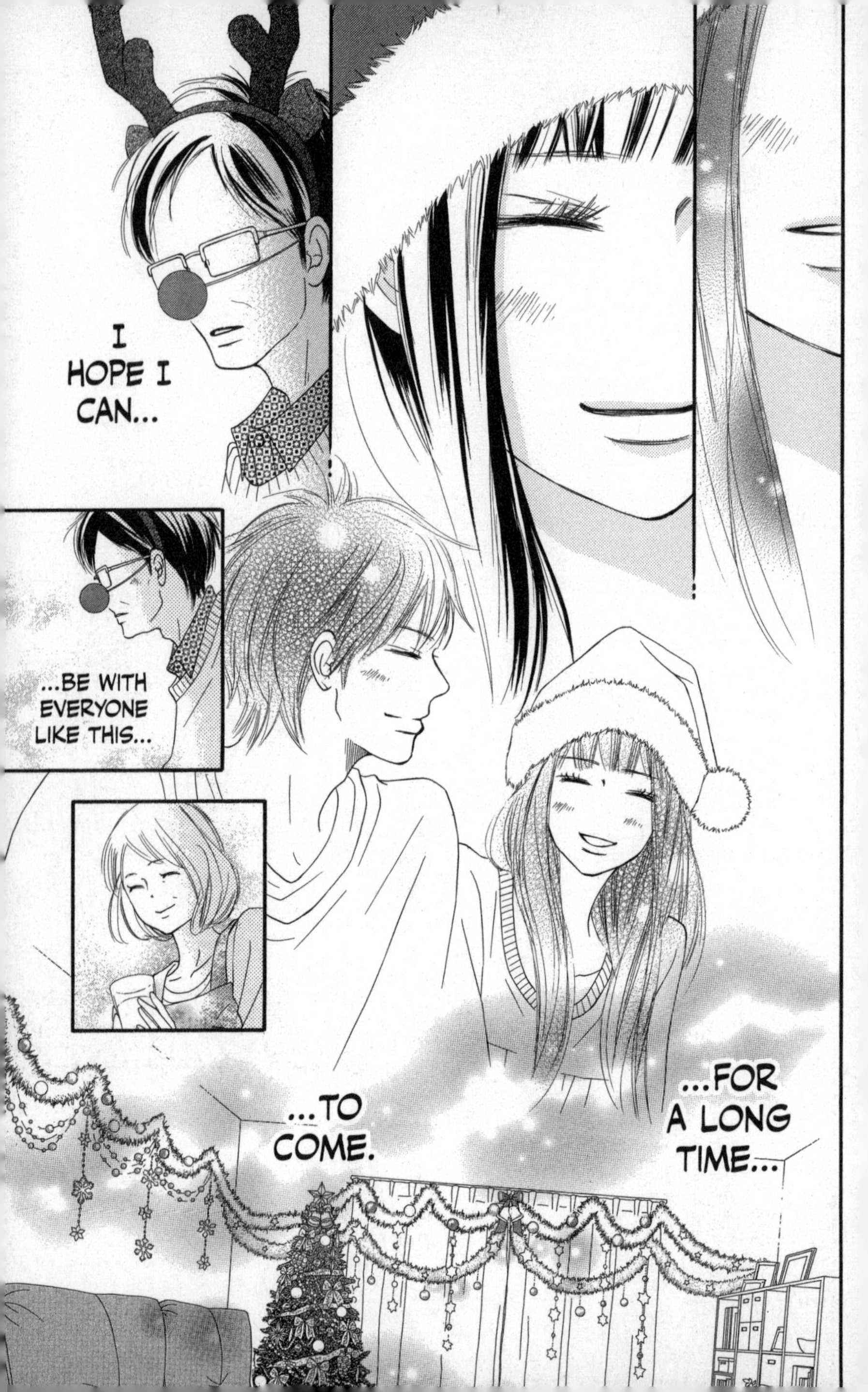
I HOPE I CAN...
...BE WITH EVERYONE LIKE THIS...
...FOR A LONG TIME...
...TO COME.

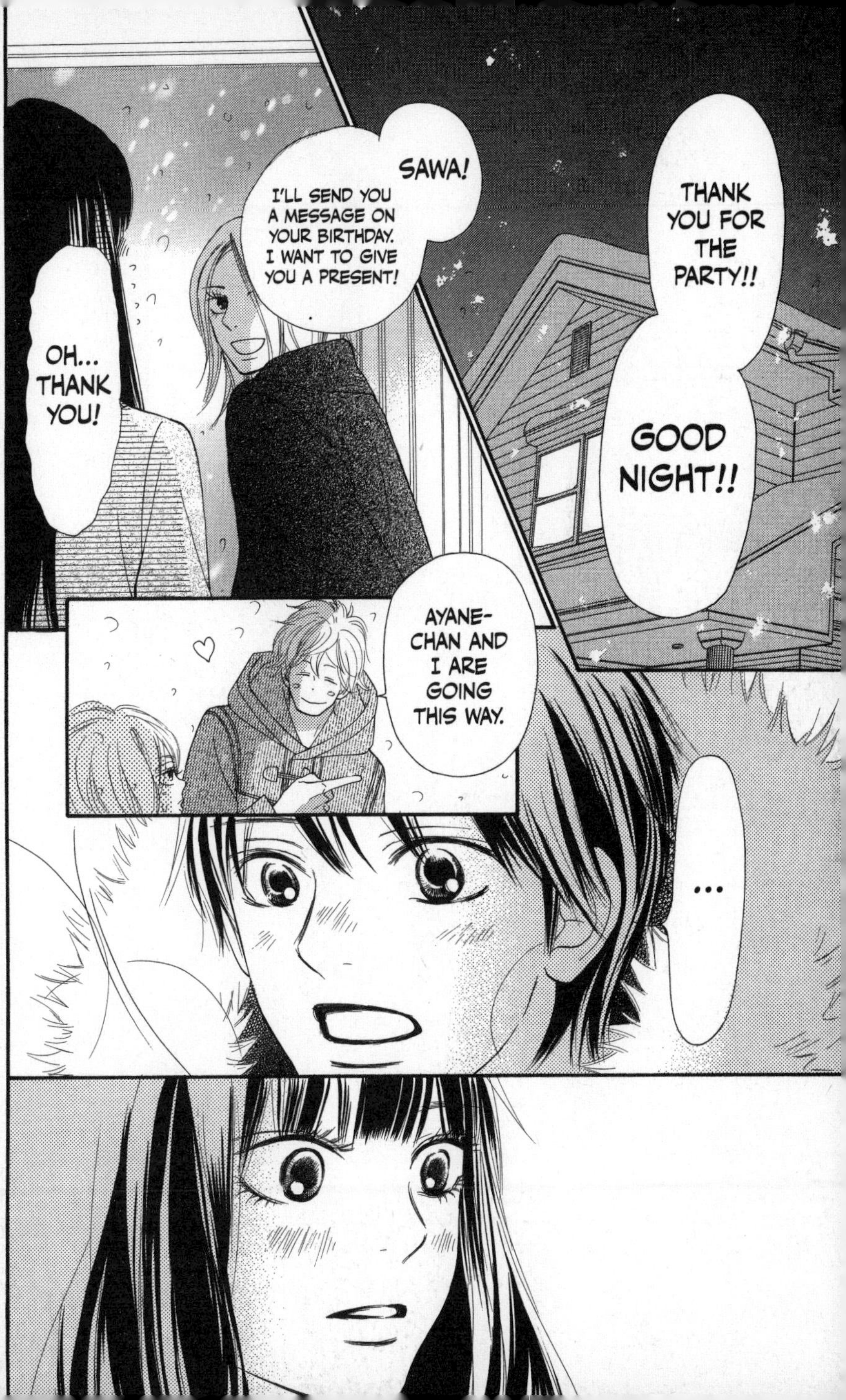
THANK YOU FOR THE PARTY!!
GOOD NIGHT!!
SAWA!
I'LL SEND YOU A MESSAGE ON YOUR BIRTHDAY. I WANT TO GIVE YOU A PRESENT!
OH... THANK YOU!
AYANE-CHAN AND I ARE GOING THIS WAY.
...

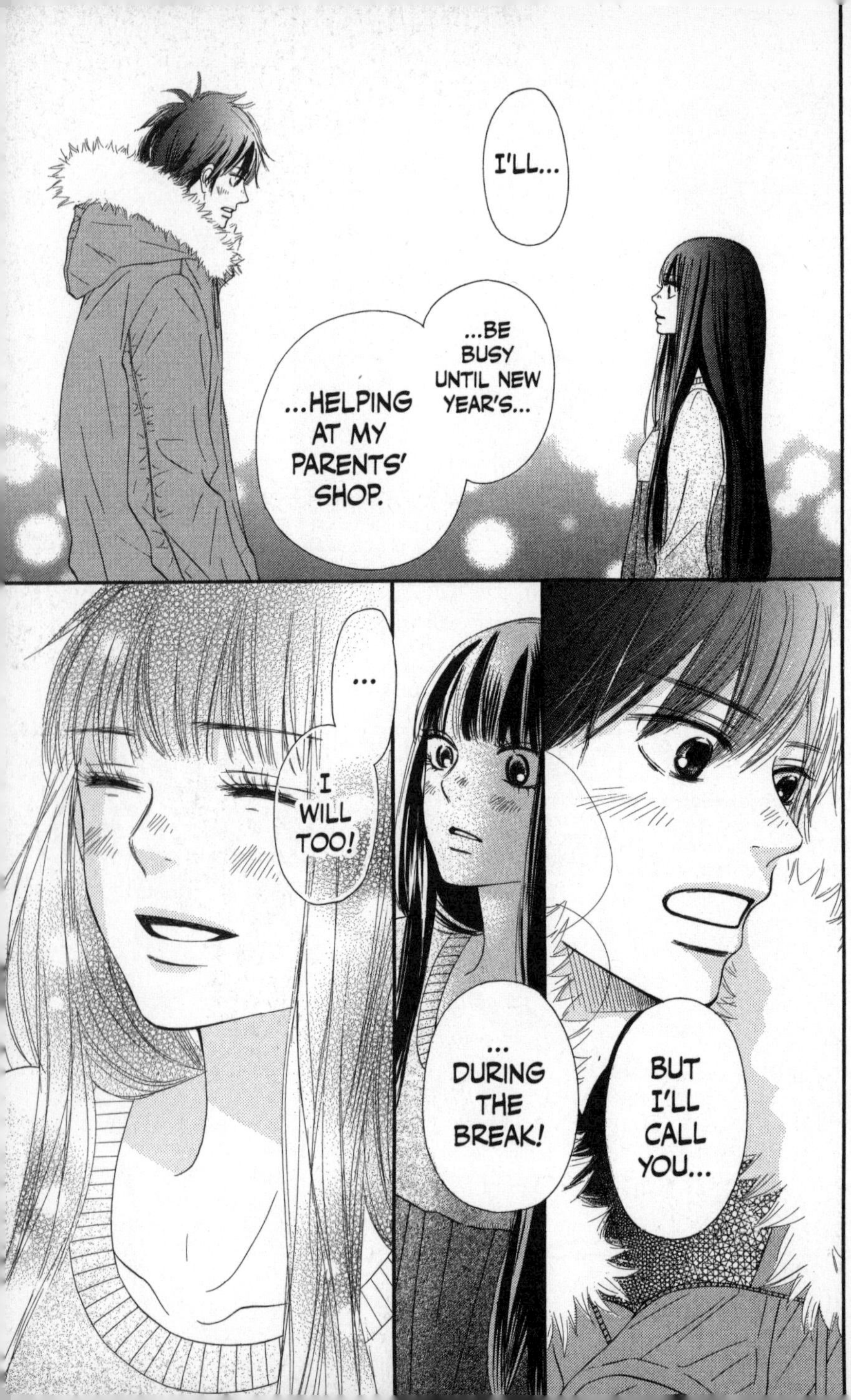
I'LL...
...BE BUSY UNTIL NEW YEAR'S...
...HELPING AT MY PARENTS' SHOP.
BUT I'LL CALL YOU...
...DURING THE BREAK!
...
I WILL TOO!

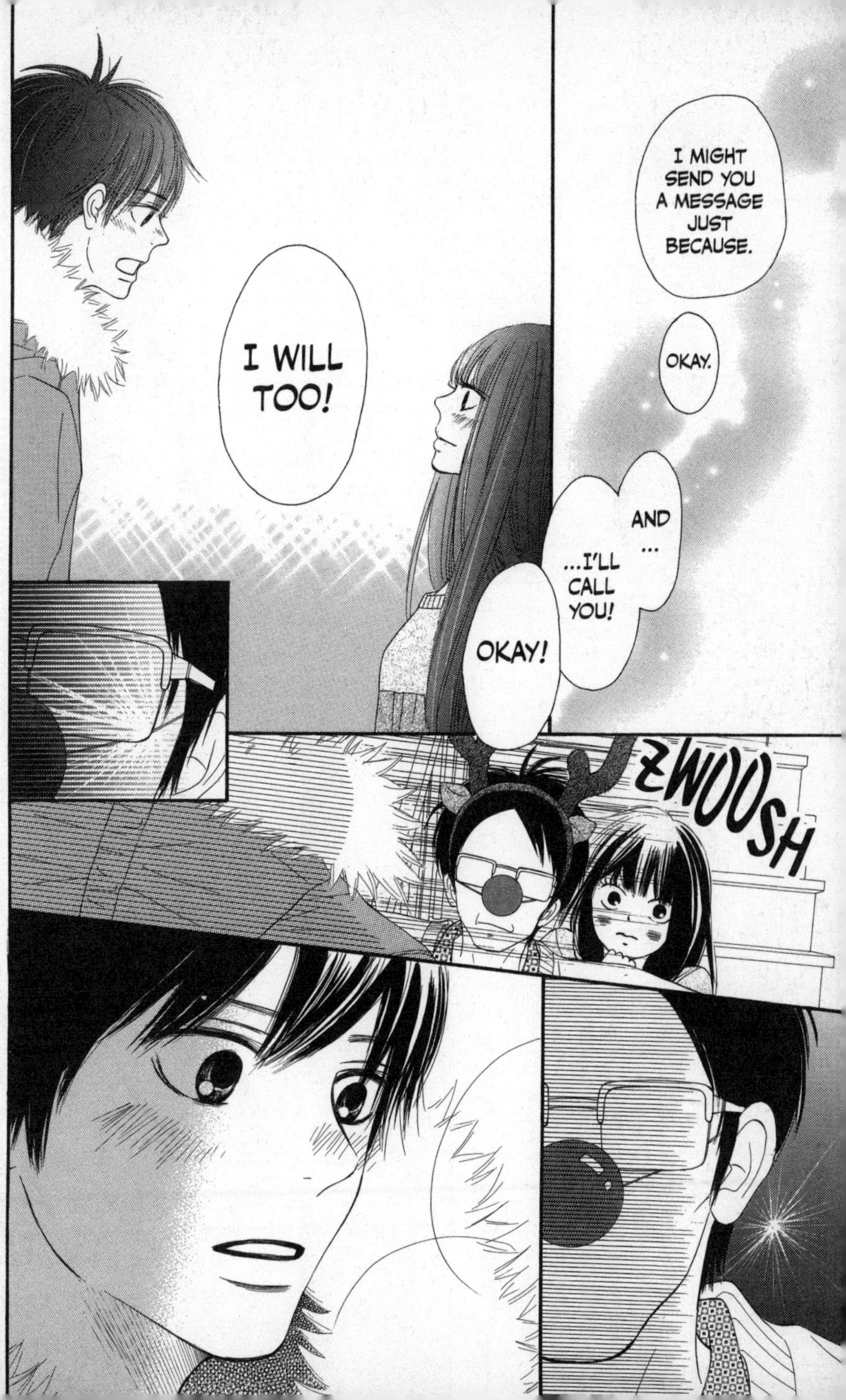
I MIGHT SEND YOU A MESSAGE JUST BECAUSE.
OKAY.
I WILL TOO!
AND ...
...I'LL CALL YOU!
OKAY!
ZWOOSH

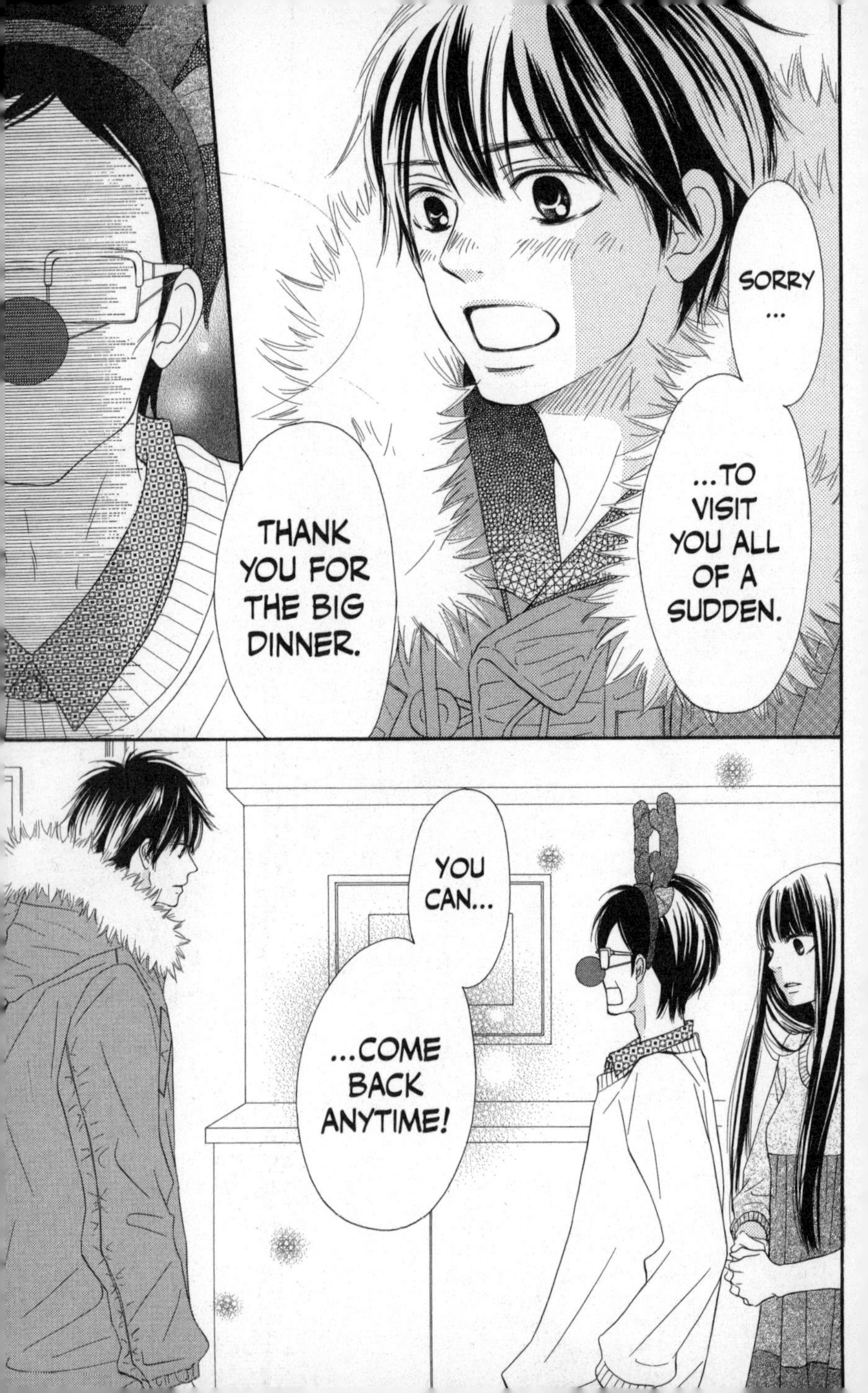
SORRY ...
...TO VISIT YOU ALL OF A SUDDEN.
THANK YOU FOR THE BIG DINNER.
YOU CAN...
...COME BACK ANYTIME!

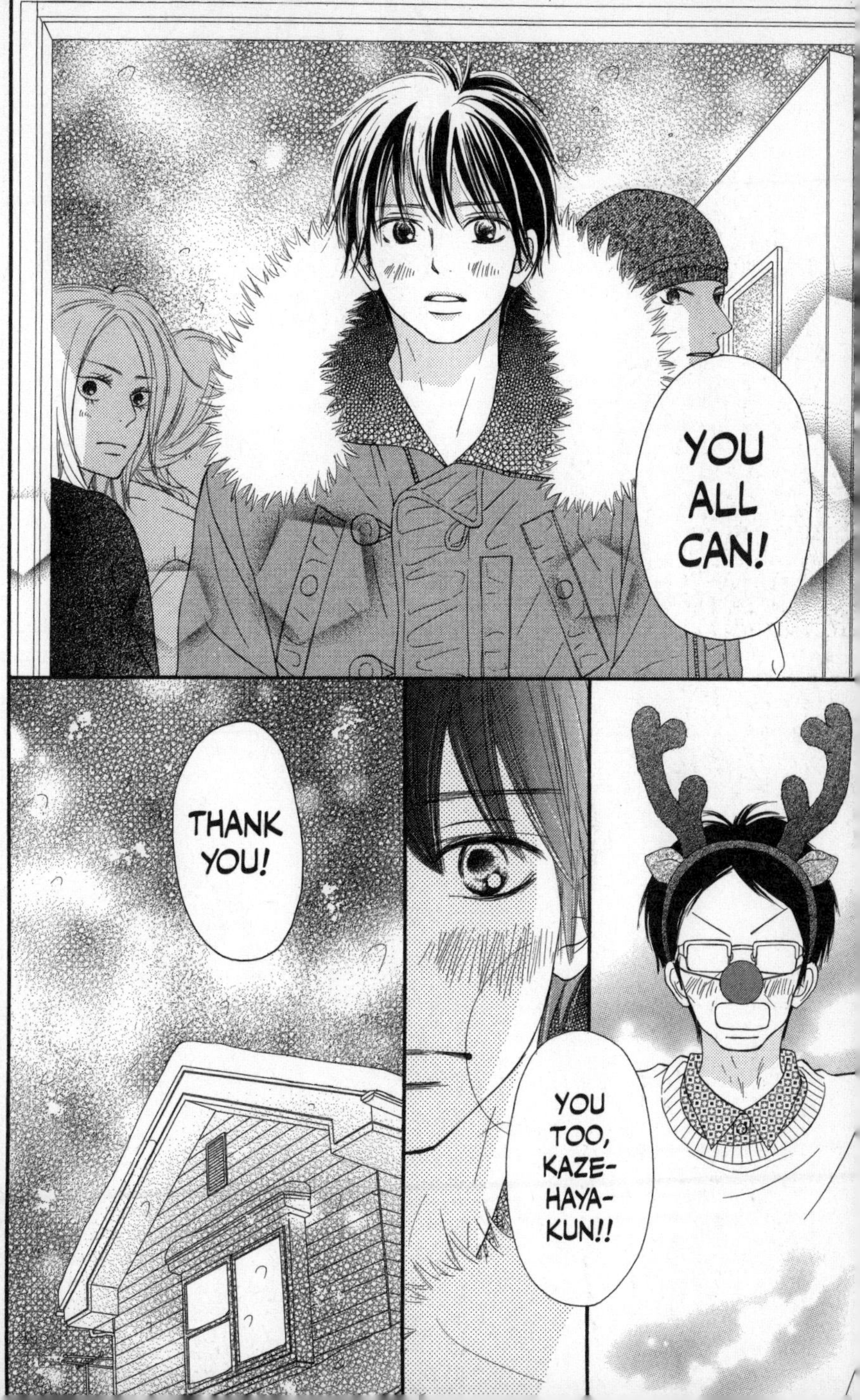
YOU ALL CAN!
YOU TOO, KAZE-HAYA-KUN!!
THANK YOU!

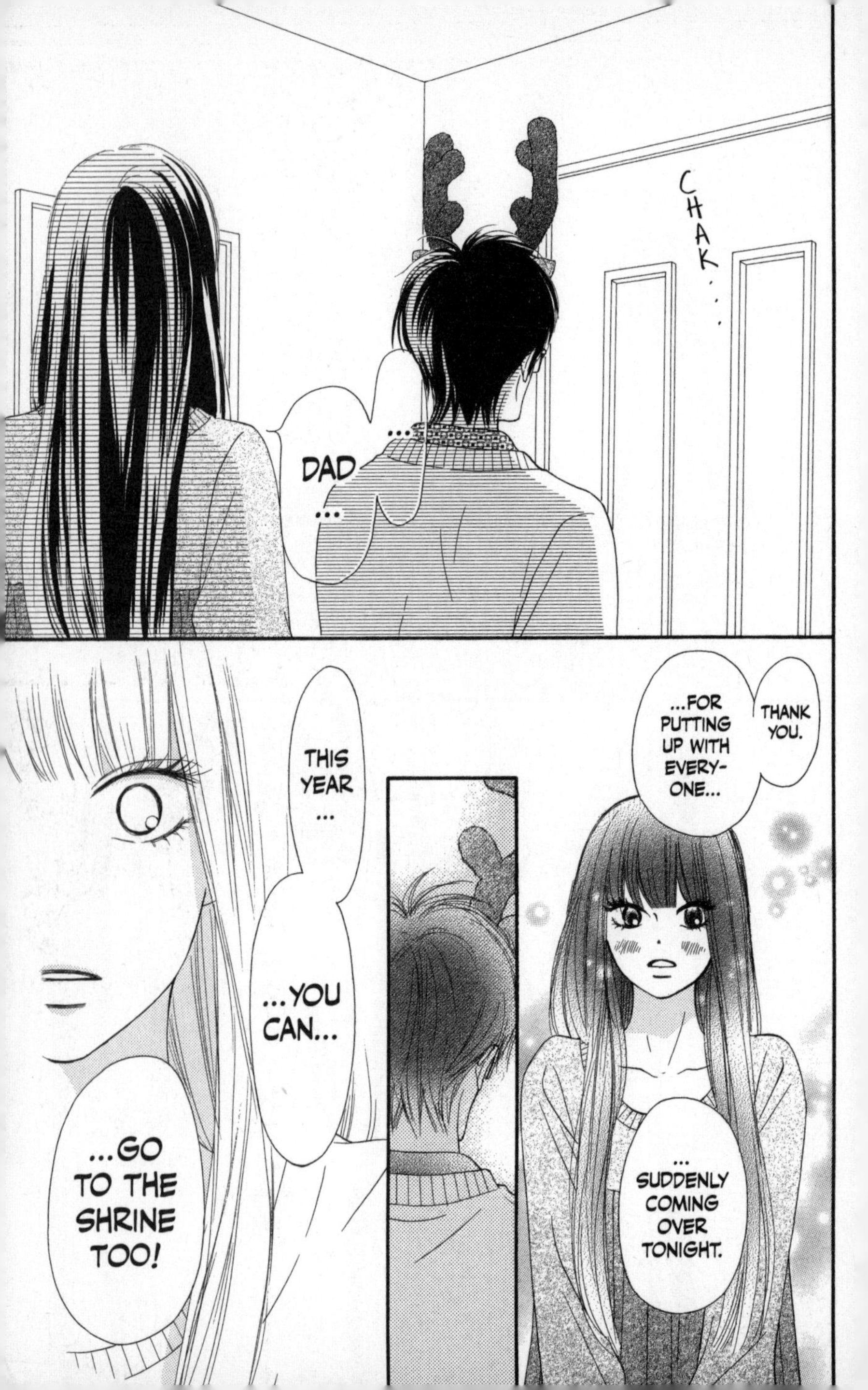
CHAK...
...DAD...
THANK YOU.
...FOR PUTTING UP WITH EVERYONE...
...SUDDENLY COMING OVER TONIGHT.
THIS YEAR...
...YOU CAN...
...GO TO THE SHRINE TOO!

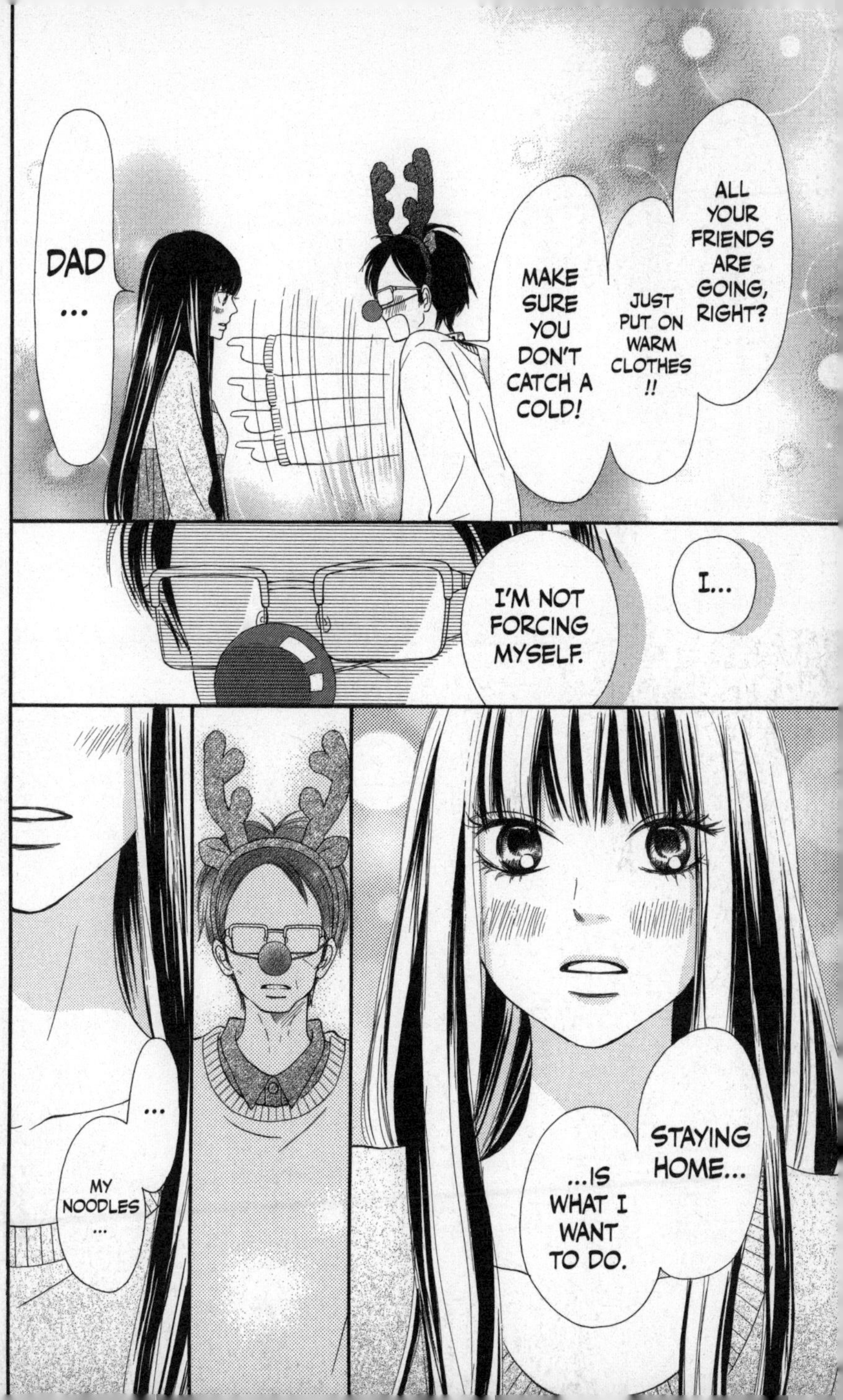
ALL YOUR FRIENDS ARE GOING, RIGHT?
JUST PUT ON WARM CLOTHES !!
MAKE SURE YOU DON'T CATCH A COLD!
DAD ...
I...
I'M NOT FORCING MYSELF.
STAYING HOME...
...IS WHAT I WANT TO DO.
...
MY NOODLES ...

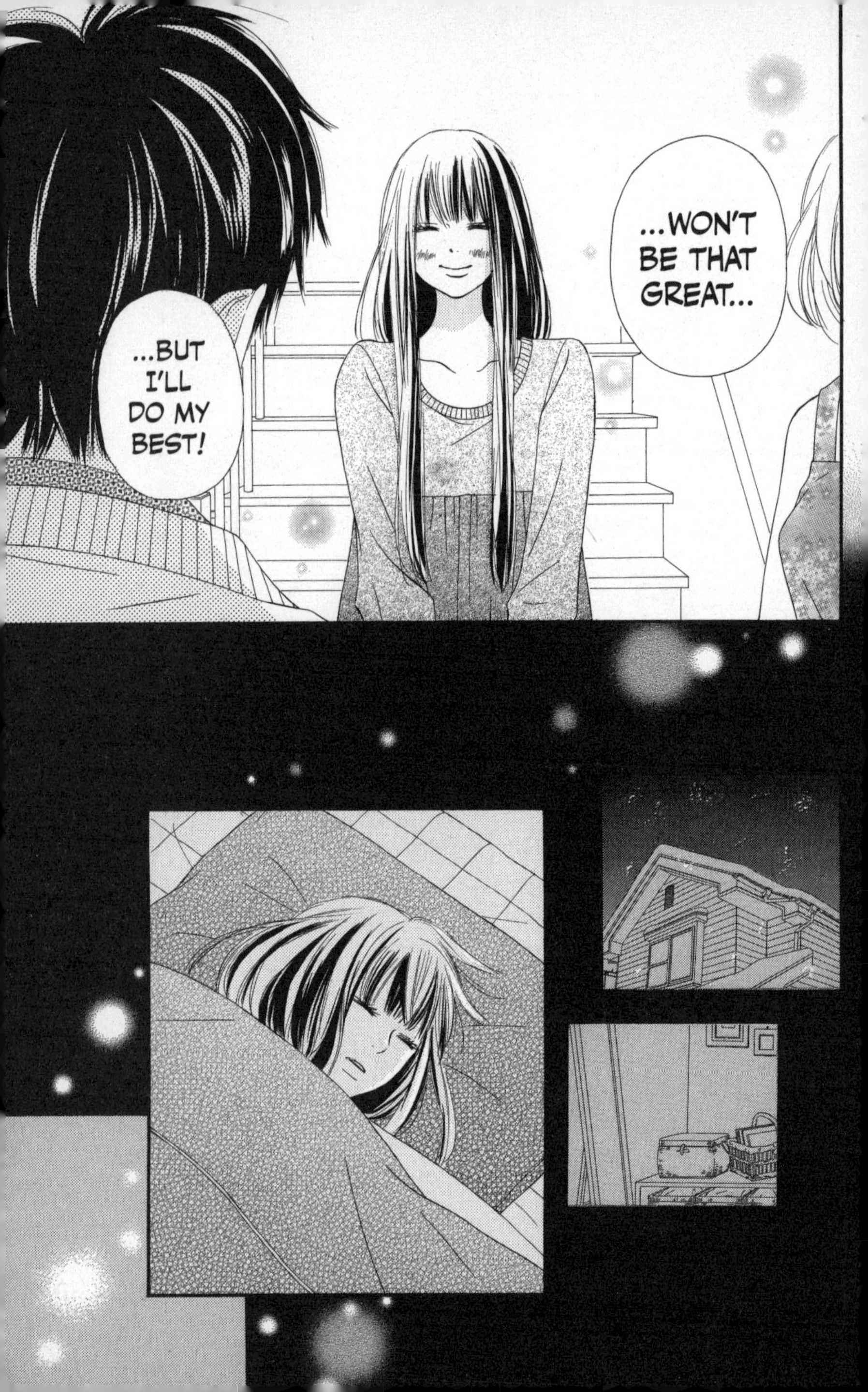
...WON'T BE THAT GREAT...
...BUT I'LL DO MY BEST!

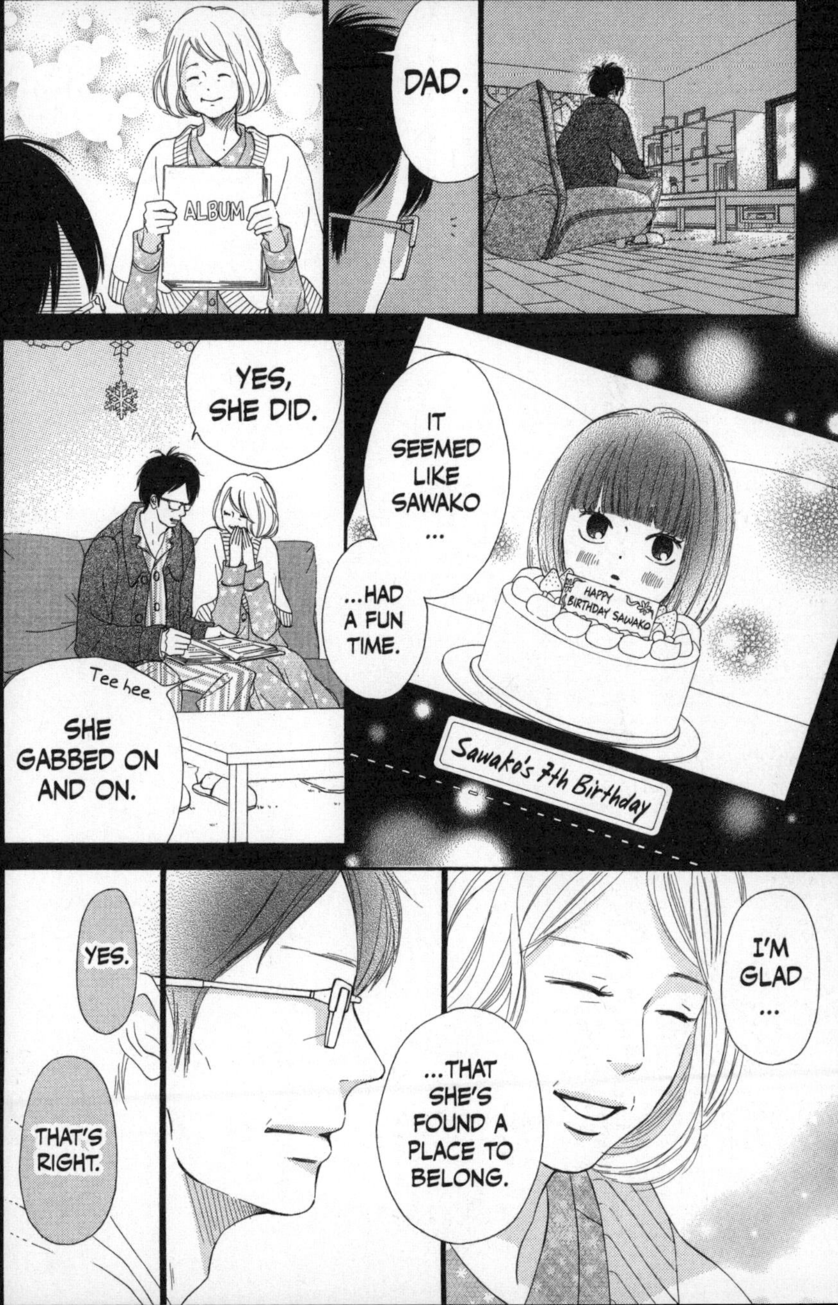
DAD.
ALBUM
IT SEEMED LIKE SAWAKO ...
...HAD A FUN TIME.
HAPPY BIRTHDAY SAWAKO
Sawako's 7th Birthday
YES, SHE DID.
Tee hee.
SHE GABBED ON AND ON.
I'M GLAD ...
...THAT SHE'S FOUND A PLACE TO BELONG.
YES.
THAT'S RIGHT.

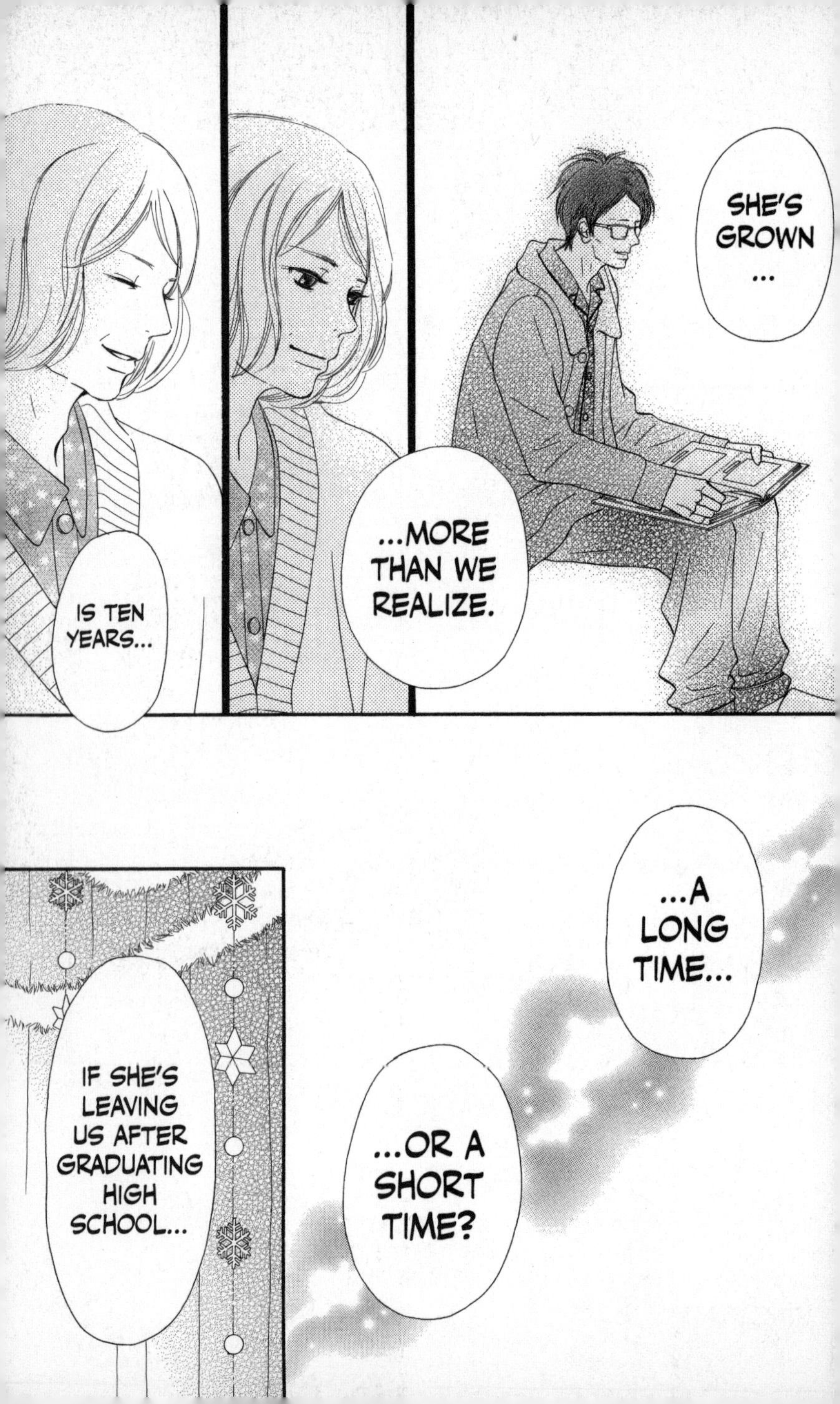
SHE'S GROWN ...
...MORE THAN WE REALIZE.
IS TEN YEARS...
...A LONG TIME...
...OR A SHORT TIME?
IF SHE'S LEAVING US AFTER GRADUATING HIGH SCHOOL...

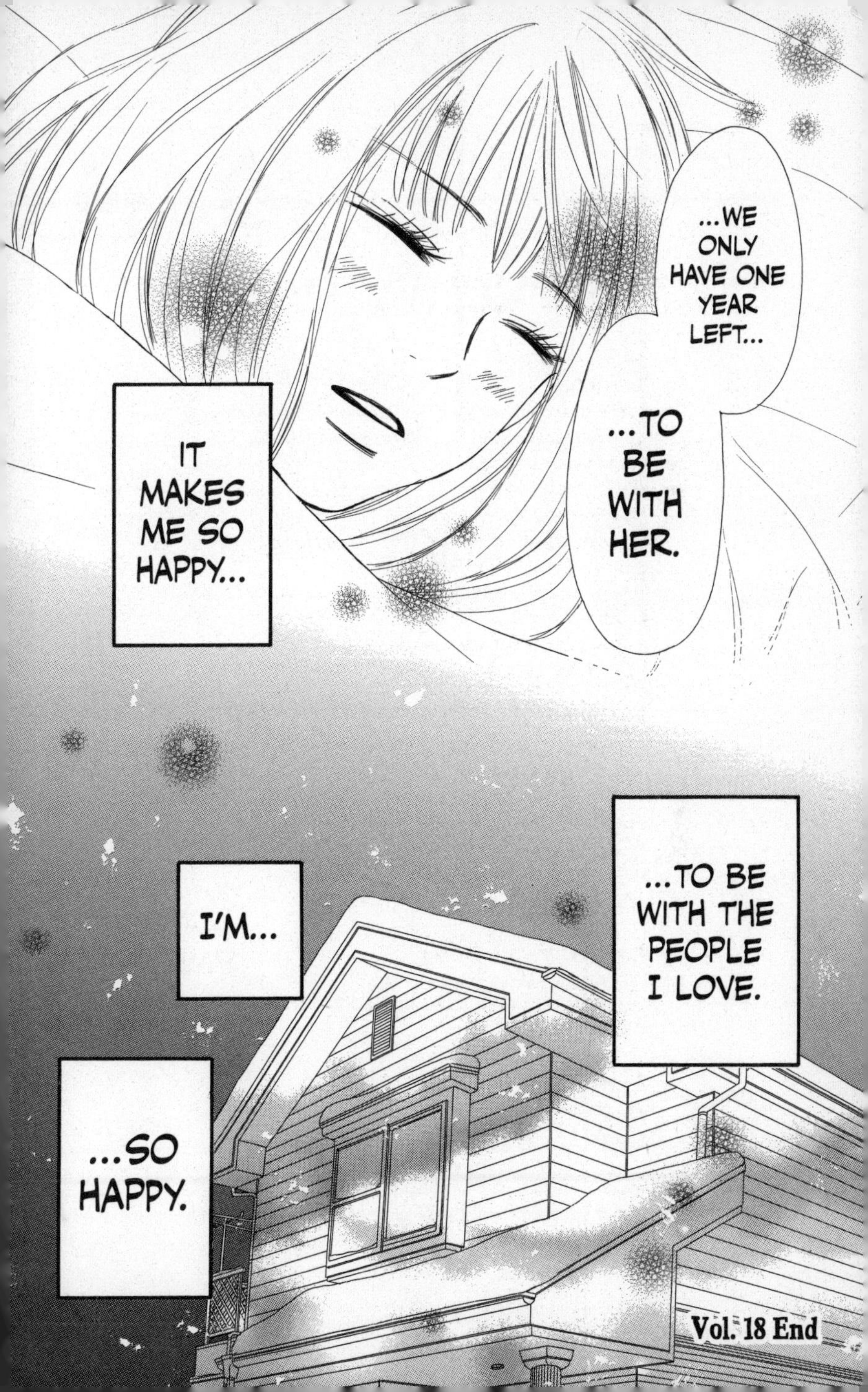
...WE ONLY HAVE ONE YEAR LEFT...
...TO BE WITH HER.
IT MAKES ME SO HAPPY...
...TO BE WITH THE PEOPLE I LOVE.
I'M...
...SO HAPPY.
Vol. 18 End

From me (the editor) to you (the reader).

Here are some Japanese culture explanations that will help you better understand the references in the *Kimi ni Todoke* world.

Honorifics:
When saying someone's name in Japanese, a suffix is often attached to indicate how familiar the speaker is with the person. Some are more polite and respectful, while others are endearing. Calling someone by just their first name is the most informal.
-kun is used for young men or boys, usually someone you are familiar with.
-chan is used for young women, girls or young children and can be used as a term of endearment.
-san is used for someone you respect or are not close to, or to be polite.

Page 127, "preverved":
Chizu tries to say the English word "preserved," echoing Ryu in volume 17.

Page 136, Japanese high school boy:
It would be unusual in traditional Japanese culture for a boy to exhibit a blatant show of romantic affection, such as gifting a bouquet of red roses.

Page 140, Christmas cake:
Often a sponge cake decorated with strawberries and cream, the Christmas cake is a fixture in Japanese Christmas celebrations.

Page 155, New Year's noodles:
In Japan, it is customary to eat buckwheat noodles (*toshikoshi soba*) on New Year's Eve.

The long, long Christmas season is finally wrapping up for Sawako and the others. It's finished. Over. It lasted a while!

So much fun stuff comes out at Christmas. I like Christmas with my friends, but also with my family. Don't point party-poppers at people!

--Karuho Shiina

Karuho Shiina was born and raised in Hokkaido, Japan. Though *Kimi ni Todoke* is only her second series following many one-shot stories, it has already racked up accolades from various "Best Manga of the Year" lists. Winner of the 2008 Kodansha Manga Award for the shojo category, *Kimi ni Todoke* also placed fifth in the first-ever Manga Taisho (Cartoon Grand Prize) contest in 2008. In Japan, an animated TV series debuted in October 2009, and a live-action film was released in 2010.

Kimi ni Todoke
VOL. 18

Shojo Beat Edition

STORY AND ART BY
KARUHO SHIINA

Translation/Ari Yasuda, HC Language Solutions, Inc.
Touch-up Art & Lettering/Vanessa Satone
Design/Nozomi Akashi
Editor/Hope Donovan

Published by VIZ Media, LLC
P.O. Box 77010
San Francisco, CA 94107

10 9 8 7 6 5 4 3 2 1
First printing, January 2014

Kyoko Mogami followed her true love Sho to Tokyo to support him while he made it big as an idol. But he's casting her out now that he's famous enough! Kyoko won't suffer in silence— she's going to get her sweet revenge by beating Sho in show biz!

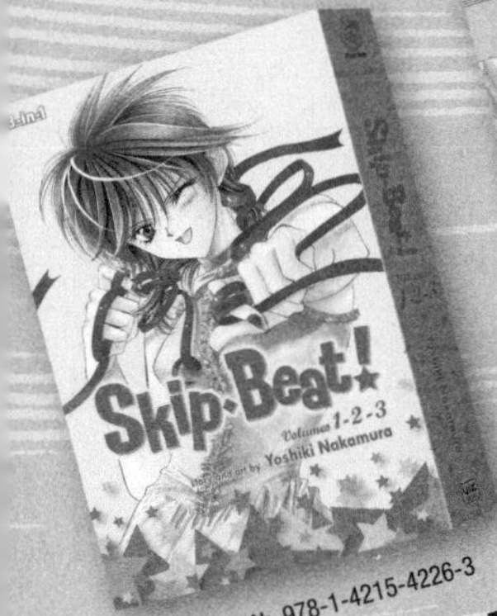
3-in-1
Skip·Beat!
Volumes 1-2-3
Story and art by Yoshiki Nakamura

Vol. 1 ISBN: 978-1-4215-4226-3

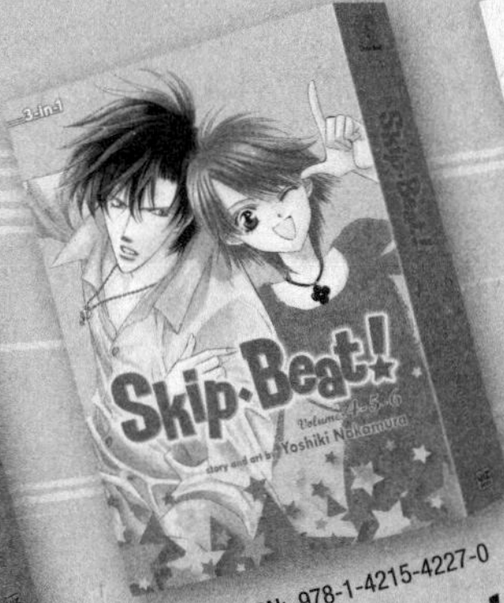
3-in-1
Skip·Beat!
Story and art by Yoshiki Nakamura

Vol. 2 ISBN: 978-1-4215-4227-0

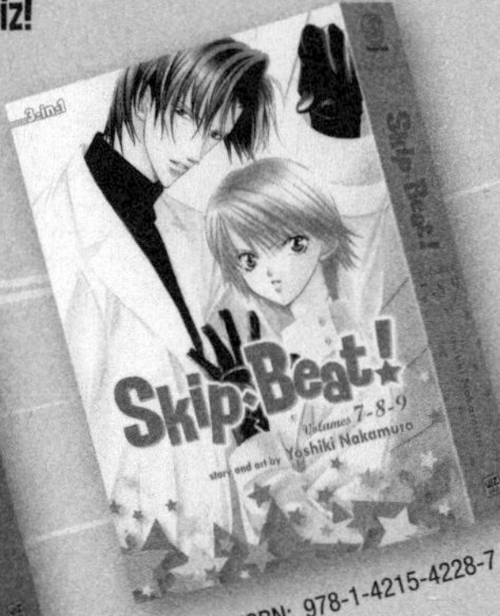
3-in-1
Skip·Beat!
Volumes 7-8-9
Story and art by Yoshiki Nakamura

Vol. 3 ISBN: 978-1-4215-4228-7

Only **$14.99** for each volume! ($16.99 in Canada)

Show biz is sweet...but revenge is sweeter!

Skip·Beat!

Story and Art by YOSHIKI NAKAMURA

In Stores Now!

RATED T FOR TEEN ratings.viz.com

Shojo Beat

VIZ media www.viz.com

Surprise!

You may be reading the wrong way!

It's true: In keeping with the original Japanese comic format, this book reads from right to left—so action, sound effects, and word balloons are completely reversed. This preserves the orientation of the original artwork—plus, it's fun! Check out the diagram shown here to get the hang of things, and then turn to the other side of the book to get started!

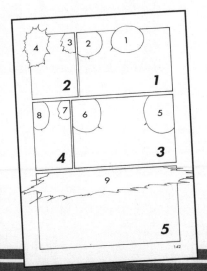